D1263794

Florissant Valley Library
St. Louis Community College
3400 Pershall Road
Ferguson, MO 63135-1499
314-595-4514

F.V.

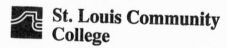
WITHDRAWN

St. Louis Community
College

Forest Park
Florissant Valley
Meramec

Instructional Resources
St. Louis, Missouri

GAYLORD

WILLA CATHER'S
NEW YORK

WILLA CATHER'S NEW YORK

New Essays on Cather in the City

Edited by

Merrill Maguire Skaggs

Madison • Teaneck
Fairleigh Dickinson University Press
London: Associated University Presses

© 2000 by Associated University Presses, Inc.

All rights reserved. Authorization to photocopy items for internal or personal use, or the internal or personal use of specific clients, is granted by the copyright owner, provided that a base fee of $10.00 plus eight cents per page, per copy is paid directly to the Copyright Clearance Center, 222 Rosewood Drive, Danvers, Massachusetts 01923. [0-8386-3857-0/00 $10.00 + 8¢ pp, pc.]

Associated University Presses
2010 Eastpark Boulevard
Cranbury, NJ 08512

Associated University Presses
16 Barter Street
London WC1A 2AH, England

Associated University Presses
P.O. Box 338, Port Credit
Mississauga, Ontario
Canada L5G 4L8

The paper used in this publication meets the requirements of the American National Standard for Permanence of Paper for Printed Library Materials Z39.48-1984.

Library of Congress Cataloging-in-Publication Data

Willa Cather's New York : new essays on Cather in the city / edited by Merrill Maguire Skaggs.
    p. cm.
Includes bibliographical references and index.
ISBN 0-8386-3857-0 (alk. paper)
1. Cather, Willa, 1873–1947—Knowledge—New York (N.Y.) 2. Woman and literature—New York (State)—New York—History—20th century. 3. City and town life in literature. 4. New York (N.Y.)—Intellectual life—20th century. 5. New York (N.Y.)—In literature. I. Skaggs, Merrill Maguire.
PS3505.A87 Z9383 2000
813'.52—dc21

00-037635

SECOND PRINTING 2002

PRINTED IN THE UNITED STATES OF AMERICA

To Angela Conrad and Karen Marquis
who made it happen

Contents

Illustrations

Preface

Countless people in museums, libraries, and homes across the nation, indeed trans-Atlantically, have helped the twenty contributors to this volume to prepare their materials, and therefore to make this book idea into a fact. To all of them, our single and collective thanks.

For permissions to reprint the illustrations essential to our volume, we thank the following: The British Library for *The Eruption of Vesuvius in 1767* by Pietro Fabris 681K13; James Camner for the photograph of Olive Fremstad; Columbia School of Architecture for the photograph of the (now demolished) Singer Tower at 149 Broadway; The Corcoran Gallery of Art for *The New York Window* by Childe Hassam; Whitney Cox for the photograph of the Church of the Ascension at Fifth Avenue and 10th St.; the GTE Corporation for the photograph of the Old Metropolitan Opera House at Broadway and 39th St.; The Historical Society of the Town of Greenwich for Cather materials held in their Holley House Collections; the Metropolitan Museum of Art for *Winter in Union Square* and *Fifth Avenue Noon* by Childe Hassam; the Museum of Modern Art for *Girl with a Mandolin* and *Les Demoiselles d'Avignon* by Pablo Picasso; the National Gallery of Art for *Allies Day, May 1917* by Childe Hassam; the New York Historical Society for the photograph of Madison Square Park Looking Northeast from Fifth Avenue and 23rd St.; the Philadelphia Museum of Art for *Nude Descending a Staircase, No. 2;* the Phillips Collection for *Washington Arch, Spring* by Childe Hassam; Schweizwerische Stiftung für die Photographie for *Naples* by Wilhelm von Gloeden; the Smith College Museum for *Union Square in Spring* and *Street Scene, Christmas Morning* by Childe Hassam; the Underwood Photo Archives for the photograph of The Cloisters at the time of its purchase by the Metropolitan Museum of Art in 1925.

Beyond specific permissions and services, however, we wish to express our hearty gratitude to those who helped with the mechanics of computer-driven editing, by far the most harrowing part of this book's production. Ray Semiraglio, head of the Faculty Development Lab of Drew University, and his staff patiently dealt with what felt like Emergency Room anxieties traceable to computer snicksnarls, all of which seemed life-threatening at the time they appeared. Without the lab and its staff, no book. We also cheerfully acknowledge the generous technical assistance rendered with competence and grace by Linda Blank, Administrative Assistant in the Caspersen School of Graduate Studies at Drew University, and Terri Green, Secretary of the English Department. Other colleagues also helped when they fortuitously wandered by.

Our most enduring gratitude and sustained applause, however, goes to Marilyn Berg Callander. Dr. Callander subsidized permissions fees for our illustrations, and always urged us to get the best we could imagine. The pictures in this volume are her contributions.

Introduction

MERRILL MAGUIRE SKAGGS

Although Willa Cather's fiction attracted a national audience from the time she published her first book of short stories, she has often been thought of as a regionalist, a Nebraska writer. There's a reason: she set eight of her great novels, and many short stories besides, either on the prairie or in states and sites that replicate the contours of her Nebraskan hometown, Red Cloud. The fact remains, however, that significant action in nine of her twelve novels also occurs in other places, as do such major stories as "Paul's Case," "A Wagner Matinée," "Coming, Aphrodite!" and "Before Breakfast." When we pinpoint those novels in which substantive action occurs specifically in New York City—*Alexander's Bridge, The Song of the Lark, One of Ours, My Mortal Enemy*—we no longer have trouble recalling that Cather chose to live most of her life in Manhattan. She knew her chosen city of residence intimately.

In recent years, especially because of the moving sites for international Cather symposia located outside of Nebraska, Cather scholars have reached consensus about the woeful inadequacy of Cather's earlier labels. In 1995 scholars gathered in Quebec to investigate the setting for *Shadows on the Rock,* with a sidetrip to Grand Manan's "Before Breakfast" location. In September of 1996 they converged on Pittsburgh, where young Willa lived when she first moved from Red Cloud after completing her college education, and where "Paul's Case" begins. In 1997 scholars collected in Winchester, Virginia, for a firsthand look at Back Creek family plots, and the places featured in *Sapphira and the Slave Girl;* for Cather lived in western Virginia till she was nine, and returned there for the setting of her last novel. In fact, as the century waned, Catherites gathered under a full moon on Mesa Verde, in October of 1999, to imagine cliff cities of the mind. But in June of 1998, the growing scholarly conclave convened at Drew University in New Jersey, in a colloquium organized by Drew graduate students Angela Conrad and Karen Marquis, to focus on Willa Cather's New York connections.

In that week Cather scholars taught each other a great deal about Cather's New York. A fraction of the lessons shared appears in this book. Predictably, the participants acknowledged first that New York

was the place *most* central to the life Cather chose for herself. It was
her permanent residence from 1906 until her death in 1947. New
York City was where Willa Cather became a literary power, through
her editing *McClure's* magazine. It was the turbulent cultural center
most crucial to her rapidly developing artistic sophistication. It nurtured her inexhaustible curiosity as it provided the opera, theater,
ballet, art galleries and museums, new books and literary conversation through which she grew and in all of which she participated
energetically. It also provided the bohemian ferment of Greenwich
Village in which she lived, which challenged and provoked her. All of
New York—its high arts and sidewalk low life, and all the sights a
habitual walker in the city glimpsed in between—enriched her mind
and imagination and fertilized her powerful, synthesizing creative
vision.

Once scholars focused on Cather's New York, the fact that sprang
out immediately was the omnipresence of the Northeast in Cather's
writing. From the "Dedicatory" poem of her first published volume—
April Twilights of 1903—Northeastern hillsides covered with apple
orchards precede her references to Nebraskan children dreaming by
a western river. As Ann Romines shows compellingly in this volume,
the shadow of cities, especially of Cather's New York, lies just beneath
the surface even of Cather's antebellum Virginia novel. Even in the
posthumous story "The Old Beauty," the turning point of the heroine's life is a sexual assault which presumably could have occurred to
the privileged protagonist only in socially mobile New York.

It is certainly no surprise that New York would be a central ingre-
dient in Willa Cather's work, once one assimilates the facts presented
in this book. John J. Murphy surveys with admirable thoroughness
the sites Cather walked by daily, knew thoroughly, and blended into
her fiction. Murphy provides a comprehensive context for subsequent facts touched on in the essays that follow his. My own essay
focuses on Cather's even earlier familiarity with Cos Cob, Connecticut, a New York getaway spot beloved of artists and *McClure's* folk
alike. Taking that connection further, Joseph Urgo carefully considers "the Cather years" at *McClure's,* during which Cather transformed journalistic practice in ways esthetic, political, cultural, and
literary, ways affecting her own later work and profoundly affecting
that magazine. Robert K. Miller discusses, through the ways Cather
fictionalized several contemporary disasters, the cultural anxieties
that surface in her work. And Jo Ann Middleton completes the first
part of this collection by looking at Cather's fiction through medical
lenses, especially the ways in which Cather's early medical "bent," as

well as medical experience, friendships, and information, is integrated into her fiction.

In part 2, "Art Capital of the World," on the arts Cather loved so well and assessed so knowledgeably when they became available around her, we see that Cather located herself in the very center of cultural, literary, and artistic activity. This section, in fact, opens several broad avenues into Cather's intensely compressed fictions. By choice she found living quarters around Washington Square's bohemia—where the most radical creations and thoughts of her time were shared. Cynthia Griffin Wolff establishes a theoretical framework for the essays to follow when she asks, "if an artist working in such a medium as prose fiction elects to refer to another medium (in the case of Cather, refer extensively), what unsuspected consequences might follow? If Willa Cather often deflects her reader's attention to painting or music, what all-but-hidden connections does her complex conjoining imply?" Cather's acquaintance with Childe Hassam and the New York he painted, as well as the artistic consequences of their volleying glances, are illustrated and documented by Kathryn Faber. Sherrill Harbison changes the subject to Cather's Wagner, and Gretel Weiss draws on a lifetime of listening to discuss Cather's use of Schubert. The breadth of Cather's cultural sophistication, however, is perhaps stretched farthest by Evelyn Haller, who adds the ballet to the art forms feeding those reverberating allusions in Cather's fiction.

Cather was before all else, of course, a writer, in a tradition as well as a community of writers. It is her relationship to other writers she associated with New York or met in New York, that opens up Cather scholarship in part 3, "City Contacts and Literary Connections." Gloria Rojas covers Cather's absorption of Walt Whitman, the celebrator of "Mannahatta." Robert Comeau reveals some consequences of Cather's personal friendship with Mark Twain, the most famous man of his age and her New York neighbor. Deborah Williams explores the problematic sisterhood offered Cather by Zona Gale, also a famous Pulitzer Prize winner and social activist. And Mona Pers traces Cather's warm friendship with Nobel Prize winner Sigfrid Undset, who lived in Brooklyn during the Second World War. Laura Winters rounds out the topic, and even projects a Cather connection into the future, as she explores Cather's influence on four contemporary writers.

In part 4, "Urban Perspectives," this collection looks broadly at urban perspectives which surface in Cather's work. Ann Romines leads off by constructing the bridge that joins rural or small town

Cather to that Cather sophisticate who never discards her city mind-set. Heather Armstrong compares the city consciousness of Cather and Dreiser, two writers profoundly shaping our views of city life through heroines curiously similar in careers, if not in character. Jessica Rabin shows how much Cather absorbs of the ethnicity which makes New York so distinctive a place to live, so full of friction and energy; and Joanne Morrissey colors in Cather's fictional response to that "bitch-goddess Success" who drove her and from whose whips and scorns she exempted her favorite characters in *Obscure Destinies*. Susan Rosowski ends the collection with a discussion of comedy, without which life seems barren in either country or city.

Willa Cather always returned to New York because, like Eudora Welty's Edna Earle Ponder, she "missed her city lights." We are sure of that fact because young Willa, from the first opportunities that came her way in her college years, headed straight for the city. The first accessible city she could get to was Chicago, and that midwestern capital precedes New York in Thea Kronborg's fictional experience, as well as literally in Cather's own. In Chicago Cather first developed her taste for opera, as well as her eye for painting and architecture. Architecturally-rich Pittsburgh was another crucial stopping place, as well as a professional editor's launching pad, before Cather found a way to her work at *McClure's,* and to her chance thereafter to locate permanently in New York. But after 1906, it was a New Yorker's eye that Cather trained on her Nebraska experiences—much as New Yorker Jim Burden looks back in *My Ántonia.* Thereafter, from the world's artistic capital, Willa Cather—a natural-born culture sponge who was interested in everything and on whom nothing was lost—assimilated what she saw and felt and knew for her stunningly sophis-ticated artistic productions about Nebraska farmers, as well as about the urban elite. Her experiences in the city inform all her fictions. Indeed, we are just beginning to learn how much.

WILLA CATHER'S
NEW YORK

Part I
Geographical City and Home Town

From Cornfield to the Big Apple Orchard: New York as School for Cather and Her Critics

JOHN J. MURPHY

Since I was born a New York boy, educated here, and raised about forty miles "out on the island," I thought it would be easy for me to consider Willa Cather and the city. But I gave the project too much thought. I decided that while my Catholic school introduction to *Death Comes for the Archbishop* and *Shadows on the Rock* generated my initial interest in Cather, that interest was quickly augmented by the New York perspective I shared with her. For in spite of Willa Cather's recognition of this city's horrors and frustrations, the energy and inventiveness of New York breathes through most of her work. As the city does, Cather combined incredibly disparate worlds and peoples. The resulting tension in both city and fiction is stimulating. Like the city, Cather is praised and blamed for what she creates, is accused of prejudice and smugness while being celebrated for her inclusiveness and sympathy. Rereading made me realize that Cather was a New Yorker more than a Nebraskan or Virginian, and a Newyorkophile more than a Francophile or a Southwest aficionado.

Entering the City

Cather first visited New York in February 1898, while she was working in Pittsburgh. She was twenty-four, saw the great Polish actress Helena Modjeska in Schiller's *Mary Stuart* and lunched with her. We can imagine the impressionable young woman's wintry introduction to the big city and even the train ride to it from Pittsburgh in "Paul's Case" (1903), which romanticizes New York as theater and retail merchandise. After checking in and napping at the old Waldorf Astoria (where the Empire State Building now stands), Paul takes a cab up Fifth Avenue and sees "whole flower gardens blooming under glass cases . . . vastly more lovely and alluring that they blossomed thus unnaturally in the snow. [Central] Park itself was a wonderful stage winter-piece."[1] Cather's youthful introduction is tapped again in *My Mortal Enemy* (1926); the hazy city inspiring an effective Impressionist's response: "The snow blurred everything a little, and the buildings on the Battery all ran together—looked like an enormous fortress with a thousand windows. From the mass, the dull gold dome of the *World* building emerged like a ruddy autumn moon at twilight."[2] To narrator Nellie Birdseye, Madison Square is "like an open-air drawing-room," and Saint-Gaudens' Diana on the tower of Stanford White's Garden (gone now like the old Waldorf) "stepped out freely and fearlessly into the grey air." "Here," Nellie feels, "winter brought no desolation" (544). Cather's 1898 meeting with Modjeska is worked into the novel—the actress in her cloak framed by a window, "the moonlight falling across her knees" (555).

Although New York as a somewhat undefined locale appears in Cather prior to her 1898 introduction to it (for example, the 1897 story "Nanette: An Aside" takes place in an opera diva's rooms in the Hotel Savoy, built five years earlier at the southeast corner of Central Park), the city becomes as Cather's acquaintance increases a cohesive reference point for characters involved in faraway places like Hong Kong, Naples, the West Indies, and even Nebraska. In "Eric Hermannson's Soul" (1900), a New York society girl engaged to a dabbler in theater management and art collecting (he is importing a Puvis de Chavannes to New York from Paris) can only experience passion with a crude Norseman of the plains. Nebraska and New York are again juxtaposed in "The Treasure of Far Island" (1902), when playwright Douglas Burnham (prairie boy made good) discusses his New York activities with the small town girl he rediscovers back home. By "A Death in the Desert" (1903) Cather felt familiar enough with the city to pen Katharine Gaylord's lament at being exiled in Wyoming, thousands of miles away: "Do tell me about New York. . . . How does it look and taste and smell just now? . . . [W]hat misguided aspirants practice their scales in the rookeries about Carnegie Hall? What do people go to see at the theatres, and what do they eat and drink there in the world nowadays? You see, I'm homesick for it all, from the Battery to Riverside" (*EN & S*, 69). In two 1905 stories, "The Garden Lodge" and "Flavia and Her Artists," the heroines (the first a practical Brooklyn girl) shelter artists in New York suburbs, one near Long Island Sound, "steel-blue and dotted with white sails" and "splendidly seen from the windows of the lodge" (*EN & S*, 49), and the other in Tarrytown "on the historic Hudson" because "the best" artists "could not be lured so far away from the seaport" (*EN & S*, 10).

In 1906 Cather came to New York as associate editor for *McClure's* on East 23rd Street, taking up residence at the Hotel Griffin on West 9th Street and then at 60 Washington Square South in the building

Madison Square Park, Looking Northeast from Fifth Avenue and 23 Street, Winter 1910–11. Courtesy of the New York Historical Society.

where Edith Lewis was living. Assignments in Boston for the Mary Baker Eddy project and then in London interrupted these first years, and permanent residence was delayed until 1909 when Cather and Lewis began to share (in Lewis's words) a "not very comfortable apartment . . . on Washington Place, just off Washington Square."[3] The New York strain continues during this time and reflects growing intimacy with the city. For example, in "The Namesake" (1907), Lyon Hartwell's identification of his sculptor father draws upon Cather's acquaintance with the Metropolitan Museum's collection of American sculpture. The elder Hartwell, says his son, "was one of those first fellows who went over after [William Wetmore] Story and [Hiram] Powers—went to Italy for 'Art' quite simply; to lift from its native bough the willing, iridescent bird. Their story is told, informingly enough, by some of those ingenuous marble things at the Metropolitan" (*SP & OW*, 56). In "The Willing Muse" (1907) the narrator reveals Cather's knowledge of Manhattan social geography: popular author Bertha Gray overwhelms her fragile husband by (among other things) dislodging him from their downtown flat and "into a new apartment house on Eighty-Fifth Street" with a servant who took cards.[4] "On the Gulls' Road" (1908) indicates Cather's exposure to the Impressionist paintings she saw in New York, to which the wandering narrator returns to receive an intimate letter from the deceased woman he had drawn in red chalk and fallen in love with during a voyage from Genoa.

The City in Story

In the fall of 1912 Cather and Lewis moved into 5 Bank Street, their home for fifteen years, where, according to Lewis, "Cather did her happiest writing. . . . it was there that she completed *O Pioneers!*, and worked at all her other books through *Death Comes for the Archbishop*. Although she wrote parts of them in other places," adds Lewis, "they all came back to 5 Bank Street, it was there they had their home."[5] A few months prior to this move Cather published a story emphatically about New York as futuristic American city, "Behind the Singer Tower," complementing the theme of destructive ambition in her first novel, *Alexander's Bridge* (which also came out in 1912), and anticipating Carl Linstrum's complaint in *O Pioneers!* (1913) about the city's tendency to overwhelm its citizens. The occasion for this story is a devastating fire in a high-rise hotel called the Mont Blanc, a fictional event probably based on smaller hotel fires in New York and Syracuse. The incident generates a discussion by six professional men (one an engineer) of Manhattan as "an irregular parallelogram pressed between two hemispheres, and, like any other solid squeezed in a vise, [shooting] upward" (*CSF*, 44). The energetic thrust of the city is linked to the scores of rich and famous lives claimed in the hotel fire: "Never before, in a single day, had so many of the names that feed and furnish the newspapers appeared in their columns all together, and for the last time" (45). The fatal toll of irresponsible and unregulated building motivates the disgruntled engineer, Hallet, to expose the ongoing victimization of anonymous blue collar workers in an account of an Italian immigrant killed in the construction of the Mont Blanc. Stanley Merryweather, New York's "most successful manipulator of structural steel" (47), had allowed worn cables to be used in order to increase profits. Thus greed, victimization of immigrant laborers otherwise unwelcome in New York, the materialistic vengeance of discriminated-against Jews (Merryweather is part Jewish), and the general waiving of humanitarian principles to the detriment of the poor combine as themes.

The symbol of the city's destructive energy is the Singer Tower, an ornate skyscraper of 612 feet designed by Ernest Flagg and completed in 1908 at 149 Broadway, which dominated lower Manhattan for eighteen months as the tallest building until eclipsed by the Metropolitan Life Tower off Madison Square. (The Singer Tower was demolished in 1968.) Against the new materialism this turbinlike structure represents to Hallet, "the Statue of Liberty, holding her feeble taper," seems "but an archeological survival" (46). The burial of the workers (including Hallet's little Italian friend) when a dredging bucket drops upon them from its worn cable, "like a brick . . . on an ant hill" (51), is an interesting contrast to Cather's own experience of New York as an escape from death in a Nebraska cornfield, for the city represented for Cather the alternative to burial and oblivion. During the *McClure's* years, writes Lewis, "[t]he city itself, so open to the sea and freedom . . . stimulated and excited her";[6] subsequently, the "years from 1912 to 1927 were for her years of absorbing and delightful experiment and discovery."[7] Yet, Cather was aware of the social stifling of millions among the city's lower classes and concludes her story by extending their fate to all of society. Hallet speculates on the sacrificing of humanity in the city's vertical thrust toward the unknown, "a new idea of some sort . . . that's what we are all the slaves of. . . . It's the whip that cracks over us till we drop. Even Merryweather . . . will never know anything about [it]. Some day it will dawn, serene and clear, and your Moloch on the Singer Tower over there will get down and do the Asian obeisance" (*CSF*, 54).

During the next several years, between the writing of novels, Cather acknowledged New York's difficult realities in several stories revealing significant knowledge of the city's landscape and lifestyles. In "Consequences" (1915) a "young man of pleasure," Kier Kavenaugh, who knows the ins and outs of handling working girls ("broilers" he calls them) from various ethnic backgrounds, is pursued unto suicide by the shabby ghost of his ruined future. In this exposé of personal waste, Cather takes us from the Flatiron Building on 23rd Street, up Fifth Avenue past the Public Library, then up Sixth to Central Park South (59th Street), where Kavenaugh has his rooms, and includes a Steichen-like portrait of the *Times* Building hung with vapor as well as references to Long Island watering places on both the south shore (Long Beach) and north (Huntington Bay). In a moment of self-pity for pleasure-seekers like himself, Kavenaugh laments, "Queer place, New York; rough on the little fellows. Don't you feel sorry for them, the girls, especially? I do. What a fight they put up for a little fun!" (*SP & OW*, 151). In "The Bookkeeper's Wife" (1916),

Singer Tower, 149 Broadway, Looking Southwest. Courtesy of Columbia University School of Architecture.

a commentary on domestic collapse, Percy Bixby goes uptown to 123rd Street to win the hand of social-climbing stenographer Stella Brown, to whom he must lie about his bookkeeper's salary and supplement it with embezzlement. But Stella resumes her career due to boredom after the marriage and replaces Percy with a high-roller. "You might as well live in Newark if you're to sit at home in the evening," she tells him. "You oughtn't to have married a business woman; you need somebody domestic" (*SP & OW*, 165–66). In "Ardessa" (1918) Cather offers a slice of the magazine publishing business while tracing the rise of young Jewish businesswomen Becky Tietelbaum and Rena Kalski, who replace a Christian woman grown lazy and privileged enough to take vacations in East Hampton. Economic and social upheaval are implied in Ardessa's demotion scene as editor O'Mally (a thinly disguised S. S. McClure) "looked out of the window at a new sky-scraper that was building, while [Ardessa] retired without a word" (*SP & OW*, 181).

The meaninglessness of both social climbing and business success comes home to corporate lawyer Paul Wanning in "Her Boss" (1919) when he is diagnosed with a fatal illness: "How [he wonders] had a short-lived race of beings the energy and courage valiantly . . . to throw up towers and build sea-monsters and found great businesses, when the frailest of the materials with which they worked . . . had more permanence in this world than they?" (*SP & OW*, 198). Neither his wife nor children (spoiled daughters and an unproduced playwright son) can provide the kind of comfort Wanning receives from legal firm copyist Annie Wooley, who gives him her time and sympathy as he dictates his autobiography during his final days. Taking Wanning to Annie's tenement house on Eighth Avenue allows Cather to expound on the conditions of "a typical poor family of New York":

> Of eight children, only four lived to grow up. . . . Illness and death and funerals . . . had come at frequent intervals in Annie's life. . . . Annie had often given up things . . . because there was sickness at home, and now she was patient with her boss. . . . [S]he was not interested in getting all she could for her time, or in laying up for the future. . . . [T]he present is . . . all [girls like her] have. (202)

In a depressing coda we discover that Annie is dismissed from the firm after Wanning dies and is cheated out of the thousand dollar bequest he intended for her.

Playing the Art Mart

Such stories reflect Cather's periodic exasperation with the crass values and vulgarity of New York. After completing *The Professor's House* (1925) Cather threatened to leave the city for good, yet she returned to Bank Street after sojourns in New Mexico and New Hampshire. When the Bank Street building was pulled down to make way for a new apartment building, Cather moved into small sunless rooms in the Grosvenor, an old apartment hotel at 35 Fifth Avenue (across from the Church of the Ascension), rather than leave the city. Five years later, Cather found an apartment at 570 Park Avenue, near the upscale shops of Madison Avenue and the treasures of the Metropolitan Museum. "She still professed to hate New York and to say that it was becoming ever less attractive as a place to live," writes Woodress, "but she couldn't bring herself to leave."[8] Neither did she waste much time castigating the city in fiction. She was an artist, not a social critic, and New York, the nation's literary capital, with its increasingly rich array of art life, music, and theater, was ultimately conducive to the kind of artist she was. Two passages in "Coming, Aphrodite!" (1920), perhaps her best New York story, suggest to me what the city contributed to Cather. The first lists its offerings to singer Eden Bower, an artist discovering herself: "She had time to look about, to watch without being watched; to select diamonds in one window and furs in another, to select shoulders and moustaches in the big hotels where she went to lunch. She had the easy freedom of obscurity and the consciousness of power. She enjoyed both. She was in no hurry" (*SP & OW*, 375). Cather adds that these opportunities "really did a great deal toward making her an artist." The second passage details the workday of experimental painter Don Hedger: "He forgot there was anything of importance going on in the world outside of his third floor studio. Nobody had ever taught him that he ought to be interested in other people; in the Pittsburgh steel strike, in the Fresh Air Fund, in the scandal about the Babies' Hospital. A grey wolf, living in a Wyoming canyon, would hardly have been less concerned about these things than was Don Hedger" (363–64). The opportunity to plunge into life at its highest pitch and then withdraw from it and, like Hedger, plunge into "more tempestuous adventures" in a dark studio are characteristic of Cather and her artists in New York.

Indeed, this story and two others clustered with it in *Youth and the Bright Medusa* (1920) create Cather's version of New York as the place where artists contend with the free enterprise system the city itself symbolizes. Don Hedger, we are told, "had twice been on the verge of becoming a marketable product," but he had resisted the temptation and worked as a draughtsman when in need of money (361). Burton Ives, who had the marks of success Eden Bower understood (a Japanese servant, a wine cellar, and a riding horse), represents the kind of artist Hedger refuses to become but that Eden herself seems to have become on her return to New York, "her thoughts . . . entirely upon stocks" in gold mining (394). This compromise between singing and marketability is examined both in "The Diamond Mine" (1916) and "Scandal" (1919). In "Scandal" Kitty Ayrshire has become a commodity in a society invaded by wealthy Jews. Siegmund Stein, Cather's representative of this class, has risen in the garment industry and become a factor in the arts, the decorative frosting on his solid financial cake. While climbing the social ladder, Stein "cultivated the society of . . . poets, actors, musicians. He entertained them sumptuously, and they regarded him as a deep mysterious Jew who had the secret of gold, which they had not" (*SP & OW,* 460). Kitty is exploited by Stein through a lookalike garment factory girl he uses (and tosses) to get his name linked to Kitty's, and then, after marrying a Jewish department store heiress and dislodging an old New York family from its historic Fifth Avenue mansion, Stein tricks Kitty into singing at his housewarming. Kitty helplessly concludes that the Steins will "get you in the end," that for victims of circumstance in New York "so many of the circumstances are Steins" (467). Lest Cather be charged with discriminating solely against Jews, in "The Diamond Mine" the leeches living off Metropolitan Opera diva Cressida Garnet's voice are dour Ohio Christians. The Jew in Cressida's life, Miletus Poppas, her accompanist (actually her mentor), although "a vulture of the vulture race" (*SP & OW,* 402), is the only one to protect "the goose that laid the golden eggs" (410). Cressida is "not musically intelligent" (409) and must struggle to master her roles; she is one of those workhorse artists, conscientious, sane, sure, preferred by managers over more gifted singers. We never know if she has or ever had any potential for the artistic "revelations" of her rivals (422), for her commitment "to make [her undeserving] family happy" (406) forces her to be pragmatic to a stifling degree. She continues to sing long past her prime to bail out her fourth husband's investments, and she goes down with the *Titanic,* having booked passage on the maiden voyage because she considered "all advertising . . . good" (430).

Such portraits are essentially depressing and would confine the city to the negative light of Cather's periodic disapproval if they were not relieved by setting. If a context of struggle and frustration, New York also becomes in Cather's juxtaposition of outdoor and interior scenes a stimulating place where artists live, work, and congregate. In "Coming, Aphrodite!" Washington Square inspires a lively pastiche of crying Italian babies being splashed by the fountain as plump robins hop in the soil and Stanford White's Arch frames the bright leaves of young poplars along Fifth Avenue; it is "a stream of things that were bright and beautiful and alive" (359). The excursion to Coney Island becomes a more extensive holiday set-piece of tall steins of beer in the noisy balcony restaurant, shifting parasols, red-faced barkers, shining fat women, balloons, and shouting little boys. Perched on his roof back in Washington Square with his dog on a May night of silver stars, Hedger looks out over the blue stillness and "dark and mournful" chimneys of other roofs as he listens to Eden singing "the tempestuous, overlapping phrases of Signor Puccini" (362–63). Returning from Long Island expecting to take up with Eden, Hedger sees "the East River, and the bridges, and the city to the west . . . burning in the conflagration of the sunset" (391). In "The Diamond Mine" Cressida and the narrator find exhilaration after a snowstorm in a painterly Central Park indebted perhaps to Childe Hassam's *Late Afternoon, New York: Winter* (1900) or *Winter in Union Square* (1894):

> Overhead it was a soft, rainy blue, and to the west a smoky gold. All around the horizon everything became misty and silvery; even the big, brutal buildings looked like pale violet water-colours on a silver ground. Under the elm trees along the Mall the air was purple as wisterias. The sheep-field, toward Broadway, was smooth and white, with a thin gold wash over it. (411)

Alternating with these depictions are picturesque interiors: the restaurant with the frescoed Italian scenes and built around a court where Cressida meets her third husband, an erratic Bohemian composer and violinist; the basement oyster house with the handleless cups and sawdust floor Hedger takes his meals at; Kitty Ayrshire's study in "Scandal," where she huddles in "folds of diaphanous white over . . . diaphonous rose" in the corner of a couch in a long room full of flowers, owing (I think) to Hassam's *The Room of Flowers* (1894), and with a painting of a Paris salon at the opposite end. This interior is of particular interest for it links New York's art life to Europe's. The painted interior depicts Kitty's Paris friends: a composer, a sculptor, the painter's wife, an historian, and others; it "made, as it were, another room; so that Kitty's study on Central Park West seemed to open into that charming French interior, into one of the most highly harmonized and richly associated rooms in Paris" (454). Eyeing the

Winter in Union Square (1894) by Childe Hassam. Courtesy of the Metropolitan Museum of Art, gift of Miss Ethelyn McKinney, 1943, in memory of her brother, Glenn Ford McKinney.

canvas, Kitty's New York visitor exclaims, "[Y]our own room, too, is charming," adding that the lamp in the painting "shines upon you and me" (455).

The Writer's Alembic

Through such scenes (and there are many, many more) Willa Cather acknowledges her attachment to and occasional enthusiasm for New York, recognizing it as the perspective of her art. The importance of this perspective struck me emphatically when I was putting together my analysis of *My Ántonia* for Twayne's Masterwork Studies. I titled the strategic chapter "The Alembic of Art," an alembic being a distilling device for refining and changing material poured into it. The alembic in Cather's case involved literature of other writers (both canonical and contemporary), theater, music, and painting. While Cather experienced the arts wherever she traveled (and traveled to many places to experience the arts), she was in New York more than other places (as Lewis indicates, it was the home base), and New York was emerging as a comprehensive and international arts community. The material Cather poured into her alembic included Nebraska, but what came out should be labeled a New York product. As the narrator of the Introduction in *My Ántonia* makes clear, "Jim Burden and I both live in New York" (*EN & S*, 711), and the original version underscores that fact. Jim writes his book about his formative years and Ántonia in New York, where he finishes and titles it. As we observe what survives of Willa Cather's New York and piece together the lost city, as we locate what she would have seen when she shopped around Bank Street or made her way up Broadway to the opera, as we rediscover what was being performed in theaters and concert halls or being displayed at the Metropolitan Museum during those years, clues to her fiction emerge that are as pertinent as those available in Webster County, Nebraska.

Cather's early fiction, editing, and theater-reviewing in Lincoln, Pittsburgh, and Washington D.C. prepared her for her plunge into New York's frantic literary scene in 1906. "New York is a vast mart," wrote Howells, "and literature is one of the things marketed here."9 The Knickerbocker tradition established by Washington Irving, James Fenimore Cooper, Herman Melville, and Walt Whitman included Howells and Twain by the century's turn. Henry James and Edith Wharton were born in the city and made it a fashionable subject of fiction. Stephen Crane, Frank Norris, and Theodore Dreiser had preceded Cather to New York; and during her lifetime fellow novelists like Sinclair Lewis, Ellen Glasgow, Edna Ferber, Nathanael West, John Dos Passos, F. Scott Fitzgerald, Thomas Wolfe, John Steinbeck, John O'Hara, Zora Neale Hurston, and Richard Wright made New York home. The city's poets included Hart Crane, E. E. Cummings, Edna St. Vincent Millay, Wallace Stevens, Marianne Moore, Mark Van Doren, and W. H. Auden. The theater, as it moved from Union Square to Times Square and then developed off Broadway, was being defined by Eugene O'Neill, Clifford Odets, Elmer Rice, George Kaufman, Marc Connelly, and others. Cather's tenure at *McClure's* placed her at the center of much of this activity, and she continued theater reviewing into the 1912–13 season, critiquing plays by Pinero, Shaw, Stanley Houghton, and Arnold Bennett and Edward Knoblauch.[10] Elsie Sergeant lost patience when Cather boycotted the O'Neill plays being produced at the Sheridan Square Theatre near Bank Street and voiced a preference for Galsworthy moral comedies on Broadway. (Cather did socialize with one of O'Neill's actors, Paul Robeson, as a guest of the Menuhins.)[11] She attended ceremonial dinners in New York for Twain, Howells, and Robert Frost, met often with Edward Arlington Robinson, and developed a lasting friendship with the actor George Arliss and his wife. Cather and Lewis often held open house at 5 Bank Street and later entertained on Park Avenue, where their guests included Alfred and Blanche Knopf, and Sigrid Undset, the Norwegian novelist who made her home in Brooklyn Heights during World War II. Although somewhat reclusive in her later years, Willa Cather remained involved in the literary scene.

Literary activities, of course, even when social, bordered on business for Cather, but she enjoyed the visual arts and especially music as recreation, even though they often provided the creative impetus for her fiction. (Her critical statements, like Henry James's, abound in the terminology of and references to the fine arts.) Edith Lewis recalls that their economies in Washington Place made them hesitate to purchase a coffeepot but never prevented their going to the opera (74). Old New Yorkers bent on competing with European capitals were joined by thousands of Italian, German, and Russian Jewish immigrants in establishing the city as a world musical center by the turn of the century. Tchaikovsky had come to preside at the opening concerts in Carnegie Hall in 1891; Antonin Dvořák composed his symphony "From the New World" while directing the city's National Conservatory in 1892–93; Gustav Mahler conducted the Philharmonic and at the Metropolitan Opera from 1908 to 1911, and Arturo Toscanini left Italy in 1908 to become artistic director of the Met. Charles Ives, Virgil Thomson, George Gershwin, and Aaron Copland were among the classical composers at home in the city, and during World War II Hungarian refugee Béla Bartók fled to New York, where he had his Piano Concerto no. 3 premiered by Yehudi Menuhin.

Willa Cather regularly took advantage of this musical activity. In the early years opera was her primary passion, and she attended Met performances conducted by both Mahler and Toscanini. Indeed, she heard an astounding number of famous singers, whose names Lewis carefully records in her brief biography:[12] Polish tenor Jean de Reszke and his brother Edouard, a bass; French bass Pol Plancon;

Lillian Nordica, American soprano; French soprano Emma Calvé; Polish coloratura Marcella Sembrich; Nellie Melba, Australian soprano; French baritone Maurice Renaud; American soprano Emma Eames; Antonio Scotti, Italian baritone; Swedish-born American soprano Olive Fremstad, who inspired *The Song of the Lark;* American contralto Louise Homer; Italian coloratura Luisa Tetrazzini; Enrico Caruso, Italian tenor; Russian bass Feodor Chaliapin; Mary Garden, Scottish soprano; Italian baritone Pasquale Amato; Emmy Destinn, Bohemian soprano; and Geraldine Farrar, American soprano. After her move to Park Avenue in 1932, Cather seemed to favor symphony and chamber music concerts. During these years Toscanini was principal conductor at the Philharmonic and developed the orchestra's reputation for Beethoven, Brahms, Verdi, and Wagner. Among Cather's closest friends at this time were British pianist Myra Hess and the Menuhin family, whose prodigy children, Yehudi, Yaltah, and Hepzibah, Cather adopted as nephew and nieces.

As a New Yorker, Cather had access to the visual arts more than anywhere outside Europe. By 1901 the Metropolitan had become the richest art museum in the world. In 1913 the International Exhibit of Modern Art at the 69th Regiment Armory, Lexington Avenue and 25th Street, established the city as a center of avant garde art activity. (Cather's friend Mabel Dodge was one of the organizing sponsors of this Armory Show.) The Museum of Modern Art was set up in 1929, and the Whitney Museum of American Art a year later. At this time the Met was rehousing and adding the medieval collection acquired for it by John D. Rockefeller's purchase in 1925 of George Grey Barnard's museum of medieval art. By 1938 the supplemented medieval collection opened to the public in the Cloisters, a section of a Romanesque Benedictine monastery transported from southern France to Fort Tryon Park in upper Manhattan. We know Cather frequented the Metropolitan from her use of Jehan George Vibert's painting *The Missionary's Story* (displayed there in 1925) as the basis of the Prologue to *Death Comes for the Archbishop* (1927).[13] What else impressed her at the Met is impossible to know, although we can identify some of the works the museum had acquired by 1929 that would have been of interest to her. Among numerous American landscapes, Cole's *The Oxbow* and Bierstadt's *Rocky Mountains, Lander's Peak* had become familiar items. American Impressionists were represented by Sargent's *Madame X.,* Whistler's *Cremore Gardens,* Homer Martin's *Harp of the Winds,* Cassatt's *Lady at the Tea Table,* and Hassam's *Church at Gloucester.* Among Italian paintings of significance were Giotto's *Epiphany,* Botticelli's *Last Communion of St. Jerome,* Di

Olive Fremstad. Courtesy of James Camner.

"The Cloisters." George Grey Barnard's Museum for Gothic Art at the time of its purchase by the Metropolitan Museum of Art in 1925. International Newsreel. Courtesy of Underwood Photo Archives, San Francisco.

Paolo's *Paradise,* Raphael's *Madonna and Child Enthroned,* Carpaccio's *Meditation on the Passion,* Bellini's *Madonna and Child,* Mantegna's *Holy Family with Mary Magdalen,* and Maroni's *Abbess Lucrezia Vertova.* Spanish acquisitions included El Greco's *View of Toledo* and *Portrait of a Cardinal.* On exhibit from the Flemish and Dutch schools were Van der Weyden's *Christ Appearing to His Mother,* Christus's *Lamentation,* Bosch's *Adoration of the Magi,* Brueghel's *Harvesters,* Rembrandt's 1660 *Self-Portrait,* Vermeer's *Young Woman with a Water Jug,* and Maes's *Young Girl Peeling Apples.* The German collection included Dürer's *Virgin and Child with St. Anne.* Among French works were Barbizon painter Rousseau's *Forest in Winter Sunset;* several studies by Pierre Puvis de Chavannes, whose work inspired *Death Comes for the Archbishop;* Bastien-LePage's *Joan of Arc,* Manet's *Boating,* Degas's *Woman with Chrysanthemums,* Cézanne's *Gulf of Marseilles;* Renoir's *Mme. Charpentier and Children,* and Monet's *Rouen Cathedral in Mid-Afternoon.* In the medieval collection predating the Cloisters, Cather would have

The Church of the Ascension, Fifth Avenue at 10th Street. Courtesy of Whitney Cox.

noticed a thirteenth century carved wooden Virgin and Child from Auvergne and several French tapestries.

Art was also available outside museums. Lewis notes Cather's frequent visits to the Church of the Ascension directly across Fifth Avenue from the Grosvenor because "she loved the beautiful altar, with John La Farge's great fresco above" (151). The fresco, *The Ascension of Our Lord,* fills the round arch of the sanctuary, which also features a bas-relief by Saint-Gaudens of two angels holding a chalice. Cather had convenient access to this church during the writing of *Shadows on the Rock* (1931), using it perhaps as a refuge from the sunless hotel bedroom she had brightened with allegorical scenes from the *Lady and Unicorn* tapestries. I am convinced that the aesthetic shaping of religious mystery evident in the church's altar, fresco, and stained glass windows, depicting parables and scenes of the Christian story from the Annunciation to the Vision of St. John by such distinguished artists as La Farge, J. Alden Weir, and Louis Comfort Tiffany, contributes to "the world of the mind" of the devout nuns in her novel, that "well-ordered universe . . . created by God for a great purpose, the sun . . . made to light it by day, the moon . . . to light it by night,—and the stars, made to beautify the vault of heaven like frescoes . . . safe, lovingly arranged, and . . . congenial. . . ."[14]

The Critic in the City

This city is for me the greatest revealer of Willa Cather's eclectic creative process. While I was reading Cather as a college student here (picking up first editions along Fourth Avenue for a dollar or two and then carelessly scribbling in them with ink), I was also discovering the city block by block and its cultural offerings. The New York City Ballet was then in its infancy and housed in the old Mecca Temple on West 55th Street, where one could get upper balcony seats for $1.50 and then move close to the stage after intermission. The muscular strain and beads of perspiration on Maria Tallchief and Andre Aglevsky revealed the strenuous effort behind the illusion of ease in writing as well as dance. I recall as achievements of Helen Hayes both gentle play with her audience and subtle understatement, theatrical equivalents of Cather's "inexplicable presence of the thing not named" (*SP & OW*, 837). In Shaw's *Saint Joan*, Irish actress Siobhan McKenna artfully employed a thick brogue and rustic gestures to emphasize, like Cather through Jim Burden, the peasant qualities of her heroine. As I got to know Cather better and read *The Song of the Lark* I felt physically close at the Metropolitan Opera's old home at Broadway and 39th Street, where she spent so much time. She would have known if not heard the singers I heard there, for they were among those who staffed the Met during the war, when international travel was restricted. Italian bass Salvatore Baccaloni and French coloratura Lily Pons made their careers at the Met; the others were American: tenors Jan Peerce and Richard Tucker; baritone Leonard Warren; mezzo-soprano Risë Stevens, and soprano Eleanor Steber.

This is not meant to be a nostalgia trip but to indicate an ongoing aesthetic approach to Cather's work. During a week in Manhattan about five years ago, I attended a special exhibit on Belgian surrealist René Magritte at the Metropolitan Museum. While looking at the art and listening to the curator's audio commentary, not only did I begin to appreciate Phyllis Rose's comparison of the "massive dislocation" of the structure of *The Professor's House* (1925) to Magritte's surrealism[15] but discovered that Godfrey St. Peter's psychological diffi-

Metropolitan Opera House, Broadway and 39th St. (1883–1966). Courtesy of GTE Corporation.

culties and their resolution could be approached through these paintings. Magritte's *Daring Sleeper,* in which the subject is suspended in a coffinlike box over a void camouflaged with a concoction of familiar images in a lead tablet, illustrated clearly the meaning of the near-death experience of Cather's subject.[16] After the Cather seminar in Winchester in June of 1997, I made a visit to the Cloisters for the first time in many years to compare it to the Cluny I had visited in Paris a month earlier. One of the highlights of the Cloisters is the Campin Room, named for the fifteenth-century Flemish painter Robert Campin, whose Altarpiece of the Annunciation (*circa* 1425) is the room's object of focus. The museum has furnished this room with contemporary pieces similar to those in the central panel of the triptych: table, bench, iron candle bracket, brass candlestick, laver (basin), majolica jug holding a lily, even a beamed ceiling. According to what Craig Harbison defines in this tradition of painting as "a descriptive realism of particulars,"[17] the domestic possessions of donors are depicted objectively but used in a symbolic way to support religious themes. In the Campin altarpiece, for example, the "brass laver is . . . a symbol of Mary's purity, like the Madonna lily in the vase . . . . The candle on the table is a symbol of Christ; the candlestick represents the Virgin who bore him."[18] Campin seats Mary on the floor instead of the bench to demonstrate her humility, but the bench itself becomes meaningful in the finials or ornaments on its arms, the dog and the lion. This kind of realism is Cather's approach in *Shadows on the Rock,* in which domestic routine and objects develop sacred significance. Cather had been acquainted prior to *The Professor's House* with the warmly furnished living rooms and kitchens full of coppers in northern Renaissance paintings, and in "Tom Outland's Story" she utilizes the window scenes opening from such interiors to harbors and seas beyond (*SP & OW,* 974). However, in *Shadows* she focuses on the interiors themselves and their furnishings: the walnut dining-table, white cloth, silver candlesticks, decanters of red and white wine, and high-backed sofa upholstered in red velvet in the Auclair living room; Count Frontenac's colored glass fruit; Jacques' carved beaver; Cécile's engraved silver cup; the brooms, clouts and brushes that transfigure life into a sacred experience.

✷

New York City is unsurpassed as a school for Cather the artist and her art; its essential connection to that art explains why she continued to live in the city. She was at the top of a world where, as John Steinbeck wrote, "[a]ll of everything is concentrated, . . . population, theatre, art, writing, publishing, importing, business, murder, mugging, luxury, poverty. It is all of everything. It goes all night. It is tireless and its air is charged with energy."[19]

Notes

1. Willa Cather, *Early Novels and Stories,* ed. Sharon O'Brien (New York: Library of America, 1987), 125–26. Cited as *EN & S.*
2. Willa Cather, *Stories, Poems, and Other Writings,* ed. Sharon O'Brien (New York: Library of America, 1992), 543. Cited as *SP & OW.*
3. Edith Lewis, *Willa Cather Living* (New York: Knopf, 1953), 74.
4. Willa Cather, *Collected Short Fiction, 1892–1912,* ed. Virginia Faulkner (Lincoln: University of Nebraska Press, 118). Cited as *CSF.*
5. Lewis, *Living,* 148.
6. Ibid., xvii.
7. Ibid., 148.
8. James Woodress, *Willa Cather: A Literary Life* (Lincoln: University of Nebraska Press, 1987), 446.
9. Kenneth T. Jackson, ed., *The Encyclopedia of New York City* (New Haven: Yale University Press, 1995), 682.
10. Woodress, *WC,* 236.
11. Ibid., 488.
12. Lewis, *Living,* 74–75, 90.
13. James Woodress, "The Genesis of the Prologue of *Death Comes for the Archbishop,*" *American Literature* 50 (1978–79): 475.
14. Willa Cather, *Later Novels,* ed. Sharon O'Brien (New York: Library of America, 1987), 526. Cited as *LN.*
15. Phyllis Rose, "Modernism: The Case of Willa Cather," *Modernism Reconsidered,* ed. Robert Kiely (Cambridge: Harvard University Press, 1983), 127–28.
16. John J. Murphy, "The Modernist Conversion of Willa Cather's Professor," *The Calvinist Roots of the Modern Era,* ed. Aliki Barnstone, Michael T. Manson, and Carol J. Singley (Hanover: University Press of New England, 1997), 67.
17. Craig Harbison, *The Mirror of the Artist: Northern Renaissance Art in Its Historical Context* (New York: Abrams, 1995), 27.
18. Bonnie Young, *A Walk through the Cloisters* (New York: Metropolitan Museum of Art, 1988), 125–26.
19. Jackson, *Encyclopedia,* 683.

Bibliography

Camner, James, ed. *The Great Opera Stars in Historic Photographs.* New York: Dover, 1978.

Cather, Willa. *Collected Short Fiction, 1892–1912.* Ed. Virginia Faulkner. Lincoln: University of Nebraska Press, 1970.

———. *Early Novels and Stories.* Ed. Sharon O'Brien. New York: Library of America, 1987.

———. *Later Novels.* Ed. Sharon O'Brien. New York: Library of America, 1990.

———. *Stories, Poems, and Other Writings.* Ed. Sharon O'Brien. New York: Library of America, 1992.

Gray, Christopher, ed. *Fifth Avenue, 1911, from Start to Finish in Historic Block by Block Photographs.* New York: Dover, 1994.

Harbison, Craig. *The Mirror of the Artist: Northern Renaissance Art in Its Historical Context.* New York: Abrams, 1995.

Howard, Kathleen. *The Metropolitan Museum of Art Guide.* New York: Metropolitan Museum of Art, 1983.

Jackson, Kenneth T., ed. *The Encyclopedia of New York City.* New Haven: Yale University Press, 1995.

Lewis, Edith. *Willa Cather Living.* New York: Knopf, 1953.

Murphy, John J. "The Modernist Conversion of Willa Cather's Professor." In *The Calvinist Roots of the Modern Era.* Ed. Aliki Barnstone, Michael T. Manson, and Carol J. Singley. Hanover: University Press of New England, 1997. 53–72.

———. *My Antonia: The Road Home.* Boston: Twayne, 1989.

Rose, Phyllis. "Modernism: The Case of Willa Cather." In *Modernism Reconsidered,* Ed. Robert Kiely. Cambridge: Harvard University Press, 1983. 123–45.

Sergeant, Elizabeth Shepley. *Willa Cather: A Memoir.* Lincoln: University of Nebraska Press, 1963.

Silver, Nathan. *Lost New York.* New York: Wings, 1967.

Weinberg, H. Barbara et al. *American Impressionism and Realism: The Painting of Modern Life, 1885–1915.* New York: Metropolitan Museum of Art, 1994.

Whitfield, Sarah. *Magritte.* London: South Bank Centre, 1992.

Woodress, James. "The Genesis of the Prologue of *Death Comes for the Archbishop.*" *American Literature* 50 (1978–79): 473–78.

———. *Willa Cather: A Literary Life.* Lincoln: University Nebraska Press, 1987.

Young, Bonnie. *A Walk through the Cloisters.* New York: Metropolitan Museum of Art, 1988.

Young Willa Cather and the Road to Cos Cob

MERRILL MAGUIRE SKAGGS

When Willa Cather forbade the publication of her personal letters and notes, she guaranteed that we readers would speculate about her private life. We guess because we want to know exactly what she was thinking in the months she wasn't guiding her meticulously edited work into print. I wish here to speculate about a hidden chapter of young Cather's private life around New York. The action I'll trace eventually culminates in the Bush-Holley House of Cos Cob, the present day headquarters of The Historical Society of the Town of Greenwich, Connecticut. That fact is lucky for us scholars because the present proprietors have good archives and excellent archivists,[1] and the former owners saved just about everything. That oddly familiar (because so often painted) Bush-Holley house was once thought a "picturesque" seventeenth-century farm house;[2] two centuries later it was advertised as a boarding house easily reached in an hour or less by train from New York.[3] Amateurs and geniuses captured it on canvas hundreds of times and from every angle because it served also as headquarters of the "Cos Cob art colony."[4] The "Cos Cob clapboard school" of art,[5] in turn, embraced many American Impressionist painters such as Childe Hassam, Leonard Ochtman, J. Alden Weir, Theodore Robinson, John Twachtman, and Elmer MacRae.

Willa Cather, too, stayed here. While she carefully obfuscated this interlude in her life, I believe it significantly affected her career, her life choices, and her future fiction. The story I'll construct will require remembering simultaneously several places important to Cather—Nebraska, Chicago, Pittsburgh, England, France and Connecticut. But if we can hold all these places in our minds at once, I think we can guess something new about how a determined genius-to-be named Willa Cather acquired skills she would put to use when she depicted a world and a parish.

The evidence about Cather which I will use in this essay either derives from sources well-known already, or else is illustrated here. The reproduced documents are from the HSTG Archives, which also contains seven unautographed Cather volumes, mostly first editions,[6] and a revised edition of *April Twilights,* inscribed emphatically on April 27, 1924, "For Constance MacRae, one of my 'public' when

43

The Old Holley House c. 1895. Courtesy of HSTG Archives, Holley House Collection.

it was small indeed," and signed *Willa Cather. Constant* Holley MacRae, for the record, helped manage her mother's boarding house and eventually married Elmer MacRae, one of the artists who gathered on the porch or on the property to paint.[7] Willa got the name wrong in her publicly personalized greeting, as her friend Viola Roseboro' often did also. Also among archival papers is a 1920's postcard signed "Willa R," though clearly in Cather's handwriting,[8] and a Christmas card from "Adele and Willa," as clearly written by the mysterious Adele who cannot yet be identified, though the *Willa* signature duplicates "Willa R."

Local lore has it that when Willa Cather came to stay at the Holley boarding house, Childe Hassam had to move out of the best bedroom. Be that as it may, Hassam painted many views, front and back, of Holley House. His undated painting of a reclining woman reading on the Holley House porch is felt by residents of Greenwich to be of Willa Cather, because of her hairstyle. Put local tales, postcards, and inscribed book together and we know that Willa Cather did stay at Holley House and later fondly recalled the place and the pro-

Title Page of revised *April Twilights* (1923), inscribed, "For Constance MacRae, one of my 'public' when it was small indeed. Willa Cather. Cos Cob April 27th *1924*. Courtesy of HSTG Archives, Holley House Collection.

Vassar Lake, Vassar College, Poughkeepsie, N.Y. Courtesy of HSTG Archives, Holley House Collection.

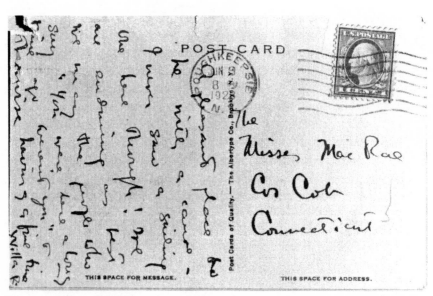

Postcard from "Willa R" to "The Misses MacRae." Courtesy of HSTG Archives, Holley House Collection.

Christmas card signed "Love and best wishes for a Merry Christmas from Adele and Willa." Courtesy of HSTG Archives, Holley House Collection.

prietress. Beyond that, we do not know exactly when, why, with whom, or with what professional results.

I would like to propose here a slightly revised biographical story line for Cather. I believe Willa was certainly in Cos Cob soon after she returned from Europe in the fall of 1902, and that while there she was hobnobbing with artists as well as *McClure's* magazine folk. For the McClure's crowd used Holley House too, for a handy getaway. Lincoln Steffens was its enthusiastic promoter,[9] and among its recorded guests were not only Steffens and his first wife Josephine, but also Ida Tarbell, Viola Roseboro', and Jean Webster. Auguste Jaccaci, a *McClure's* art editor, owned property nearby.[10] Jaccaci went on to direct the art of *Scribner's* after Mr. McClure fired him in 1902, because, as McClure told his wife, "I do not like the way he keeps a diary of all I say to him in our personal relations."[11] One surmises that the magazine stories told on the Holley House porch could be spicey.

As far as Cather goes, I believe that her visits triggered the astonishing burst of creativity out of which she wrote her first two books, *April Twilights* (1903) and *The Troll Garden* (1905), both connected in some way or another with S. S. McClure. Just as important, I think Cather heard in Cos Cob the artists' talk about techniques for capturing motion, mood, color and light that, translated to fiction, helped make her stories so startlingly memorable.[12]

The story about young Willa Cather that makes the most sense to me involves a somewhat rearranged chronology of events. But the biographer's tracks I still happily follow at several turns were left by Sharon O'Brien, to whom I am grateful. Our new sequence of events starts when 28-year-old Willa and her friend Isabel McClung land in England in late June, 1902. By now Willa Cather has written and published both stories and poems, has functioned as a successful journalist and reviewer, has edited magazines, taught school, and acquired a startlingly fine education in literature, music, theater, and opera, and a noteworthy exposure to the very significant architecture in Chicago and Pittsburgh. She has also had the opportunity in those two cities to view painting and public sculpture, though her knowledge of painting at this point may have been "academic," that is, shaped by the reigning tastes in Chicago and Pittsburgh, as expressed by the works on public display.

Here a key fact comes into focus. The first significant collections of French Impressionist paintings in this country were amassed around Chicago. An apocryphal story I heard from a distinguished Yale art historian concerns the New York debutante, just after the turn of the twentieth century, who visited Chicago to meet her fiance's family for the first time. As she toured his family home she gasped to recognize on its walls the most breathtaking paintings. She turned roundeyed to her future mother-in-law and gushed appreciatively, "But where do you get your Impressionists?"

The older woman stopped dead still and then replied firmly, "My dear, in Chicago we do not *get* our Impressionists. We *inherit* them— from our grandmothers!"

I'm repeating this joke to explain two personal opinions. First, when young Willa Cather came back east to Pittsburgh to claim her first fulltime editorial job, she would have become aware of a certain eastern condescension toward midwest culture; it can still pop up. But she also had to know that where French Impressionist art was concerned, Chicago got there first. With six years of practiced cultural counterpunching behind her by 1902, she was primed to pound any British who might look like they were thinking condescending thoughts about America, who were asking, "Who reads an American book?" Indeed, the savaging she gives England in her Lincoln newspaper letters home may be partially understood as vented ire first aroused in Pittsburgh.

Having been in England a whole week, Cather pronounces the voices of girls "strident,"[13] their dress "frankly a shock at first" (7), and their "unfortunate" carriage "so universal that it amounts to a national disfigurement among the women" (7). Later, Cather derisively foregrounds British painting stained by "that muck of sentimentality which has choked all truth and courage and vividness out of English art" (73).

My second opinion related to Chicago art history concerns Cather's disproportionately warm responses to French art scenes. Soon after leaving England she set up almost chauvinistically the superior French Barbizon and Provence landscapes. To her, the wheatfields of Millet's work looked like Bladen—"more familiar than anything I have seen on this side the Atlantic" (122)—and the Van Gogh and Cezanne-rendered scenes of Provence provided "the excitement of continual novelty" (170). Even the women of Arles, she points out, are superior, "noted all over France for their beauty" (172).

In between Barbizon and Arles, Cather discovers the wonderful landscape of the Côte d'Azur. She describes Le Lavandou as "a fishing village of less than a hundred souls, that lies in a beautiful little bay" (155), with houses built "between the steep hillside and the sea" (155), arranged "on either side of one narrow street" (155) accommodating "one very fairly good hotel, built on the sea" (155). In that hideaway, "There is a long veranda running the full length of the house on the side facing the sea" (155). In short, she finds a place Cos Cob replicates—or that replicates Cos Cob. She mentions good fare, a little train connecting the retreat to the outside world, and "singing—always singing" (157). She concludes rhapsodically,

> Nothing else in England or France has given anything like this sense of immeasurable possession and immeasurable content. I am sure I do not know why a wretched little fishing village, with nothing but green pines and blue sea and a sky of porcelain, should mean more than a dozen places that I have wanted to see all my life. No books have ever been written about Lavandou, no music or pictures ever came from here, but I know well enough that I shall yearn for it long after I have forgotten London and Paris. One cannot divine nor forecast the conditions that will make happiness; one only stumbles upon them by chance, in a lucky hour, at the world's end somewhere, and holds fast to the days, as to fortune or fame. (157–58)

Once Cather had located such a place, it seems to me that she would want to duplicate it. The question becomes, however, which place is the original and which the mirror image? The descriptive phrases she records about Le Lavandou uncannily match the scene a guest might view from the veranda of Holley House in the fishing village of Cos Cob, in Connecticut. In fact, Steffens begins his description, "Cos Cob, Conn., is a little old fishing-village strung along one side of one long street facing Cos Cob harbor in the town of Greenwich, which is the first New England community the New York, New Haven and Hartford Railroad passes on the way east" (436). My second suggestion about this happy scenic echo effect, however, is that one as knowledgeable about the current American cultural scene as Cather was, would already know by 1902 that painters identifying themselves as American impressionists had been producing for fifteen years what Childe Hassam jokingly called "the Cos Cob clapboard school" of art. The colony was well known and regularly featured in newspaper articles by the 1890's.[14] In fact, Cather could have glimpsed Cos Cob before her first trip abroad, and taken "possession" of its analog as Tom Outland takes possession of the Blue Mesa. The main question is how Willa Cather got to Holley House in the first place, and the likeliest answer involves Viola Roseboro'.

Viola Roseboro', daughter of a Congregationalist minister from Tennessee, had for over a decade been earning her living in New York as an actor, a journalist, and a free-lance writer and writing coach, when she interviewed for a job with S. S. McClure. McClure hired her in 1896 partially because, he explained, "I can't find any expression to describe that woman's talk. It is too varied."[15] Her job was to discover fresh writing talent and uncover genius. She did: O. Henry, Booth Tarkington, Damon Runyon, and Willa Cather, it would seem, all came to McClure's attention with her imprimatur.[16] Roseboro' also worked as a freelance editor and coach; Gertrude Hall said of her work, "Since I have experienced the benefit of Miss Roseboro's critical help I would not dare send a manuscript to a publisher till she saw it."[17]

Roseboro' was one of the three loyalists to remain in McClure's offices after the exodus of staffers in May, 1906. She remained until the end of McClure's tenure and stayed in touch with him until his death at age 92. Because *McClure's,* at its peak, was the world's best general magazine with the world's best-paid feature writers and a risk-taking propensity to publish unknowns, ambitious young writers of self-confidence and sound judgment would certainly have sent their work there. All unsolicited prose writing was assessed by Viola Roseboro'. I assume that is the obvious way she and Willa Cather met.

That Roseboro' was a familiar guest at Holley House by the spring of 1903 is established by her gift of the novel she published in April of that year, inscribed, "For the Holly House Library with the grateful good wishes of the author."[18] By April of 1903, when Cather's *April Twilights* was published, Roseboro' clearly knows Cos Cob well. In previous months, once the Holley House painters were mentioned, Roseboro' should have had little trouble persuading young Willa Cather to visit it for an outing. But Cather may well have been as eager to meet other *McClure's* notables as she was to scrutinize American Impressionism in progress. In any case, I believe Cather's biography at this point makes more sense if we assume that her Cos Cob visits preceded her first two books and occurred, at the least, between October of 1902 and late April of 1903. At Holley House Cather would have gotten to know key players in the magazine, as well as the art, world. Such contacts could explain why Samuel McClure, a hyperactive, impulsive and impetuous go-getter and entirely indiscriminate reader of verse,[19] then demanded of Cather, whom he had not met, within a week after the publication of her vanity-press, slender volume of derivative poems called *April Twilights,* that she come to New York for a meeting, even though she was, of course, a young midwestern woman then living in Pittsburgh. Obviously, somebody McClure trusted put the book in his hands and told him it was written by a winner he ought to meet. The one he had hired to give him that kind of advice was Viola Roseboro'. Typically McClure grabbed where Roseboro' pointed. If we assume further that Cather had already met several literary people with pull, like the Cos Cob/publishing crowd, before her little book appeared, we could also understand (in my case for the first time), how *April Twilights* got reviewed in the New York *Times:* then as now, the *Times* was not quick to review respectfully the new and small first volumes of poetry published by earnest mid-western young women.

I believe the Cos Cob connection between important painters and Willa Cather opens up yet-untold possibilities for study of Cather's prose techniques, especially since the Armory Show of 1913—that defining marker of Modernism—featured Holley House painters. The basic story is told fancifully by Anya Seton in the catalog program for the show of Elmer MacRae's painting, held at the Milch Galleries of New York March 23-April 18, 1959, and called "Forgotten Artist of the 1913 Armory Show":[20]

> On the crest of a hill, out behind the ancient Bush-Holley House at Cos Cob, Connecticut, there stands a picturesque barn . . . its weathered siding scarred by the sun, the rains and the ceaseless winds from across the nearby waters of Long Island Sound.
>
> . . . And it was there, in the barn, that two of the most important art discoveries of decades have just been made by fellow members of the Greenwich Historical Society which has acquired and is restoring this exquisitely beautiful Colonial homestead. . . . Our immediate interest starts with the purchase of the property some seventy-five years ago, by Mr. Edward P. Holley. In the mid-1890's, after living there for several years, Mr. Holley and his wife converted the house into "The Holley Inn"—soon to become a favorite summering place for budding artists and writers. Among this group was Elmer Livingston MacRae, a talented young New York artist with a host of friends. On October 16th, 1900, Mr. MacRae married the Holley's only daughter, Constant, and it was in the old house that the couple's twin daughters were born.
>
> The barn provided the perfect setting for a studio and before long it had become the headquarters for that now famous group of American artists known as the "Cos Cob School"—with the great John H. Twacht-man as its mentor.
>
> Cos Cob was a paintable spot and it was frequented by artists who worked and painters who painted: John H. Twachtman and his son Al-den; Childe Hassam, Louis Comfort Tiffany . . . and countless others. Then there were those who "just dropped by," like Walt Kuhn, George Luks, Jo Davidson, Arthur B. Davies, William Glackens, Jerome Myers, and a host of other friends of Elmer Livingston MacRae.
>
> . . . Among the many writers and editors who stayed or visited at "The Holley Inn" were such prominent people as Lincoln Steffens. . . . Willa Cather, who did some of her most exquisite writing in the old north bedroom; . . . Jean Webster, who wrote "Daddy Long-legs"; Don Seitz of

the *World;* Moody of the *Evening Sun;* Gilman Hall of *Ainslee's* and *Every-body's* and my father, Ernest Thompson Seton.

. . . "The concept of holding a great exhibition (International Exhibition of Modern Art, celebrated as the Armory Show, in 1913)" writes Ira Glackens, . . . "originated with Elmer MacRae, Jerome Myers, Walt Kuhn and Henry Fitch Taylor."

For years the intimate details of the "Armory Show" have been mysteriously lost. . . . It was left to several well-qualified researchers of the Greenwich Historical Society to discover the long lost records of the Show, high *in the hayloft of the ancient barn in Cos Cob! And here, too, were found the early paintings by MacRae! Not in years have two such important art discoveries been made and both in a single day!*

But I must leave further work on Holley House Modernism to American art historians.

What I would like to concentrate on here is what a Cos Cob connection might suggest about Cather's early work. Most obviously, she wrote about artists in *The Troll Garden* because she was observantly among them at this time. But if, as Professor St. Peter argues, great artists get their "splendid effects by excision,"[21] then we ought to be able to learn some things worth knowing by considering the poems excised from the revised edition of *April Twilights,* and the stories omitted from collections printed after *The Troll Garden.*[22] For starters, it's possible that Cather deliberately "planted" a revised edition of *April Twilights* in the Holley House library to *obscure* or camouflage the absence of thirteen missing and too-personal early poems which revealed too much about this place and time in her life, which connections she had tried to erase when she excised those poems from the revised edition.

"Dedicatory," the first excised poem, for example, begins by evoking an April twilight experienced in a setting typical of Connecticut—with hills hid in violet shadow, still meadow brooks, a snowy orchard and still-naked oaks and beeches—before the poem passes on, through memory, to "three who lay and planned at moonrise, / On an island in a western river." The poem "Asphodel," whose speaker is analogous to a slain warrior's pale shade, ends with the intriguing lines, "So I recall our day of passion yet, / With sighs and tenderness, but no regret." "The Mills of Montmartre" features "crimson sails" that "turn all the night-time long," notably converting to dust the yellow grain brought in by lasses, while those sails turn luridly in the dark. "On Cydnus," and "The Namesake," on facing pages, actually seem to deal with similar themes: "On Cydnus" is about throwing a world away, and "The Namesake" is about throwing a life away. "Eurydice" ends with the exclamation, "Sweetheart! the way from Hell's so long, so long." And most intriguingly, the title of the next-to-last poem seems to gulp, "I Have No House For Love to Shelter Him." When Cather's syntax stumbles, even in a poem title, her readers probably ought to stop and ponder. And the last excised poem salutes Paris, the city of "pride and power."

Equally intriguing are the three stories Cather eliminated from all story volumes that followed *The Troll Garden*. We know that she prepared her first volume of stories in the same adrenaline rush that produced her poems, though McClure's publishing house delayed book publication until 1905. Yet all those poems and stories seem to start to life in that same winter and early Spring of 1902–1903. Coincidentally, Viola Roseboro' also experienced a creative burst at this time which produced her novel *The Joyous Heart*, also published in April of 1903. Even more coincidentally, the heroine of that novel is named *Vella Carruthers*, a name not entirely unlike Willa Cather. When Vella is first described, we are told, "It was granted in time that she had an April charm of her own."[23] And for what it's worth, this Vella dies nobly at the end, in childbirth.

In any case, what arrests my attention in Cather's early tales is that the three "excised" stories—"Flavia and Her Artists," "The Marriage of Phaedra," and "The Garden Lodge"—all share a theme or suggest obliquely a confluence of adultery and incest: a most forbidden package of sins. *Phaedra*, of course, signals such sins through the name of that Greek matron who lusted after Hippolytus, her step- son. That reference indicates adulterous mother-son incest. The young girl from whose point of view "Flavia and Her Artists" is told is named *Imogen*, after the daughter of Shakespeare's *Cymbeline*. Imogen is threatened by the lusts of her step-mother's son Cloten, who knows she is already married to her true love. Shakespeare's Imogen fights threatened brother-sister incest and adultery, though the young lass of Cather's story actually longs for reconnection with her once-loving host, in a kind of symbolic incest of the daughter-father variety. But it's "The Garden Lodge" that seems to me the most interesting story of the three. Here the implied incest and adultery is conveyed through music. As we start into this story we register that the setting is a ringer for Cos Cob, seen from the windows of the Bush-Holley House, where I'm guessing this adrenaline rush may have begun.[24]

After we get past the names of the principle characters in "The Garden Lodge"—Caroline Noble and Raymond d'Esquerré (or

Moonbeam Esquire)—the first thing to notice is the setting. It's a "place on the Sound" in the magic month of May, in fact, "the most mild and florescent of all the blue-and-white Mays the middle coast had known in years," where a lodge "in the apple orchard" produces "the sound of the tenor's voice and of Caroline's crashing accompaniment" floating through air from which one can spot that "[t]he Sound, steel-blue and dotted with white sails was splendidly seen from the windows." Concomitantly, garden and orchard are "riotous with spring and had burst into impassioned bloom, as if to accommodate Caroline, though she was certainly the last woman to whom the witchery of Freya could be attributed."[25] We spot all the symbols of sexually charged fertility from blooming apple orchards to Freya, also called Frigge, for whom Fridays are named and to whom Friday the 13th is sacred.

Caroline Noble, our heroine, is a disciplined woman whose rearing in a slackly-run house among distractable musicians has led to her profound hatred of poverty: "She was young and pretty, and she had worn turned gowns and soiled gloves and improvised hats all her life. She wanted the luxury of being like other people, of being honest from her hat to her boots, of having nothing to hide, not even in the matter of stockings, and she was willing to work for it" (190). That is, Caroline wants everything Cather had derided British shop girls, in her summer letters of 1902, for not wanting: "the American idea of neatness, of being genuine as far as you go, of having little and having it good" (7). Beyond the poverty that produces shoddy clothes, however, "[t]here were two things she feared even more than poverty; the part of one that sets up an idol and the part of one that bows down and worships it" (190). One could paraphrase these fears as "falling in love." In "The Garden Lodge," Caroline Noble fears falling in love.

Disciplined and determined Caroline can make money by playing accompaniments at song recitals. By age twenty-four she meets and marries a wealthy, forty-year-old widower whose fortune is associated with New York's Wall Street, and settles into an affluent life. Trouble begins when a famous tenor artist accepts the Nobles' hospitality for a month, and then practices his art in their garden lodge, accompanied by Caroline. After he leaves, Caroline's husband offers to build a more substantial summer house in place of the garden lodge, and Caroline immediately objects. Later unable to sleep because "the night was close and warm, presaging storm" (191), Caroline slips back to the garden lodge and begins to play that solo from the first act of the *Walküre* which she and Raymond had practiced together: it translates, "Thou art the Spring for which I sighed in Winter's cold embraces." It is sung by Siegmund to his sister Sieglinde, who is already another man's wife. Hence, adultery and incest again. Bursting into sobs as she realizes her own intense longing, Caroline discovers,

> The horror was that it had not come from without but from within. The dream was no blind chance; it was the expression of something she had kept so close a prisoner that she had never seen it herself; it was the wail from the donjon deeps when the watch slept. Only as the outcome of such a night of sorcery could the thing have been loosed to straighten its limbs and measure itself with her. . . . The fact that d'Esquerré happened to be on the other side of the world meant nothing; had he been here, beside her, it could scarcely have hurt her self-respect so much. (196)

Caroline gets a grip on herself and tells her husband at breakfast to tear that lodge down. Her response tallies with that refrain from the excised 1903 poem: "I have no house for Love to shelter him."

So what does this all add up to? I'm guessing that Cather experienced in the winter of 1902–3 that rush of energy and exhilarating release everybody calls "falling in love." It happened in a place that looked a great deal like Holley House, which was visited at that time by the most talented artists of all kinds, and the most interesting people in the Northeast. Cather's passion was strong and threatening enough to feel equivalent to the most tabooed package of sins she could conjure, combined adultery and incest. That may have been so because to realize such a passion required Cather to do the one thing she had most staunchly forbidden herself: to live the vicarious, marginalized, self-sacrificial, supportive life of a second fiddle, an accompanist. The very idea damaged her self-respect, for she knew very clearly, as she had known for a long time, that she was destined to be The Star.

My guess is that Willa Cather put Cos Cob behind her and never looked back. She wrote patronizingly about accompanists from time to time, for an accompanist can live only through the art of another. She did mention in her study of Thea Kronborg, the starring diva of *The Song of the Lark,* that Thea's accompanist Oliver Landry grew up "on a rocky Connecticut farm not far from Cos Cob."[26] When Cather remembered that Cos Cob moment twenty years later, however, she saluted the proprietress of Holley House with a rush of warm feeling. She might even, in reminding Constant MacRae of sympathy felt years before, have hoped that Constant had once held Cather's *first* volume of poems, just printed, with wonder. Cather might have hoped there was that moment when the young MacRaes said, as

Cather's beloved Emerson had said wonderingly to an unknown named Walt Whitman, "I greet you at the beginning of a great career."

Notes

1. Susan Richardson, the exceptionally efficient, knowledgeable, and generous archivist, was a crucial help to me in documenting this essay.

2. Theodore Robinson records in his diary that the house "was built in 1664 they say." Susan G. Larkin, "Light, Time, and Tide: Theodore Robinson at Cos Cob," *The American Art Journal* 23 No. 2 (1991): 85.

3. Larkin publishes a map of Cos Cob in 1900, showing the railroad line (Ibid., 77). Advertisements of Holley Farm (where art students could stay) stressed "wide piazzas, ample grounds, splendid shade; no mosquitoes, no chills and fever: one hour from New York to Coscob; all trains stop; ten minutes from depot; references required."

The Holley House itself was advertised, "First class board, large rooms, piazzas, shade, fresh vegetables, milk, etc.; one minute from boating, bathing and fishing; three minutes walk from Coscob depot; 45 minutes by express; all trains stop; Rooms in adjoining cottage at reduced rates; liberal arrangements for winter months." The William E. Finch, Jr. Archives of the Historical Society of the Town of Greenwich (the HSTG Archives) contains four such advertisements.

4. For the most complete account, see dissertation by Susan G. Larkin, "'A Regular Rendezvous for Impressionists': The Cos Cob Art Colony 1882–1920," CUNY, 1996. Two copies are in the HSTG Archives.

5. The joking phrase originated with Childe Hassam. See Susan G. Larkin, "'Moss Grown and Worm Eaten': Images of Cos Cob's Architecture," *Greenwich History* 2 (Fall 1997): 27.

6. These include a first edition of *A Lost Lady*, a fifteenth printing of *A Lost Lady* (1939), a first edition of *Shadows on the Rock*, a first edition of *The Old Beauty*, a first edition of *Sapphira and the Slave Girl*, a fourth printing of *One of Ours*, and a first edition of *December Night*, the special issue of 1933, which was presented to Constant and Elmer McRae by Martha Twachtman. The special printing issue which Cather herself clearly sent and inscribed is numbered 76 of 450.

7. See Larkin, "Moss Grown," 33–35, and also the Anya Seton account quoted in the text.

8. I am indebted to Marilyn Callander (*Willa Cather and the Fairy Tale*, 1989) for comparing the handwriting on the card to handwritten letters from Cather which Callander owns. Her conclusion: "Unquestionably Willa." Her opinion is confirmed by Bruce Baker, after his months of work with Cather letters in the WCPM Archives in Red Cloud.

9. Steffens devotes a chapter of his *Autobiography* to Cos Cob and Holley House.

10. *The Autobiography of Lincoln Steffens* (Complete in One Volume), (New York: Harcourt, Brace, 1931), 440.

11. Peter Lyon, *Success Story: The Life and Times of S. S. McClure* (New York: Scribner's, 1963), 200 n.

12. Steffens gives a vivid account of such conversations: "The Holly House [sic] was a great, rambling, beautiful old accident—so old that it had its slave quarters up

under the roof; and it looked out from under elms as high as oaks upon the inner harbor and an abandoned boat-building house with sail lofts. There was a long veranda where the breezes blew down from the river, up from the Sound, and cooled the debaters and settled the dinner debates that Twachtman started. We dined all together at one long table in a fine, dark, beflowered dining-room. The game was always the same. Twachtman would whisper to me as he passed on to his place, 'I'll say there can be no art except under a monarchy.' Waiting for a lull in the conversation, he would declare aloud his assertion, which was my cue to declare the opposite." (*Autobiography,* 437)

13. *Willa Cather in Europe: Her Own Story of the First Journey,* Introduction and Notes by George N. Kates (Lincoln: University of Nebraska Press, 1984), 6.

14. The Larkin dissertation title—"'A Regular Rendezvous for Impressionists': The Cos Cob Art Colony 1882–1920"—tells this story. Larkins's dissertation includes impressive lists of local or visiting artists, writers or publishing people, notables, and art students.

Steffens also confirms these facts: "Quiet, almost dead, it was a paintable spot frequented by artists who worked, painters who actually painted: Twachtman and the Murphys, Childe Hassam and Elmer McRae; by writers who wrote: Bert Leston Taylor, Wallace Irwin, Thompson Seton [Anya Seton's father]; by editors and publishers: Gilman Hall of *Ainslee's* and *Everybody's,* Don Seitz of the *World,* Moody of the *Evening Sun.* . . . It was an 'art colony'; the painters there were sometimes called 'the Cos Cob school'; we talked art, and we had a contempt for people who talked business and politics." (*Autobiography,* 436)

15. Lyon, *Success,* 141.

16. Ibid., 154, 158n, 296.

17. HSTG Archives: summary information sheet on Viola Roseboro'. Gertrude Hall, of course, wrote a book on opera which Cather praised in "Gertrude Hall's *The Wagnerian Romances,*" *On Writing* (Lincoln: University of Nebraska Press, 1988), 60–66.

18. Roseboro' appears to have been one of the many *McClure's* and New York publishing people attracted to Cos Cob in the wake of Steffens' enthusiasm. We can also tell, however, that when a time lapse occurs between publication of her work and its presentation as a gift, Roseboro' records the fact. Her next novel, *Players and Vagabonds* (1904), is also in the Holley House collection. It is inscribed, "For dear Constance MacRae, given Nov. 22, '06." A notable postscript written on Cather's first birthday at *McClure's,* adds on the same flyleaf, "Presentation edited and amended Dec. 7, '06 (From V. R.)"

19. Half the disgust about McClure's affair with Frances Wilkinson was aroused by the fact that he insisted on publishing her doggerel alongside the poetry of A. E. Housman and W. B. Yeats. (Lyons, *Success,* 260)

20. Seton's account is occasionally inaccurate and was intended more as publicity than scholarship. Yet Claire Vanderbilt, the current Chair of The Historical Society of the Town of Greenwich, explained in an interview how deeply she regretted the sale (by the Milch Gallery on behalf of the HSTG) of two trunkloads of papers detailing this planning process to Joseph Hirshhorn, who subsequently donated the papers to the Smithsonian Museum. Money from the sale was used to restore and open the Bush-Holley House under auspices of the HSTG (6 December 1996).

21. Willa Cather, *The Professor's House* (New York: Knopf, 1925), 76.

22. Professor Robert Thacker generously notified me of finding a letter in Harvard's library from Cather to her editor Ferris Greenslet, dated 23 October [1915] and saying, "Yes, I'd like to bring out an expurgated and revised edition of *April*

Twilights sometime. You are good to offer to do it." Professor Thacker kindly added, "Given your contentions about Cather's rewriting herself with the 1923 *April Twilights,* the word 'expurgated' is pretty much confirmation, I'd say." (email 14 Sept. 1999)

23. Viola Roseboro', *The Joyous Heart* (New York: McClure, Phillips, 1903), 7.

24. Because I-95 now mars this view, it may be easier to consult the canvases painted from the porch or around the house.

25. Willa Cather, *Collected Short Fiction,* Introduction by Mildred Bennett (Lincoln: University of Nebraska Press, 1965), 187.

26. Willa Cather, *The Song of the Lark* (Lincoln: University of Nebraska Press, 1978), 445.

Bibliography

Cather, Willa. *Collected Short Fiction, 1892–1912.* Ed. Virginia Faulkner. Lincoln: University of Nebraska Press, 1970.

———. *On Writing: Critical Studies on Writing as an Art.* Lincoln: University of Nebraska Press, 1988.

———. *The Professor's House.* New York: Knopf, 1925.

———. *The Song of the Lark.* Lincoln: University of Nebraska Press, 1978.

Kates, George N., Introduction and Notes. *Willa Cather in Europe: Her Own Story of the First Journey.* Lincoln: University of Nebraska Press, 1988.

Larkin, Susan G. "'A Regular Rendezvous for Impressionists': The Cos Cob Art Colony 1882–1920." Ph. D. diss., CUNY, 1996.

———. "Light, Time, and Tide: Theodore Robinson at Cos Cob." *The American Art Journal.* 23. No. 2. (1991): 75–108.

———. "'Moss Grown and Worm Eaten': Images of Cos Cob's Architecture." *Greenwich History* 2 (Fall, 1997): 27–49.

Lyon, Peter. *Success Story: The Life and Times of S. S. McClure.* New York: Scribner's, 1963.

Roseboro', Viola. *The Joyous Heart.* New York: McClure, Phillips, 1903.

Seton, Anya. "Forgotten Artist of the 1913 Armory Show." New York: Milch Gallery Catalog. Elmer MacRae Paintings, March 23–April 19, 1959.

Steffens, Lincoln. *The Autobiography of Lincoln Steffens* (Complete in One Volume). New York: Harcourt, Brace, 1931.

Willa Cather's Political Apprenticeship at *McClure's* Magazine

JOSEPH R. URGO

I

Willa Cather's final literary apprenticeship was spent as writer and editor at *McClure's* Magazine in New York City from 1906 until 1911, years referred to by Ellen Moers as "the Cather era" at that publication.[1] She was promoted to Managing Editor in 1908. The work Cather did while associated with *McClure's* accomplished what today we would call modernist, or cultural, politics where aesthetics are employed to prod cognitive changes and to question the modes of thought that buttressed social institutions. Aided by a prior association with members of the staff, Cather participated in a significant redirection of *McClure's* editorial policies, away from 19th-century paternalism toward a more eclectic, less overtly doctrinaire (but still quite evident) politics of social and cultural engagement. *McClure's* historian Harold Wilson defines this era at *McClure's* as the period when the magazine attempted to "portray more positive aspects of society." This meant moving away from the position "that reform consisted in getting various laws obeyed to the position that certain new laws and new organizational structures were necessary to preserve the old ideals. Indeed, this was the direction of the whole progressive movement" at the time.[2] And most interesting for Cather critics, whereas muckraking had "relegated literature to a secondary status"[3] in the magazine, the Cather era would employ literature to lead, rather than to adorn, its social agenda. However, it would be a mistake to see *McClure's* as less politically engaged as a result of these changes. If the magazine's revised mission was to create *new laws* and *new organizational structures,* then we know, at the end of the 20th century (after civil rights, feminist, and other cultural reform movements), that what was necessary was the institution of new ways of thinking.

In 1906, *McClure's* magazine was in crisis. A division emerged, partially fueled by S. S. McClure's eccentric and sometimes erratic personal style, which pitted those who supported a change in editorial policy against those who did not.[4] After 1906, the stress on reporting lawlessness would be replaced by more positive advocacy for social renewal. The emphasis on the literary might thus be seen as part of a general move at *McClure's* away from condemning toward creating. As one would expect, the positivists who had contributed so much to making the old *McClure's* a success, Ida Tarbell and Lincoln Steffens, for example, were not pleased when they left the magazine. The emotional content of the situation was aggravated further when President Roosevelt openly criticized *McClure's* for having gone too far in its muckraking condemnations. According to Wilson, "The President's growing impatience with muckraking only further encouraged McClure to emphasize what he called the upbuilding nature of the American people,"[5] though it also led his adversaries at *McClure's* to conclude that he was selling out.[6]

Perhaps because historians rather than cultural or literary critics have told the story of *McClure's,* the idea that it abandoned its political agenda in 1906 has been accepted without qualification. Historians have followed the lead (and the memoirs) of the influential and prolific journalists, Steffens and Tarbell, and their perspective has largely informed the historical record. Cather was brought to the magazine through the efforts of its literary staff, including a woman who had read her previous submissions to the magazine, Viola Roseboro'.[7] Within its renewed mission, the literary would play a more central role. Readers would encounter literary selections that prodded and queried the magazine's reportage, sometimes in direct contradiction, sometimes in playful disregard for the gravity of the events covered. During the Cather era, *McClure's* editorial policies participated in a general, social redefinition of the place of the arts within public discourse. In the coming age of mass media, as we know, arts and politics would no longer assume distinct public spheres. Literary historians may thus come to agree with Robert Thacker, who describes S. S. McClure's commitment to "publishing a magazine as imaginatively various as could be made," and Cather's attraction to that project.[8]

Careful examination of the editions of *McClure's* in which Cather's fiction appears reveals a cohesive quality between Cather's writing and the salient issues and ideas of the magazine. It also reveals that Cather's literary concerns were consistent with its social and political agenda. The magazine was carefully crafted, with a number of particular editions in this era achieving thematic or other forms of unity. Throughout *McClure's* in this period, there is evidence of a deft editorial hand regarding the placement of features, reportage, and fiction. Cather's personal engagement with political and intellectual issues may be discerned by attending to the particular social context provided by the magazine for her fiction.

Three editorial methods characterize the way in which fiction was encountered in *McClure's*. First, the literary work may bear some topical connection to the nonfiction selections in the issue. In this way, fiction and nonfiction would share matters of setting and theme. In months directly before March 1907, there were very few features with Southern themes, or stories set in the South. The March 1907 issue, however, has a number of Southern concerns. March 1907 opens upon a full-color frontispiece illustration of "Lyon," with its caption, "See 'The Namesake' p 492," juxtaposed with the first Civil War installment of Carl Schurz's reminiscences.[9] Two additional Southern features are included in this issue, an essay by Thomas Nelson Page,[10] and Grace King's plantation tale, "The Clodhopper."[11] Cather's story itself is accompanied by a second color illustration, at a time when color was very expensive, and rare in the magazine. The Southern setting of Cather's "The Namesake" is thus featured prominently and complemented in the March 1907 issue by additional features concerning the same region, in both fiction and nonfiction.

In a second, and more sophisticated editorial method, readers would encounter fiction that commented upon or illustrated cognitive issues raised by other features in the magazine. Readers would thus find literary features playfully interacting with reportage, teasing out concepts and modes of thought. The October 1907 edition features a long essay by Hugo Munsterberg, titled "The Third Degree, or The Science of the Association of Ideas." Munsterberg describes a process that involves the use of association therapy to elicit from subjects what they wish to hide. Association therapy measures time duration to responses, and studies reactions to "dangerous words," or terms closely related to suppressed information. "The psychologist who seeks to discover the secret connections of ideas may then, by his association method, not only protect the innocent and unmask the guilty, but bring health and strength to the nervous wreck."[12] One nervous wreck in the magazine is Harold, the husband in Willa Cather's story "Eleanor's House," whose health and strength is restored once he faces the secret connections of ideas that have oppressed him in his second marriage. Of course, his current wife's health and strength is compromised seriously by the revelation that her husband believes it ludicrous to think his dead wife would be jealous of her.

The frontispiece to the October 1907 issue is an illustration from

"Eleanor's House," a psychological tale about the necessity of confronting suppressed anxieties while letting go the past. At Fortuney, Harold's dead first wife Eleanor "is living still,"[13] and interfering with his ability to live in peace with his new wife Ethel. The depicted scene shows Ethel collapsed after learning her husband's true assessment of her. The caption reads, "The girl had slipped to the floor as if she had been cut down" (109). By meeting at Fortuney, Eleanor and Harold's mansion, the couple engages in a dramatization of association therapy, and while the truth is good for the subject Harold, we can see that revelations can also be quite costly, and not always so healthy.

Munsterberg explains that when psychologists question their subjects using "The Science of the Association of Ideas," they are interested in "the conditions under which [ideas or images] arise, the influence under which the frequency or the recency [sic] or the vividness of the combination of special experiences has on the choice of the resulting idea."[14] This is, in many respects, a quest for the thing not named by the subject. Munsterberg directs our attention to cognitive processes, processes at the center of modernism, including modernist cultural politics. In criminal cases, idea association is used to create the psychological circumstances under which the guilty person may "slip" and speak the concealed truth, such as when Harold "slips" and blurts his preference for his first wife Eleanor.

Munsterberg's essay thus may have provided Cather further confirmation of her developing, narrative aesthetics,[15] and may allow us to tie those aesthetics to intellectual currents at *McClure's*. The doctor advocates the replacement of brutal, physical pressure with the psychological process of "time-measurement of association" in order to determine what the criminal is *not saying*—to postulate truth by studying the associations made by the suspect, to see what is spontaneous and what is held back. A similar evolution had already occurred at *McClure's* when it moved away from the more brutal approach of political confrontation and took on more subtle, modernist cultural work. Modernism demonstrates that far from escaping social and intellectual issues, aesthetic approaches to contemporary politics may develop into a legitimate form of engagement, not to say intellectual activism. To a developing modernist like Cather, aesthetics were serious business, especially those that would affect readers cognitively. It is in this sense that Cather's work at *McClure's* provided her a political apprenticeship, for as editor and contributor she sharpened her ability to engage in social and political issues without resorting to bluntness and ideological overtness. Success is

thus accomplished by revealing secret connections, by eliciting sub-
conscious associations. According to the doctor, "Just as the bodily
facts have to be examined by the chemist or the physiologist, the
mental facts must be examined also, not by the layman, but by the
scientific psychologist with the training of a psychological laboratory."[16] Or, by the novelist, who would write, "Whatever is felt upon
the page without being specifically named there—, the overtone
divined by the ear but not heard by it."[17]

The third context in which a reader of *McClure's* magazine encountered Cather's creative work was through an implicit relationship to
other pictorial subject matter. Fiction was almost always illustrated in
some fashion, as we have seen. However, in 1906–1912 there was a
growing tendency for fictional subject matter to be coincidentally
illustrated by other, seemingly unrelated pictorial matter in the magazine. Just as literature and reportage could be combined for effect,
fiction and other arts could serve to augment the effect of each, and
again, to provide knowledge by juxtaposition.

In the December 1908 issue of *McClure's*, Cather's "On the Gull's
Road" is immediately preceded by "One Hundred Masterpieces of
Painting," subtitled "Sacred Conversations." This heavily illustrated
feature explores the cognitive power of Renaissance art through
such examples as *Madonna and the Saints*, by Mantegna, *Saint Basil
Dictating his Doctrine*, by Herrera, and *The Dispute on the Trinity*, by
Andrea del Sarto. The artistically rendered conversations, according
to the text, solved crucial theological problems, and, in the artist's
rendition, provided eternal reminders of sacred revelations to us.
The role of art in human progress, the capacity of art to communi-
cate new knowledge, is unmistakable in the feature. Raphael's *Saint
Cecilia* is explained as an image of "people meeting *outside of time*,"[18]
in some aesthetic realm where matters of great importance are
discussed. Depicted as well, Rubens' *The Infant Jesus with Saint John
and Angels* is described as "*a conversation without words*,"[19] where ideas
are communicated by mood, sensation, and transcendence—or by
association therapy.

Cather's "On the Gull's Road," triggered by a red chalk drawing in
the narrator's study, provides an extended gloss on the power of the
visual arts. A young painter visits "on a matter of business, and upon
seeing my drawing of Alexandra Ebbling, straightway forgot his er-
rand" (*CSF*, 79), as if moved "outside time" and into the realm of art.
The artist's contemplation of the drawing provides the frame for the
narrative as a whole, which fills in the "conversation without words"
represented by the artwork. The placement of this story directly after

"One Hundred Masterpieces of Painting" has the effect of allowing the narrative to serve as contemporary, fictional illustration of the power of the image to evoke emotional realities, and to conjure worlds outside time, in aesthetic realms of living.

II

Cather's fiction at *McClure's* culminates with the serialization of "Alexander's Masquerade" in the spring of 1912. Readers of Cather's first novel encountered a text with strong thematic links, cognitive connections, and pictorial juxtaposition to other features of the magazine. Thematically, the editions in which the three installments appear are concerned to a great extent with prominent, powerful figures in politics and industry, and raise questions about the era's "great man" theory of history. The *McClure's* series about the bridge maker, where one man must hold together the forces of history and social progress, is the primary agent of the magazine's interrogation of this contemporary ideology. The series provides an important cultural inquiry into the idea of the heroic individual who leads social progress. Cather introduces the idea of collapse as a result of exaggerated individualism, and in its magazine context, suggests that those who rely upon individuals for security or protection will in time be abandoned. "Alexander's Masquerade" thus plays off major concerns of the magazine, and displays an uncanny level of intellectual engagement.

The "Alexander's Masquerade" series begins in February 1912, in an issue dominated by stories of heroic figures and their antagonists. The lead article is "Gompers and Burns on Unionism and Dynamite." The story concerns an incident in which Bridge-Workers' union activist J. J. McNamara dynamited the quarterly meeting of the Executive Council of the Union. The article centers on the phenomenon of union violence. The page layout for this feature represents a curious departure for *McClure's*. The text is bordered on the left and right by sidebars into which representations of bridges have been drawn. The architecture of the page is thus framed by industrial images, while the pages chronicle the human forces that lay stress to the represented phenomena. Examples of union violence fill the space between the sidebars:

A nice crowd. There was one workman in Indianapolis, an old man, whom they got after. He had a job on an iron smokestack. So they went up and cut off all but one of the rivets around one length of the pipe. The idea was that this one bolt would hold until he started working on it next day, and then it would give way and the pipe would telescope down and shear the man in two. It fell during the night, instead; so they fixed one of the ropes on his derrick, and he fell and was crippled for life. . . . When McManigal spoke to J. J. McNamara about the Los Angeles *Times* and its twenty-odd men that were killed, "I guess they'll come across now," said McNamara. That's all he was interested in.[20]

Various examples of bribery and muscling by union men during labor-violence trials are provided in the Gompers story, and the article ends with a call for the union membership to clean its house of corrupt labor leaders. The call to the workers is followed immediately by an interview with Gompers, who defends his union against the implication that isolated acts represent the values and aims of the labor movement as a whole. His statement includes a thorough defense of the union mission in America, including progressive programs in child labor, work conditions, and the "material, moral, and social uplift of the men and women of labor."[21]

In between "Unionism and Dynamite" and the first installment of Willa Cather's novel are a series of full-page, minimally captioned portraits of the "Leaders of the New Democracy." Photographs of six men whom *McClure's* advocates for consideration as potential Democratic Presidential nominees are included. They are: Eugene N. Foss (Massachusetts governor); Judson Harmon (Ohio governor); Woodrow Wilson; Champ Clark (Speaker of the House); Joseph W. Folk (ex-governor of Missouri); and Thomas R. Marshall (Indiana governor).[22] Now, curiously, as the reader turns the Marshall page, we come immediately upon the Cather tale, and its first illustration. The caption reads, "Alexander switched on the lights and stood in the archway, glowing with strength and cordiality."[23]

It is not possible to read about Bartley Alexander apart from the Leaders featured in the magazine. "There were other bridge-builders in the world, certainly, but it was always Alexander's picture that the Sunday Supplement men wanted, because he looked as a tamer of rivers ought to look."[24] At the same time, we cannot separate Alexander from his status as builder, from the technique that is a part of his temperament, and the fame owing from the Moorlock Bridge in Canada, "the longest cantilever in existence." And finally, we know him as a man who must deal with corruption in both management and unions. "He was cramped in every way by a niggardly commission, and was using lighter structural materials than he thought proper. He had vexations enough, too, with his work at home. He had several bridges underway in the United States, and they were always being held up by strikes and delays resulting from a general industrial unrest."[25] Nonetheless, Bartley Alexander voices no cognizance of the material, moral, and social uplift of the men and women of labor.

In the context of *McClure's*, Cather's tale of the bridge-maker raises serious questions about the era's professed faith in the powers of great men. Alexander "had expected that success would bring him freedom and power; but it had brought him power that was only another kind of restraint. He had always meant to keep his personal liberty at all costs."[26] We have read Cather's novel as the story of personal limitations. We might also consider it as contributing to *McClure's* inquiry into the standard ideology of her age, the belief that strong men guided historical events. Indeed, if "power . . . was only another kind of restraint," then what kind of faith should we place in those Leaders of a New Democracy? Surely men in groups—whether the forces of democracy itself or the fact of labor organization—provided powerful constraints on men who sought to act alone, or who felt as if they would determine the progress of the nation.

The second installment of "Alexander's Masquerade" appeared in March, an issue that continued *McClure's* concern with greatness, but this time in two major stories of human frailty and decline at high levels of social and economic power. The feature article is "The Passing of a Great Railroad Dynasty," and it concerns the way in which Jay Gould's children were losing control of the family's railroad empire. The family head, George J. Gould, is known as the "Sick Man of Wall Street" for his financial mismanagement.[27] Hence, despite Jay Gould's use of "all possible expedients" to assure the survival of his railroad empire,[28] the empire collapsed. Why? *McClure's* is very clear: "The Goulds are losing control of their ancestral domains because, like the Vanderbilts, they have attempted to do two incompatible things—live lives of idleness and luxury, and at the same time personally control great enterprises."[29] Specifically, George J. Gould's taste for luxury has led him to display an "inattention to business in recent years." That inattention is specifically embodied in Miss Edith Kingdon, "a charming New York actress of high personal character" whom Gould romanced and married, very much in the public spotlight. George Gould's inattention is replicated in the lives of his siblings, documented at length, all of whom attempted what *McClure's* judged "incompatible."

Brother Howard married Kathrine (sic) Clemmons, "an actress

who had once conspicuously figured in the retinue of Buffalo Bill's Wild West Show," who lavished Gould money on sending architects to Ireland to reproduce Kilkenny Castle on the shores of Long Island Sound.[30]

Brother Frank participated in a highly publicized divorce, after which "a well-known dancer sued him for breach of promise."

Sister Anna, heir to a one-million-dollar annual income, married "a little curly-headed, pink-cheeked, blue-eyed, faintly mustached Frenchman" popularly known on the boulevards as the "Powder-Puff," but recorded in more dignified fashion in Parisian social circles as the Count Paul Marie Boniface de Castellane. Count Boni's claim to membership in the Castellane family was seriously questioned in social circles; nonetheless, he created something of a stir when he appeared in New York, in 1895, as the active suitor of Anna Gould. He was so penniless that the moneylenders of Paris had to finance his courtship. The Gould-Castellane marriage marked the first conspicuous appearance of the Goulds in New York "society." However, the marriage was marked by creditors, gambling debts, lavish building projects in Paris such as "buying the Pallazo della Scala at Verona because it contained several ceilings by Tiepolo, which Boni transferred to Paris." The Goulds finally offered the Count "$200,000 down and $30,000 a year if he would leave them alone." As for Madame Gould—soon after the divorce she married the Prince de Sagan, Boni's cousin.

The tone of the article is a mixture of amusement at the romantic entanglements and outrage at the waste of economic promise. Money for improvements on New York City elevated lines is wasted on luxuries for Gould siblings. Jay Gould's ownership of Western Union is sold to the American Telegraph Company for cash. Finally, "the whole so-called Gould railroad system, from Toledo to Salt Lake City, from Omaha to New Orleans and El Paso, is a great neglected estate." The article documents the defeat of George Gould in the railroad wars with the new financiers, led by E. H. Harriman, who worked with banking interests and other powerful forces to wrest control of the railroad from Gould. Why did Gould lose the war? "The real explanation," according to *McClure's,* is "simple. It is found in the character of the Goulds themselves. The complex forces controlling modern American industrialism proved too much for them."[31]

Meanwhile, in part two of "Alexander's Masquerade," Bartley visited but "got no word with Hilda alone, and he left in a discontented state of mind. For the rest of the week he was nervous and unsettled, and kept rushing his work as if he were preparing for immediate departure. On Thursday afternoon he cut short a committee meeting, jumped into a hansom, and drove to Bedford Square"[32] to see his actress friend. On board ship, Bartley is seen pacing in the evening. "From his abstraction and the determined set of his jaw, they fancied he must be thinking about his bridge. Everyone had heard of the new cantilever bridge in Canada. . . . But Alexander was not thinking about his bridge."[33] He was thinking about Hilda and what to do about his luxurious relationship with her.

The Alexander series, in its published context, dates Cather's concern with the decline of great figures (and with collapse in general) to a specific set of journalistic materials. In keeping with *McClure's* methods, the series about the bridge-maker called into question the assumption, implicit in much of the reportage, that powerful men controlled historical events. In its *McClure's* context, "Alexander's Masquerade" shares as much in common with *A Lost Lady* as it does with its more familiar parallel, *The Professor's House*. In *McClure's* it is not so much Bartley Alexander's psychological trauma that arrests attention as it is the social drama of powerful men who "attempted to do two incompatible things—live lives of idleness and luxury, and at the same time personally control great enterprises." The March 1912 issue of *McClure's* closes with editorial commentary on its contents, including this assessment of the Goulds: "The pioneers who built up these great structures were men of extraordinary force or craft. . . . But is it very clear now that, in twenty-five or at most fifty years, there will be no Goulds, or Vanderbilts, or Harrimans, or Hills, or Rockefellers, or Morgans dominating the industries of this country. . . . There are to be no permanent railroad and oil and iron 'dynasties' in the United States."[34] In ten years, Cather would write this story herself, when she imagined the decline of Captain Forrester in his efforts to manage the "incompatible." The Progressive implication is clear, as readers would easily conclude that institutions, not individuals, ought to be entrusted with social progress.

The last installment of "Alexander's Masquerade," which leaves Mrs. Alexander alone, abandoned and widowed, was published in April 1912, in an issue that turns *McClure's* attention to marriage.[35] Readers encountered the dramatic conclusion of Bartley Alexander's life in the context of two distinctive pieces on marriages that prove less than sustaining for the wives involved. In each case, the woman's subordination to an individual man leaves her to fend for herself when he dies. "Great French Mysteries: The Strange Case of Marie LaFarge" tells the true story of a "young, gifted, beautiful" woman who "inch by inch destroyed the life of the husband she did not love."[36] It turns out that LaFarge discovered, after her honeymoon, "that she had married a man very unlike herself, one who cared nothing for books, for music, for society, or for anything except business."[37] So, she kills him—or, at least, she is convicted of the crime, and spends the rest of her life in prison.

The second article on marriage is satirical and unsigned. "Matrimony: Our Most Neglected Profession" has as its subtitle, "The Confessions of a Wife who was forced to earn her own living." The Wife in question enters marriage without the necessary training to perform her role as home manager and as "purchaser" in the household partnership. When her husband David dies, she goes to work. She gets a housekeeper named Sarah. As a result, she experiences the man's role as "producer" in the marriage partnership, reliant on the purchaser at home. "I had suddenly taken David's place as the producing partner; Sarah had taken my place as the purchasing member of the firm." Eventually Sarah leaves when the Wife asks her to keep a budget. In place of Sarah, the Wife hires a woman with training in domestic science.

> "Here is a man masquerading as a woman," I hear someone say. "No! I am a successful business woman—a wife who was forced to earn her own living. But, because I have been in business for fourteen years, I can see the partnership of marriage as man, the producing member of the firm, sees it. And because I was an unsuccessful wife before I became a successful business woman, I dare to write what follows."[38]

The death of the husband compels her to see the world in a new way. Subsequently, by transforming her vision of the world, she participates in changing it. The story is thus vintage *McClure's,* and also reflects the era's growing concern with the new arts of consumption. What will become of Winifred Alexander, now that she must be both producer and purchaser?

As editor, Willa Cather was present during an important change in focus at *McClure's,* the significance of which is greatly misunderstood if dismissed or categorized as a political softening. *McClure's* continued its evolution as a modernist cultural outlet, where political ideas are approached at the level of cognitive processes as well as at the level of ideological and public policy arguments. In literary history, similar issues arise between social realists and high modernists, each vying for influence throughout this century. Cather's aesthetics are, in many ways, born of the crossing between high modernism and social realism, and her fiction often arches the spectrum. Her sense

of balance between aesthetic and representational concerns was certainly influenced by her political work at this very prominent magazine. *McClure's* forged a similar bridge in the Progressive era. Rather
than simple, representational advocacy, the magazine embarked on a
number of sustained examinations of public issues by using a variety
of narrative and pictorial methods, and employing a range of inter-
rogative perspectives. "Alexander's Masquerade" works in conjunction with the magazine's simultaneous belief in strong leadership, as
seen in the series on Democratic Leaders, while expressing serious
doubt that such leadership can be sustained, as evidenced by the
exposé on the Gould family. In addition to gathering materials that
would appear in her mature fiction, Cather sharpened her aesthetic
vision at *McClure's,* a vision that would transcend immediate political
issues and approach social and political reality on cognitive grounds.
McClure's Magazine in the Cather era is a harbinger of the twentieth-
century merger of arts and politics in the mass media. As such, the
magazine embodied the modernist assumption that progressive
change is accomplished less through force or enforcement, and
more through the creation of new modes of thought, new social
institutions, and new alignments in the human structures that govern
and embody social behavior. At *McClure's* Magazine, Willa Cather was
at the forefront of this movement, and it was one reason she came to
New York City with such enthusiasm in the early years of this century.
I don't think she ever left it behind.

Notes

1. Qtd. in Peter Lyon, *Success Story: The Life and Times of S. S. McClure* (Deland, FL:
Everett / Edwards, 1967), x.

2. Harold S. Wilson, *McClure's Magazine and the Muckrakers* (Princeton: Princeton
University Press, 1970), 150–51.

3. Ibid., 166.

4. According to Wilson, "Several members of the staff felt an indictment of
lawlessness might appeal to the middle class but that the magazine needed to balance its rather negative attitude with something more positive." Ibid.

5. Ibid.

6. Amy Ahearn was kind enough to read an earlier draft of this paper. Ahearn is
researching *McClure's* for her dissertation at the University of Nebraska-Lincoln, and
adds that the historical record on this period at the magazine is still highly debata-
ble. For example, there is evidence for Roosevelt's denying any dissatisfaction with
the magazine, and recanting the public statements Wilson cites.

7. V. R. Roseboro's biographer, Jane Kirkland Graham, relates a rather remarkable story of how it was that Willa Cather came to work at *McClure's:*

> Viola began pointing out the quiet beauty of the poems by Willa Cather, collected under the
> title *April Twilight* [sic]. V.R. had become deeply interested in this woman, a Virginian who as

a child has been transplanted in a Nebraska prairie town where she rubbed shoulders with gifted immigrants, but who was now working in Pittsburgh. From the inception of *McClure's* she had submitted manuscript; it had been Viola's privilege in [sic] behalf of the McClure, Phillips Co. to interest Mr. McClure in Willa's first volume of short stories; later, perhaps as late as 1906, when trouble arose "with the firm" (not the publishing house), Isabelle McClung called on Viola and appealed to her; V.R. immediately sent Willa her picture, "a speaking likeness," along with reassurance, dragging her out of despair.

Although Roseboro' and Cather "were never intimate friends," their relationship is part of a larger network of professional women in which Cather seems to have been well connected throughout her life. There was a serious rift between the two women in the 1940s, when Cather asked Roseboro' to return all of her letters. Roseboro' thought that Cather was attempting to retract any credit that she had given her for her editorial assistance early in Cather's career. Direct correspondence between the two women began in the 1890s, when Cather submitted poetry to *McClure's*. "During the Pittsburgh period, Viola sent personal letters that dragged Willa Cather out of periods of despair, and gave her new hope. Even then, it seems that Viola had urged her to come to New York." It was at that time that Roseboro' interested McClure in Cather; and later, according to Graham, "when the *McClure's* staff walked out, it was Viola who induced Mr. McClure to get Miss Cather on the new staff." Roseboro's claims complicate but also make more credible the intervention of S. S. McClure in Cather's life. Jane Kirkland Graham, *Viola, The Duchess of New Dorp: A Biography of Viola Roseboro'*, 2 vols. (Danville, IL: Illinois Printing Company, 1955), 79–80, 123–124, 127.

Woodress explains that Cather came to McClure's attention when a Lincoln newspaper editor recommended her to his cousin, H. H. McClure, who "passed though Lincoln looking for talent" in 1903. However, it seems unlikely that this second-hand reference alone would cause S. S. McClure to summon her to New York by telegram. Equally plausible, the message delivered by his cousin may have confirmed the promise seen in her by the woman who had already rejected a number of Cather manuscripts, but had encouraged her to keep submitting. Roseboro' claims that Cather continued to send her manuscripts all her life because she valued Roseboro's judgment, based upon important early advice she got from her. Woodress confirms that Cather sent Roseboro' an advance copy of *Sapphira and the Slave Girl*, and continued to correspond with her toward the end of her life. Roseboro' would have found *Sapphira* an interesting read, as she came from a family of southern abolitionists and often told a story of the family's flight from St. Joseph, Missouri, while posters were mounted in town calling for her father's execution. James Woodress, *Willa Cather: A Literary Life* (Lincoln: University of Nebraska Press, 1987), 170, 481, 487, 496, 499.

Finally, we may have to add Viola Roseboro' to Sarah Orne Jewett's more famous advice that Cather stop emulating others and write what she knew. In a letter to her biographer, Roseboro' recalls telling Cather "that she better write something she had some *feeling* about. I was immensely disgusted with her. I knew she had genius, it was in the best of her talk, and she was pouring out one dead pretentious story after another that nobody could read and she got published only because Mr. McClure knew she had genius" (qtd. in Graham). Roseboro' was critical of Cather for ignoring her once she became managing editor of *McClure's*: "she would over-step the Fiction Editor, and put her own stories into the magazine without showing them to anyone except S. S. McClure and not always him, because he was often away." Roseboro's largest claim has to do with *My Ántonia*. According to Roseboro', she read the novel in manuscript "and told her to rewrite it because it was told through the wrong character's point of view." In a letter quoted by Graham, Roseboro' writes: "But here is what I loved to hear best of all: (It is she who was the little boy and bigger through the tale . . .)." Graham, *Viola,* 129, 124, 125, 132.

8. Willa Cather, *The Autobiography of S. S. McClure* (1914), Introduction to the Bison Books Edition by Robert Thacker (Lincoln: University of Nebraska Press, 1997), vii.

9. Carl Schurz, "Reminiscences of a Long Life: The Breaking out of the War." Schurz was minister to Spain during the war.

10. "The Great American Question: A Special Plea from a Southerner."

11. Grace King's story concerns a steadfast slave-woman named Maria, illustrated along with her plow. The narrative ends: "He watched them turn from the long road into the cross one, beyond which the sun was just rising. . . . And as they passed across the golden disk of the sun, each one shot into clear distinctness, and the Master then saw that Maria, as of old, led the race" (Ibid., 491). The strong woman and the backdrop of the golden disk of the sun, and something about the South, a crossroads, and a plow, would stay in Cather's mind for some time.

12. *McClure's* 29:6 (October 1907): 622.

13. *Willa Cather's Collected Short Fiction: 1892–1912,* ed. Virginia Faulkner (Lincoln: University of Nebraska Press, 1970), 97. Page references to Cather's short stories are to this volume (*CSF*), where they are reprinted and readily available. References to "Alexander's Masquerade," on the other hand, are to *McClure's,* because it was revised for separate publication as *Alexander's Bridge.*

14. *McClure's* 29:6 (October 1907): 615.

15. Munsterberg's work may have contributed to the refinement of ideas Cather had been working on since at least 1896, when she described the power of Paul Verlaine's poetry. "Facts and incidents count for nothing, it is all the mood. He does not write of a night or a woman or a passion, but of a sensation." *The Kingdom of Art: Willa Cather's First Principles and Critical Statements, 1893–1896,* ed. Bernice Slote (Lincoln: University of Nebraska Press, 1966), 395. I wish to thank Susan Rosowski for pointing out this correspondence, and for a very helpful reading of an early draft of this essay.

16. *McClure's* 29:6 (October 1907): 622.

17. Willa Cather, "The Novel Démueblé," *Not Under Forty* (New York: Knopf, 1936), 50.

18. *McClure's* 32:2 (December 1908): 135. The article was written by John La Farge.

19. Ibid., 144. Emphasis in the original, as if to make sure the cognitive effects are not missed.

20. *McClure's* 37:4 (February 1912): 366.

21. Ibid., 376.

22. One additional Leader, Oscar Underwood, is mentioned but not photographed. A feature story about the Southern party leader follows "Alexander's Masquerade."

23. *McClure's* 37:4 (February 1912): 384.

24. Ibid., 387.

25. Ibid., 393.

26. Ibid., 393.

27. *McClure's* 38:5 (March 1912): 483. The article was written by Burton J. Hendrick.

28. "The Gould system" contained 19,000 miles of railroad track and was considered to hold "possibilities of development such as have opened upon the vision of no other American railway 'magnate'" (Ibid., 484).

29. Ibid., 484.

30. This and subsequent illustrations are ibid., 489–91.

31. Ibid., 501.

32. Ibid., 523.

33. Ibid., 533.

34. "The World We Live In: The Downfall of American Dynasties," Ibid., 599. No byline listed.

35. At the same time, a biographical profile of Judson Harmon, a fictional account of a British man who seeks to be ranked as a gentleman, and a photographic series on "Progressive Leaders of Both Parties" continue the magazine's interest in powerful individuals.

36. *McClure's* 28:6 (April 1912): 608. The article was written by Marie Belloc Lowndes and is part of a series of accounts of similarly intriguing legal cases.

37. Ibid.

38. Ibid., 626.

Bibliography

Brady, Kathleen. *Ida Tarbell: Portrait of a Muckraker.* New York: Seaview/Putnam, 1984.

Cather, Willa. *The Autobiography of S. S. McClure.* Lincoln: University of Nebraska Press, 1997.

———. "The Novel Démeublé." *Not Under Forty.* New York: Knopf, 1922.

Graham, Jane Kirkland. *Viola, The Duchess of New Dorp: A Biography of Viola Roseboro'.* 2 Vols. Danville, IL: Illinois Printing Company, 1955.

Faulkner, Virginia, ed. *Willa Cather's Collected Short Fiction: 1892–1912.* Lincoln: University of Nebraska Press, 1970.

Lyon, Peter. *Success Story: The Life and Times of S. S. McClure.* Deland, FL: Everett/Edwards, 1967.

McClure's Magazine. 28–38 (1906–1912).

Slote, Bernice, ed. *The Kingdom of Art: Willa Cather's First Principles and Critical Statements, 1893–1896.* Lincoln: University of Nebraska Press, 1966.

Wilson, Harold S. *McClure's Magazine and the Muckrakers.* Princeton: Princeton University Press, 1970.

Woodress, James. *Willa Cather: A Literary Life.* Lincoln: University of Nebraska Press, 1987.

"Behind the Singer Tower": A Transatlantic Tale

ROBERT K. MILLER

When "Behind the Singer Tower" was first published on May 18, 1912, American readers had good reason to receive with interest a story about a major disaster in which hundreds of prominent people lost their lives at a time when they felt safely protected by modern engineering and opulent furnishings. The *Titanic* had sunk the previous month, and journalists were still reporting news of what had gone wrong on that April night in the North Atlantic. We know, of course, that Cather had completed "Behind the Singer Tower" in 1911 and that she had based it on other real-life disasters including the Windsor Hotel fire of 1899[1] and The Triangle Waist Company fire of 1911, a short distance from her home in Greenwich Village.[2] Nevertheless, in choosing to write about the vulnerability of an exceptionally large object devoted to housing people in transit and in which lives are suddenly and sensationally consumed, Cather seems to have been remarkably prescient. Although Leonardo DiCaprio is unlikely to star in a multimillion dollar production of "Behind the Singer Tower," Cather's "night to remember" can, like the sinking of the *Titanic,* help us to better understand the cultural anxieties running beneath the surface of the century we have so recently left behind.

As we all know, the *Titanic* set sail for New York but never reached the safety of its harbor. Hundreds of other boats did, however—many of them, like the *Titanic,* carrying great numbers of immigrants hoping to find a new home on this side of the Atlantic. "Behind the Singer Tower" is written in the midst of a period of mass immigration to the United States that was prompting alarm—remarkably similar to some of the opinions being expressed in current debates over immigration policy and multicultural curriculums—that our country was at risk of losing its identity. At that time, critics of American immigration policy were especially concerned by the number of Italians and Jews then entering the country—the two cultural "others" that appear most prominently in "Behind the Singer Tower." For example, in a 1908 article published in the *Atlantic Monthly,* Harvard

professor William Z. Ripley notes that Italian immigration had increased from 20,000 in 1876 to "an army of 300,000" in 1907; complains that we have "tapped the political sinks of Europe"; and raises
the possibility that our nation's "Anglo-Saxon stock be physically
inundated by the engulfing flood."[3]

Apparently focused upon two occasions involving sudden death at
a New York hotel, "Behind the Singer Tower" is told from a boat in
New York harbor, a boat surrounded by other boats and in sight of
that "much-traveled highway, the road to the open sea" (*CSF*, 43). In
my reading, the story is very much concerned with the people and
values that are traveling this highway—especially those who are using
it to come here—and whether these new arrivals will cause the cultural and financial capital of the New World to suffer the decline
experienced by ancient cities on the other side of the Atlantic. Evelyn
Haller has demonstrated how Cather draws upon Flaubert's *Salamm-
bo* to compare New York with Carthage. Like Haller, I believe that
"Behind the Singer Tower" is not only about class conflict, as other
critics have pointed out,[4] but also about the cultural conflicts that
follow when people of different nations cross territorial boundaries.
It is significant, in this respect, that Cather names her fictional luxury
hotel the Mont Blanc. The highest mountain in Europe, Mont Blanc
is a useful image in a story that addresses the "perpendicular" nature
of New York life (46). But we should also note that Mont Blanc is at
the border of three countries, one of which is Italy. With this in mind,
I want to explore why Cather makes so many references to Italy in
"Behind the Singer Tower"—especially to the city of Naples—and
this journey will require a brief side trip to Berlin.

The primary narrative is inspired by the burning of the thirty-five
story Mont Blanc Hotel in Manhattan. The fire had begun on the
twelfth story and moved rapidly upwards, trapping the guests on the
upper floors and causing more than three hundred deaths.[5] In the
hope of calming their nerves after a day of work related to the fire,
two journalists, a draftsman, a lawyer, and a physician accept an
invitation to go boating with Fred Hallet, the engineer who had
supervised "the foundation work" (47) for the Mont Blanc. Out on
the water, Hallet tells the story of an earlier tragedy at the hotel. A
worn cable had broken during construction causing equipment and
a large load of sand to fall without warning on a team of Italian
workmen. Although Stanley Merryweather, the head engineer, had
been repeatedly warned by Hallet that the cable needed to be replaced, he had ignored these warnings. As a result, six men die—
including Caesarino, a young workman whom Hallett had be-

friended and encouraged to return to Italy. At the hour of his death, Caesarino had within his pocket a steamer ticket for Naples.

It is, of course, significant that Hallet tells this tale as one of six men in a boat.[6] When the cabling broke during the hotel's construction, six workers had been buried alive in sand. By establishing a parallel between two groups of six men, Cather suggests that all men are, so to speak, in the same boat. When cables break, fire breaks out, or a great liner sinks at sea, death does not strike the poor alone. Nor is it possible for survivors to discern differences among the victims of disaster. "The lists were still vague," after the fire, "for whether the victims had jumped or not, identification was difficult, and in either case, they had met with obliteration, absolute effacement, as when a drop of water falls into the sea" (44).

As obvious as this idea may be, it is easily forgotten in a culture in which people are raised to believe that you get what you pay for—from which it follows that the more you pay, the more you get. This idea—so close to the American heart—is introduced in the opening paragraphs of the story. "We were in a kind of stupor," the narrator—who is one of two journalists—claims.

> When the launch ran out into the harbor, we saw an Atlantic liner come steaming up the big sea road. She passed so near to us that we could see her crowded steerage decks.
>
> "It's the *Re di Napoli*," said Johnson of the *Herald*. "She's going to land her first cabin passengers tonight, evidently. Those people are terribly proud of their new docks in the North River; feel they've come up in the world." (43)

The irony here is clear. Although the steerage decks are crowded, third class passengers will have to wait until morning to disembark. Only the first class passengers will be allowed off the boat that evening—a privilege they had earned by the size of their fare. The reference to "those people," presumably the Italian owners of the liner, introduces the racism that is so prevalent in the story. And the belief that these owners are "proud of their new docks" and "feel they've come up in the world" raises a question central to the story: Is it morally sound to take pride in new docks; or, by extension, any new work of construction, including the Singer Tower?

The great fallacy of "coming up in the world" is the belief that upward movement is, in itself, a worthy goal, whether it be in the engineering of taller and taller buildings or in acquiring sufficient wealth to occupy the upper floors of such buildings. People who follow this path can easily convince themselves that coming up in the world allows them to occupy space which is more protected and secure than the space they had left behind. But the fire at the Mont Blanc Hotel proves how dangerous such thinking can be. In this case, the people at the greatest risk are the wealthy guests who could command the highest rooms.

Only one of these guests is described in any detail, and this brings me to one of the oddest passages in all of Cather's work. A man's severed hand is found on a window ledge and identified as the hand of Graziani, an Italian tenor, thanks to a "little-finger ring" that had been the gift of the German Emperor. "Yes it was the same hand," the narrator observes.

> I had seen it often enough when he placed it so confidently over his chest as he began his "Celeste Aida." . . . When he toured the world he must have whatever was most costly and most characteristic in every city; in New York he had the thirty-second floor, poor fellow! He had plunged from there toward the cobwebby life nets stretched five hundred feet below on the asphalt. Well, at any rate, he would never drag out an obese old age in the English country house he had built near Naples. (45)

The reference to Naples establishes a link with Caesarino, the Italian workman befriended by Hallet, as well as to the earlier reference to the *Re di Napoli,* or King of Naples, arriving in New York. I'm also struck by the heartlessness with which the tenor's death is written off, which prompts me to consider what's really going on here. Readers of *The Professor's House* will recognize that Cather probably would have seen something grotesque about building an English country house near Naples, just as she saw something unseemly about building a Norwegian manor house on the shores of Lake Michigan, or a New York office tower that looks, we are told, as if it "had come out of Asia quietly in the night" (46). Then there's that "little finger ring," and the implications established by its provenance at a court associated, in the early twentieth century, with homosexuality. I will return shortly to why these implications are significant. But the tenor is dismembered and killed not because of his sexual history, his obesity, or his taste in architecture. No, he dies because of a particular kind of self-indulgence: "When he toured the world he must have whatever was most costly and most characteristic in every city; in New York he had to have the thirty-second floor, poor fellow!" In this case, a room high in the air is not only the most characteristic feature of New York, but also the most costly. Focusing on an Italian who has, it seems, risen too high in New York, Cather is challenging the belief that value can be measured in terms of price.

In this respect, I am reminded of Oscar Wilde's definition of a cynic as "a man who knows the price of everything and the value of nothing,"[7] a line that might well serve as the epitaph for Stanley Merryweather, "the most successful manipulator of structural steel in New York" (47). As his name suggests, Merryweather has an astonishing ability to avoid dwelling upon anything unpleasant or troubling—including the death of the Italian workmen, which leaves him "pleasurably excited" (52) despite his responsibility for these deaths. Remembering their days in college together, Hallet observes, "If you made a fool of him tonight—well, 'Tomorrow's another day,' he'd say lightly, and tomorrow he'd blossom out in a new suit of clothes and a necktie of some unusual weave and haunting color" (47–48). While this kind of emotional resiliency is surely preferable to carrying a grudge or falling into despair, Merryweather's temperament keeps him from understanding the consequences his behavior has upon others—especially the men in his employ. According to Hallet, "He made amazing mistakes, harrowing blunders. . . .One of his maxims was that men are cheaper than machinery. He smashed up a lot of hands, but he always got out under the fellow-servant act. 'Never been caught yet, huh?' he used to say with his pleasant, confiding wink" (51).[8]

When Hallet finishes his story about the Italian immigrants who had been killed during the hotel's construction, he reflects that the episode of the broken cable "was only a little accident, such as happens in New York every day in the year" (53). He then continues in a passage that is infused with the language of a fiery furnace:[9]

> There's a lot of waste about building a city. Usually the destruction all goes on in the cellar; it's only when it hits high, as it did last night, that it sets us all thinking. Wherever there is the greatest output of energy, wherever the blind human race is exerting itself most furiously, there's bound to be tumult and disaster. Here we are, six men, with our pitiful few years to live and our own little chance for happiness, throwing everything we have into that conflagration on Manhattan Island, helping, with every nerve in us, with everything our brain cells can generate, with our very creature heat, to swell its glare, its noise, its luxury, and its power. Why do we do it? (53)

Struggling to find a comforting answer to this question, he lamely concludes, "There must be something wonderful coming . . . a new idea of some sort" (53–54) will emerge in fiery Manhattan "[w]hen the frenzy is over, when the furnace is cooled" (53–54).

As comforting as this idea may be, it is hard to take it seriously. Aside from the fact that the buildings of New York are growing taller, there is no reason to believe that "something wonderful is coming," least of all some wonderful new idea that will justify, somehow, whatever is wrong with the present. In advancing such wishful thinking, Hallet is unconsciously allying himself with Merryweather who has a genius for overlooking unpleasant realities because of his optimistic belief in a future in which everything turns out just fine. If there is anything wrong with what Cather calls "the New York idea," it is this blind belief in progress which enables men to justify the kind of social injustice which makes a rosy future unlikely—even for people at the top, like the guests on the upper floors of the Mont Blanc Hotel. As Marilyn Arnold has argued, "Behind the Singer Tower" is a story "that reminds us that the cost of a thing can be measured by the amount of human life expended in acquiring it; and by this standard the cost of the New York dream is staggering."[10]

By invoking the idea of Naples, Cather suggests that the New York dream is becoming a kind of nightmare. Reflecting on the human cost of maintaining buildings like the Singer Tower, the narrator casually notes,

> the average for window cleaners, who, for one reason or another, dropped to the pavement was something over one a day. In a city with so many millions of windows that was not perhaps an unreasonable percentage. But we felt that the Mont Blanc disaster would bring our particular type of building into unpleasant prominence, as the cholera used to make Naples and the conditions of life there too much a matter of discussion." (45)

Naples, like New York, happens to be a city close to my heart, and I have spent some time reflecting upon why Cather makes so many Neapolitan references in this story, a story, after all, that begins with "the King of Naples" arriving in New York and in which there are repeated references to *dagos*. These references contribute, of course, to one of the story's themes: the idea that American culture, as seen most vividly in New York, is becoming culturally diverse—imperilling the Anglo-Saxon ascendancy. Naples was a port from which thousands of Italian immigrants left for America. More importantly, it was, by 1911, a city in decline. In the eighteenth century, Naples had been the cultural capital of Italy, and the third largest city in Europe—an essential stop on the grand tour thanks to a splendid setting that inspired the saying "See Naples and die," as if life could offer nothing more wonderful than a visit there. Misgoverned through the nineteenth century, Naples was ravaged by a cholera epidemic in 1884 and became increasingly associated in the American imagination with disease, crime, and licentiousness—so that the arrival of the "King of Naples" in New York would inspire mixed feelings at best.[11]

In my eye, Naples is still one of the most beautiful and interesting cities in the world, a city filled with a wealth of architectural and artistic treasures. Nevertheless, this city of palaces and churches is also the site of much poverty. One need not walk far, especially in the Quartieri Spagnoli, without seeing arresting contrasts of grandeur and squalor. It is for this reason that the Neapolitan references in "Behind the Singer Tower" are significant. By associating Naples and New York—and specifically by introducing a Neapolitan boat, a Neapolitan tenor, and Neapolitan workers into New York—Cather is inviting readers to ask if New York is likely to suffer the same fate as Naples.

If social injustice transforms New York into a city peopled primarily by the very rich and the very poor—life there will be as dangerous as it is within a city built at the base of an active volcano. According to this narrator, the Singer Tower is the "presiding Genius" (46) watching New York City and its harbor; for Naples and its harbor, the "presiding genius" is Mt. Vesuvius. During the eighteenth and nineteenth centuries thousands of pictures had been painted of this mountain towering over a great city; indeed the view of Vesuvius from Naples or its harbor may well be the most frequently painted landscape in Western art. It would certainly be the image most likely to occur to cultivated readers in 1912 when invited to picture the city.[12] Cather's New York, like Naples, is associated with both water and fire, and described with the kind of romantic language that could apply equally well to paintings of the Bay of Naples, many of which are nocturnal in order to convey the drama of living at the base of an active volcano: "There was a brooding mournfulness over the harbor," we are told, "as if the ghost of helplessness and terror were abroad in the darkness" (43). Moreover, Vesuvius had a major eruption in 1906, and any eruption of Vesuvius evokes the historical memory of the eruption in the year 79 when people in Pompeii and Herculaneum were buried alive[13]—an image that links back to the Italian workman buried alive during the construction of the Mont Blanc Hotel. When we revisit the scene of that tragedy, we find that we are in a deep hole[14] heated to "a temperature that was beyond anything the human frame was meant to endure" (51)—a perfect description for the interior of a volcano. Caesarino's father had been

The Eruption of Vesuvius in 1767 by Pietro Fabris, Item 681K13. Courtesy of the British Library.

buried in "volcanic soil" (49), and his son, in turn, is buried within the New York equivalent.

Initially associated with "panting little animals that roll around in the dust and somehow worry through famine" (48) and with "wild little water dogs" (49), Caesarino emerges as an individual because he is "so eager to please" (49) and Hallet is able to speak some Italian. The older man befriends the younger and they fall into the habit of going to the beach together, where Caesarino looks at Hallet "like a girl in love" (50). I don't think it's a stretch to read a queer subtext here, and a link to the Neapolitan tenor who had received a little finger ring from the Kaiser.

In the early twentieth century, Naples was known as a city in which it was possible to enjoy homosexual liaisons, just as Berlin had this reputation in the 1920s and San Francisco in the 1970s. One factor behind this reputation is that southern Italians are accustomed to physical intimacy between people of the same gender; it is common throughout the south for men to walk arm in arm with other men simply because they care for each other and are unafraid to touch. Another factor was the poverty that prompted young Neapolitan men to make themselves available to the wealthy foreigners who vacationed there.[15] Many of these visitors were German.[16] I referred earlier to how the German court was also associated with homosexuality—most directly through the trials in 1908 and 1909 of Philipp Prince zu Eulenburg-Hertefeld, a close friend of the Kaiser, and General Kuno Count von Moltke, the military commandant of Berlin, through which dozens of other prominent Germans were implicated, including the imperial chancellor, Bernhard Prince von Bülow.[17] These scandals were widely reported shortly before Cather composed "Behind the Singer Tower," as was an even more sensational scandal in 1902 when Friedrich Alfred Krupp, one of the wealthiest men in the world, committed suicide after being deported from Italy when photographs became circulated in which he was shown making love to young boys at his villa on Capri.[18] Capri is in the Bay of Naples, as is the nearby island of Ischia where Caesarino had spent his childhood, "swimming and diving and sprawling about among the nets on the beach" without "ever having had any clothes on in the summer until he was ten" (49). Images such as these evoke associations with the work of Wilhelm von Gloeden, a Prussian aristocrat whose photographs of naked Italian boys were very much in vogue when Cather visited Naples in 1908.[19] The iconography of the photograph he called "Naples" illustrates the homoeroticism associated with that city—an association that was, I believe, very much in Cather's mind when she wrote "Behind the Singer Tower."

Naples by **Wilhelm von Gloeden. Courtesy of Schwiezerische Stiftung für die Photographie, Zürich.**

Meanwhile, back in New York, the male culture of Italian immigrants—many of whom were bachelors living in close proximity to one another—seems to have played a significant role in the development of the city's gay life during the early twentieth century. The historian George Chauncey has shown how New York's gay bars were then located in Italian enclaves on the Lower East Side, Greenwich Village and East Harlem.[20] Without turning to the problematic and much discussed question of Cather's own sexuality, I think it safe to assume that she would be familiar with this urban pattern as the editor of a major muckraking magazine based in New York. Seen from a queer perspective, the apparently gratuitous references to the German emperor and Hallet's fondness for taking Caesarino to the beach become means through which Cather suggests that American culture is becoming more cosmopolitan than folks back home in Nebraska might guess.

How we view these changes is influenced by how we view Hallet. He is, after all, an engineer responsible for "foundation work" in New York, and the story is told primarily from his point of view—two reasons for paying close attention to what he says and believing that his views may be shared by others. The extent to which he speaks for Cather is questionable, however. Having demonstrated Hallet's anti-Semitism, Loretta Wasserman argues that Cather intended to distance herself from this character because his "callousness is so extreme."[21] Hallet seems less threatened by Italians, but his patronizing attitude towards them is no less callous than his hostility towards Jews. His tone shifts depending upon the degree to which he thinks his authority might be challenged by others, but his views are consistently racist. There is certainly little reason to take seriously the superficial empathy he expresses when briefly imagining what it would be like to live like the men he employs.

> Haven't you ever noticed how, when a dago is hurt on the railroad and they trundle him into the station on a truck, another dago runs alongside him, holding his hand and looking more scared of the two? . . . Suppose we went to work for some great and powerful nation in Asia that had a civilization built on sciences we knew nothing of, as ours is built on physics and chemistry and higher mathematics; and suppose we knew that to these people we were absolutely meaningless as social beings, were waste to clean their engines . . . that we were there to do the dangerous work, to be poisoned in caissons under rivers, blown up by blasts, drowned in coal mines, and that these masters of ours were as indifferent to us individually as the Carthaginians were to their mercenaries? I'll tell you we'd guard the precious little spark of life with trembling hands. (49)

Despite its grandiloquence, the passage amounts to a cliché: "There but for the grace of God go I." He's right, of course, but he's mouthing a pious formula rather than revealing any real growth. Speaking of immigrants shortly after this passage, he declares: "*We* don't want 'em, God knows" (49). And he apparently remains committed to practicing a profession that exploits those who do arrive.

There is a limit, however, to the extent we can use the "unreliable narrator" argument as a way to exempt Cather from holding views that make us uncomfortable. Racism is pervasive through this story and, like the more subtle use of homophobia, it serves Cather's purpose. As both Marilyn Arnold[22] and Susan J. Rosowski[23] have shown, "Behind the Singer Tower" offers a sustained attack upon "the perpendicular idea" of New York symbolized by the construction of ever-taller office towers. In Cather's words:

> Our whole scheme of life and progress and profit were perpendicular.
>   There was nothing for us but height. We were whipped up the ladder. (46)

A perpendicular city is, without question, problematic—primarily because its architecture creates structures in which some people live on top of others. The image of being "whipped up the ladder," as if we have no choice and must necessarily suffer as the result of upward movement, is also troubling. But if we reject the "perpendicular idea" of the city, we lose the very reason why cities have flourished: they represent opportunity, the possibility of remaking our lives and living with greater comfort than might be the case in a village. Millions of immigrants recognized this opportunity, and cities like New York have also offered a relatively safe haven for their gay, lesbian, and bisexual citizens. Whatever the shortcomings of the perpendicular city—and there are more than a few—how many Americans would be content to live in a world so level that it is flat, and in which departures from prevailing norms are routinely punished? Cather herself found New York, the most perpendicular of our cities, the perfect site for advancing her own career. What seems to trouble her is that the "ladder" of the city is also available for people (be they Italian, Jewish, gay, or all three) she is reluctant to accept as neighbors.[24] Although I recognize that there are political and spiritual risks to attaching undue importance to the idea of "coming up in the world," I must point out that the risks are just as grave for those who sneer at upward mobility.

In "Behind the Singer Tower," Cather challenges the direction in which American culture seems headed, and with good reason. The "foundation work" of twentieth-century New York may, like the *Titanic,* have a structural flaw. In particular, Cather asks us to see how both rich and poor alike are at risk when we lose a sense of political and spiritual direction by focusing obsessively upon the acquisition of wealth and the construction of increasingly elaborate buildings. She also draws attention to the exploitation of immigrants in a city where, as she points out, the Singer Tower had come to overwhelm the Statue of Liberty. These are important ideas, and I believe that "Behind the Singer Tower" is one of Cather's most compelling stories. Having said that, I must also say that I deeply regret the extent to which she evokes both racism and homophobia to make her point. She asks, in effect, do we want New York to become another Naples, and she fully expects her readers to answer *no.* In doing so, she is exploiting the kind of fear that is now once again being used to divide us from our neighbors and betraying the sympathetic imagination that would characterize her work at its best.

Notes

1. Mildred Bennett, Introduction, *Willa Cather's Collected Short Fiction, 1892–1912,* ed. Virginia Faulkner (Lincoln: University of Nebraska Press, 1970), xli; cited as *CSF.*

Sharon O'Brien, *Willa Cather: The Emerging Voice* (New York: Oxford University Press, 1987), 383.

2. Evelyn Haller, "'Behind the Singer Tower: Willa Cather and Flaubert,'" *Modern Fiction Studies* 36 (1990): 41.

3. William Z. Ripley, "Races in the United States," *Atlantic Monthly* 102 (December 1908): 746, 747, 759. Views like Ripley's can be found in many articles from this period. Even Elizabeth Shepley Sergeant, who wrote to expose the exploitation of Italian workers, reveals a racist perspective. After noting that Italians "form the largest racial unit in recent immigration," she links them to "other dark-skinned races who have swarmed and spread through New York." Elizabeth Shepley Sergeant, "Toilers of the Tenements," *McClure's* 35 (July 1910): 232. The *swarmed* is telling, as is the reference to color. Sergeant's successful submission of this article to *McClure's* marked the beginning of her friendship with Cather.

4. Bennett, xli; Marilyn Arnold, *Willa Cather's Short Fiction* (Athens: Ohio University Press, 1984), 92–97.

5. The six-story Windsor Hotel was considerably smaller, and the fire there consumed the entire building. Sixteen people were killed and sixty-four injured. (For detailed description of the Windsor fire, see the New York *Times,* March 18–20, 1899.) The idea of people trapped by fire in the top stories of a tall building is more likely to come from the Triangle Waist Company fire on March 25, 1911, a fire in which 146 women and girls died after being trapped on the top three floors of the building. Many of the victims were Italian or Jewish immigrants.

6. Drawing attention to Cather's use of the boat, Joan Hall connects "Behind the Singer Tower" with Conrad's "The Heart of Darkness." Joan Hall, "Cather's 'Deep Foundation Work': Reconstructing 'Behind the Singer Tower,'" *Studies in Short Fiction* 26 (1989): 81–86.

7. Oscar Wilde, *Lady Windermere's Fan* (1892). Reprinted in *The Plays of Oscar Wilde* (New York: Vintage, 1988), 3.

8. A common-law ruling that dates from 1842, the fellow-servant act protected employers from liability; it held that a worker injured on the job could sue another worker for negligence but not the employer. The Federal Employees Liability Act of 1908, which improved protection for railroad workers, was the first significant change in fellow-servant liability. Employers would continue to enjoy considerable protection until states passed worker-compensation laws, a process not completed until 1949.

9. When read in context with the description of the Singer Tower as a building "like the Jewish high priest in old Bible dictionaries" (46), the idea that New York is a kind of "furnace" evokes the story of Shadrach, Meshach, and Abednego. See *Daniel: 3.*

10. Arnold, *Short Fiction,* 92.

11. The Bourbon kings who ruled Naples in the nineteenth century, Ferdinand I and Ferdinand II, were notorious for their stupidity and cruelty. For an engaging description of Ferdinand I in fiction, see Susan Sontag's *The Volcano Lover.*

12. Cather enjoyed this view during her visit to Naples in 1908 with Isabelle McClung. Paraphrasing a letter Cather sent to one of her old teachers, James Woodress writes: "Naples itself was a marvel and their hotel overlooked the bay, which Cather thought the most beautiful body of water in the world. She was sitting on her balcony every afternoon and watching Mt. Vesuvius change from violet to lilac to purple." James Woodress, *Willa Cather: A Literary Life* (Lincoln: University of Nebraska Press, 1987), 198. For representative paintings of this scene, see Carlo Knight's *Les Fureurs du Vésuve* and *Vases and Volcanos* by Ian Jenks and Kim Sloan.

13. When visiting Italy in 1908, Cather devoted two days to Pompeii (Woodress 198).

14. Susan J. Rosowski notes that the hole is "like a mass grave." "Willa Cather as City Novelist," *Writing the City: Eden, Babylon, and the New Jerusalem,* ed. Peter Preston and Paul Simpson-Housely (London: Routledge, 1994), 151.

15. George Chauncey, *Gay New York: Gender, Urban Culture, and the Making of the Gay Male World, 1890–1940* (New York: Basic, 1994), 74.

16. See Robert Aldrich, *The Seduction of the Mediterranean: Writing, Art, and Homosexual Fantasy* (New York: Routledge, 1993), 56–68; 108–16; 143–52; 162–78.

17. James D. Steakley, "Iconography of a Scandal: Political Cartoons and the Eulenburg Affair in Wilhelmin Germany," *Hidden from History: Reclaiming the Gay and Lesbian Past,* ed. Martin Duberman, Martha Vicinus, and George Chauncey, Jr. (New York: Meridian, 1990), 236–40.

18. William Manchester, *The Arms of Krupp 1587–1968* (Boston: Little, 1968), 229–40. Homosexuality was not a criminal offense in Italy, although there were strict laws against it in Germany (one reason why gay and bisexual Germans vacationed in Italy during the nineteenth and early twentieth century). Krupp was deported for molesting children, in this case male children, and having done so in such a public manner that Italian authorities could not overlook the case. Socialist newspapers in Germany and elsewhere emphasized how the Krupp case illustrated how powerful capitalists thought they could live above the law. Much was made of the Kaiser's decision to attend Krupp's funeral.

19. Von Gloeden (1856–1931) established his studio in Taormina, Sicily; his visitors there included Edward VII, J. P. Morgan, Oscar Wilde, and Eleanor Duse. Reproductions of his work could be ordered through catalogs. In Naples, his work was marketed by another Prussian aristocrat, Wilhelm von Plüschow. Peter Weiermair, *Wilhelm von Gloeden* (Cologne: Taschen, 1996), 4–19.

20. Chauncey, *Gay New York,* 73–74.

21. Loretta Wasserman, "Cather's Semitism," *Cather Studies* 2 (1993): 7.

22. Arnold, *Short Fiction,* 92–96.

23. Rosowski, "City Novelist," 150–51.

24. I am reminded, in this respect, of a passage in "Neighbour Rosicky": "In the country, if you had a mean neighbour, you could keep off his land and make him keep off yours. But in the city, all the foulness and misery and brutality of your neighbours was part of your life" (*Obscure Destinies,* 59).

Bibliography

Aldrich, Robert. *The Seduction of the Mediterranean: Writing, Art and Homosexual Fantasy.* New York: Routledge, 1993.

Arnold, Marilyn. *Willa Cather's Short Fiction.* Athens: Ohio University Press, 1984.

Bennett, Mildred. Introduction. *Willa Cather's Collected Short Fiction, 1892–1912.* Ed. Virginia Faulkner. Lincoln: University of Nebraska Press, 1970.

Cather, Willa. *Collected Short Fiction, 1892–1912.* Ed. Virginia Faulkner. Lincoln: University of Nebraska Press, 1970.

———. *Obscure Destinies.* New York: Knopf, 1932.

Chauncey, George. *Gay New York: Gender, Urban Culture, and the Making of the Gay Male World, 1890–1940.* New York: Basic, 1994.

Hall, Joan. "Cather's 'Deep Foundation Work': Reconstructing 'Behind the Singer Tower.'" *Studies in Short Fiction* 26 (1989): 81–86.

Haller, Evelyn. "'Behind the Singer Tower': Willa Cather and Flaubert." *Modern Fiction Studies* 36 (1990): 39–55.

Jenks, Ian and Kim Sloan. *Vases and Volcanoes: Sir William Hamilton and his Collection.* London: British Museum Press, 1996.

Knight, Carlo. *Les Fureurs du Vésuve.* Paris: Gallimard, 1992.

Manchester, William. *The Arms of Krupp 1587–1968.* Boston: Little, Brown, 1968.

O'Brien, Sharon. *Willa Cather: The Emerging Voice.* New York: Oxford University Press, 1987.

Ripley, William Z. "Races in the United States." *Atlantic Monthly* 102 (December 1908): 745–759.

Rosowski, Susan J. "Willa Cather as City Novelist." *Writing the City: Eden, Babylon, and the New Jerusalem.* Ed. Peter Preston and Paul Simpson-Housely. London: Routledge, 1994. 149–70.

Sergeant, Elizabeth S. "Toilers of the Tenements." *McClure's* 35 (July 1910): 231–48.

Sontag, Susan. *The Volcano Lover.* New York: Anchor, 1992.

Steakley, James D. "Iconography of a Scandal: Political Cartoons and the Eulenburg Affair in Wilhelmin Germany." *Hidden from History: Reclaiming the Gay and Lesbian Past.* Ed. Martin Duberman, Martha Vicinus, and George Chauncey, Jr. New York: Meridian, 1990. 233–57.

Wasserman, Loretta. "Cather's Semitism." *Cather Studies* 2 (1993): 1–22.

Weiermair, Peter. *Wilhelm von Gloeden.* Cologne: Taschen, 1996.

Wilde, Oscar. *Lady Windermere's Fan.* (1892). Rpt. in *The Plays of Oscar Wilde.* New York: Vintage, 1988. 1–82.

Woodress, James. *Willa Cather: A Literary Life.* Lincoln: University of Nebraska Press, 1987.

Willa Cather and Modern Medicine

JO ANN MIDDLETON

Medical circles joke that one instance of an unusual case provides an anecdote, two make a series, and three allow the doctor to say, "In my experience. . . ." My own experience covers teaching Cather to medical residents. The first time I read "Neighbour Rosicky" with a group of young doctors at a Medical Humanities Conference, we were talking about the American Dream, when a Russian physician told us with great emotion that he had come to this country, like Rosicky, to find a unique place for himself: "in France, you see, I would always be just a Russian." Cather would have liked that personalizing response to her story, since she believed that "feeling is the simplest evidence of some reality created through the imagination."[1] As she said, "The absolute necessity in art is the personal encounter. The artist or the work succeeds if the thing works—if there is a response."[2] The second time I read the story with another group of residents, they focused on Dr. Burleigh's sensitive relationship with his patient and his diagnosis of Rosicky's heart disease from accurate symptoms; "she had the details right," they conceded. Cather would also be pleased with these discriminating medical readers who noticed the details, because she knew that "the hand, fastidious and bold, which selected and placed—it was that that made the difference."[3] It occurred to me that I could now speak from "my own experience" when a young doctor in a strictly medical conference recently characterized a patient as a man with qualities "just like Neighbour Rosicky." Cather would indeed be pleased to know that this receptive reader retained "an intangible residue of pleasure" from her story that he "can remember without the volume at hand."[4] Cather and the New Jersey-New York medical community do, indeed, seem "perfect together."

Of all the American writers we have read over the years, Cather is the only writer medical residents ask to read again. They appreciate "Two Friends" as an exploration of the consequences of miscommunication and foolish narrow-mindedness; they correctly diagnose "Old Mrs. Harris" with congestive heart failure and plan to become doctors who, like Mrs. Rosen, know when to help without intruding, and not doctors who, like Mrs. Jackson, run roughshod over the very people who most need compassion. But they always love the bond

between "Neighbour Rosicky" and Dr. Burleigh most. Given this experience, of course, I must ask why Willa Cather, who abandoned
medicine for literature, evokes such a strong and overwhelmingly
pleasurable response from medical women and men, who sometimes
know very little about American culture? I would like to propose that
looking through a medical lens offers yet another way into Cather's
fiction.

Willa Cather's earliest recorded delight was "slicing frogs and
toads" and her chief ambition "To be an M.D."[5] As an adolescent she
shared Will Drucker's interest in scientific experiments as well as in
the classics, set up a makeshift lab in the basement where she first
dissected frogs and toads, then progressed to cats and dogs. Cather
remembered accompanying Red Cloud's physicians, Dr. McKeeby
and Dr. Damerell, on their rounds; "How I loved the long rambling
rides we used to take. . . . I could tell who lived at every place and
about the ailments of his family."[6] Dr. Damerell even let her adminis-
ter chloroform before he performed an amputation.

In her graduation speech, Cather argued that "Scientific investigation is the hope of our age, as it must precede all progress. . . . We do
not withhold from a few great scientists the right of the hospital, the
post-mortem, or experimenting with animal life, but we are prone to
think that the right of experimenting with life too sacred a thing to
be placed in the hands of inexperienced persons. . . . If we bar our
novices from advancement, whence shall come our experts," she
asked, adding, "would all the life destroyed in experimenting from
the beginning of the world until today be as an atom to the life saved
by that one great discovery for which Harvey sacrificed his practice
and his reputation, the circulation of the blood?"[7]

When Cather got to the University of Nebraska, she studied the
sciences; she was granted advanced credit for chemistry and did perfectly well dissecting frogs, but math almost proved her undoing. In
fact, she didn't pass freshman math until the second semester of her
senior year. What happened when her essay on Thomas Carlyle was
published has been well documented: "Up to that time . . . I had
planned to specialize in science; I thought I would like to study
medicine. But what youthful vanity can be unaffected by the sight of
itself in print. It has a kind of hypnotic effect."[8] Cather's extraor-
dinarily successful involvement in literary pursuits during her college
years attests to the vigor with which she turned to the arts; indeed,
scholars have been inclined to agree with Edward Wagenknecht that
"about all that seems to have survived her shift away from science to
the humanities was her love for the stars, . . . yet even those who find

her scientific period hardest to understand must admit that it does link up with her characteristic tendency to blink nothing."[9] However, when Cather said that "most of the basic material a writer works with is acquired by the age of fifteen,"[10] she didn't exclude her youthful experiments or her medical ambitions; therefore it seems reasonable to question whether she truly did lose interest in the things of science as she turned her creative energy to the art of fiction.

When we look for them, there are a surprising number of doctors among Cather's friends. Besides the previously mentioned Dr. McKeeby and Dr. Damerell, we must add Dr. Love, who delivered her, whose daughter she played with and whose name she took for a while as her own middle name. Dr. Julius Tyndale, Mrs. Westermann's brother, came to Lincoln from New York and shared her interest in music and letters as well as in medicine and science; he was instrumental in arranging the trip to Chicago for a week of opera that marked the end of her college years. Dr. Joseph Wiener, Jr., nephew of Charles, came from New York in 1893 to operate on Fanny Weiner; and there was also the as-yet unidentified doctor in Pittsburgh who proposed marriage and of whom Dorothy Canfield approved. Another Pittsburgh physician and friend of Isabelle McClung, Dr. Edmund Esquerré, avoided Cather because he thought she regarded people as potential characters in her fiction; since she appropriated Godfrey St. Peter's physical characteristics and lecture style from him and used his last name in "The Garden Lodge," perhaps he was right. Dr. Ernest Albert Creighton, who married Mary Miner, was the model for Dr. Ed Burleigh, just as the George Seibels' physician, William Burleigh, contributed his name. Among her later friends were Dr. Frederick Sweeney, from whom she "stole" the wartime diary on which she based the shipboard epidemic in *One of Ours;* Dr. Macaulay, one of the very few Grand Manan natives with whom she socialized; Dr. William H. Glafke, gastroenterologist, and Dr. Frank Ober, orthopedist, two of the numerous physicians Cather needed in New York; and, of course, Dr. Richard Mellen, the orthopedic surgeon who married her favorite niece Mary Virginia Auld.

Cather's interest in medicine was also sustained by her close relationship with her Grandmother Boak, well known for her skill as a nurse. James Woodress notes that Cather wrote an article on nursing as a profession for the *Home Monthly,* referring to her grandmother as "one of those unprofessional nurses who served without recompense, from the mere love of it," adding that "the man who went to town for the doctor always stopped for her on the way. . . . I have heard the old folks tell how, during those dreadful diphtheria scourges that used to sweep over the country in the fifties, she would go into a house where eight or ten children were all down with the disease, nurse and cook for the living and 'lay out' the dead."[11] Following her grandmother's example, Cather nursed and nurtured her mother and younger brothers and sisters throughout her life, taking great joy in her skill at domestic duties. In 1940, when she was 67 years old, she spent most of the summer in NY taking care of Mary Virginia, hospitalized that year for a serious illness.

Cather could not help but be up-to-date on changes in the scientific and medical worlds during her tenure at *McClure's*. When S. S. McClure read in the paper about Roentgen rays, he had dispatched a reporter to Germany to get a story on this new medical marvel. Editing and rewriting Georgine Milmine's biography of Mary Baker Eddy must have had a special interest for a former pre-med student; Cather's series of articles was taken as a satirical attack on Christian Science by church leaders and, as Guy Reynolds points out, is still proscribed.[12] A review of articles published in *McClure's* during Cather's tenure as managing editor includes more than twenty-five scientific articles dealing with medicine, including a detailed report on work at the Rockefeller Institute and two tracking Paul Erlich's progress on Drug 606 (arsenobenzol), which promised to cure syphilis.[13] Interestingly, the sources for the Pittsburgh steel strike and the Fresh Air Fund, about which Don Hedger knows nothing in "Coming, Aphrodite!," as well as "the scandal about the Babies' Hospital," which has eluded researchers, can be found in *McClure's* articles. Appearing in the same number as Constance Leupp's "Campaigning for Babies' Lives" (*McClure's* 39 [August 1912]) is "The Bohemian Girl" by Willa Cather. These articles, I suspect, will prove to be enormously rewarding to scholars tracking other medical, social, and political allusions in Cather's work.

From Elizabeth Shepley Sergeant we know that Cather was well aware of contributions made by medicine to the war effort. In May 1919, Sergeant told her about Dr. Thomas Salmon, chief consultant in psychiatry of the AEF—the first psychiatrist honored in any army, who "would hold sessions with soldiers who had retreated out of fear, and Dr. Alfred E. Cohn of the Rockefeller Institute, who had noticed a nervous heart disease, which proved curable as it was not organic.[14] And a newspaper account of Cather's 1928 tour of the new Superior, Nebraska, hospital "from cellar to garret" alludes to her personal knowledge of hospitals: "Visiting the operating room she stated that her experiences in such places would not permit her to enthuse very much over them, but that she thought it was as pleasant as a room of its kind possibly could be."[15] A significant source of Cather's intimacy with medicine is, in fact, her own experience of the "healthcare system" as she knew it.

Although Cather writes about tennis, target practice and six-mile hikes, although she "thought nothing of a 12-mile walk on Grand Manan or an afternoon stroll around the reservoir in Central Park,"[16] although she rode a bicycle to work and raced a streetcar, spent the night lost on Mesa Verde, skated with Red Cloud friends and family in 1922, and made a trip with Roscoe through the Big Horn Mountains in Wyoming in 1927, she did have first-hand experience of the effects of illness on the patient. During her New York years, she became familiar herself with many of the city's hospitals: St. Luke's, Roosevelt, Presbyterian; and Isabelle was diagnosed with her fatal kidney disease, probably nephrocalcinosis leading to hydronephrosis, at Lennox Hill.

There is no record of serious illness during Cather's childhood; she had the usual colds (perhaps the most famous of which can be found in *Sapphira and the Slave Girl*), when Mary Anderson would come to help nurse her. There is some evidence that she had polio as a girl in Red Cloud; Carrie Sherwood remembered that the doctor said she would never walk again. However, as she grew older, Cather had a series of medical problems and illnesses, some of which made their way into her fiction. It is, in fact, a fascinating exercise to look at Cather's medical history in terms of what was available to her, and in light of what we know now.

I begin with what I am sure Cather would consider the most troubling of her physical ailments, the injuries to her wrists which prevented her from writing for long periods of time in her later years. In 1934 she sprained the big tendon in her left wrist, didn't go to the doctor, and ended up with a serious inflammation. In 1938 someone accidentally smashed one of her hands while she was shopping in a drugstore, and in 1941 her right wrist became painfully swollen. Her doctor diagnosed it as a serious inflammation of the sheath of the tendon and devised a steel and leather brace that immobilized her thumb, but left her fingers free, so that with difficulty she was able to sign her name.

The only recorded illness of Cather's college years occurred in 1895 when she returned from her opera trip to Chicago with "typhoid-pneumonia" which kept her in bed for a couple of weeks and brought her mother from Red Cloud to nurse her. She records frequent colds, an attack of bronchitis for two weeks in 1917, and influenza in 1909, 1919, 1928, 1938, and 1945. Of note is that she usually had the flu in February (prime flu season) and that, not only did she survive the terrible flu epidemic of 1918–19, but also she met Dr. Sweeney when she became sick with that flu at Jaffrey.

In the fall of 1898, Cather, then living in Pittsburgh, had a six-week bout with "grippe." We hear nothing more about any gastrointestinal problems until 1921, when she describes her appointment with Dr. William H. Glafke, head of the Stomach Clinic at St. Luke's Hospital: "He said he would have rather written *My Ántonia* than any other book ever written in America . . . . she thought he would try to do his best for her. The only trouble was that he wanted to talk all the time about her job instead of her misbehaving colon."[17] In 1923, Cather had two attacks of "appendicitis" and another in 1935, but no surgery; she was probably suffering from colitis or, perhaps, diverticulitis. But in April 1942, Cather went to see her doctor to have a sore throat painted with Argyrol. He found that she was running a high fever and conducted her personally to the hospital, where she was found to have an inflamed gall bladder. Cather refused to have the advised operation, and went home when her temperature dropped to normal. Yet the respite was only temporary, and in the summer she had to have the gall bladder removed.

Since sulfa appeared only in the 1930s and penicillin in the 1940s, we shouldn't be surprised to find stubborn infections. In 1911, Cather suffered an acute mastoiditis that required surgery and several weeks of hospitalization. A suspected mastoid process in 1922 turned out to be infected tonsils, and Cather had them out, losing a lot of blood in the process. Her most famous infection, though, is the blood poisoning she got in 1914 from a hatpin. She got a nasty pinprick on the back of her head, didn't pay much attention to it, and the scratch got infected. The infection led to blood poisoning, an operation on her scalp, three weeks in Roosevelt Hospital, and a bandaged head for five more weeks. It has been suggested that Cather's depression, rage at the illness that kept her from working, and bitterness at the foolishness of her accident indicate her fear and disgust at any physical deformity. On the other hand, her reactions to the pain of her injury, the helplessness a patient often feels, her guilt at having been the cause of her own misfortune, and the frustration of inactivity, all seem perfectly reasonable to me.

Two further medical mysteries await our investigation: In January 1912, Cather was hospitalized for several weeks for a "sharp illness and an exhausting little surgical procedure," and in 1928, when she left Red Cloud, she returned to New York by way of Rochester, Minnesota, stopping off at the Mayo Clinic (which was originally established for the treatment of thyroid disease) for some sort of examination. She described her problem as "a bothering hurt," but after she had spent two weeks at the Clinic, it was pronounced "a slight matter" and she returned to New York.

So, does this record add up to anything worth remembering? I think it does. In *Bergson and American Culture,* Tom Quirk refers to a 1912 letter from Cather to Sergeant in which Cather makes clear that "from an intellectual point of view, she was rather more attracted to the scientific rather than the purely philosophical dimensions of [Bergson's] *Creative Evolution.*"[18] In fact, she found the early chapters magnificent, but the final, essentially philosophical one significantly less interesting. Quirk then suggests that "from a literary point of view . . . the book seems to have suggested to her a means to coordinate and integrate imaginative materials."[19] Scholars have long realized that nothing was ever lost on Cather. I propose that the integration of her medical "bent" into the art of her fiction, suggested in part by Bergson's integration of philosophy and science, is yet another instance of her sophisticated modernist sensibility.

Within the past few years, there has been a concerted effort to return the "art" to the art of medicine. Investigators such as Kathryn Montgomery Hunter have studied the narrative basis of medicine, proposing that narrative ethics impact those essential medical histories. She points out that "understanding medicine as a narrative activity enables us—both physicians and patients—to shift the focus of medicine to the care of what ails the patient and away from the relatively simple matter of the diagnosis of disease."[20] Patients tell stories as authors create narratives while doctors listen to those stories (decoding or interpreting) in much the same way that readers read texts. Doctors have always been trained to listen for the telling detail, to find the significant fact, to select and arrange the elements in a patient's story. Now doctors are also being encouraged to hone their analytic skills by close reading of literature in order to grasp what patients say and leave unsaid, to listen for stories of illness, not just catalogues of disease, and to devise ways to heal, not just to cure. Modernist Willa Cather anticipated this focus years ago. One result was Elizabeth Sergeant's pique that Cather wasn't a bit interested in Freud: "Her intolerance began to trouble me. She was truly skeptical about the post-war world. Take this Viennese Freud: Why was everybody reading him? Tolstoy knew as much about psychology—with no isms attached—as any fiction writer needed."[21] When Cather was fourteen, she became enthralled with Tolstoy, and owned a paperback copy of "The Death of Ivan Illich." She was right; that text is used extensively in medical training as a magnificent depiction of human suffering and death.

How then does Cather connect medicine with literature? First of all, we can find a goodly number of doctors in her fiction. In "On the Gulls' Road," Dr. Niels Nannestad, Alexandra Ebbling's doctor-father, can do nothing for her heart disease; Scott Spinney has alienated all the doctors in town, including Dr. Jones, and refuses to call Dr. Tom until it is too late for him to save Nelly in "The Joy of Nelly Deane"; Dr. Zablowski in "Behind the Singer Tower" works for the Rockefeller Institute; although he gets to his patient, Dr. Paradis cannot save Amédée's life in *O Pioneers!;* Dr. Miles Creedon appears in "Scandal"; Dr. Seares and an unnamed specialist in "Her Boss"; both Dr. Truman, the army doctor who calls on Claude's assistance during the flu epidemic, and Dr. Chessup, the ship's doctor, figure in *One of Ours;* Dr. Dennison, a close friend of the Forresters, sets Niel's arm and attends Captain Forrester in his long illness, and so on, to the end of her work.[22]

The point is, when Cather selects medical detail, it is accurate and appropriate to the story. Two of the more peculiar instances are Thea's Swedish Movements, physical therapeutics that seem to be making a comeback; and Enid's visit with her mother to a Vegetarian Sanitarium, modeled on the one established at Battle Creek, Michigan, by Dr. John Harvey Kellogg. The brown paste used in *One of Ours* is ichthyol ointment once used to treat erysipelas—a streptococcal infection; and in the same novel we even get a folk cure for rheumatism: take a guinea pig to bed and he will draw out all the pain. Auclair relates to Cécile the relative merits of contemporary medical therapies: Unicorn's Horn (norwhale), viper broth, liquorice, and cod liver oil, all historically correct. And Cather's characters have to deal with a wide range of diseases, too: tuberculosis, heart disease, gangrene, yellow fever, cholera, and, of course, influenza, which was prevalent in the United States for several years before 1918–19 epidemic in which 500,000 people died.

In a 1906 letter to Witter Bynner, Cather appropriates medical imagery to describe Henry James's act of "diagnosing" her work: "she felt as if she were about to undergo a searching physical examination that might undermine her confidence in the dependableness of her organs, confirming her own doubts."[23] Elizabeth Sergeant recalls a conversation in which Cather told her, "Novelists, opera singers, even doctors . . . have in common the unique and marvelous experience of entering into the very skin of another human being. What can compare with it? she said, her eyes shining."[24] And in 1925, Cather wrote to Dorothy Canfield Fisher that she was delighted with a book she had just read, *The Doctor Looks at Literature,* particularly the chapters on D. H. Lawrence and Proust.[25]

Sharon O'Brien proposes "[t]hat Cather associated the doctor's profession with creative power . . . mingling the literal and metaphoric powers of entry and transformation. . . . Equating the doctor with phallic potency and creativity, she links the patient with helplessness and emptiness."[26] Conversely, Nadeane Trowse notes the number of diseases, doctors and patients in Cather's work as a reaction against authoritarian and patriarchal naming of lesbianism as a disease.[27] I would like to suggest a third reading of the medical in Cather that hinges on the congruency between a physician's ability to immerse himself or herself in the patient's story and Cather's recollection: "I have never felt any intellectual excitement any more intense than I used to feel when I spent a morning with one of these old women at her baking or butter-making. I used to ride home in the most unseasonable state of excitement; I always felt . . . as if I had actually got inside another person's skin."[28] Getting inside another person's skin is what novelists and doctors do have in common. Cather learned from the medical way of seeing, from scientific scrutiny, just as she welcomed and learned from all new visions of the human condition. "The magnitude of the subject matter is not of primary importance," she tells us; a writer "achieves anything noble, anything enduring . . . by giving himself absolutely to his material." And that "this gift of sympathy is his great gift; is the fine thing in him that alone can make his work fine."[29] Robert Coles agrees: "It is the everyday life that clinicians also contend with—the unique nature of each human being. Since no patient is quite like any other, the doctor has to step from well-learned abstractions to the individual person at hand—an important move indeed. Novelists as well are wedded to the specific, the everyday; their job is to conjure up details for us. And . . . everyday life has its own ethical conflicts. No wonder novelists do so well examining the trials and temptations that intervene, say, in a doctor's life."[30]

The impetus to teach doctors to read more closely, to reflect on the ethical and philosophical through literature, might be a recent development in medical education, but thoughtful physicians and scientists have long recognized twentieth-century duality between technology and art as detrimental to the human condition. Albert Einstein, Jacob Bronowski, and Bruce Mazlish have all observed that the central problem of contemporary man is to find a way to reconcile science and the humanities. As Merrill Skaggs has pointed out, much of Cather's artistic project was to reconcile dualities, and I believe that much of her genius lies in her ability to integrate her wide-ranging interests into that apparently simple whole that continues to engage her readers so thoroughly.[31] Yehudi Menuhin said of Cather that "[h]er interest in human beings and her desire to understand them was not confined to a source of material for the practice of her art. It was far more genuine and generous than that for she loved not only with a full heart but with not a little curiosity!"[32] That curiosity which she never lost and which reveals itself in her continuing fascination with medicine is, I believe, one key to that gift of integration in her apparently pure and unalloyed art.

In a letter to the *St. Paul Daily News* Cather pointed out that "[t]he writer does not efface himself, as you say; he loses himself in the amplitude of his impressions, and in the exciting business of finding all his memories, long-forgotten scenes and faces, running off his pen, as if they were in the ink, and not in his brain at all."[33] William Carlos Williams, physician-poet, recalls much the same experience in seeing his patients:

> I lost myself in the very properties of their minds: for the moment at least I actually became *them*, whoever they should be, so that when I detached myself from them at the end of a half-hour of intense concentration over some illness which was affecting them, it was as though I were reawakening from a sleep. For the moment I myself did not exist, nothing of myself affected me.[34]

From the supposedly scientific sector come a surprising number of medical professionals—doctors, almost doctors, and nurses—who have made important contributions to literature: Anton Chekhov, John Keats, John Locke, Sir Arthur Conan Doyle, Louisa May Alcott, Walt Whitman, Gertrude Stein, Somerset Maugham, William Carlos Williams, Walker Percy, Lewis Thomas and yes, Willa Cather.

What does Willa Cather have to do with modern medicine? I believe that those young doctors who respond so strongly to Cather come to realize through her work the possibility of their own integration of the sciences and the humanities in the art and practice of medicine. They find in her stories opportunities to reflect on the ethical questions and responsibilities of contemporary life. Willa Cather pointed out that "[w]e like a writer much as we like an individual; for what he is simply, underneath his accomplishments. Oftener than we realize, it is for some moral quality, some ideal which he himself cherishes, though it may be little discernible in his behavior in the world. It is the light behind his books and it is the living quality in his sentences."[35] Medical readers recognize in Cather a kindred spirit, a close observer of humanity in all its variety, and someone, like them, who finds ways to integrate art and science in order to remedy and restore.

Notes

1. Bernice Slote, ed., *The Kingdom of Art: Willa Cather's First Principles and Critical Statements 1893–1896* (Lincoln: University of Nebraska Press, 1967),46.
2. Willa Cather, interview with Rose C. Feld, "Restlessness Such as Ours Does Not Make For Beauty," *New York Times,* 21 December 1924, in *Willa Cather in Person,* ed. L. Brent Bohlke (Lincoln: University of Nebraska Press, 1986), 68–69.
3. Willa Cather, *The Professor's House* (New York: Vintage, 1973), 75.
4. Willa Cather, "Miss Jewett," in *Not Under Forty* (New York: Knopf, 1964), 78–79.
5. See James Woodress, *Willa Cather: A Literary Life* (Lincoln: University of Nebraska Press, 1987); Sharon O'Brien, *Willa Cather: The Emerging Voice* (New York: Oxford, 1987); E. K. Brown, *Willa Cather: A Critical Biography,* completed by Leon Edel (New York: Knopf, 1953); Mildred Bennett, *The World of Willa Cather* (Lincoln: University of Nebraska Press, 1989); Edith Lewis, *Willa Cather Living* (New York: Knopf, 1953); Elizabeth Shepley Sergeant, *Willa Cather: A Memoir* (Athens: Ohio University Press, 1992); Kathleen D. Byrne and Richard C. Snyder, *Chrysalis: Willa Cather in Pittsburgh* (Pittsburgh: Historical Society of Western Pennsylvania, 1982); Marion Marsh Brown and Ruth Crone, *Only One Point of the Compass: Willa Cather in the Northeast* (Danbury CT: Archer Editions Press, 1980); and Edward Wagenknecht, *Willa Cather* (New York: Continuum, 1994) for biographical details.
6. Cather, quoted in Woodress, *WC,* 114.
7. Cather, "Superstition vs. Investigation," in Bolke, *Person,* 142.
8. Cather, quoted in Woodress, *WC,* 73.
9. Wagenknecht, *Cather,* 143.
10. Latrobe Carroll, "Willa Sibert Cather," in Bolke, *Person,* 20.
11. Woodress, *WC,* 19.
12. Guy Reynolds, *Willa Cather in Context: Progress, Race, Empire* (New York: St. Martin's Press, 1996), 156.
13. Among the articles in *McClure's,* Vols. 30–40 (1907–12) are Cleveland Moffit's "The Edge of the Future in Science"; Samuel Hopkins Adams's "Guardians of the Public Health"; Richard C. Cabot's "One Hundred Christian Science Cures"; George Kennan's "Problems of Suicide"; Dr. Henry Smith Williams's "Alcohol and the Individual"; Carolyn Conant Van Blarcom and Marion Hamilton Carter's "Preventable Blindness"; E.T. Brewster's "Studying the Animal Mind in Laboratories," "The Animal Mind from the Inside," and "The Fly—The Disease of the House"; Burton J. Hendrick's "Cancer, What We Know About It," "New Facts on Cancer," "Some Modern Ideas on Food," "Pellagra, The Medical Mystery of Today" (accompanied by notes on Pellagra "by noted authorities in Europe and America"), "The New Anesthetic—Stovane," "Work at the Rockefeller Institute: The Transplanting of Animal Organs," and "Conquering Spinal Meningitis"; Hereward Carrington's "Eusapia Pallidino, The Despair of Science"; "A Defense of the New Orleans Health Authorities"; Marguerite Mark's "Professor Erlich's Discoveries," followed in the next issue by "Paul Erlich: The Man and His Work"; "When a Man Marries: Selection and

Heredity as They Apply to the Individual"; Dr. Henry Smith Williams's "Alcohol and the Community" and "The Scientific Solution of the Liquor Problem"; Dr. Brandreth Symonds's "The Mortality of Overweights and Underweights"; Prof. M. A. Rosanoff and Dr. A. J. Rosenoff's "Evidence Against Alcohol"; "In Justice to American Manufacturers of Serum," an early example of the "medical letter" by John F. Anderson, Dir, Hygenic Laboratory; and "A Scientific Study of Fools." What I find surprising is that so many titles sound as if they came from today's magazines!

14. Sergeant, *Memoir,* 166.

15. Bolke, *Person,* 102.

16. Brown, *Biography* , 320.

17. Woodress, *WC,* 321.

18. Tom Quirk, *Bergson and American Culture: The Worlds of Willa Cather and Wallace Stevens* (Chapel Hill: The University of North Carolina Press, 1990), 124–25.

19. Ibid.

20. Kathryn Montgomery Hunter, *Doctor's Stories: The Narrative Structure of Medical Knowledge* (Princeton: Princeton University Press, 1991), xxi.

21. Sergeant, *Memoir,* 173–74.

22. Gervaise Beaudoin, whom Auclair treats in *Shadows on the Rock,* was known as a man of honor and a good doctor, more concerned with practicing his art and healing people than making money; and Euclide Auclair, himself, was based on Michel Sarrazin, a barber-surgeon who practiced seventeenth-century advances in medicine and anatomy and "new" treatments of disease. Dr. Ed Burleigh, my residents' favorite physician, is drawn from Mary Miner's husband Dr. Ernest Albert Creighton; and, we have a pair of medical men in *Sapphira and the Slave Girl:* Dr. Clavenger, an "intelligent, devoted doctor," and Dr. Brush, the uneducated country doctor who practices by referring to Buchan's Family Medical Book, as well as Rachel Blake, who has a "knack for caring for the sick."

23. O'Brien, *Voice,* 309.

24. Sergeant, *Memoir,* 58.

25. I am indebted to Mark Madigan for calling this letter of 27 February 1925 to my attention.

26. O'Brien, *Voice,* 92.

27. Nadeane Trowse, "Willa Cather's Condition: Disease, Doctors and Diagnoses as Social Action" in *Cather Studies, Volume IV,* eds. Michael Peterman and Robert Thacker (Lincoln: University of Nebraska, 1999).

28. Woodress, *WC,* 38–39.

29. Cather, "Miss Jewett," in *Not Under Forty* (Lincoln: University of Nebraska Press, 1988), 79–80.

30. Robert Coles, "Medical Ethics and Living a Life" in *On Doctoring,* ed. Richard Reynolds, M.D., and John Stone, M.D. (New York: Simon & Shuster, 1995), 283.

31. See Merrill M. Skaggs, *After the World Broke in Two: The Later Novels of Willa Cather* (Charlottesville: University Press of Virginia, 1990) for a thoughtful and incisive discussion of Cather's attempt to repair the "break" in consciousness that results from biographical, philosophical, and intellectual dualities, of which Cather was acutely aware.

32. *Miracles of Perception: The Art of Willa Cather* (Charlottesville: Alderman Library, University of Virginia, 1980), 7.

33. Cather in Bolke, *Person,* 178.

34. William Carlos Williams, "The Practice," in *On Doctoring,* 68.

35. Cather, "Miss Jewett," 94.

Bibliography

Bennett, Mildred. *The World of Willa Cather.* Lincoln: University of Nebraska Press, 1989.

Bohlke, L. Brent, ed. *Willa Cather in Person.* Lincoln: University of Nebraska Press, 1986.

Brown, E. K. Completed by Leon Edel. *Willa Cather: A Critical Biography.* Lincoln: University of Nebraska Press, 1987.

Cather, Willa. *The Professor's House.* New York: Vintage Books, 1973.

———. *Not Under Forty.* New York: Alfred A. Knopf, 1964.

Hunter, Kathryn Montgomery. *Doctor's Stories: The Narrative Structure of Medical Knowledge.* Princeton: Princeton University Press, 1991.

Lewis, Edith. *Willa Cather Living.* New York: Alfred A. Knopf, 1953.

Miracles of Perception: The Art of Willa Cather. Charlottesville: Alderman Library, University of Virginia, 1980.

O'Brien, Sharon. *Willa Cather: The Emerging Voice.* New York: Oxford, 1987.

Quirk, Tom. *Bergson and American Culture: The Worlds of Willa Cather and Wallace Stevens.* Chapel Hill: The University of North Carolina Press, 1990.

Reynolds, Guy. *Willa Cather in Context: Progress, Race, Empire.* New York: St. Martin's Press, 1996.

Reynolds, Richard, M.D. and John Stone, M.D., eds. *On Doctoring.* New York: Simon & Shuster, 1995.

Sergeant, Elizabeth Shepley. *Willa Cather: A Memoir.* Athens: Ohio University Press, 1992.

Skaggs, Merrill. *After the World Broke in Two: The Later Novels of Willa Cather.* Charlottesville: University Press of Virginia, 1990.

Slote, Bernice, ed. *The Kingdom of Art: Willa Cather's First Principles and Critical Statements 1893–1896.* Lincoln: University of Nebraska Press, 1967.

Trowse, Nadeane. "Willa Cather's Condition: Disease, Doctors and Diagnoses as Social Action" in *Cather Studies, Volume IV.* ed. Michael Peterman and Robert Thacker. Lincoln: University of Nebraska, 1999.

Wagenknecht, Edward. *Willa Cather.* New York: Continuum, 1984.

Woodress, James. *Willa Cather: A Literary Life.* Lincoln: University of Nebraska, 1987.

Part II
Art Capital of the World

Morality and the Naked Lady

CYNTHIA GRIFFIN WOLFF

Wallace Stevens once observed that Willa Cather "takes so much pains to conceal her sophistication . . . it is easy to miss her quality."[1] In fact, she concealed sophistication so well that scholars have only recently begun to discover the subtle web of echoes and allusions that give depth and texture to her apparently transparent prose. We have discovered traces of earlier writers from Homer to Henry James. Cather's debt to music is revealed not merely in the surprising number of narratives devoted to musicians, but more subtly in the lyrical cadences of her prose and the musical structures that can inform her novels. References to the visual arts are everywhere—surfacing almost casually, both by direct reference and by descriptive echo. Perhaps it is not surprising, then, that the task of relating Cather's fiction to her sources has usually surveyed surfaces—that is, the texts themselves—and studied content or, occasionally, form.

There are, however, larger, more subtle, and perhaps more important, questions of "reference." These questions investigate the ontology of a given artistic form: the implications, limitations, and boundary conditions of its existence. One can ask, if an artist working in such a medium as prose fiction elects to refer to another medium (in the case of Cather, refer extensively), what unsuspected consequences might follow? If Willa Cather often deflects her reader's attention to painting or music, what all-but-hidden connections does her complex conjoining imply?

To some degree Cather's interests reflect the creative innovations of her age. The implications of both visual art and music came under intense scrutiny during her apprenticeship: and by 1912 and 1913, when she wrote her "two" first novels, painters and musicians had begun to renounce conventional limitations with an almost anarchic glee. Avant garde artists in both media resolved to overcome the temporal limitations traditionally imposed on their work. Musicians and painters were linked in this endeavor; but music and visual art exhibit converse relationships to temporal constraints: they delimit opposite poles of the dilemma that the artists of Cather's day attacked.

Once created, visual art is comprehensive, intact, static, and complete. The viewer apprehends it at one time and all at once: there is no 'past' or 'future' in this form. (We may imagine that the fruit in the still life grew on a limb, but that imaginary tree-life is inconsequential for painter or viewer.) And as Keats wryly observed, the lover on the Grecian Urn is forever suspended in a state of yearning: he will neither age nor ever possess his beloved. Although the "completed" visual art can still offer the viewer a complex moral/aesthetic vision, with careful examination and analysis perceptive viewers can grasp the "meaning" of the work in its entirety; and although the process of understanding any given work completely may require considerable time, the static visual image will always present its complications simultaneously. Thus a viewer can retain the *whole* of it in memory, not merely some part (as its beginning, middle, etc.).

By contrast, music glides through time, embodying motion. In music, there is nothing *but* past and future, for music offers its listener no stationary "now": while music is being performed, "now" after "now" streams from future into past leaving a brilliant penumbra, but no stable whole. Certainly a talented musician can retain entire symphonies in her head; however, even the most talented musician recalls these symphonies sequentially. Music's serial relationship to time is intrinsic to the form: and no artist can escape this transience. (Clearly Willa Cather pondered this enigmatic fact about music, for in her fictions, she often uses music to intensify tragic transience. The connection of music to transience lies at the heart of *Lucy Gayheart*.)

A long convention links narrative fiction to painting, particularly portrait painting (one thinks of *The Portrait of a Lady, The Picture of Dorian Gray,* and *A Portrait of the Artist as a Young Man,* for example); and casual reflection suggests that painting seems to have some "natural" relationship to characterization in a novel. Yet this surface association overlooks a number of complex issues, perhaps even falsifies examinations of them. People, even people in novels, are neither fixed nor static. People live in—and through—time. Or, to put it differently, time is intrinsic to our understanding of human life. For this reason, then, fiction is really quite unlike portraiture. In its intractably sequential fluidity, it may be more like music—moving through time, always changing, always just beyond our grasp as a completed entity.

Having acknowledged this fact, however, we have added to our problem, not solved it. For example, certain fixed elements within all fictions make the analogy to painting seem not merely apt, but inevitable. In Western culture, especially in post-Puritan culture, we usually assume that a death signals a "finished" life. The American Puritan heritage has left the residual conviction that one can "understand" or "evaluate" men and women by their characters at death. As a prior assumption, we assumed that some "Divine Architect" has set a "time" for each life; and that death, in its finality, represents both Transcendent Will and Ultimate Judgment.

A great many readers unthinkingly accept the conclusion of a novel (like the moment of death) as the signal permitting a summary "definition" of character. Yet in a novel, the only "Creator" is the author; it is the author who sets the "Time" for birth and death. Further, an author decides to begin the "life" of each character according to narrative needs (seldom with birth); the author decides how much to disclose about a character's "life"; she has absolute command over the character's finale in the fictional world (which may or may not be death). And she deploys all of these decisions to shape and articulate her notion of the novel's "reality" for the reader. In short, although any given novel may seem to offer the reader an inevitable, and absolutely "reliable" world, this sense of "completeness" is entirely contrived and may even be deliberately deceptive.

Another way of understanding this ontological puzzle is to say that in a piece of fiction, the author is that "Higher Power" who has the absolute authority to define the relationship between time and character. Although this right cannot be relinquished, its power can be a source of great difficulty; and the implications of any artist's management of time, so hotly debated in the worlds of music and art during Willa Cather's early years, may have presented even more trouble for her as a writer of fiction than the analogous problems did for her contemporaries who worked in music and the visual arts.

We can understand Cather's concern with the subtle, sometimes paradoxical, implications of time if we articulate several of the especially vexing puzzles that interested her. For example:

1. Does a person's death (or the end of a novel) offer a reliable "definition" of his or her character? Should we suppose that at this moment we can make conclusive moral judgements about that person? If so, can we commit ourselves to certain baffling corollaries that follow:
   - Those who die young predictably seem "better" than those who live longer, because they never fail, or become bitter or vicious, or grow unattractive. (The adolescent Juliet is univer-

sally appealing; a slatternly middle-aged Juliet might seem more like the nurse.)
- Conversely, if a person has led a good-enough life while young but has slipped into bitterness after old age has imposed pain and hardship, must we wish an early death had circumvented the ignoble behavior of old age? Should we remember a "good" youth when evaluating an elderly character? And how should we weight the several phases of life?

2. To consider the relationship between time and character, must we acknowledge the related problem of circumstance and character—the "what if" dilemma? What if, at some time, an accidental benefit befalls a person. Should that person get moral "credit" for consequent good behavior?
- "What if" a person suddenly finds it easy to be "good" because she has been "helped"—by a small inheritance, say, or the death of a powerful enemy?
- "What if" a sickly person becomes querulous and spiteful after a charitable, good-natured, and healthy youth? How should we assess the "meaning" of such a life? Can we even acquire the information we must have to judge it?
- "What if" some ruinous circumstantial tragedy befalls a person, something beyond his control, after which he indulges in "unscrupulous" behavior which might never have occurred had the bad luck been averted. How are we to judge this "weakness"?

3. Finally, in a novel, there is a unique narrative fact that further complicates the morality/character/time situation: an author gets to determine the circumstances in which the reader initially encounters a character; and the moment of this first meeting may indelibly color the reader's attitude.
- If a character is first represented in her unsympathetic old age, while mitigating information about her earlier life is withheld until later, the reader's capacity to approve of the character may have been fatally compromised. The vision of an embittered old woman may never be erased.
- Conversely, if a sympathetic young person is traced through "tragic" or "piteous" decline, we may remain sympathetic even though he sinks into a state of spite or malice.

All of these problems attend the manipulation of time within a fiction. To some extent, all serious novelists of Cather's generation pondered them and attempted to adjust their fictions to the increasingly obvious moral limitations of the genre.

I have presented these particular problems because Cather herself seems quite consciously to have wrestled with them and to have invited her readers to understand these ensuing moral paradoxes. Many of her novels embody the puzzles just outlined.

Let us begin with the death of a promising young person of unfulfilled potential. Claude Wheeler is just such a boy: surely his is the bold, bright beginning of some wonderful tale cut short. If we make these optimistic assumptions, however, we confer an unearned heroism upon him, for everything in his life was as yet merely possibility. And after all, not all who die young are "good."

And what of the obverse: what of youthful high spirits that wither and decay into bitter old age; what of Myra Henshaw? Should we pity (or censure) Myra Henshaw for having *failed* to die young in fiery defiance and reciprocated passion? Might not she too have seemed, once, the stuff of greatness-cut-short? Might we have judged Myra quite differently had it been her youthful self we first came to know?

The Professor's wife has collected a small inheritance from her father, a sum of money that has "made all the difference" in her nature. Is Lillian's equanimity conditional upon Time's having delivered the small competence that allowed her to be generous and amiable? Can anyone legitimately evaluate some hypothetical other self?

Perhaps Cather's most interesting experiment with presentation is in *Sapphira and the Slave Girl*. The reader's introduction to Sapphira all but compels revulsion: a vicious voice, harsh with anger—a voice followed by the sound of a slap. Patently, we are not meant to love Sapphira. However, the *timing* of this moment (before we know anything else about her history or the larger situation) may unfairly kill our sympathy. Once we have learned more about her life, can we find pity for the spirited girl who consigned herself to Back Creek and eventually became dropsical and crippled? Can we understand the resentment of a woman whose husband is inattentive and emotionally cold to her, while he becomes sentimentally, if chastely, involved with the lissome young slave? The sequential nature of fiction thwarts our capacity to evaluate our own judgments. And with such a beginning, can anyone ever feel the compassion for Sapphira that her servant Till does?

Willa Cather understood the artistic foment of her era. Moreover, she knew that the issue of "time," especially in the visual arts, had become the subject of serious study. Always aware of contemporary innovations, even when she deplored them (as she increasingly did), Cather occasionally chose to study them and learn. The post-Impressionist transformations of painting proved to be one of these exceptional cases. The post-Impressionists introduced her to new modes of understanding and new ways of representing reality—what Cather would call "a new way of seeing";[2] and this new vision clarified the kind of ambiguities and complexities we have just examined. Her education escalated in the spring and summer of 1913.

Elizabeth Shepley Sergeant, who had been in France for an extended visit, returned to America in late June of 1913. Edith Lewis was away, so a room was available; Willa Cather, who had only recently moved into the new apartment at 5 Bank Street, urged her friend to stay in New York as her guest. For the most part this invitation expressed simply her desire to spend time with Sergeant, for whom Cather always had great fondness; in part, however, it also revealed Cather's desire to get help in mastering the "new art" that had taken New York by storm earlier that year—"new art" that had sprung largely from France. "My portrait [had been] painted by a Cubist from a vineyard—*un sauvage,* a wild man," Sergeant remembers.

> He called himself, a *"Fauve,"* who had already exhibited in New York.
>   Willa was intrigued [by the new visions of experimental art and] especially by the Cubist. She determined [that] I should expound modern art to her. [And when the canvases of this *"Fauve"* were unpacked], she began at once to study [them] with interest, since they represented a new way of *seeing.* . . . She asked me many questions about the wild man from a Provencal vineyard, a *petit bourgeois* by birth, who had got to painting in this new and startling way. In later life, nothing interested her less than what the French call *le mouvement,* in poetry or novels, the *avant-garde.* But in 1913, the story of *le sauvage,* as his mother called him, and above all, his new way of painting, piqued her interest.[3]

Perhaps the "Fauve" whose paintings were "exhibited in New York," had found some patron with an available gallery; more likely, however, his work had been part of the "International Exhibition of Modern Art" in the Armory at Lexington and 25th St.—that explosive American *début* of modern art—the introduction of Matisse, Braque, Picasso, Duchamp, and many others to a general audience in this country, and without question the most controversial artistic event that ever took place in America. The Armory Exhibition (as it came to be known) ran for an entire month, from February 15, 1913 to March 13, 1913. And it was located just a brisk walk away from Willa Cather's new apartment.

Although Willa Cather had just moved into the Bank St. apartment in Greenwich Village, we have no proof that she took the walk uptown to see this controversial Exhibition—although her long, well-documented history of curiosity, along with her fondness for taking very extended walks, would argue that she must have. Yet whether she did is of little importance. The Exhibition provoked such a violent and wide-spread reaction, had become the object of such heated dispute, that no one who read the New York City newspapers could escape its shock waves. Nor could they avoid knowing of iconoclastic art.

Every major daily in the city ran not one, but many articles on the Exhibition—most of them illustrated. Major journals of opinion like *Harper's, The Outlook, The Literary Digest, The Independent, Current Opinion, The Nation* ran at least one feature article on the Exhibition—generally several; and these were also generously illustrated. (*The Nation* also maintained an active debate in its "Letters to the Editor" section.) Even former President Theodore Roosevelt wrote an essay on The Exhibition for *The Outlook*. Noncommittally, he expressed admiration for the energy that "shake[s] off the dead hand, often the fossilized dead hand, of the reactionaries," while voicing suspicion of that "lunatic fringe [which] was fully in evidence, especially in the rooms devoted to the Cubists and the Futurists, of Near-Impressions."[4] Eventually his essay became the object of dispute in and of itself. After a week or two, not merely the contents of the Armory Exhibition, but also the terms of the various controversies about it, had come to be so widely known that cartoons about the affair sprang up all over the country.

What tenets of Cubism did Cather find useful for her fiction? The most basic eschewed "resolution" in a work of art. All students of Willa Cather's work are familiar with her refusal to provide definitive endings and clear-cut conclusions; to some extent, this fictional maneuver has its antecedent in the tenets of the modernist movement in visual art.

> For the traditional distinction between solid form and the space around it, Cubism substituted a radically new fusion of mass and void. In place of earlier perspective systems that determined the precise location of discrete objects in illusory depth, Cubism offered an unstable structure of dismembered planes in indeterminate spatial positions. Instead of assuming that the work of art was an illusion of a reality that lay beyond it, Cubism proposed that the work of art was itself a reality that represented the very process by which nature is transformed into art. . . .

Girl with a Mandolin (1910) by Pablo Picasso. Courtesy of the Museum of Modern Art. Nelson A. Rockefeller Bequest.

For a century that questioned the very concept of absolute truth or value, Cubism created an artistic language of intentional ambiguity. In front of a Cubist work of art, the spectator was to realize that no single interpretation of the fluctuating shapes, textures, spaces, and objects could be complete in itself.[5]

These assumptions were the basis for a form of art whose *visual* rendition of reality was "an unstable structure of dismembered planes"; similarly, novelists would demand a form whose *narrative* validity lay not in a story's cohesion and conclusion, but in a skillful management of the various types of incoherence that are intrinsic to the process of story-telling. (Thus in *My Ántonia,* Jim's tale might or might not be more valid than the independent tale that the reader concocts as she follows Jim's narrative.) Or, the aesthetic authenticity of a novel might lie in the complex, unresolved intersection of *many* stories (as in *Shadows on the Rock*), no one of which offers absolute or sufficient "truth," and no one of which is entirely false. Or "truth" might lie entirely *outside* of the novel. (Thus the "told story" will never summon the shimmering presence that haunts the footprint or the wild memory of the girl herself in *Lucy Gayheart.*)

Cubist theory does not suggest merely that there may be many "points of view" of some stable (real or fictional) world. Instead it insists that there are as many fictional worlds as there are people—as many stories about these worlds as can be told. That "truth" (if one can speak of truth) must lie in an agglomeration of stories—not in the tale, but in the process of telling—perhaps, necessarily, in a multiplicity of tellings.

Visual artists were well aware that these radical theories combined many of the elements of their art with those of music. Not surprisingly, their renditions of the "still-life" often explicitly acknowledged the evanescent, "musical" element of these artistic theories by featuring musical instruments prominently in pictures whose various planes floated in space. The message such pictures delivered was that even if some coherent and stable "real world" existed (somewhere), no single, stable vision of it could capture its enigmatic equipoise: no two visions could share the same existential reality; and art should not impose coherence and balance upon a situation where such radical instability was the "norm."

If the still-life speaks to modernist visions of the material world, post-impressionist portraiture in its many forms addresses issues of "character" or "human nature." And perhaps because we all enjoy looking at others (as a part of looking for ourselves), two depictions

Nude Descending a Staircase, No. 2 (1912) by Marcel Duchamp. Courtesy of the Philadelphia Museum of Art: The Louise and Walter Arensberg Collection.

of nudes in the Armory Exhibition attracted special attention: Picasso's *Demoiselles d'Avignon* and Duchamp's *Nude descending a staircase.* The latter was reproduced countless times; in fact, it was reproduced more often than anything else in the show. Its attraction seems to have been hypnotic.

> There was usually such a crowd before the Duchamp *Nude descending a staircase* that it was difficult to see. The buzz of excitement was exhilarating. Some tried to understand, others tried to explain, the great majority either laughed or were infuriated. It could be seen as a symbol of the ultimate in moral degeneracy or as a mad and irresponsible joke. . . . Because of a certain incongruity in its title and the puzzle which it presented, the *Nude* became the focal point of the Exhibition.[6]

One element of outrage had less to do with artistic innovation than with the repudiation of certain well-established prerogatives: "This mockery of the human, and especially the female, nude was deeply offensive to the American art-loving public. . . . Beautiful paintings of female nudes—seen, often, simply as objects to be owned by powerful men . . . were an essential, perhaps the essential part of the traditional world of nineteenth century art."[7]

Picasso's *Demoiselles* raised many of the same problems. Paradoxically, although these "Desmoiselles" are prostitutes, Picasso's painting suggests anything but ownership; for with its puzzling sense of vibration or motion, the images have the frustrating quality of first appearing to be available, but then of mysteriously disintegrating into evasive inaccessibility as the eye moves from left to right.

> This inconsistency is an integral part of *Les Demoiselles.* The irrepressible energy behind its creation demanded a vocabulary of change and impulse rather than of measured statement in a style already articulated. The breathless tempo of this pregnant historical moment virtually obligated its first masterpiece to carry within itself the very process of artistic evolution.[8]

The idiosyncratic, vexing sense of movement in *Les Demoiselles* echoes many of the aesthetic problems with which we began. Cubist art, like literary art, addressed the difficulty of "placing" a human life within some permanent frame[work] so that we might understand its nature and moral significance.

Les Demoiselles achieves its effect of nervous movement by treating a group of figures; *Nude descending a staircase* compressed its renunciation of customary expectations by rendering a single figure that

Les Demoiselles d'Avignon (1907) by Pablo Picasso. Courtesy of the Museum of Modern Art, New York. Acquired through the Lillie P. Bliss Bequest.

defied all standard anticipations. The figure is erect, when supine passivity is usual; the figure's gender is uncertain, when centuries of tradition had dictated the explicitly female; the figure's identity is hidden, when titillating candor had long been the norm; in fact, in this picture, the figure could not even be "found," much less "gendered."

Deeply religious, Willa Cather was unlike a good many "modernist" authors who dismissed moral questions. Yet although Cather focused on moral quandaries, she differed from her conservative predecessors by repeatedly frustrating our attempts to resolve these dilemmas in some safe and definite way. She entices us into seeking complete, coherent, and morally "fixed" characters, characters whose ethical and emotional "selves" we can discover; then repeatedly, she withholds satisfaction. "What are we to make of the real Thea Kronborg? Who is the real Marian Forrester? When is Ántonia most authentically herself?" Serious questions must be asked, enigmas examined; and paradoxically, the crucial moral act is engaging in this exercise itself, not in discovering some final answer.

Like the *Nude*, no essence of these characters exists as culmination: they are not creatures whose lives come to some resolution defining "who they really are" (although narrators like Jim Burden and Niel Herbert attempt to fit them into just such paradigms). Instead, their nature is comprehensive and inclusive. Like the *Nude*, their "reality" does not cohere in a static finale. The "meaning" of these characters is everywhere in their lives, not just in the narrow, most recent "now." (After all, from Eternity's, or from an author's, point of view—that is, from a view outside of time—any moment in a person's life is equipresent with any other moment.) Thus, although Cather has never suggested that decisions about "character" and/or "morality" are pointless, she does suggest that these dilemmas are difficult in ways that have not yet been investigated; that all "conclusions" must be only tentative; and that we can never limit our analysis to some "time-present" that ignores past conduct or future possibilities.

The first novel to follow Cather's examination of cubism was *The Song of the Lark*. Suggestively, the title conflates visual and musical arts by simultaneously naming a (static) picture and the (fluid) music to which Thea has devoted her life; and it explicitly raises some of these existential enigmas in terms of Thea's own art. At the moment when Thea discovers the Indian pottery, she wonders

> What was any art but an effort to make a sheath, a mould in which to imprison for a moment the shining, elusive element which is life itself— life hurrying past us and running away, too strong to stop, too sweet to lose? The Indian women had held it in their jars. . . . In singing, one made a vessel of one's throat and nostrils and held it on one's breath, caught the stream [of life] in a scale of natural intervals.[9]

Yet Cather's attempts to create an extra-temporal character are not entirely successful here. The ruthless result of Thea's "success," that is, the force of a fiercely self-preoccupied woman, so thoroughly cancels the poignancy of her earlier life that the lingering image of the finished, hardened *prima donna* eclipses the more sympathetic figure of the struggling girl. Yet clearly we are intended to comprehend Thea in terms of an entire span of time: the sturdy child who pulled her little brother in his wagon, the almost-woman who wept over Ray Kennedy's death, the nascent singer who found her inspiration in Panther Canyon, and the audacious understudy, all these have been assimilated into "Kronborg." And as with the *Nude* on the staircase, we must not seek to isolate just one image and proclaim it definitive.[10]

In subsequent novels, Cather found many ways to make character comprehensive and inclusive. In *The Professor's House,* St. Peter has lost touch with that "boy that he had long ago left behind him in Kansas, in the Solomon Valley. . . . This boy and he had meant, back in those far-away days, to live some sort of life together and to share good and bad fortunes."[11] Ambitiously thrusting ahead, the Professor has jettisoned shreds of self along the way; hence his need for Tom Outland, or perhaps his need for the abstract potency of Tom Outland's perpetual youth—or even for his obsessive illusion that such a youth is possible. Yet in his more lucid moments, St. Peter realizes that his yearning for the boy's presence is symptomatic of some profound, desolate emptiness within: "[L]ife with this Kansas boy [that he had once been himself], little as there had been of it, was the realest of his lives, and that all the years between had been accidental and ordered from the outside" (240). Having lost the sense of life as comprehensive and organic, St. Peter is not so much dying as falling apart. The redemptive moment in his ruminations may be his ultimate acknowledgment that in the real world, Tom would have changed: "His fellow scientists, his wife, the town and State, would have required many duties. . . . [He] would have had to write thousands of useless letters, frame thousands of false excuses . . ." (236–237). Tom's "self" would have moved on in ways the Professor cannot envision, accumulating all of those collective components that would have shaped some subsequent identity; and the Professor's "Tom Outland" could never have been sustained as a rehabilitating recollection.

In *My Ántonia* and *A Lost Lady* Jim Burden and Niel Herbert both pursue a singular woman from the past, a woman whom they seek to define not as the composite of complex experiences, but as a creature frozen in time, suspended—unchanging in some single, perfect moment.[12] The reader understands that their quest has less to do with the lady than it does with their need for some complete, absolute, and comforting vision of themselves; and the reader also discerns that this misguided quest causes them to lose the most valuable thing of all—the richly complex woman as she really is.

Death Comes for the Archbishop presents the most complex examination of these dilemmas. What distinguishes the Archbishop from all of these other characters, however, is not merely his piety, but also his powerfully organic sense of self—the emotional counterpart of this piety. He remembers the boy-self lovingly, and he loves New Mexico because "In New Mexico he always awoke a young man . . . a wind that made one's body feel light and one's heart cry 'To-day, to-day,' like a child's."[13] Equally, "there were many passages in [his] missionary life that he loved to recall; and how often and fondly he recalled the beginning of it!" (285). Passing back and forth over his lifetime like sensitive hands over a keyboard, the Bishop celebrates the entirety of his time on earth for what it was—Life, only life, precarious, imperfect life: God's supreme gift. And when he contemplates his coming Death, it seems no more than a passage toward the realm of ultimate understanding.

> He observed . . . that there was no longer any perspective in his memories. He remembered his winters with his cousins on the Mediterranean when he was a little boy, his student days in the Holy City, as clearly as he remembered the arrival of M. Molny and the building of his Cathedral. He was soon to have done with calendared time, and it had already ceased to count for him. He sat in the middle of his own consciousness; none of his former states of mind were lost or outgrown. They were all within reach of his hand, and all comprehensible. (293)

A singular creation in Cather's fictions, the Bishop comprehends the balanced, musical mingling of his many "selves": in death, he reaches immaculate harmony. And in attaining unity, he gains that *consciousness* of unity which is the singular sign of an authentic and "achieved" self.

Notes

1. *Letters of Wallace Stevens,* Selected and edited by Holly Stevens, Foreword by Richard Howard (Berkeley: University of California Press, 1996), 381.

2. Elizabeth Shepley Sergeant, *Willa Cather: A Memoir* (Athens: Ohio University Press, 1992), 108.

3. Sergeant, *Memoir,* 108. As she grew older, Cather retained her interest in the subtleties of cubism. She respected D. H. Lawrence more than any other "modern" artist, and in later years asked Sergeant, "'Have you ever read *Sea and Sardinia?* Lawrence there used the language of *cubisme*'" (Sargeant, *Memoir,* 210).

4. Theodore Roosevelt, "A Layman's Views of An Art Exhibition," *The Outlook* (March 29, 1913): 719.

5. Robert Rosenblum, *Cubism and Twentieth-century Art* (New York: Harry N. Abrams, 1976), 13–14.

6. Milton W. Brown, *The Story of the Armory Show* (New York: The Joseph H. Hirshhorn Foundation, 1963), 109.

7. Martin Green, *New York 1913: The Armory Show and the Paterson Strike Pageant* (New York: Scribner's, 1988), 179.

8. Rosenblum, *Cubism,* 16 (my emphasis).

9. Willa Cather, *The Song of the Lark* (Boston: Houghton Mifflin, 1943), 378.

10. Never fully satisfied with the novel, Cather wrote a rather apologetic "Preface" in 1932 and revised ruthlessly in 1937, and she directs us to a process, not to a single moment. Later, she would insist in an often-quoted aphorism: "The end is nothing; the road is all [fr. Michelet]," and this, too, evokes process. Interestingly, the epigram listed just under the title of this novel *also* demands that we understand Thea in terms of movement: "It was a wond'rous lovely storm that drove me! Lenau's *Don Juan.*" See *SL,* v-vi.

11. Willa Cather, *The Professor's House* (New York: Vintage, 1990), 239.

12. Interestingly, there is a powerfully *judgmental* streak in both of these men. Repeatedly, Cather is interested in our tendency to understand and evaluate in terms of some single, isolated moment.

13. Willa Cather, *Death Comes for the Archbishop* (New York: Knopf, 1927), 276.

Bibliography

Brown, Milton W. *The Story of the Armory Show.* New York: The Joseph H. Hirshhorn Foundation,1963.

Cather, Willa. *The Song of the Lark.* Boston: Houghton, Mifflin, 1943.

———. *The Professor's House.* New York: Vintage, 1990.

———. *Death Come for the Archbishop.* New York: Knopf, 1927.

Martin Green. *New York 1913: The Armory Show and the Paterson Strike Pageant.* New York: Scribner's, 1988.

Roosevelt, Theodore. "A Layman's Views of An Art Exhibition," in *The Outlook,* (March 29, 1913): 718–720.

Rosenblum, Robert. *Cubism and Twentieth-century Art.* New York: Harry N. Abrams, Inc., 1976.

Sargeant, Elizabeth Shepley. *Willa Cather: A Memoir.* Athens: Ohio University Press, 1992.

Stevens, Wallace. *Letters of Wallace Stevens.* Selected and edited by Holly Stevens. Foreword by Richard Howard. Berkeley: University of California Press, 1996.

In the City of New York: Two Artists at Work

KATHRYN H. FABER

Elizabeth Shepley Sergeant writes in her memoir that Willa Cather "stands out as closer than any other writer of stature that I have known to living Goethe's dictum: 'We approach the world through art, and art is our link with it.' "[1] Cather, who devoted her life to observing the world around her and learning all she could about music, opera, art, and the theater, sought to create stories that unobtrusively utilized all that knowledge. Thus, her move to New York in 1906 marked a significant point: the city became her landscape. Likewise, Childe Hassam, the American painter whom she knew at the Cos Cob summer colony for painters and writers, had begun in the early 1890s to turn the city into a vista he painted. Throughout the rest of their lives, these two artists and acquaintances experimented with styles of rendering cityscapes. They visited Europe, traveled in America, escaped to the Connecticut countryside; but they returned to their New York homes to capture the urban places and people who intrigued them. In New York both reached the peaks of their careers: Hassam as the leading American Impressionist, Cather as the best woman writer of her time. Hassam strongly believed that "'one who paints the life he sees around him . . . makes a record of his own epoch.' "[2] Cather painted with words meant to describe the locales and emotions of city people: "Nobody yet ever knew anything thoroughly through study. . . . To know anything about any class of people, one must ascertain how and what they feel, and to do that one must not only observe but feel himself."[3] Thus Cather and Hassam looked at the same New York places that also felt like home. As we shall see, a link emerges between several Hassam paintings of Fifth Avenue, midtown, and the three Squares, and Cather's New York cityscapes described in particular short stories or novels.

Even as Cather and Hassam reveled in New York's advantages, their relaxation and reflection outside the city offered them opportunities to share impressions of New York. Quite possibly, Cather must have found provocative the insights emerging from her own observations, as well as her conversations with Hassam about his pictorial images. Their simultaneous visits to Cos Cob have been documented in Dorothy Weir Young's biography of her father, J. Alden

Weir, Hassam's colleague at the Cos Cob Summer Art Colony and a fellow member of the Ten, those American Impressionists who favored some retention of realism. Art historian Susan Larkin states that Cather and Hassam boarded at Holley House—probably for the same weeks in 1914 and 1915. After a 1924 visit, Cather inscribed a copy of *April Twilights:* "For Constance MacRae, one of my 'public' when it was small indeed." In her 1925 Christmas gift to Mrs. MacRae—a copy of *The Best Stories of Sarah Orne Jewett*—Cather also inscribed greetings over her signature. Larkin reports that Hassam, too, was "possibly at Holley Farm before 1882" and certainly almost every year until 1922, "exhibiting with the Greenwich Society of Artists in 1914, 1919, and 1922."[4] And Adeline Adams notes in her Hassam biography: a "favorite painting ground was Cos Cob, a lovable little town on the Connecticut side of Long Island Sound . . . not far from the great city."[5] Larkin suggests that Hassam sees the city in relation to the country, as well as vice versa; he portrays a city that is the "locus of modernity, change, and sophistication," and a country that is "tradition, nature, and simplistic."[6]

An affection for Connecticut farms near Cos Cob further connects Cather and Hassam. In *The Song of the Lark,* fictional Thea Kronborg's accompanist Oliver Landry had lived near his Cos Cob birthplace until he was fifteen, "on a rocky . . . farm . . . [in a] farmhouse, dilapidated and damp . . . beside a marshy pond."[7] In a similar location, Hassam visited his friend J. Alden Weir at the painter's Branchville farm near Cos Cob—"a quiet, plain little house among the rocks."[8] In New York the fictional Landry lives in the Washington Square area not far from both artists' homes, in "a three-story brick house on Jane Street, in Greenwich Village." Landry, we are told, "had an affection for the house on Jane Street . . . where he had first learned what cleanliness and order and courtesy were" (*SL,* 669), as Cather had an affection for her Bank Street apartment just three blocks north of Jane Street, and where she entertained—courteously.

When they returned to the city, these artists found both the emotions and the variety of physical locations that rendered rich material for their work. For the Nebraskan born in Virginia, New York and its people provided every kind of diversity and a place to advance her career as a journalist. Edith Lewis writes that Cather arrived in New York filled with the self-possession that would characterize her life at five separate New York addresses, the first at Washington Square. Although his Eastern, urban roots in Boston differed from Cather's

Back Creek origins, Hassam, too, chose New York to advance his career. Upon returning to America in 1889 after a three-year stay in Europe, Hassam settled at 95 Fifth Avenue, only a few blocks from Washington Square. Adams recounts that "As time passed, he loved his adopted city more and more, both for his wide circle of congenial friends . . . and for what he found of beauty in its daily life, its street scenes, vistas, parks, and countless horizons."[9]

Central to Hassam's New York paintings and to Cather's New York fiction is Fifth Avenue. Hassam's early subjects derived from the action on the street below his apartment window. Hassam told art critic A. E. Ives, "There is nothing so interesting to me as people . . . as they hurry through the streets on business or saunter down the promenade on pleasure. Humanity in motion is a continual study to me."[10] In a 1913 article for *The New York Sun,* he asserted, "There is no boulevard . . . that compares to our own Fifth Avenue."[11] Likewise, Sergeant describes Cather's Fifth Avenue as "suspended in the vistas of a comfortable world not yet at war, halfway between the Age of Innocence and the Age of the Skyscraper, free of traffic jams."[12]

The essential fact about lower Fifth Avenue is that it debouches into Washington Square. To paint one of his best-known works, *Washington Arch, Spring,* Hassam chose a vantage point from his studio apartment just north of Washington Square looking south toward the Stanford White-designed arch. The monument frames the elegant life on the north and only hints at a world less attractive south of the square. As shadows fall across the whitened sidewalks and the street beyond, dominant Impressionist violets and blues reflect in the bright open air, and shimmering light suggests life in the tree that has just burst forth its new gold and green leaves. An elegant woman in gown of white with lavender and yellow folds commands the composition, while other strollers pass small, neatly-maintained gardens at the townhouse stoops. Movement characterizes the urban scene: street sweepers maintaining the park's beauty, horses and drivers ready to transport residents uptown. Although Hoopes argues that Hassam "was content to portray the world without subjective judgement or commentary," he admits in paintings of New York Squares "something akin to commentary here in the juxtaposition of gentle, delicate forms and colors . . . and the harsh angularity . . . " of new buildings.[13] In another reflection, the clarity of the day as well as Hassam's faith in the city is depicted in *Fifth Avenue at Washington Square:* a genteel lady walks south beneath poplar trees, enjoying the bright sunshine—perhaps Edith Lewis on her way home. Using

Washington Arch, Spring (1890) **by Childe Hassam. Courtesy of the Phillips Collection, Washingotn, D.C.**

watercolor and oil, throughout the 1890s Hassam painted Fifth Avenue as a residential arena. According to the *New York Sun,* by 1918 Hassam had been Fifth Avenue's historian for years.[14]

Cather's, as Hassam's, Washington Square was "brimming over with vitality, with eagerness for life."[15] Having spent her first weeks in temporary quarters just off Fifth Avenue at the Hotel Griffon on West Ninth Street, Cather moved first to nearby South Washington Square and later to 82 Washington Place. According to her companion Edith Lewis, the city was for Cather "so open to the sea and free-dom[;] the people she met . . . the work she was doing, all stimulated her" as much as did the "charming places. On the north side . . . the long row of houses of rose-red brick, residences of aristocratic old New York families, gave it an aura of gentility and dignity. On the south side, writers and artists lived. . . ."[16] These surroundings come alive in "Coming, Aphrodite!" where Cather captures the life of poor artists as well as the charm of the Square they walk. Lewis documents the similarity:

> Cather has recalled not only the physical aspects of the old studio build-ing at Number 60 [South Washington Square] and its surrounding neigh-borhood, but even more, the youthful, lighthearted, and rather poetic mood of those days before the automobile, the radio, and the motion picture—and before two wars— . . . [when] young people were younger, more ingenuous, less initiated. Life seemed more unknown to them—and its possibilities more boundless.[17]

Artist Don Hedger is one of those "young people who came to New York to 'write' or 'paint'—who proposed to live by the sweat of the brow rather than of the hand, and who desired artistic surround-ings."[18] He "had lived on the top floor of an old house on the south side of Washington Square . . . [in a room] very cheerless, since he never got a ray of direct sunlight [and] the south corners were always in shadow" (63). But when Hedger walks his dog along University Place and West Street, he looks "up the avenue through the arch" and sees Hassam images: "young poplars with their bright, sticky leaves . . . and shining horses and carriages . . . a stream of things that were bright and beautiful and alive." Like Cather, he bemoans the sight of an automobile, "mis-shapen and sullen, like an ugly threat to the city's natural beauty" (65).

That natural beauty of the area drew Cather to another Greenwich Village apartment at #5 Bank Street, a short walk west of Washington Arch. Here, for fifteen years, Cather felt a "continuous ascent in artistic accomplishment." Bank Street was her "sanctuary [and] sen-suous,"[19] akin to Hedger's small spot, which he found "affluent com-pared to anything he had ever known before" (67). Hedger observes the city, as did Hassam, from vantage points above the city's action. On the roof of his building, Hedger feels "a kind of heaven" (69).

And his neighbor, the beautiful singer Eden Bower with her goddess luminosity, befits the Impressionist imagery so familiar in Hassam's paintings. Looking through the knothole of his new neighbor's door, Hedger sees Eden "in a pool of sunlight . . . positively glorious in action. . . . The soft flush of exercise and the gold of afternoon sun played over her flesh together, enveloped her in a luminous mist." And Cather indicates, "The spot was enchanted" (72). His once dreary apartment has taken on the outdoor beauty of Washington Square, and Hedger enters a "new chapter" of sensuousness: "This thing, whatever it was, drank him up as ideas had sometimes done." His image of women changes. Hedger had felt "an unreasoning antipathy toward the well-dressed women he saw coming out of shops or driving in the Park, the women of Hassam's paintings. He saw them enslaved by desire of merchandise and manufactured articles. . . . They were enough, he thought, to make one almost forget woman as she existed in art, in thought, and in the universe" (74–75). Equating Eden with the moon over the Square, the "immortal conception" of woman, Hedger envisions her as the personification of art: "You see I'm trying to learn to paint what people think and feel; to get away from all that photographic stuff" (87).

But Hedger, like Cather and Hassam, has not come to his credo without trial. Eden Bower's materialism has frightened and irritated Hedger. In his experimentation with new art forms, he discovers that he prefers "painting for painters—who haven't been born" (94). Like Hassam and Cather, he must be true to his convictions, even at the cost of giving up Eden. When—five days after his decision to pursue his art—he returns in search of Eden Bower, the goddess, he rides in a hansom "down lower Fifth Avenue into the Square." And the scene that Cather describes mirrors the Impressionist images of Hassam's *Washington Arch, Spring:*

> through the Arch behind [him] were the two long rows of pale violet lights that used to bloom so beautifully against the grey stone and asphalt. Here and yonder about the Square hung globes that shed a radiance not unlike the blue mists of evening, emerging softly when daylight died, as the stars emerged in the thin blue sky. Under them the sharp shadows of trees fell on the pavement and the sleeping grass. (97)

Although Eden has left, she will return 18 years later to Washington Square and learn that Hedger, like Hassam, "is one of the first among the moderns . . . [,] a great name with all the young men, and . . . decidedly an influence in art" (100–101).

Cather's and Hassam's feelings about Fifth Avenue were to change with each of their experiences in the city. Throughout the 1890s, Hassam's images depict changes in time, weather, and social attitudes. *Fifth Avenue in Winter* memorializes his view from the window at #95. It recalls Fred Ottenburg's seductive drive with Edith Beers down Fifth Avenue on a "bright winter day . . . bitterly cold" (*SL,* 579). Writing of a later time, Cather defines a less elegant atmosphere in "Coming, Aphrodite!," but she speaks of Fifth Avenue with some longing for "the very last . . . of the old horse stages on Fifth Avenue" (65). She also divulges the social snobbery of Fifth Avenue. Ever the artist, she maligns pretension. Don Hedger sees "a pretty girl standing on the steps of one of the houses on upper Fifth Avenue . . . [and he] believed [such girls] to be artificial" (74–75). In "Scandal," Kitty Ayrshire's admirer Pierce Tevis gossips: "The Steins now inhabit a great house on Fifth Avenue that used to belong to people of a very different sort. To old New Yorkers it's an historic house."[20]

Hassam's 1916 and 1919 paintings, *Fifth Avenue. Noon* and *Fifth Avenue,* likewise depict a city on the move. They distinctly show social and architectural changes: crowds of people and scores of vehicles seem like thin fragments, stick-figures hemmed in by massive buildings, the latter suggesting a current mood of patriotism with two small American flags at the back of the canvas. Hassam's changing view parallels Cather's. In "Behind the Singer Tower" she looks at the city "enveloped in a tragic self-consciousness. Those incredible towers of stone and steel" suggest that "the city was protesting, was asserting its helplessness, its irresponsibility for its physical conformation, for the direction it had taken."[21] And both artists' portrayals correspond to the condition of Anton Rosicky, the Czech immigrant who "was tormented by a longing to run away . . . [from s]o much stone and asphalt . . . so many empty windows. It struck young Rosicky that this was the trouble with big cities; they built you in from the earth itself, cemented you away from any contact with the ground."[22]

As Hassam adds his image of optimism in the flags, Rosicky can forgive the starkness by praising "the finest, richest, friendliest city in the world" where he saved enough money "to buy his freedom" (242–244). In his flag series Hassam suggests deep appreciation for the opportunity he felt in his "ardent . . . promotion of America as a land of liberty and freedom."[23] Between 1916 and 1919, he created approximately thirty flag paintings, which convey his sense of "the poetry, the romance and beauty of the people [on] Fifth Avenue, . . . a patriotic and zealous love of this street."[24] *Allies Day, 1917,* the most

Fifth Avenue, Noon. **Etching by Childe Hassam. Courtesy of the Metropolitan Museum of Art. Gift of Mrs. Childe Hassam, 1940.**

famous of these flag paintings, creates a pattern of French, British, and American flags draped over Fifth Avenue as masses of people move below. Art historian William H. Gerdts comments on Hassam's use of Impressionist techniques for symbolic purpose. The war effort is greater than the individuals who participate.[25]

Allies Day, May 1917 by Childe Hassam. Courtesy of the National Gallery of Art, Washington, D.C. Gift of Ethelyn McKinney in memory of her brother, Glenn Ford McKinney.

Cather, too, "felt strongly about the war from the beginning, for it threatened everything in the world of the mind that was most precious to her." After hearing about the death of a cousin and visiting the battle sites with her friends Jan and Isabelle Hambourg, Cather— in the tradition of the Impressionist painter—wrote *One of Ours,* a novel "born from personal experience."[26] Although her fiction does

not wave the flags, when Claude Wheeler and his troops sail from
Hoboken and look toward the skyline of New York, their first sight of
the "Goddess of Liberty" evokes the same spirit of national pride that
penetrates the Hassam flag paintings:

> Blue sky broke overhead, and the pale silhouette of buildings . . . grew
> sharp and hard. Windows flashed flame-coloured in their grey sides; the
> gold and bronze tops of towers began to gleam where the sunlight strug-
> gled through. . . . Post cards had given them no idea of the energy of her
> large gesture. . . . [T]he scene was ageless; youth were sailing away to die
> for an idea."[27]

Not only patriotism but also gratitude to the French who gave America the great monument provoke the men to song with a "gay, indom-
itable resolution of that jaunty air" (1152). Their song invades the air
as colorfully as Hassam's flags fly over Fifth Avenue.

As Fifth Avenue offered Hassam and Cather moments of conflict as
well as the sublime, Union Square—where Broadway meets Fourth
Avenue at the foot of Park Avenue South—also provided them with a
charged locale. Looking from the window of his first studio close to
Union Square, Hassam observed an area of commercial establish-
ments and small factories—all surrounded by park. While the
blanket of snow in *Winter in Union Square* depicts a feeling of calm,
Hassam's trolleys and hansoms connote progress. His *Union Square in
Spring* projects constant activity, though devoid of obvious social commentary, because it is mainly a topographical study of the wide-open
park and nonthreatening buildings. Gerdts contends that "Hassam
may have assumed a position high up in the Everett House" to observe his view of this serene spring scene.[28] His painting again connects Hassam to Cather, who places Thea Kronborg at Everett House,
a respectable hotel on the north side of Union Square. Respectable it
may have been, but Cather finds it a place of dark moods. When a
dejected Fred Ottenburg first visits Thea, her rooms seem "brown
with time, dark in spite of two windows that opened on Union
Square" (*SL*, 591). Later, on a "fresh spring" day, her sitting room is
"flooded by thin, clear sunshine" (599). This time the atmosphere is
colored by the same light that permeates both Hassam paintings of
Union Square.

Another form of changing atmosphere appears in the artists' views
of Madison Square, just sixteen blocks north of Washington Square
and close to Cather's office at *McClure's* on Twenty-third Street. In *My
Mortal Enemy* Cather sees a "double personality" in the Madison
Square she "remembered from about 1904," and Cather is likely

Winter in Union Square by Childe Hassam. Courtesy of the Metropolitan Museum of Art. Gift of Miss Ethelyn McKinney, 1943, in memory of her brother Glenn Ford McKinney.

smiling when Nellie Birdseye thinks naively that the Square looks like "an open-air drawing room." For Nellie could "imagine a winter dancing party being given there, or a reception of some distinguished European visitor."[29] Naive or not, however, Nellie sees with Hassam-like eyes. Arriving at Jersey City on "a soft, grey December morning, with a little falling snow," Nellie looks with "straining eyes to catch through the fine, reluctant snow [her] first glimpse of the city. The snow blurred everything a little, and the buildings on the Battery all ran together" (18–19). Nellie projects this "blurred" vision in all she sees of Myra and Oswald Henshawe throughout the novel.[30]

Union Square in Spring (1896) by **Childe Hassam. Courtesy of Smith College Museum of Art.**

But the effect—that snowy atmosphere, however grey or white—fills Hassam's *Madison Square—Snowstorm,* casting the same dim vision that Cather projects. Very possibly from a window at the Fifth Avenue Hotel, where he dined and met with colleagues, Hassam painted his Impressionist response to the Square's activity on a blustery day. Pedestrians cross snow-covered streets at the corners of the Square; horse-drawn carriages and a new trolley move along suggesting that not even the elements can disrupt the busy life of New Yorkers. One critic comments on the painter's personal conflict: "poetic hazes of gold, rose, and lavender hues 'deprived the skyscraper of its rawness and effective realism.'"[31] Although the view is blurred by the heavy falling snow, beyond the Square's open space stands the muted Madison Square Garden with the magnificent bronze Diana offering the painting a pious reverie. However blurred the image of the skyscrapers may seem, Hassam has created a strong impression of the city.

Cather interprets the same scene in *My Mortal Enemy* when the Henshawes welcome their Midwestern guests to Madison Square. Nellie Birdseye's first visit to New York—for all her blurred memories of the place—is filled with admiration as strong as Hassam's painting. After unpacking at Hassam's familiar Fifth Avenue Hotel, Nellie gazes "wistful[ly]," so that Myra Henshawe suggests Nellie spend time alone in Madison Square. With snow falling on the Square, men sweeping paths, and trees looking like friendly people, the scene is inviting. Nellie sees the city as a glamorous blur, Cather's choice for her and one much like Hassam's painting:

> The trees and shrubbery seemed well-groomed and sociable, like pleasant people. The snow lay in clinging folds on the bushes, and outlined every twig—a line of white upon a line of black. . . . Madison Square Garden, new and spacious then, looked at me so light and fanciful, and Saint Gaudens' Diana . . . stepped out freely and fearlessly into grey air. I lingered long by the intermittent fountain. Its rhythmical splash was like the voice of the place. (21)

The young Midwestern girl sees with the eye of that Impressionist painter whom Hamlin Garland calls a person "concerned with atmosphere always . . . with nature for his teacher [and whose] attitude toward nature is a personal one."[32] As she listens to the splash of the Square's fountain and watches "an old man selling violets, each bunch wrapped in oiled paper to protect them from the snow," Nellie appears to the returning Myra as "fair moon struck," for she now feels a part of this happy scene: "Here, I felt winter brought no desolation" (22).

Whether it is snow or rain, the picture of inclement weather renders a paradoxical atmosphere for both artists. *Winter Mist, Madison Square* depicts a weather pattern so familiar to New Yorkers that Hassam chose to include this seldom seen work in his 1880 collection of paintings in *Three Cities*. The blurred winter scene that greets Nellie Birdseye parallels the foggy summer haze that Claude Wheeler sees. Looking toward the city, Claude discerns that the "day had come on hot and misty," and the "tall buildings [were] mere shadows of grey and pink and blue that might dissolve with the mist and fade away." He "wanted to see the city clearly; . . . couldn't make anything of these uneven towers that rose dimly through the vapors" (*OO*, 1150). Once again Cather chooses the colors, shadows, and tones that Hassam has used in creating his impression of Madison Square, and he suggests through the cloudy images as many possibilities as do the imaginations of Nellie and Claude. Because he will soon sail for the war front in France and will not know New York, Claude is disappointed. Through the smog, both Nellie and Claude try to identify buildings they might recognize, and both see traces of the World Building, once the home of a New York newspaper. Nellie views its "dull gold dome . . . [that] emerged like a ruddy autumn moon at twilight" (*MME*, 20). Claude asks: "What was the gold dome glinting through the fog?" and finds that none of his fellow soldiers can identify it" (*OO*, 1150). For the mist of both snow and fog suggest awe and majesty, but also convey a mystery about the obscure city.

A sense of wonder like Claude's emerges in another Hassam painting, *Late Afternoon, New York: Winter,* which connects to snow scenes in *My Mortal Enemy.* With touches of shimmering light and shades of blue and purple, Hassam poetically juxtaposes commercial buildings to the naturalness of a snowy scene at twilight. The one blurred figure of a woman moves amidst slightly more distinct hansoms and a trolley on a street lined with small barren trees. The serene painting illustrates the state of reverie that Nellie experiences alone in Madison Square. While it seems unlikely that Cather saw Nellie's "half-commercial, half-social" city as a place that was "neat after the raggedness of our Western cities," the writer did have memories of "good manners and courtesy" among the people she knew in New York. And the late afternoon that Cather paints for Nellie is as poetic as the one Hassam draws:

> About the Square the pale blue shadows grew denser and drew closer. The street lamps flashed out all along the Avenue, and soft lights began to twinkle in the tall buildings while it was yet day—violet buildings, just a little denser in substance and colour than the violet sky. (21–22)

At the same time Nellie remembers her own "gazing" at the impressionistic sight, she welcomes Myra Henshawe's arm in hers, a first sign of the closeness that would keep Nellie searching for the person who symbolized the New York woman.

That New York woman is the subject of a Hassam painting, *Street Scene, Christmas Morning,* illustrative of another scene in *My Mortal Enemy.* Hassam's beautifully dressed, veiled woman walks along the

Street Scene, Christmas Morning (1892) by Childe Hassam. Courtesy of Smith College Museum of Art.

snow-covered street that commands the background for his figure. Shades of blue and thick strokes of white bring clear light into the painting; touches of purple and contemporary colors of the red trolley and green package that the woman carries soften the canvas that contains just a portion of a dimly-lit shop window. As Nellie and Aunt Lydia leave the hotel on Christmas morning, their early view of New York connects to Hassam's painting: "the sun shone blindingly on the snow-covered park, the gold Diana flashed against a green-blue sky" (27). They walk toward Grace Episcopal Church, located at Broadway and Tenth Street. Or is it really Grace Church? When Cather lived at the Grosvenor Hotel at Fifth Avenue and Tenth Street, Lewis tells us that "the Church of the Ascension was her favourite church in New York; . . . and for years she went regularly to the vesper services."[33] Although the specific designation of church is uncertain, the irony of hypocrisy on the way to church is clear. In his movement toward deceit of his wife, Oswald slips into Lydia's muff "a flat little package . . . some sleeve-buttons given to me by a young woman who means no harm" (27). The atmosphere is bright, but the promise of what will follow is as veiled as Hassam's lady. Although the Madison Square sunlight "seemed safe and friendly and smiling" (43), Nellie's memory of her visit with the Henshawes in New York reminds us of her "blurred vision."

Two more Hassam paintings illustrate Madison Square scenes in *My Mortal Enemy*. *New York Window* juxtaposes interior serenity to a newer, larger world beyond. A woman, draped in a gown of soft blues, purple, and white, sits before a window decorated in dark purple draperies that seem to protect her from that other lighter world. Into the Henshawes' room Cather brings the Polish actress, Helena Modjeska. Then, after most guests have left, "Modjeska . . . went to the window, drew back the plum-coloured curtains, and looked out . . . [to see] the Square is white with moonlight." Having asked her companion Emelia to sing, Modjeska sits "by the window, half draped in her cloak, the moonlight falling over her knees" (38–39). In Modjeska's friend we recall another Hassam painting, *The Sonata,* which portrays a young woman at her piano in typical Impressionist white brushstroke, her gown touched with folds of blue and violet, her head downcast with the emotion wrought by one who plays her sonata passionately. With the addition of a candle, Hassam places light within as well as from outside the composition, thus illuminating the soul of the artist. Art critic David Curry tells us that in creating this "most impassioned work," Hassam remembered the music of Beethoven's *Appassionata*.[34] How ironic to note, then, Cather's im-

The New York Window by Childe Hassam. Courtesy of The Corcoran Gallery of Art, Washington, D.C.

pression of the same music: Edith Lewis writes that a young German pianist who lived in their Bank Street building "never practiced but one thing—Beethoven's *Appassionata;* . . . Willa Cather came to like this practicing—she said it was a signal to work and she associated it with her working hours."[35] As Modjeska turns out the interior light, Emelia begins to sing. And from Emelia's song Nellie draws a memory she will always equate with Myra Henshawe: "a compelling, passionate, overmastering something for which I had no name, but which was audible, visible in the air that night" (40). Emelia is Hassam's figure, and the scene is filled with as much emotion as the painting.

As Hassam's woman who plays the sonata sits downcast, her back to the viewer concealing her passion or exhaustion, we recall also Thea Kronborg in *The Song of the Lark.* As a young music pupil of Andor Harsanyi, Thea is dejected about her art. Even her posture betrays her emotions: "stiff back, stiff elbows, a very formal position of the hands." The teacher sees "a richly gifted nature . . . [but] her ardour had not been awakened. . . . The literature of the piano was an undiscovered world to her" (446). Then, years later in New York, Thea and Dr. Archie look out the window of her Riverside Drive apartment, and the singer who has found her flame sits down on the piano bench. Thea tells Dr. Archie: "What one really strives for [in art] is so far away, so deep, so beautiful." While she plays a song they sang long ago in Moonstone, Archie watches "her bent head . . . as if she were seeing down through the years" (682). The memory is not blurred for Thea as it is for Nellie. Just a week later after Thea has sung a marvelous Sieglinde at the Metropolitan, Mrs. Harsanyi remembers the "clumsy girl, hunched up over the piano," who labored at the musical instrument she would abandon for a career in voice. But on that delightful evening, her husband rejoices in a different memory: his belief in the artist's secret—"passion"—for he has seen her realize that she "had only to touch an idea to make it live" (697). Hassam's impassioned musician-pianist is Cather's passionate musician-singer.

Because of Hassam's influence on the art community in New York, the contemporary art critic Albert Gallatin named him "beyond any doubt the greatest exponent of Impressionism in America."[36] To work nearer to other artists, Hassam was drawn to midtown, which became known for its artists' studios. In 1908 he moved to 130 West 57th Street. Considered "the major interpreter of New York . . . , his involvement with the city was inexhaustible."[37] A founder of the Watercolor Society of New York in 1890, he exhibited actively with the Society of Painters in Pastels, the Society of American Artists, and the National Academy long before he helped found the group of Ten American painters in 1898. His midtown scenes depict the changes taking place. While his 1892 *Central Park* portrays a sedate scene of upperclass women and children strolling in a well-manicured landscape, *Hovel and Skyscraper* of 1904 commemorates urban progress. In the later painting, Hassam creates a realistic depiction that juxtaposes ordinary construction equipment to elaborate riding stables in Central Park. Workers on scaffolds and riders on horses symbolize the mingling of two social classes in the midtown that Hassam called home until his death in 1935. These interpretations remind us that Cather, too, rendered in her fiction characters as diverse as Don Hedger and Kitty Ayrshire, characters as comfortable with New York's social scene as Myra Henshawe or as naive as Nellie Birdseye.

Midtown—with its easy access to Central Park and Carnegie Hall—became home to Cather, as it was to Hassam. After five years in and out of the Grosvenor Hotel at Tenth Street and Fifth Avenue, Cather moved finally to Park Avenue, "number 570, at Sixty-third Street in a building with a uniformed doorman, a rather ritzy address for a person with Cather's distaste for ostentation."[38] Lewis tells us she enjoyed many concerts, undoubtedly ones such as Thea Kronborg's former teacher Andor Harsanyi plays at Carnegie Hall. Sergeant remembers that her friend "brimmed with physical life. . . . You could see she was country-bred"[39] when they took walks in the Park—probably the inspiration for Nellie Birdseye's "delightful afternoon" there (*MME,* 33). Or perhaps a winter walk offered the image Cather recalled in "The Diamond Mine" when Cressida walked in Central Park

> after the first heavy storm of the year. . . . The air grew much warmer and the sky cleared. Overhead it was a soft, rainy blue, and to the west a smoky gold. All the horizon became misty and silvery; even the big brutal buildings looked like pale violet water-colours on a silver ground. Under the elm tree along the Mall the air was purple with wisterias. The sheep-field toward Broadway was smooth and white, with a thin gold wash over it.[40]

Clearly, Cather is as much the Impressionist painter as is Hassam; her interpretation dips into the same palette that he utilized.

As Hassam commented on urban progress, so did Cather. Myra Henshawe "condescendingly" snubs a woman who waves to her as she rides through the Park. Kitty Ayrshire, like one of Hassam's women and one of the "ritzy," lives "on Central Park West . . . where her friends sat or stood about." Mockingly, Cather describes the "men distinguished, women at once plain and beautiful, with their furs and bonnets, their clothes that were so distinctly not smart—all held together by the warm lamp-light, by an indescribable atmosphere of graceful and gracious human living" (*CS,* 157). One guesses that Kitty may have resembled a Cather neighbor near that Park Avenue apartment, one who would have driven Cather to leave the city for fresher air!

Hassam and Cather both sought that fresher air. Often "fed up with New York and society,"[41] Cather recaptured old delights during her summers away from the city. But she continued to play with verbal images of New York, and in her essay "On the Art of Fiction," she offers an explanation for both an artistic credo and an attitude toward the city: a writer experiences "phases of natural development. In the beginning, the artist, like his public, is wedded to old forms, old ideals, and his vision is blurred by the memory of old delights he would like to recapture."[42] Until her death in 1947, she always returned "naturally" to the city she called home—a place that held memories "of old delights." Whatever activities captivated his enthusiasm within the city, Hassam also fled New York during the summer months, and eventually built a home at East Hampton. With the great urban changes, he became somewhat distressed, as he told his friend Florence Griswold: "I don't know that I wish a very large dose of New York for any of my friends."[43] Long before they left the city for long periods of time, however, Cos Cob's proximity to New York— first stop out of the city on the railroad—had enticed Cather and Hassam to that quiet, unspoiled village that seemed like wide-open country.

From the 1890s until the 1930s, New York's mingling of tradition continuously captured the enthusiasm of the artists who lived and worked there. For Willa Cather and Childe Hassam, those traditions of diverse people and various locales inspired poetic depictions in fiction and painting. In a 1913 article for the *New York Sun,* Hassam conveyed the connection in words that might have been Cather's own: "The portrait of a city . . . is in a way like the portrait of a person—the difficulty is to catch not only the superficial resemblance but the inner self."[44] In her essay of 1922, "The Novel Démeublé," Cather acknowledges an author's debt to modern art. She cautions the writer to select good details, which are "always so much a part of the emotions of the people that they are perfectly synthesized; they seem to exist, not so much in the author's mind, as in the emotional penumbra of the characters themselves."[45] Two artists who lived in New York have drawn upon their experiences "[o]ut of the teeming, gleaming stream of [their] present [to] select the eternal material of art" (*NUF,* 48). We might well assert that the essence of fictional characters, painted figures, and the artists themselves emerge within New York to create well-wrought pictures on canvas and on the printed page.

Notes

1. Elizabeth Shepley Sergeant, *Willa Cather: A Memoir* (Lincoln: University of Nebraska Press, 1953), 2.

2. Quoted in A. E. Ives, "Mr. Childe Hassam on Painting Street Scenes," *Art Amateur* (October 1892): 116.

3. Willa Cather, *The World and the Parish: Willa Cather's Articles and Reviews, 1893– 1902,* ed. William H. Curtin, II (Lincoln: University of Nebraska Press, 1970), 713.

4. Susan G. Larkin, "'A Regular Rendezvous for Impressionists': The Cos Cob Art Colony 1882–1920," CUNY, 1996, 211–68. Larkin's dissertation presents an extended discussion of the American Impressionists who visited and taught at Cos Cob at the turn of the century.

5. Adeline Adams, *Childe Hassam* (New York: American Academy of Arts and Letters, 1938), 85–86.

6. Larkin, "Rendezvous," 207.

7. Cather, *Early Novels and Stories,* ed. Sharon O'Brien (New York: Library of America, 1987), 669. Subsequent references to *The Song of the Lark* will be cited parenthetically in the text as *SL.*

8. Quoted in Dorothy Weir Young, *The Life and Letters of J. Alden Weir* (New Haven: Yale University Press, 1960), 161.

9. Adams, *Hassam,* 69.

10. Quoted in Ives, "Painting," 116–17.

11. Ibid., 116.

12. Sergeant, *Memoir,* 46.

13. Donelson F. Hoopes, *Childe Hassam* (New York: Watson-Guptill, 1979), 42.

14. "Childe Hassam and the Americanization of Fifth Avenue," *New York Sun* (24 November 1918), sec. 1, p. 10.

15. Edith Lewis, *Willa Cather Living* (New York: Alfred A. Knopf, 1953), xvii.

16. Ibid., xv–xvii.

17. Ibid., xvi.

18. Willa Cather, "Coming, Aphrodite!," *Collected Stories* (New York: Vintage, 1992), 64. Subsequent references to this work are cited parenthetically in the text.

19. Sergeant, *Memoir,* 112.

20. Cather, "Scandal," *Collected Stories,* 65.

21. Willa Cather, *Collected Short Fiction 1892–1912,* ed. Virginia Faulkner (Lincoln: University of Nebraska Press, 1970), 44.

22. Cather, "Neighbour Rosicky," *Collected Stories,* 243. Subsequent references to this work are cited parenthetically in the text.

23. Ilene Susan Fort, *Childe Hassam's New York* (New York: Chameleon, 1993), xiv.

24. "Painting America Childe Hassam's Way," *Touchstone* (5 July, 1919): 272.

25. William H. Gerdts, *American Impressionism* (New York: Artabras, 1984), 304.

26. Lewis, *Living,* 117–22.

27. Cather, *EN & S,* 1151–52. Subsequent references to *One of Ours* are cited parenthetically in the text as *OO.*

28. William H. Gerdts, *Impressionist New York* (New York: Abbeville, 1994), 304.

29. Willa Cather, *My Mortal Enemy* (New York: Knopf, 1926), 21. Subsequent references to this work are cited parenthetically in the text as *MME*.

30. See Merrill Maguire Skaggs, *After the World Broke in Two: The Later Novels of Willa Cather* (Charlottesville: University Press of Virginia, 1990), 100–102. As Skaggs contends, the entire novel involves an overlay of a "blurred vision"—Cather's fiction painted with a grey palette.

31. Fort, *Hassam's New York*, xii.

32. Hamlin Garland, "Impressionism," *Crumbling Idols* (Ann Arbor: Edwards Brothers, 1952), 122–32.

33. Lewis, *Living*, 46.

34. David Park Curry, *Childe Hassam: An Island Garden Revisited* (New York: Norton, 1990), 27.

35. Lewis, *Living*, 87.

36. Quoted in Gerdts, *American Impressionism*, 98.

37. Ibid., 96.

38. James Woodress, *Willa Cather: A Literary Life* (Lincoln: University of Nebraska Press, 1987), 447.

39. Sergeant, *Memoir*, 48.

40. Cather, *Collected Stories*, 116.

41. Woodress, *WC*, 281.

42. Cather, *On Writing* (New York: Knopf, 1949), 104.

43. Quoted in Ulrich W. Hieisinger, *Childe Hassam: American Impressionist* (New York: Prestel-Verlag, 1994), 97.

44. Childe Hassam, "New York the Beauty City," *New York Sun* (23 February 1913): 16.

45. Cather, *Not Under Forty* (Lincoln: University of Nebraska Press, 1988), 48.

Bibliography

Adams, Adeline. *Childe Hassam*. New York: American Academy of Arts and Letters. 1938.

Cather, Willa. "Behind the Singer Tower," *Collected Short Fiction, 1892–1912*. Ed. Virginia Faulkner. Lincoln: University of Nebraska Press, 1970, 43–49.

———. "Coming Aphrodite!" *Collected Stories*. New York: Vintage, 1992, 63–101.

———. "The Diamond Mine," *Collected Stories*. New York: Vintage, 1992, 102–36.

———. *My Mortal Enemy*. New York: Knopf, 1926.

———. "Neighbour Rosicky," *Collected Stories*. New York: Vintage, 1992, 231–61.

———. *Not Under Forty*. Lincoln: University of Nebraska Press, 1988.

———. *On Writing*. New York: Knopf, 1949.

———. *One of Ours*. *Early Novels and Stories*. Ed. Sharon O'Brien. New York: Library of America, 1987. 943–1297.

———. "Scandal," *Collected Stories*. New York: Vintage, 1992. 153–69.

———. *The Song of the Lark*. *Early Novels and Stories*. Ed. Sharon O'Brien. New York: Library of America, 1987. 291–706.

———. *The World and the Parish: Willa Cather's Articles and Reviews, 1893–1902*. Ed. William H. Curtin. II. Lincoln: University of Nebraska Press, 1970.

"Childe Hassam and the Americanization of Fifth Avenue," *New York Sun* (24 November 1918), sec. 1, p. 10.

Curry, David Park, *Childe Hassam: An Island Garden Revisited*. New York: Norton, 1990.

Fort, Ilene Susan. *Childe Hassam's New York*. New York: Chameleon, 1993.

Gerdts, William H. *American Impressionism*. New York: Artabras, 1984.

———. *Impressionist New York*. New York: Abbeville, 1994.

Hassam, Childe. "New York the Beauty City." *New York Sun* (23 February 1913): 16.

Garland, Hamlin. "Impressionism," *Crumbling Idols*. Ann Arbor, Mich.: Edwards Brothers, 1952.

Hieisinger, Ulrich W. *Childe Hassam: American Impressionist*. New York: Prestel-Verlag, 1994.

Hoopes, Donelson F. *Childe Hassam*. New York: Watson-Guptill, 1979.

Ives, A. E. "Mr. Childe Hassam on Painting Street Scenes." *Art Amateur* (October 1892): 116.

Larkin, Susan G. "A Regular Rendezvous for Impressionists: The Cos Cob Art Colony, 1882–1920." Ph.D. Diss. CUNY, 1996.

"Painting America: Childe Hassam's Way." *Touchstone* (5 July 1919): 272.

Sergeant, Elizabeth Shepley. *Willa Cather: A Memoir*. Athens: Ohio University Press, 1953.

Skaggs, Merrill Maguire. *After the World Broke in Two: The Later Novels of Willa Cather*. Charlottesville: University Press of Virginia, 1990.

Woodress, James. *Willa Cather: A Literary Life*. Lincoln: University of Nebraska Press, 1987.

Young, Dorothy Weir. *The Life and Letters of J. Alden Weir*. New Haven: Yale University Press, 1960.

Cather, Fremstad, and Wagner

SHERRILL HARBISON

In June of 1913, Willa Cather waited on a New York pier for a steamer bringing Elizabeth Shepley Sergeant home from France. Before the two women's greetings were over, Sergeant realized that her friend was in the grip of a new enthusiasm:

> The word "Fremstad" had already appeared in her letters. Fremstad, Fremstad, wonderful Fremstad. . . . Nothing, nothing, Willa murmured in the cab, . . . could equal the bliss of entering into the very skin of another human being. Did I not agree? And if this skin were Scandinavian—then what?[1]

The Swedish-born soprano Olive Fremstad (1871–1951) had first electrified New York audiences in the role of Richard Wagner's most extreme and exotic female character, the schizoid temptress Kundry of *Parsifal,* and Willa Cather—already an ardent Wagnerite—was one of those most smitten. In the decade (1903–14) of the singer's meteoric career with the Metropolitan Opera, Cather observed in Fremstad's work "the rapid crystallization of ideas as definite, as significant, as profound as Wagner's own." For more than a year Cather had been entertaining an idea for a novel about an opera singer, and now, in preparation, she was writing a triple profile of three reigning divas—Louise Homer, Geraldine Farrar, and Olive Fremstad—for *McClure's* magazine. She already knew that Fremstad interested her most, but after meeting and interviewing her, Cather's feelings about the singer grew deeper and more complex. To Sergeant she wrote that Fremstad's presence left her profoundly moved, "choked up" by things "unutterable."[4]

From watching Fremstad both on and off stage Cather recognized how completely the singer lived through her roles, how little of the person was left for anything else. Of the three artists, Cather determined that only Fremstad was equipped with the talent, intelligence, and dedication to reach what Geraldine Farrar had called "the frozen heights" of perfection. "Work is the only thing that interests her," Cather reported; though Fremstad had tried other things which, "from a distance, seemed beautiful," art had proved "the only thing that *remains* beautiful."[5]

Fremstad's life also made clear that the single-minded pursuit of beauty destined such an artist to spend most of her time in personal and intellectual solitude. "We are born alone, we make our way alone, we die alone," Fremstad had confided, and the greatest rewards of an artist's quest were also enjoyed alone. "My work is only for serious people. If you ever really find anything in art, it is so subtle and beautiful that—well, you need never be afraid anyone will take it away from you, for the chances are that nobody will ever know you've got it."[6]

These convictions, issuing from the mouth of a stunning Scandinavian singer, set off a creative inner explosion in Cather. Well before encountering Fremstad, Cather herself had protested (to a puzzled Elizabeth Sergeant) that, while most artists "almost desperately" linked themselves to lovers, spouses, children, "as if to avoid being devoured by art," Cather herself "*wanted* to be so devoured."[7] Cather understood that lovers or children could never fully share such an impersonal mission, nor would they be satisfied with the husk of humanity left after the artist's vitality was drained away. Although personal attachments would always be alluring in times of loneliness, they could never satisfy this artist's ambition or fulfill her dreams.

Cather watched Fremstad perform every role in her repertoire. She and the singer became friends—Fremstad cheering and tending Cather when once she was hospitalized with a nasty infection; Cather spending a week visiting Fremstad's primitive cabin retreat in Maine. The singer's companion Mary Watkins also warmed to Cather, finding her a welcome ally during bouts of Madame's mercurial temper.[8]

The shared belief that art was an exacting master was not all the two women had in common. Like Cather, Fremstad had been an immigrant to the prairie in her adolescence. Born in Stockholm and raised in Oslo, she moved with her family to a frontier settlement in Minnesota when she was twelve, at about the same time the Cather family moved from Virginia to Nebraska. Young Olava (changed to Olive by her American neighbors) had already won singing competitions in Norway; on the prairie her musical talents were pressed into the service of church and revival meetings conducted by her father, a Methodist minister, and to providing piano lessons to the local population.[9]

Like Cather growing up in Red Cloud, Fremstad's artistic gifts were out of scale with her surroundings; yet those surroundings still left their mark on her, making her seem strangely familiar to Cather. She wrote Sergeant that Fremstad had the same kind of suspicious, defiant, far-seeing pioneer eyes she remembered from the Scandina-

vian farm women she had known as a child—indeed, Fremstad's
habits and manner reminded Cather of her own fictional Swedish
heroine, Alexandra Bergson of *O Pioneers!*—Alexandra with a voice.[10]

To Willa Cather, the combination of artist and Scandinavian immigrant suggested adventure of the highest order. "I have never found
any intellectual excitement any more intense," she recalled to an
interviewer later that same summer,

> than I used to feel when I spent a morning with one of those old farm
> women. I used to ride home in the most unreasonable state of excite-
> ment; I always felt as if they had told me so much more than they said—as
> if I had actually got inside another person's skin.[11]

Toward Olive Fremstad, Cather's feelings were clearly both identification and infatuation, a mature combination of these emotions
first experienced for the rugged farm women on the prairie. The
great "intellectual excitement" now before her would be to consum-
mate this attraction, to merge Fremstad and herself in the character
of Thea Kronborg, the opera singer-heroine of *The Song of the Lark*.[12]

※

The fictional Thea Kronborg, like Fremstad, reaches perfection's
"frozen heights" by placing art ahead of everything else. Work takes
every ounce of her strength, leaving her drained, aged, and often
unfit for company. When urged to take more time for personal life,
she replies, "Your work becomes your personal life. You're not much
good until it does." Her art demands the kind of perfect dedication
that Nietzsche called *chastity*, and its goal was a paradox, the kind of
"sensuous spirituality" that is also the goal of the mystic.[13]

The association of artistic achievement with religious or spiritual
discipline was hardly new to Cather. As early as her teenaged debut
essay on Thomas Carlyle she had adopted the Romantic view of the
artist as mediator between human and divine realms. Her youthful
arts reviews insisted repeatedly that the artist had a sober responsibility to a higher calling; in 1895 she wrote, "it is the veil and the cloister
which keep the priesthood of art untainted from the world."[14] Given
these convictions, it is not surprising that she was strongly attracted to
the musical ideas of Richard Wagner (1813–83), probably the most
influential artist of his century.

Today many readers seem puzzled by Cather's taste for Wagner,
whom Henry James once called a "ridiculous mixture of Nihilism and

bric-a-brac."[15] The composer's crude anti-Semitism and his intellec-tually and morally muddled exhibitionism had compromised his rep-utation well before his music was championed by the Third Reich; today Wagner's association with the Nazi era—even though post-humous—still presents an impossible hurdle for many people. The composer's ponderous seriousness can also feel quite foreign to Cather's modest, lucid, accessible style; indeed, *The Song of the Lark* is one of her most labored novels, and seems at times overburdened with the weight of its Wagnerian cargo. What, then, were these Wag-nerian ideas—so "definite, significant, and profound"—to which Cather resonated, and how did they correspond to Fremstad's performances?

They were, in the deepest sense, dramatic ideas. Richard Wagner understood better than any composer before or since the emotional and intellectual potential of opera, and he made it his mission to introduce dramatic realism and serious philosophical content to an art form first designed as stylized entertainment for a now obsolete aristocracy. His reform program for the genre was as complex and self-contradictory as the man himself, but three of his concepts left an unmistakable imprint on Cather's work. One is Schopenhauer's philosophy, which proposed that since no sensate experience could finally satisfy human cravings, spiritual peace must be sought in aes-thetic contemplation. A second is the idea of the *Gesamtkunstwerk* (variously translated as "total artwork" or "synthesis of all the arts"), and the ideal intermingling of its different formal components for sensuous effect. A third is what Carl Dahlhaus calls Wagner's "rig-orous artistic morality"—his intolerance of Philistinism, and his un-compromising belief in the value of art for its own sake. In an indus-trial age that had consigned art to a peripheral existence, Dahlhaus observes, Wagner promoted the "simultaneously despairing and ec-static conviction" that art was the sole justification for life, elevating it to a religion.[16]

These ideals appear repeatedly both in Cather's journalism and her fiction, and Wagner himself appears too, both explicitly (as in her early stories from *The Troll Garden,* and in the 1925 "Uncle Valen-tine," where his music is invoked to establish mood and theme) and implicitly (as in her 1922 novel *One of Ours,* in which she admitted having deeply embedded the *Parsifal* legend, though neither the composer nor the opera is ever mentioned[17]).

Both explicit and implicit kinds of Wagnerism appear in *The Song of the Lark.* The composer's music is of course much discussed in the book's final section, when Thea performs several Wagnerian roles.

But subtle references to Wagner appear much earlier in the book—
starting with the dedication poem to Isabelle McClung, which echoes
a passage in "The Prize Song" from *Die Meistersinger von Nürnberg*.[18]
This song is a marriage proposal, composed by the hero for a contest
in order to win the woman he loves; it is also sung at festivals by
Thea's suitor and benefactor Fred Ottenburg (227), whose role in
this novel resembles that played by Isabelle McClung in Cather's own
life.[19]

Other Wagnerian motifs float through the earlier parts of the text,
unnamed, like symbolic *leitmotifs*. As a child, Thea begins secretly to
dream of studying music in Germany, "the only place you can really
learn" (54), after reading "the strange 'Musical Memories' of the
Reverend H. R. Haweis" (75)—a reference surely lost on most of
today's readers. Haweis, a British Anglican clergyman and amateur
musician, was a serious Wagnerite who frequently used the operas as
subject of his sermons; over half of *My Musical Memories* (1884) is
devoted to his personal reminiscences of the composer, of Bayreuth,
and to analyses of the *Ring* and *Parsifal*. Other Wagnerian themes
surface later when Thea studies in Chicago: her first teacher, the one-
eyed, fatherly Harsanyi, plays Wotan to the fearless, rock-climbing
valkyrie in Panther Canyon who will one day perform Wotan's favored daughter Brünnhilde in the *Ring*. Even Thea's first experience
of Wagner's music—the Walhalla theme and the famous rainbow
bridge that "throb[s] out into the air" in *Götterdammerung*—enters
her mind as a *leitmotif*, fragmentary and tantalizing, "as people hear
things in their sleep" (170).

The most important mark of Wagner's influence on this novel,
however, is not in its structure or style but in its philosophy about art
and artists, and the links between art, eroticism, and religion. In 1899
Cather declaimed that "music first came to us as a religious chant or a
love song," and "through all its evolutions it should always express
those two cardinal needs of humanity."[20] Like so many artists of her
generation, she was bewitched by Wagner's compelling *fusion* of
these two "cardinal needs" in art, by his effort to control the risks of
ecstasy by subjecting it to artistic form. "I know nothing about the real
enjoyment of life," Wagner complained in an 1852 letter to Franz
Liszt;

> for me the "enjoyment of life and love" is something I have only imag-
> ined, not experienced. So my heart has had to move into my head and my
> living become artificial; it is only as "the artist" that I can live, as a "man" I
> have been completely absorbed into him.[21]

This was precisely the dilemma—and the achievement—that Cather recognized in Fremstad's performances. "With Mme. Fremstad," she wrote, "one feels that the idea is always more living than the emotion; perhaps it would be nearer the truth to say that the idea is so intensely experienced that it becomes emotion."[22]

Many critics have commented on Cather's tendency to circumvent love stories in her work or to punish erotic relationships between her fictional characters—in most of her novels someone is either humiliated or destroyed by love gone wrong. While most often this has been discussed autobiographically, as a sign of Cather's own sexual repression or neurosis, it is Wagner—not Freud—who provides the most useful model for her *artistic* approach to eroticism.[23]

Mary Jane Humphrey has proposed convincingly that *Tristan und Isolde*—the pivotal work of musical modernism—inspired the *Liebestod* of Emil and Marie in *O Pioneers!*[24] This should be no surprise, since Cather's earlier *Troll Garden* stories are so thickly laced with Wagnerism. As William Blissett observes, "Paul's Case" is quintessentially Wagnerian—both in its deep probing of sensual/spiritual links, and in its masterful use of symbolic motifs, which provide "the full harmony of this brief music-drama, the narrative being the mere vocal line."[25] Wagner's place is more explicit in "The Garden Lodge," a tale of the genteel, reserved matron Caroline Noble, who struggles to control her fantasies about a visiting tenor with whom she rehearses the Siegmund/Sieglinde love duet in her garden bower. Here the *leitmotif* is Klingsor's garden from *Parsifal*—a land of sensual delights where diabolical flowers lured chaste knights from their rigorous spiritual path. For Cather, who had left a comfortable life with Isabelle McClung to follow her career in New York, sensual attractions were also potent and real—and they were epitomized in Klingsor's slave Kundry, the role that made Olive Fremstad famous.

Wagner, however, had found an intellectual way (if not a physical one) around this danger. In two influential essays, "The Art Work of the Future" (1849) and "Opera and Drama" (1851) he expounded his views on art in specifically sexual terms, using procreation as a metaphor for the creative process itself. Conventional opera had been exhausted, he argued, because its components (music, poetry, drama, the visual arts) had devolved into empty formulas, become competitive rather than cooperative. He himself would "give birth" to a new music drama, born from the "marriage" of two ancient arts— music (the emotional element, what he called the "life-bearing, female organism"), joined in "the transports of love" to poetry (the intellectual element, "the fertilizing seed").[26] Neither was adequate by itself; to be fulfilled, the intellectual idea must be nurtured through the artist's "own necessary essence" and brought forth as "the realizational, redemptive expression of feeling."[27] Thus the "word-poet"'s final achievement would be measured by what he left *unsaid;* the "tone-poet," or musician, would echo the verbal silences to speak "the unutterable."[28]

Applying the gestation metaphor to artistic creativity had a curious consequence, however: it meant that in the artist, the erotic impulse must be *internalized*—masculine and feminine principles must merge in the single person of the creator. The artist thus became *androgynous*—as Wagner put it, "a social being subject to the sexual conditions of both *male and female.*"[29] This was an idea that would have important consequences in Cather's conception of Thea Kronborg—and perhaps also for her understanding of herself.

Wagner's use of the sexual metaphor stemmed both from his own erotic disposition and from his view of art as religion. He had recognized early that the most serious craving of his generation was a new channel for undirected religious emotion, cast adrift when Darwin undermined Biblical teachings, and he set about to provide such a channel with the *Gesamtkunstwerk,* a wedding of philosophical treatises with mythic structures set to music, and staged as dramas. It was Wagner who introduced the darkened theater and hidden orchestra, who first insisted on a silent audience during performances—all strategies designed to enhance the intimacy and solemnity of the event, and to give listeners an unprecedented privacy in which to relate to the sacred mysteries on stage. This was not to be "religious music" but *music as religion*—a transformative experience that would, in the medieval sense, "ravish the soul."[30] (Tellingly, Wagner designated *Parsifal*—his last, most ritualistic drama about purification of the sins of the flesh—a *"Bühnenweihfestspiel"* or "festival of consecration in a theater."[31])

With Wagner, however, nothing was ever simple. He himself was no ascetic, and in *Tristan und Isolde*—his astonishing "revision" of Schopenhauer—he proposed obsessive sexual love as a kind of *redemption* from desire, revamping the archetypal courtly love myth to embrace and flout the idea of renunciation in the same breath. Indeed, it was precisely this slippery mix of sensuality and spirituality that most aroused Wagner's audiences: the libretto spoke of salvation, but the music spoke quite a different language. Straight-laced Victorians listening to the long, unclimaxed raptures of *Tristan's Liebestod,* to the thrusting Venusberg theme in *Tannhäuser,* or to Sieg-mund and Sieglinde's incestuous melting into the spring night in *Die*

Walküre found themselves both aroused and frustrated—involved, Wagner's biographer Robert Gutman observes, in "a dream of purity and renunciation as they embraced the flesh."[32] The confusion was quite deliberate, produced by the composer's own ambivalence, and it was the secret of Wagner's power.

During the years Cather came of age Wagner had an enormous cult following, and most of it was female. As Joseph Horowitz has documented, the composer spoke particularly to Gilded Age women of passionate sensibility—young girls never instructed about sexuality, neurasthenic housewives shackled by genteel breeding and decorum, and independent, sometimes emotionally isolated or closeted New Women. For them Wagner's erotically charged scores were a source of violent excitation, provoking passionate feelings that felt dangerous, but came without the risks of personal relationships.[33]

Willa Cather was emphatically one of their number. By 1900 she had become irritable and impatient with the ornamental style of other operas, she sputtered, "all because that malicious man Wagner has stung the palate so that all other styles seem insipid."[34] Because she was an artist herself, however, her interest was intellectual as well as emotional; she studied the Wagner phenomenon at the same time she took part in it. Her *Troll Garden* story "The Wagner Matinee" shows that she was familiar with the urban Wagner societies, specializing in matinee concerts where women could indulge in their romantic fantasies unescorted if they chose.[35] She was also acquainted with the Bayreuth Wagner groupies, and in *The Song of the Lark* casts Fred Ottenburg's mother as one—a member of the flock of "young women who followed Wagner about in his old age, . . . receiving now and then a gracious acknowledgment that he appreciated their homage. When the composer died [she] took to her bed and saw no one for a week" (236–37).[36]

Cather borrowed what was useful to her in the Wagnerian aesthetic, honing and developing her own version of it into the 1920s. Her Fremstad profile makes clear that she understood and emulated the ideal relationship between description and suggestion that Wagner believed essential for drama, which he defined as "an act of music made visible." Wagner had understood, she wrote, that the libretto "must retain the simplicity of a legend, that the characters must be indicated rather than actualized." It was the music that made the poem "flower," that drew the legend out "from the low relief of archaic simplicity" to make it "present and passionate and personal."[37] In Olive Fremstad's histrionic minimalism—her ability to convey emotion through music alone, ignoring the melodramatic conventions of her time—Cather felt she had witnessed the perfect realization of the composer's aims.

By 1922 (the same year she published *One of Ours* with its unnamed *Parsifal* motif) Cather had developed her own minimalist aesthetic called "the unfurnished novel" ("novel démeublé"), and she used musical language to describe it:

> Whatever is felt on the page without being specifically named there— that, one might say, is created. It is the inexplicable presence of the thing not named, of the overtone divined by the ear but not heard by it, the verbal mood, the emotional aura of the fact or the thing or the deed, that gives high quality to the novel or the drama, as well as to poetry itself.[38]

The idea of suggesting mood through the senses instead of using explicit description resembles the synaesthesia favored by the Symbolist poets, who also had built their aesthetic platform on Wagnerian ideas.[39]

Cather's work on *The Song of the Lark* came at mid-point in her long intellectual relationship with Wagner. This novel experiments a great deal with subtle suggestion, but it is not minimalist and spare, as Fremstad's acting was and as Cather's later books would be. Its Wagnerism is expansive and lush, full of gorgeous sensuality like the operas themselves. And like the operas too, Cather's *text* tells about chaste dedication to a spiritual goal, while its "emotional aura"—the "overtone divined by the ear but not heard by it"—speaks a very different language.

There are, for example, no explicit sexual encounters in *The Song of the Lark*. Although Thea is always surrounded by admiring men, their lack of prurient interest in her is one of the most remarkable things about them. There is, however, a powerful erotic undercurrent in the book, beginning with Thea's intense physical response to the natural world in childhood. This sensuality is, like music, *diffused*—it envelops all her experience, rather than being directed at a particular human object.

Thea has a lifelong pattern of such responses, all experienced in solitude, and all translated into artistic emotion. On her thirteenth birthday, when she is "shaken with passionate excitement" after an intense music lesson with Wunsch, Thea wanders about "looking into the yellow prickly-pear blossoms with their thousand stamens," looking at the sand hills "until she wished she *were* a sand hill" (71). At fifteen, after a moving discussion with Dr. Archie on a languid summer night, she lies on the floor by her bedroom window "vibrating with excitement," while "her chest ached and it seemed as if her heart were spreading all over the desert." Thea is not "sentimental" about her mentors, as some young girls might be—she is a Wagnerian androgyne, containing all generativity in herself. To underscore this point, Cather's authorial voice here intervenes to explain that "[t]here is no work of art so big or so beautiful that it was not once all contained in some youthful body, like this one which lay on the floor in the moonlight, pulsing with ardor and anticipation" (122).

Wunsch, who had noticed Thea's androgynous nature early, compares her to the prickly pear blossoms of the desert—"thornier and sturdier than the maiden flowers" he dreamed of from his youth—"not so sweet, but wonderful" (87). Years later, Fred Ottenburg would observe it as a quality of her voice—"the high voice we dream of; so pure and yet so virile and human" (349).[40] Indeed, the fact that descriptions of the act of singing—translating music through the physical body—are among this novel's most erotic passages is highest Wagnerism on Cather's part. Harsanyi, laying his hand on Thea's throat to evaluate the newly-discovered voice, responds to the experience like a lover with a virgin: "He loved to hear a big voice throb in a relaxed, natural throat, and he was thinking that no one had ever felt this voice vibrate before" (159–60).[41] When Thea spends an evening singing with her Mexican friends in Moonstone, Cather transposes male and female imagery in a passage describing how "at the appointed, at the acute, moment, the soprano voice, like a fountain jet, shot up into the light. . . . How it leaped from among those dusky male voices!" (199).[42] Thea's artistic epiphany takes place in what Ellen Moers first described as literature's "most thoroughly elaborated female landscape"[43]—Panther Canyon, a gorge of shelved pink cliffs "lightly fringed with piñons and dwarf cedars." Enfolded in this shelter, Thea has a series of dream-raptures which are described orgasmically but without climax, recalling the insistent music of Wagner's *Tristan und Isolde:* "A song would go through her head all morning, as a spring keeps welling up, and it was like a pleasant sensation indefinitely prolonged" (251). When Fred later visits Thea in her refuge, the swift trajectory of an eagle swooping in and out of the gorge heightens the scene's erotic suggestiveness.[44]

In "The Art Work of the Future" Wagner defined true dramatic action as "*a bough from the Tree of Life*" whose fruit had been "*planted in the soil of art.*"[44] Thea Kronborg absorbs this lesson deeply. In perfect accommodation, she reaches the pinnacle of her powers as an artist who communicates the spiritual message of her art by means of a similar metaphor. In her final performance in the novel, a transcendent portrayal of Sieglinde in *Die Walküre,* her body becomes

> absolutely the instrument of her idea. Not for nothing had she kept it so severely, kept it filled with such energy and fire. All that deep-rooted vitality flowered in her voice, her face, in her very finger tips. She felt like a tree bursting into bloom. (395)

And in equally Wagnerian tradition, Cather uses theological language to explain how such a thing could happen: Thea had merely "entered into the inheritance that she herself had laid up, into the fullness of the faith she had kept before she knew its name or its meaning" (395).

Notes

Copyright © Sherrill Harbison 1999. This essay is an abbreviated version of the Introduction to the title in the Penguin Twentieth Century Classics edition of *The Song of the Lark* by Willa Cather. All text citations in this essay are from this edition.

1. Elizabeth Shepley Sergeant, *Willa Cather: A Memoir* (Lincoln: University of Nebraska Press, 1963), 111.

2. From 1903 until her retirement in 1914, Fremstad also appeared at the Met as Sieglinde, Brünnhilde, Fricka, Isolde, Brangaene, Venus, Elisabeth, and Elsa, as well as in half a dozen non-Wagnerian roles. Her merciless 1907 interpretation of Richard Strauss's *Salome*—a character even more depraved than Kundry, and still worse to audiences at the time, unredeemed—caused the opera to be shut down after its first performance. See Joseph Horowitz, *Wagner Nights: An American History* (Berkeley: University of California Press, 1994), 283–85; and John Dizikes, *Opera in America, A Cultural History* (New Haven: Yale University Press, 1993), 333–34.

3. Willa Cather, "Three American Singers," *McClure's* (December, 1913): 42. Hereafter TAS.

4. James Woodress, *Willa Cather: A Literary Life* (Lincoln: University of Nebraska Press, 1987), 253. Hereafter *WC.*

5. TAS, 42.

6. Ibid.

7. Sergeant, *Memoir,* 3.

8. Mary Watkins Cushing, *The Rainbow Bridge* (New York: Putnam, 1954), 244.

9. Ibid., 71–75.

10. Woodress, *WC,* 253.

11. L. Brent Bohlke, ed., *Willa Cather in Person: Interviews, Speeches and Letters* (Lincoln: University of Nebraska Press, 1996), 10–11.

12. Cather was not alone in her fascination with Fremstad. The singer inspired some decadent fiction by the music critic James Gibbons Huneker—a story, "The Last of the Valkyries" (1896, collected as "Venus and Valkyr" in *Bedouins,* 1926), and novel *Painted Veils* (1920, presumed to be a composite of Fremstad and Mary Garden); as well as novels by Gertrude Atherton (*Tower of Ivory,* 1910) and Marcia Davenport (*Of Lena Geyer,* 1936, a combined portrait of Fremstad and the author's mother, the soprano Alma Gluck).

13. Friedrich Nietzsche, reflecting on Wagner's interest in asceticism in *The Genealogy of Morals* (1887), explained that "there is no necessary antithesis between chastity and sensuality; . . . every authentic heart-felt love transcends this antithesis." *The Philosophy of Nietzsche*, trans. Horace B. Samuel (New York: Modern Library, 1954), 718–19. In "Willa Cather and the Human Voice" Richard Giannone describes Cather's artistic sensibility as a "sensuous spirituality," (*Five Essays on Willa Cather*, ed. John J. Murphy [No. Andover, MA: Merrimack College, 1974], 24), a phrase Cather herself had used to describe the music of Massenet in 1897 (William M. Curtin, ed., *The World and the Parish: Willa Cather's Articles and Reviews*, II [Lincoln: University of Nebraska Press, 1970], 520. Hereafter *Parish*).

14. *Parish*, I, 208.

15. Robert W. Gutman, *Richard Wagner: The Man, His Mind, and His Music* (New York: Harcourt, Brace Jovanovich, 1990), 403.

16. John Deathridge and Carl Dahlhaus, *The New Grove Wagner* (New York: Norton, 1984), 94–95.

17. In correspondence Cather explained that she had originally planned to call the final section of *One of Ours* "The Blameless Fool By Pity Enlightened," after Parsifal (Woodress, *WC*, 328). In her admiring 1925 Introduction to Gertrude Hall's *The Wagnerian Romances*, Cather acknowledged her own frustrations in trying to translate Wagner's method to prose. See *Willa Cather on Writing* (Lincoln: University of Nebraska Press, 1988), 60–66.

18. Wagner's text of the "Prize Song," as translated by Peter Branscombe:

> Shining in the rosy light of morning,
> the air heavy
> with blossom and scent,
> full of every
> unthought-of-joy,
> a garden invited me
> to be its guest.
> (*Morgenlich leuchtend in rosigem schien, / von Blüt' und Duft / geschwellt die Luft, / voll aller Wonen / nie ersonnen, / ein Garten lud mich ein, / Gast ihm zu sein.*) Act 3, Scene 1, Libretto p. 143.

Compare Cather's dedicatory poem in the 1915 edition:

> On uplands,
> At morning,
> The world was young, the winds were free;
> A garden fair,
> In that blue desert air,
> Its guest invited me to be.

19. This also explains why, in the 1932 edition of *The Song of the Lark*, Cather removed the poem but not the dedication itself. By 1932 she had adjusted to Isabelle's unexpected and unwelcome marriage to the violinist Jan Hambourg in 1916, a year after *The Song of the Lark* was first published, but including a poem that was also a proposal was no longer appropriate.

20. *Parish*, II, 645.

21. Deathridge and Dahlhaus, *New Grove*, 94.

22. Cather, TAS, 46.

23. See, among the early examples of the autobiographical reading, Blanche Gelfant, "The Forgotten Reaping Hook: Sex in *My Ántonia,*" *Critical Essays on Willa Cather,* ed. John J. Murphy (Boston: G. K. Hall, 1984), 147–64. Also, Sharon O'Brien, *Willa Cather: The Emerging Voice* (Oxford and New York: Oxford University Press, 1987). Cather was vehement and explicit in her dislike of Freud; see Sergeant, *Memoir,* 163–64; and Cather's own 1922 essay, "Miss Jewett," *Not Under Forty.* 1936 (Lincoln: University of Nebraska Press, 1988), 93. Cather's link with Wagner has not been widely explored. The best discussions are in William Blissett, "Wagnerian Fiction in English," *Criticism* 5 (Summer 1963): 239–60; Richard Giannone, *Music in Willa Cather's Fiction* (Lincoln: University of Nebraska Press, 1968); Hermione Lee, *Willa Cather: Double Lives* (New York: Vintage, 1989); and Mary Jane Humphrey, "The White Mulberry Tree as Opera," *Cather Studies 3,* ed. Susan J. Rosowski (Lincoln: University of Nebraska Press, 1996): 51–66.

24. Humphrey, "Tree as Opera," 52.

25. Blissett, "Wagnerian Fiction," 254.

26. Wagner's *Opera and Drama* comprises Vol. II of *Richard Wagner's Prose Works,* trans. William Ashton Ellis (1893, reprinted by Broude Brothers, New York, 1966). This concept appears on 110–11, 236, 247. I have here quoted Stewart Spencer's translation of a Wagner letter discussing his essay, cited in Jean-Jacques Nattiez, *Wagner Androgyne* (Princeton: Princeton University Press, 1993), 38.

27. Nattiez, *Androgyne,* 36.

28. Richard Wagner, *Opera and Drama,* 276, 317. The "unutterable" became a watchword of Symbolism, which was deeply indebted to Wagner's ideas; it is surely no coincidence that Fremstad's impact on Cather was to leave her "choked up" with things "unutterable."

29. *Opera and Drama,* 107; see also Nattiez, *Androgyne,* 41.

30. Richard Wagner, "The Art Work of the Future," *The Art Work of the Future and Other Works.* 1895, trans. W. Aston Ellis, *Richard Wagner's Prose Works* I (Lincoln: University of Nebraska Press, 1993), 155 and passim.

31. Deathridge and Dahlhaus, *New Grove,* 161.

32. Gutman, *Richard Wagner,* 253.

33. Joseph Horowitz, *Wagner Nights: An American History* (Berkeley: University of California Press, 1994) 215, 226.

34. *Parish,* II, 658.

35. Horowitz, *Wagner Nights,* 191–192.

36. One such Wagner acolyte was Mabel Dodge Luhan, the *bohémienne* socialite who later would become one of Cather's friends. For her description of the Bayreuth experience see Horowitz, *Wagner Nights,* 218. Another visitor, Mark Twain, marvelled in 1891 over the Bayreuth "pilgrims" who after the daily "services" returned to their hotels with "heart and soul and . . . body exhausted by long hours of tremendous emotion, . . . in no fit condition to do anything but lie torpid and slowly gather back life and strength for the next service." Calling it "one of the most extraordinary experiences of my life," he confessed he had "never seen anything so great and fine and real as this devotion." Mark Twain, "At the Shrine of St. Wagner," quoted in Horowitz, *Wagner Nights,* 226–27.

37. Cather, TAS, 46.

38. Willa Cather, "The Novel Démeublé, *WC On Writing,* 41–42.

39. Deathridge and Dahlhaus, *New Grove,* 76–77. Wagner's prolific theoretical writings had brought his ideas into circulation even before most of his music was heard or performed, and he had influential intellectual champions in Baudelaire

and Nietzsche. The French Symbolist poets were inspired by Wagner's idea of the *Gesamtkunstwerk*. In 1885 they adopted the composer as their patron saint, and named their literary journal the *Revue wagnérienne*. Other major literary figures indebted to Wagner include Thomas Mann, Virginia Woolf, and James Joyce.

40. For analyses of Thea's androgynous voice, see John H. Flannigan, "Thea Kronborg's Vocal Transvestitism: Willa Cather and the 'Voz Contralto,'" *Modern Fiction Studies* 40.4 (Winter 1994): 737–63; and Elizabeth Wood, "Sapphonics," *Queering the Pitch: The New Gay and Lesbian Musicology*, eds. Philip Brett, Elizabeth Wood, and Gary C. Thomas (New York: Routledge, 1994), 27–66. Wood also discusses Olive Fremstad's androgyny, and her possible place in the lesbian *demi-monde* of her era. For observations on Richard Wagner's own personal androgyny, see Horowitz, *Wagner Nights*, 220–21, and (less appreciatively) Gutman, *Richard Wagner.*

41. For discussions of physiological similarities between singing and orgasm see Wayne Koestenbaum, *The Queen's Throat: Opera, Homosexuality, and the Mystery of Desire* (New York: Poseidon, 1993), Chapter 5; and Wood, "Sapphonics."

42. Flannigan describes this remarkable passage as "a kind of male ejaculation in prose rhythms" ("Vocal Transvestitism", 755).

43. Ellen Moers, *Literary Women* (Garden City, NY: Doubleday, 1976), 252.

44. Susan J. Rosowski discusses the masculine elements in this sexually charged landscape in "Willa Cather's Female Landscapes: *The Song of the Lark* and *Lucy Gayheart*" *Women's Studies 11* (1984), 236–37.

45. Wagner, "The Art Work of the Future, 196–97.

Bibliography

Blissett, William. "Wagnerian Fiction in English." *Criticism* 5 (Summer 1963): 239–60.

Bohlke, L. Brent, ed. *Willa Cather in Person: Interviews, Speeches, and Letters.* Lincoln: University of Nebraska Press, 1986.

Cather, Willa. *On Writing, Critical Studies on Writing as an Art.* Foreword by Stephen A. Tennant. Lincoln: University of Nebraska Press, 1988.

———. "Miss Jewett." *Not Under Forty.* 1936. Lincoln: University of Nebraska Press, 1988: 76–95.

———. *The Song of the Lark.* 1915. Edited, with Introduction and Notes by Sherrill Harbison. New York: Penguin, 1999.

———. "Three American Singers." *McClure's* (December 1913): 33–48.

———. The Troll Garden. 1905. Afterword by Katherine Anne Porter. New York: Meridian, 1984.

———. *Uncle Valentine and Other Stories: Willa Cather's Uncollected Short Fiction, 1915–1929.* Ed. Bernice Slote. Lincoln: University of Nebraska Press, 1973.

Curtin, William M., ed. *The World and the Parish: Willa Cather's Articles and Reviews, 1893–1902.* Lincoln: University of Nebraska Press, 1970.

Cushing, Mary Watkins. *The Rainbow Bridge.* New York: Putnam, 1954.

Deathridge, John, and Carl Dahlhaus. *The New Grove Wagner.* New York: Norton, 1984.

Dizikes, John. *Opera in America: A Cultural History.* New Haven: Yale University Press, 1993.

Flannigan, John H. "Thea Kronborg's Vocal Transvestitism: Willa Cather and the 'Voz Contralto'." *Modern Fiction Studies* 40.4 (Winter 1994): 737–63.

Gelfant, Blanche. "The Forgotten Reaping Hook: Sex in *My Ántonia.*" *Critical Essays on Willa Cather.* Ed. John J. Murphy. Boston: G.K. Hall, 1984: 147–64.

Giannone, Richard. *Music in Willa Cather's Fiction.* Lincoln: University of Nebraska Press, 1968.

———. "Willa Cather and the Human Voice." *Five Essays on Willa Cather.* Merrimack Symposium, Ed. John J. Murphy. No. Andover, MA: Merrimack College, 1974: 21–49.

Gutman, Robert W. *Richard Wagner: The Man, His Mind, and His Music.* New York: Harcourt Brace Jovanovich, 1990.

Haweis, Hugh Reginald. *My Musical Memories* (1884). London & New York: Funk & Wagnalls, 1892.

Horowitz, Joseph. *Wagner Nights: An American History.* Berkeley: University of California Press, 1994.

Humphrey, Mary Jane. "The White Mulberry Tree as Opera." *Cather Studies 3,* Ed. Susan J. Rosowski. Lincoln: University of Nebraska Press, 1996: 51–66.

Koestenbaum, Wayne. *The Queen's Throat: Opera, Homosexuality, and the Mystery of Desire.* New York: Poseidon, 1993.

Lee, Hermione. *Willa Cather: Double Lives.* New York: Vintage, 1989.

Moers, Ellen. *Literary Women.* Garden City, N.Y.: Doubleday, 1976.

Nattiez, Jean-Jacques. *Wagner Androgyne.* Trans. Stewart Spencer. Princeton: Princeton University Press, 1993.

Nietzsche, Friedrich. "The Genealogy of Morals." Trans. Horace B. Samuel. *The Philosophy of Nietzsche.* NewYork: Modern Library, 1954: 617–807.

O'Brien, Sharon. *Willa Cather: The Emerging Voice.* Oxford & New York: Oxford University Press, 1987.

Rosowski, Susan J. "Willa Cather's Female Landscapes: *The Song of the Lark* and *Lucy Gayheart*" *Women's Studies* 11 (1984) 233–46.

Sergeant, Elizabeth Shepley. *Willa Cather: A Memoir* (1953). Lincoln: University of Nebraska Press, 1963.

Wagner, Richard. *The Art Work of the Future and Other Works.* Trans. W. Ashton Ellis (1895); Vol. I of *Richard Wagner's Prose Works.* Lincoln: University of Nebraska Press, 1993.

———. *Die Meistersinger von Nürnberg* (1867). Chicago Symphony Orchestra, Sir Georg Solti, London 462 606–2. Libretto, trans. Peter Branscombe, p. 143.

———. *Opera and Drama.* Trans. W. Ashton Ellis (1893); Vol. II of *Richard Wagner's Prose Works.* New York: Broude Brothers, 1966.

Wood, Elizabeth. "Sapphonics." In Philip Brett, Elizabeth Wood, and Gary C. Thomas, Eds. *Queering the Pitch: The New Gay and Lesbian Musicology.* New York: Routledge, 1994; 27–66.

Woodress, James. *Willa Cather: A Literary Life.* Lincoln: University of Nebraska Press, 1987.

Lucy Gayheart and Schubert

GRETEL D. WEISS

There is no question that music was very important in Willa Cather's life and work. Music is everywhere—from the bell of the sleigh to the musical laugh, from Mr. Shimerda's violin to the Saint-Saëns concerto, or from Thea Kronborg's dramatic soprano to Clement Sebastian's baritone. Although Cather does not neglect any type of music, however broadly defined, she had a special affinity for the voice, from the spontaneous trilling in moonlight to the high art of Wagner and to that of the art song.

It is not surprising that Cather's interest progresses from Wagner operas to Schubert Lieder in the twenty-year interval between *The Song of the Lark* and *Lucy Gayheart.* Interestingly, Dietrich Fischer-Dieskau, the great Schubert interpreter and scholar, points out that there is a close connection between Wagner and Schubert, and that some Schubert songs "held enormous importance for the development of dramatic singing, particularly as far as Wagner was concerned."[1] In a Wagner opera orchestra and stage spectacle make a highly charged dramatic whole. Although on a smaller scale and without a visual setting, a Schubert Lied is a dramatic event in its own right, and voice, text and accompaniment contribute equally to this drama in miniature.

In Cather's 1935 novel *Lucy Gayheart,* Schubert songs are integral parts of the text. Lucy, a young woman from a small Nebraska town, is pretty, delights in everything and, says Cather, has something "direct and unhesitating and joyous in her nature." Her walk is "like an expression of irrepressible lightheartedness. . . . Life seemed to lie very near the surface in her."[2] A piano pupil of her father's, the town's watchmaker and bandleader, she goes to Chicago at age eighteen to study music. Cather makes it clear from the beginning that Lucy does not possess the outstanding talent or irrepressible ambition to become an accomplished artist. Merrill Skaggs points out that Thea and Lucy are "opposite sides of a rug—or contrapuntal inversion."[3] In other words, Thea and Lucy are very different. Cather says that Lucy was "talented, but too careless and lighthearted to take herself seriously. She never dreamed of a 'career.' She thought of

159

music as a natural form of pleasure, and as a means of earning money to help her father when she came home" (4).

Since I am a long-time devotee of Schubert Lieder, the centrality of these works in *Lucy Gayheart* intrigued me. After reading all the critical commentary, however, I still found myself perplexed. Richard Giannone, for example, in his *Music in Willa Cather's Fiction,* devotes an entire chapter to *Lucy Gayheart;* and his discussion, to which I shall return, is thorough, challenging and fascinating. Yet after acknowledging Cather's assessment of Lucy's limited aspirations, I still wondered whether an analysis of the songs Lucy hears might illuminate the novel further than it has yet been lighted. I hope to do so here.

After her Christmas holiday Lucy returns to Chicago and attends a song recital by the famous baritone Clement Sebastian, who sings several Schubert songs. From the first Lucy idealizes Sebastian. "Yes, a great artist should look like that," she says, and feels that "there was something profoundly tragic about this man" (24–25). In her imagination the songs and the singer become one.

Yet Lucy's interpretation of "Der Doppelgänger" ("The Double"), one of Clement's songs, is startling because it is so shockingly wrong. "Der Doppelgänger," a poem by Heinrich Heine, was composed during the last year of Schubert's life. It is the penultimate song of *Schwanengesang (Swan's Song),* one of Schubert's three song cycles. Unlike *Die Schöne Müllerin (The Beautiful Miller Maid)* and *Winterreise (Winter's Journey),* *Schwanengesang* is not a coherent whole that tells a continuous story but a collection of unrelated songs.

"Der Doppelgänger"	"The Double"
Still ist die Nacht, es ruhen die Gassen,	Still is the night. The streets are at rest.
In diesem Hause wohnt mein Schatz;	Here is the house where my loved-one lived;
Sie hat schon längst die Stadt verlassen,	Long it is, since she left town,
Doch steht noch das Haus auf demselben Platz.	Yet the house still stands where it did.
Da steht auch ein Mensch und starrt in die Höhe,	A man stands there too, staring up,
Und ringt die Hände vor Schmerzensgewalt;	Wringing his hands in agony;
Mir graut es, wenn ich sein Antlitz sehe—	Horror grips me as I see his face—
Der Mond zeigt mir meine eigne Gestalt.	The moon shows me my own self.

Du Doppelgänger, du bleicher Geselle!	Double! Pale companion!
Was äffst du nach mein Liebesleid,	Why do you ape the torment of love
Das mich gequält auf dieser Stelle	That I suffered here
So manche Nacht, in alter Zeit?	So many a night in time past?[4]

Lucy's reaction to the song is as follows:

> When he began "Der Doppelgänger," the last song of the group (Still ist die Nacht, es ruhen die Gassen), it was like moonlight pouring down on the narrow streets of an old German town. With every phrase that picture deepened—moonlight, intense and calm, sleeping on old human houses; and somewhere a lonely black cloud in the sky. So manche Nacht in alter Zeit? The moon was gone, and the silent street—and Sebastian was gone, though Lucy had not been aware of his exit. (25)

Lucy's is hardly an adequate translation of a song about which Fischer-Dieskau writes: "fourteen years of resignation preceded this dramatic outburst at the end of Schubert's life, and he seems to have rid himself of a life-long yearning with this one cry."[5] The first stanza could be described the way Lucy does, but then the song changes dramatically. Whereas the first stanza is sung very softly, the second and third are rendered "forte." The second stanza is full of unbearable despair and horror, and the third stanza is angry and mocking, although the last line has some consolation. The effect on the comprehending listener is shattering.

How did this misinterpretation, this wrong note, find its way into Cather's work? One can speculate on several possibilities. The first that comes to mind is that Cather herself misunderstood the poem and the song; the second, that Sebastian sang the song so badly, it could easily be misinterpreted.[6] I reject both these possibilities—the first because Cather seems to know her Schubert and because there are always good reasons for everything she does, albeit analyzing her subtlety may require some work on the reader's part. But the second is equally unacceptable, because even a poor artist would have a hard time distorting the song to such a degree as to obliterate its meaning entirely; the meaning is unavoidable in both the music and the text.

Two other possibilities have more promise. It certainly is no secret that Lucy is naive and that she is unschooled and inexperienced musically. Surely her reaction underscores the depth of these shortcomings. Equally possible is this: Although Lucy does not understand the meaning of the song, her hearing it affects her profoundly. She reacts not to the song but to the singer:

She was struggling with something she had never felt before. . . . It was a discovery about life, a revelation of love as a tragic force, not a melting mood, a passion that drowns like black water. As she sat listening to this man the outside world seemed to her dark and terrifying, full of fears and dangers that had never come close to her until now.

And further:

Some people's lives are affected by what happens to their person or their property; but for others fate is what happens to their feelings and their thoughts—that and nothing more. (26–27)

Giannone's observation may be helpful here: "[Cather's] sympathy cuts across many kinds of musical aptitudes. . . . In the end it is never the quality of musicianship or the finish of musical knowledge alone which wins the novelist's favor."[7] He suggests, perhaps mistaking the artist for her subject, that it is the effects and the feelings that matter to Cather. We might also consider that Lucy's failure to comprehend the meaning of the song is a crucial prophetic device. Does Lucy's inattentiveness, for example, lead her to skate carelessly on thin ice and thus die?

Another misunderstood song is "Die Forelle" ("The Trout") which Lucy encounters at a time when her relationship with Sebastian creates a great deal of happiness for her. "Life was resolved into something simple and noble—yes, and joyous, a joyousness which seemed safe from time and change, like that in Schubert's 'Die Forelle,' which Sebastian often sang" (63–64). The irony here is that in the third stanza the trusting trout is betrayed by the cunning fisherman, though the cheerful, even somewhat rollicking, rhythm of the song and its accompaniment does not change dramatically when happiness changes to tragedy.

The major work in *Lucy Gayheart* is *Winterreise (Winter's Journey)*, also written in the year of Schubert's death. Lucy's observations are rather scant. She hears the work for the first time, and Cather describes her reaction:

She attributed to the artist much that belonged to the composer. She kept feeling that this was not an interpretation, this was the thing itself, with one man and one nature behind every song. The singing was not dramatic in any way she knew. Sebastian did not identify himself with the melancholy youth; he presented him as if he were a memory, not to be brought too near into the present. One felt a long distance between the singer and the scenes he was recalling, a long perspective. (32)

A subdued mood of passive recollection to convey Schubert's greatest vocal work is surprisingly unconventional and puzzling. The effect may be due to the quality of the performance, or again, to Lucy's "unmusicality." *Winterreise,* the story of a rejected lover's journey, is a profoundly moving and disturbing work. Fischer-Dieskau, who has sung and recorded the work many times, asks: "Should one perform *Die Winterreise* in public at all? Should one offer such an intimate diary of a human soul to an audience whose interests are so varied?"[8] For him the answer obviously is an affirmative one. Stefan Kunze, in notes for one of Fischer-Dieskau's recordings, comments that "in *Winterreise . . .* nature is remote and hostile in contrast with *Müllerin* where it is friendly and intimate,"[9] although in both cases the story deals with the wandering of a young man who has been jilted by his beloved, a common theme in German Romanticism. *Winterreise* is about existential despair, and the most moving song is the last, "Der Leiermann" ("The Organ Grinder"), text by Wilhelm Müller:

Drüben hinterm Dorfe	There, beyond the village
Steht ein Leiermann,	An organ grinder stands
Und mit starren Fingern	And with numb fingers
Dreht er, was er kann.	Plays as best he can.
Barfuss auf dem Eise	Barefoot on the ice
Wankt er hin und her,	He staggers to and fro,
Und sein kleiner Teller	And his little plate
Bleibt ihm immer lehr.	Stays forever empty.
Keiner mag ihn hören,	No one cares to listen,
Keiner sieht ihn an,	No one looks at him,
Und die Hunde knurren	And dogs snarl
Um den alten Mann.	Around the old man.
Und er lässt es gehen,	And he lets it happen,
Alles wie es will,	Everything as it will,
Dreht, und seine Leier	And plays on,
Steht ihm nimmer still.	His hurdy-gurdy never still.
Wunderlicher Alter!	Strange old man!
Soll ich mit dir gehn?	Shall I go with you?
Willst zu meinen Liedern	Will you, to my songs,
Deine Leier drehn?	Play your hurdy-gurdy?[10]

To quote Fischer-Dieskau again: "'Der Leiermann' is not only the emotional nadir of the cycle—this song is the culmination of every-thing Schubert ever wrote, for there is no escape from this agony . . . . Life has little more to offer in these lines. The effect on the listener is paralyzing."[11] I have often witnessed this stunned silence at the end of a *Winterreise* performance by a superb singer and his accompanist.

Giannone focuses on *Winterreise* in his *Lucy Gayheart* chapter titled after the song cycle.[12] His interpretation of "Der Leiermann" as well as that of the preceding song "Die Nebensonnen" ("The Phantom Suns") differs radically from Fischer-Dieskau's and mine, although it must be acknowledged that Brian Newbould in his recent book on Schubert also entertains the possibility of Giannone's reading.[13] The text of "Die Nebensonen" is as follows:

Drei Sonnen sah ich am Himmel steh'n,	Three suns in the sky I saw,
Hab lang und fest sie angeseh'n;	Long and hard I looked;
Und sie auch standen da so stier,	They also stopped and stared,
Als wollten sie nicht weg von mir.	As if unwilling to go away.
Ach, *meine* Sonnen seit ihr nicht!	You are not, alas, my suns!
Schau andern doch ins Angesicht!	You look other people in the face!
Nun sind hinab die besten zwei,	Lately, yes, I did have three;
Ging nur die dritt erst hinterdrein!	But the beset two are now down.
Im Dunkel wird mir wohler sein.	Would but the third go too!
	In the dark I'd fare better.[14]

Brian Newbould comments thus on this enigmatic poem: "Whether the first two of the three suns the traveler imagines he sees in the sky are love and hope, or the eyes of his lost love . . . the third sun which he hopes will also set is undoubtedly life itself."[15] Gian-none agrees that the third must be life, and although the wanderer would feel better in the dark if the third (life) went down as well, Giannone concludes that the wanderer "has really come to kneel before the mystery of life and commits himself to it. . . . The pledge of life justifies the bold self-reliance and is the positive achievement of the journey." Similarly Giannone suggests that the wanderer and the hurdy-gurdy man team up in some sort of psychic and physical union, and the wanderer's mind hunts for the meaning of life. "He learns that both love and hope deceive and that life alone is worth clinging to. The two suns of hope and love have set on the winter horizon; the third sun, life, is setting at the end of the cycle, as the youth goes off singing to the crank-organ tune of his companion, the beggar."[16]

In an article in the *New York Times*, Donal Henehan addresses himself to the interpretative dilemma in *Winterreise*. He suggests that many of the preceding songs in the cycle leave little doubt as to the outcome of this winter journey. "But what about the suggestion that the final song, 'Der Leiermann,' shows the man making some kind of last-straw human connection with the old organ grinder? Here I would go beyond the literal text and insist that 'strange old man' is not a down-and-outer but death itself who has come to claim the poor madman."[17]

If we accept Giannone's optimistic conclusion we can accept his assertion that *Lucy Gayheart* mirrors *Winterreise*. And indeed there are similarities. Lucy has her own winter journey after Sebastian drowns in a boating accident. She returns home as fall turns into winter. Sebastian's death means "to have one's heart frozen and one's world destroyed in a moment" (131). Lucy is withdrawn and depressed. She no longer hurries forward with her quick step, and she can only find solace in her beloved orchard. The two journeys complement each other, but the outcomes do not.

One night Lucy attends a performance of *The Bohemian Girl* at a provincial opera house. In a generally mediocre performance the soprano catches her attention. The singer is far from young, and her face and her voice are worn. But Lucy observes that there is sweetness, sympathy and understanding in her singing. "She gave the old songs, even the most hackneyed, their full value." Lucy wonders, "Why was it worth her while . . . Singing this humdrum music to humdrum people, why was it worth while? This poor little singer had lost everything: youth, good looks, position, the high notes in her voice. And yet she sang so well" (152–53). Lucy again reacts to the singer and to the feelings of this simple music, giving apparent support to the previous suggestion that the effects and feelings may matter more to Cather than high artistic achievement.

But while listening to the singer, Lucy has an epiphany involving her feelings. She has a strong urge to return to life and Chicago. "What if—what if life itself were the sweetheart?" (155). She feels that by going back into the world and by embracing life she will again find what Sebastian once meant to her. That is, she intends to rush back, as she once rushed forward, to life. She has learned nothing.

The novel would have ended in an ascending curve, in a major key, had Lucy not drowned in a skating accident. Yet despite one song,

"Mut" ("Courage"), the spiral for Schubert's wanderer is unfailingly downward and must end in death. The fact that Lucy's story, too, ends in death, however, does not obliterate the difference. Schubert's wanderer is a tragic figure, but Lucy is not.

Why then does Cather give *Winterreise* a prominent place in her novel? She may have believed as did Giannone, of course, that Lucy's and the wanderer's fate are the same, or that the obvious though limited similarities justify the song cycle's inclusion. And there is certainly a connection between Sebastian and *Winterreise* as well. When Lucy hears *Winterreise* she feels that "Sebastian did not identify himself with the melancholy youth; he presented him as if he were a memory not to be brought near the present" (32). As noted before, Lucy's total identification with the singer and not with the work may actually have led her to an intuitive understanding of Sebastian's melancholy state of mind, because the aging Sebastian has begun to realize that "his youth was forever and irrevocably gone" (65). For Sebastian, the approaching winter of his life has become an unavoidable presence, as it did for Cather, who was entering her sixties when she wrote *Lucy Gayheart.*

But without question Cather tells us something important about Lucy, namely that Lucy reacts only through feeling and that she is incapable of accurate intellectual comprehension. The best explanation of the presence of the Schubert songs, as well as for Lucy's inexplicable reaction, can be found in Cather's 1922 essay "The Novel Démeublé." Cather asserts that much description is like useless furniture and has no place in imaginative art unless these descriptions "are . . . so much a part of the emotions of the people that they are perfectly synthesized; they seem to exist . . . in the emotional penumbra of the characters themselves." She further suggests that "some of the younger writers are . . . following the development of modern painting by . . . suggestion rather than enumeration." Cather continues:

> Whatever is felt upon the page without being specifically named there— that, one might say, is created. It is the inexplicable presence of the things not named, of the overtone divined by the ear but not heard by it, the verbal mood, the emotional aura of the fact or the thing or the deed, that gives high quality to the novel or the drama, as well as to poetry itself.[18]

She concludes by saying that it would be wonderful to leave the room "bare for the play of emotions, great and little"[19] and without the clutter of useless furniture.

Cather follows her prescription precisely in *Lucy Gayheart*. Literalness in the interpretation of the Schubert songs is not Cather's concern; for her, it would merely clutter. Lucy's inattention defines her character, her way of relating to others, and her proficiency as an artist. And Lucy herself tells us what she considers important when she sees the Impressionist paintings at the Art Museum: "some are meant to represent objects, and others are meant to express a kind of feeling merely, and then accuracy doesn't matter" (85). Thus Cather's puzzling inconsistencies are not inconsistent. Lucy's inattention to the Schubert songs expresses her way of feeling and is fully in tune with her character and her fate. What matters to Cather is not a sophisticated interpretation of the songs, but a complex sense of Lucy's character. In Cather's bare room, center stage is given first to feelings or emotional responses, and then to facts, hard facts. What we finally comprehend, however, is that both feelings and facts— warm responses and cold acknowledgments—produce irreversible consequences.

Notes

1. Friedrich Fischer-Dieskau, *Schubert's Songs: A Biographical Study,* trans. Kenneth S. Whitton (New York: Knopf, 1977), 281–82.
2. Willa Cather, *Lucy Gayheart* (New York: Vintage, 1995), 3–4.
3. Merrill M. Skaggs, "Key Modulations in Cather's Novels about Music," *Willa Cather Pioneer Memorial Newsletter* XXXIX (Summer & Fall 1995): 25.
4. *Schubert's Songs,* 335.
5. *Schubert's Songs,* 282.
6. The Skaggs view. See note 3 above.
7. Richard Giannone, *Music in Willa Cather's Fiction* (Lincoln: University of Nebraska Press, 1968), 241.
8. *Schubert's Songs,* 266.
9. Stefan Kunze, "Schubert's Song Cycles," *Franz Schubert Lieder,* vol. 3. Deutche Grammophone, n.d.
10. Friedrich Fischer-Dieskau, *The Fischer-Dieskau Book of Lieder,* trans. George Bird and Richard Stokes (New York: Knopf, 1977), 189.
11. *Schubert Songs,* 266.
12. Giannone, *Music,* 213–231.
13. *Schubert: The Muse and the Man* (Berkeley: University of California Press, 1997), 307.
14. *Book of Lieder,* 189.
15. Brian Newbould, *Schubert: The Muse and the Man* (Berkeley: University of California Press, 1997), 306.
16. Giannone, *Music,* 219, 220.
17. Henahan, Donal, "There is real drama in *Winterreise*" (*The New York Times* 4 August 1985) 17.

18. Willa Cather, *Not Under Forty* (Lincoln: University of Nebraska Press, 1968), 48–51.

19. Ibid., 51.

Bibliography

Cather, Willa. "The Novel Démeublé." *Not Under Forty*. Lincoln: University of Nebraska Press, 1968.

———. *Lucy Gayheart*. New York: Vintage, 1995.

Fischer-Dieskau, Friedrich. *The Fisher-Dieskau Book of Lieder*. Translated by George Bird and Richard Stokes. New York: Knopf, 1977.

———. *Schubert's Songs: A Biographical Study*. Translated by Kenneth S. Whitton. New York: Knopf, 1977.

Giannone, Richard. *Music in Willa Cather's Fiction*. Lincoln: University of Nebraska Press, 1968.

Kunze, Stefan. "Schubert's Song Cycles," *Franz Schubert Lieder*, vol. 3, Deutche Grammophone, n. d.

Newbould, Brian. *Schubert: The Muse and the Man*. Berkeley: University of California Press, 1997. M.

Skaggs, Merrill. "Key Modulations in Cather's Novels about Music." *Willa Cather Pioneer Newsletter* XXXIX (1995): 25–30.

Willa Cather and Leon Bakst: Her Portraitist Who Was Designer to Diaghilev's Russian Ballet

EVELYN HALLER

The Portrait: How and Why

In Paris during September and October of 1923 Cather sat for the Russian artist, Leon Bakst, whom she had chosen when prominent Omaha citizens wished to honor her with a portrait on permanent display at the Omaha Public Library. The unveiling of the portrait was to be a significant public event, for funding was provided by the women of Omaha whose donations ranged from fifty cents to twenty-five dollars. While E. K. Brown suggests that Cather had chosen Bakst "on the advice of friends,"[1] Cather knew her own mind and was confident in her decision. A month earlier (11 August 1923) she had written to Irene Miner Weisz that Bakst happened to be in Paris just then, and he was the most interesting man in sight. Moreover, some French friends of his liked her books and had told him about them; and he said he'd like to paint her. W. D. Edson, editor and publisher of *The Webster County Argus,* had the facts right when he wrote in her home county newspaper that Bakst had met Cather at a social occasion and had offered his services at half his usual fee. Bakst was said to be "moved by Miss Cather's notable achievements in the world of letters." On 13 September 1923, Edson quoted from an article in *The Nebraska State Journal,* written by its editor, Will Owen Jones. Then travelling in Europe, Jones had visited Mrs. Jan Hambourg, the former Isabelle McClung, while Cather was "spending the summer with her Pittsburgh friend living in a Paris suburb." Jones wrote of Bakst: "The painter spent last Sunday at the Hambourg place, apparently enjoying the day as a visitor, but in fact making a psychological study of his subject. . . . Bakst would not spend his summer on this task if he did not feel that he could produce a study worthy of the place his subject has won in the world of letters."[2]

In any case, an art-lover as aesthetically astute as Cather could have extrapolated what to expect from Bakst's revolutionary work for Diaghilev's ballet productions: Bakst was likely to paint a portrait *à la*

russe of strong color and sensitivity; but he would not flatter his
subject. She would probably have looked into the matter of his other
portraits which, on the whole, suggest Bakst's exaltation of suffering
while he renders the cumulative signs of age.[3] In short, whatever
Bakst did in fulfillment of the commission was not likely to be a
crowd-pleaser, nor to satisfy Omaha. Indeed, "Cather wrote Irene
Weisz before the sittings began that the people in Omaha were not
going to like the portrait because it would not be a photographic
likeness."[4] Yet Cather thought the picture would look like her in the
end. Although Cather anticipated that her patrons would not be
satisfied with a painting by Bakst, she herself was pleased enough, I
would argue, for a variety of reasons. Indeed, she said that the
Omahans ought to know his name, as she had assumed Irene Miner
Weisz did, well enough to be grateful to have a picture by him.[5]
Moreover, such a portrait would underscore in Nebraska's largest city
the distance Cather had traveled from both the state and its collective
taste.[6]

Bakst's personal plans conveniently called for a final portrait commission in the midst of other work. Though he died, unexpectedly,
the following year, Cather enjoyed their twenty-four sittings, as W. D.
Edson related to Cather's home county readers: "The artist entertains her as he works by telling Russian folk tales, which not only
interests her, but doubtless furnishes material which will later be
incorporated into her stories." And Bakst, making the most of their
time together, spoke to Cather in French and asked her to speak to
him in English. Edith Lewis recalled, "His charm and genius, his
winning, attractive personality made these sittings a delight, and the
two became warm friends." Temperamentally, Bakst and Cather were
suited in their understanding of work; Lady Duff Gordon, the cou-
turiere known as Lucile, observed of Bakst, her studio neighbor, "He
was one of the few people I would allow to be near me when I was
working, for he had one of the quietest and most restful personalities
of anyone I have ever met. He had the rare gift of silence and never
talked a great deal, although what he had to say was always worth-
while." Lady Gordon also noted the restfulness of his surroundings:
"The man whose blending of colours on the stage was . . . so audacious it took one's breath away, decorated his own rooms in shades
of grey." Cather was photographed with Bakst in his elegant grey-
toned studio decorated with Asian art and a reproduction of Dona-
tello's "David," although the note in the Rizzoli Publishers book on
the artist does not identify her. To our amusement, author Charles
Spencer writes: "The lady, also known in another extant photograph

showing Bakst painting her portrait, is unknown." Bakst's address at 122 Boulevard Malsherbes was comprised of two apartments joined by an interior staircase to provide both home and studio. His atelier "resembled rather a rich flat of a man of taste than a painter's studio," and demonstrated Bakst's commitment to order: "Disorder is an obstacle to regular work. When everything is in order, the thoughts are in order as well, and the work is smoothly running on."[7] Similarly, in Cather's *Shadows on the Rock* the Auclaire household in Quebec is a domestic fortress against the disorder and barbarism of the wilderness. Order mattered greatly to Cécile's parents: her deceased mother who had trained her and her fastidious father who sustained her in a civilizing mode of life. Indeed, Cather demonstrates in this novel that lovingly kept space is sacred space.

Bakst's portrait shows a seated Cather, in a cream-colored silk or wool dress, holding a book open with her left hand while her right hand holds an ivory paper cutter[8] as if she had looked up to reflect on life itself, as well as on what she has been reading. While James Woodress concedes that "the painting is not flattering," he addresses a more important issue: "Bakst's sitter was a middle-aged woman going through a profound physical, emotional, and spiritual crisis. The portrait bares the soul of Professor St. Peter, whose similar problems Cather had already begun to describe."[9] The subject of the portrait would not look happy or pleased with her comparatively secure fortunes which included a recently awarded Pulitzer Prize for *One of Ours*. Rather, she would look like a middle aged woman of letters who valued the life of the soil and who had read Tolstoy, Gogol, and Turgenev as well as Flaubert—a writer who, in other words, was both Slavophile and Francophile. The poet Louise Bogan understood this mix: "she admires the power and breadth of the Russians even more than the delicacy and form of the French."[10] Cather, moreover, understood suffering and respected the Russian capacity for it.

A dimension of the Russian capacity for suffering was evidenced by Nijinsky when Cather met him in Bakst's studio; after kissing her hand, the dancer went to stand in a corner, thinking he was a horse. Four years earlier Nijinsky had been diagnosed in Zurich by Dr. Eugen Bleuler, who defined the clinical category Joan Acocella describes: "From 1919 onward, [Nijinsky] was basically a chronic schizophrenic. He was helpless; he could not brush his teeth or tie his shoelaces by himself. When [his wife] Romola settled in a place where she could keep him, she took him home. The rest of the time, he lived in institutions."[11] Nijinsky's visit to Bakst's studio while

Cather was sitting for her portrait must have occurred while he was staying with his family.

Like Cather and Bakst, Nijinsky was an experimental artist. Lincoln Kirstein observed that Nijinsky evinced "theories as profound as had ever been articulated about the classical theatrical dance." As Acocella observes, "above all, he needed to choreograph." Cather, as the acclaimed author of a novel about World War I, met in Nijinsky a great artist whose final performance also concerned war. It was a dance concert before an invited audience at the Suvretta House, a hotel in Paris, 19 January 1919. First Nijinsky, having seated himself on a chair, stared at his audience for perhaps half an hour. "Eventually, he unrolled two lengths of velvet, one white, one black to form a cross on the floor. Standing at the head of the cross, he addressed the audience: 'Now I will dance you the war, the war which you did not prevent.' He then launched into a violent solo, presumably improvised, and at some point stopped."[12]

Cather, either coincidentally or serendipitously, made use of a graphic device similar to Nijinsky's black and white cross. In her war novel, the Nebraska farmboy Claude Wheeler, now a lieutenant, stops at a military cemetery for Allied and enemy soldiers while waiting for nightfall before continuing to the front in the company of his sergeant:

> Hicks, too had been lost in his reflections. Now he broke the silence. "Somehow, Lieutenant, '*mort*' seems deader than 'dead.' It has a coffinish sound. And over there they're all '*tod*,' and it's all the same damned silly thing. Look at them set out here, black and white, like a checkerboard. The next question is, who put 'em here, and what's the good of it?"
> "Search me," the other murmured absently.[13]

Here, like Nijinsky, Cather demonstrates the power of the visual image. As Wheeler and Hicks depart, "The white crosses were now violet, and the black ones had altogether melted in the shadow. Behind the dead trees in the west, a long smear of red still burned" (*OO*, 1246). Indeed, as I argue elsewhere, Cather structured her war novel with the metaphor of quilts both named and alluded to in the text.[14]

The power of the simplified or abstracted image informed modernist visual arts. During his youth in St. Petersburg, Nijinsky had taken instruction in drawing from Leon Bakst. Starting in January, 1919, Nijinsky sometimes drew through the night. Romola Nijinsky describes her fright at his drawings: "'eyes peering from every corner, red and black." When she asked, "What are those masks?" he replied, "Soldiers' faces. It is the war."[15]

In her 1931 *New Yorker* profile, Louise Bogan, following the common misconception, congratulated "the ladies of Omaha" for making "an extremely appropriate choice" with Bakst, for Cather "has a strain of Tartar in her temperament." Certainly the reflexive choices and temperamental responses of this painter and his subject seem similar. Both found the theatre a source for play as children: Cather by reciting poetry and acting; Bakst by making toy theatres to entertain his younger siblings. Both had enjoyed magic lanterns. Both voiced extraordinary ambition at an early age: Cather's single-minded focus on art we are familiar with; "When his friends played the truth game Bakst frankly admitted, "I would like to be the most famous artist in the world." Both erased chronological fact: Bakst attempted "to lop off" two years from his age, as Cather lopped off three. Young Willa preferred boyish attire, while Bakst prophesied to an interviewer in New York in 1922, "Eventually it will be, I believe, that men and women will dress much alike."[16]

1998: Cather's Choice of Bakst: Wise or Unwise?

In their presentations at the Cather Colloquium at Drew in 1998, both Sharon O'Brien and Philip Gerber asserted that Cather was unhappy with her portrait by Bakst. Her dislike of the "unflattering" Bakst painting, O'Brien suggested, was a contributing factor in the development of her depression. E. K. Brown gives not only a scenario of Cather's regret at disappointing the generous people of Omaha, but also of Bakst's desperation at how badly the portrait was going. Brown further suggests that Bakst's need for money was driven by his support of a number of impoverished White Russians in Paris. Hence, Cather's compassion would not allow her to discharge Bakst. While Brown is persuasive, his interpretation of what transpired in Bakst's studio is challenged by the success of the portrait both as a depiction of Cather and as a painting.[17] The consanguinity of Cather and Bakst can be argued from Cather's literary texts and Bakst's visual art.

Did Cather care about ballet? Helen Cather Southwick spoke to me of her aunt's mailing ballet programs to her family. Given the considerable stretches of time Cather spent in London and Paris as well as in New York, it is very probable that she was acquainted with developments within this astonishing art form. Starting in 1909, the Russian dancers performed both in Paris and in London. In 1916 Nijinsky was with Diaghilev's company for a season at the Metropolitan Opera House in New York. A second season in the United States was followed by a cross-country tour of fifty-two cities in four months. Be it noted that the performances of Diaghilev's company astonished the Russians themselves. Russian embassies were admonished to avoid giving any impression of official support. Newspapers and magazines kept the public aware of the art form wherein the impresario Diaghilev and his colleagues combined music, dance, and the visual arts. As a result, fashions in clothing and interior decoration were changed dramatically. Alison Settle attributes "the true basis for the birth of Paris couture" to "the arrival in Paris in 1909 of the Diaghilev Ballet. What changed not only couture, but also interior decoration was . . . the colour which Bakst put into the background."[18]

Not only did Cather delight in the theatre—a long-standing interest, but she also chose to wear bright colors in the fashionable although theatrical fabrics of the time: velvet and silk. Indeed, Burton Rasco writing in *Arts and Decorations* in 1924 commented on Cather's "extraordinary courage to wear at the same time salmon and green" which she does "with complete success." Rasco, repeating the misconception, had "wondered why the women of Omaha had chosen that artistic Tartar barbarian, of all painters." But no longer was he in doubt: "there is probably no portraitist who would be more understanding and appreciative of the strength and subtleties of her character and handsomeness." Obviously, Cather's taste coincided with Bakst's to a remarkable degree. Consider Bakst's set for "Cleopatra": "A temple of pure rose and gold and a strip of Nile green seen between the columns." In 1924 Cather described Bakst as an artist who "does not become conventionalized by any art, not even his own. And it is in his perfectly relaxed hours when he is simply playing with his material as he played with his magic lantern when he was a boy, that he does his very best work. He has a playful idea about the scaly hide of a monster or the tight little skullcap of a Grecian queen, and then sends the Paris costumers racing about everywhere for material that will take the particular shape or give off the particular color he has in his mind."[19]

Because Cather cited Bakst's use of color, his own commentary on color bears quoting:

I have often noticed that in each colour of the prism there exists a gradation which sometimes expresses frankness and chastity, sometimes sensuality and even bestiality, sometimes pride, sometimes despair. This can be felt and given over to the public by the effect one makes of the various shadings. That is what I tried to do in Scheherazade. Against a lugubrious green I put a blue full of despair, paradoxical as it may seem. There are reds which are triumphal and there are reds which assassinate. . . . The painter who knows how to make use of this, the director who can with one movement of his baton put all this in motion, without crossing them, who can let flow the thousand tones from the end of his stick, without making a mistake, can draw from the spectator the exact emotion which he wants them to feel.

Clearly it was not merely a matter of color, but of what color signified. As Propert observed, "Two untranslatable French words give us the keynote of his work—*volupte* and *luxe* are written all over them." Ancient times in Russia, Greece, India, and Persia provided inspiration as Bakst's set designs, costumes, and program covers for the Ballet Russes demonstrate.[20] The exotic also offered opportunities for representation of violence and generation of erotic tension.

As with Bakst, one can often find both violence and eroticism in Cather's treatments. Like Bakst, Cather was aware of the heightening of drama through the presence of "the other," the perpetual stranger which she employed in her 1892 story, "A Tale of the White Pyramid." The Egyptian narrator says of the Hebrew: "my eyes were upon him continually, for I had seen no other man like unto him for beauty of face or form."[21] Unlike Cather, Bakst's use of Hebrew material was personal, for Bakst strongly identified with his Jewish heritage despite a temporary conversion to Christianity.[22] Bakst designed notably sensuous costumes for "Hebrews" in the 1909 ballet "Cleopatra."

Ancient Statues

That Cather and Bakst both drew inspiration from ancient statues is a further element of synchronicity in how they structured their art. In 1892 the nineteen-year-old Cather wrote "A Tale of the White Pyramid." Cather's description of the Hebrew's act of life-threatening bravery—a leap "over eighteen cubits" onto "the uppermost end" of the apex stone of a pyramid, as he guides it into place after a rope breaks—conveys the stance of a major Egyptian god: "He stood with both hands clenched at his side, his right foot a little before his left, erect and fair as the statue of Houris [Horus], watching the farther end of the stone" (*CSF,* 532).

By the age of thirty when her collection of poems, *April Twilights,* was published in 1903, Cather had written a poem expressive of erotic grief on Antinous, the Emperor Hadrian's lover who drowned in the Nile or, perhaps, as Marguerite Yourcenar was later to suggest in *Memoirs of Hadrian* (1951), committed ritual suicide. Bernice Slote ascribes Cather's source for her description of Antinous—"With attributes of gods they sculptured him, / Hermes, Osiris"—to the statue in the Farnese Collection in Naples, adding, "Though she did not visit Naples until 1908, Cather must have seen pictures or replicas of this statue." The speaker asks Antinous, "Did the perfection of thy beauty pain / Thy limbs to bear it? Did it ache to be, / As song hath ached in men, or passion vain?" (*AT,* 18) As Slote wisely observes of Cather, "Nothing in her work is unrelated to the whole. In the poems (as in the first stories . . .), we find the early sketches, the first motifs, the suggested design of her major work."[23]

At approximately the same time, Bakst drew on his 1905 trip to Greece to paint a monumental oil on canvas (2.85 by 3.0 meters) which he named "Terror Antiquus." Huntley Carter notes in a 1912 catalogue to an exhibition of Bakst's work for The Fine Arts Society that Bakst's aim was "to realize a vast landscape groaning beneath the terror of a cataclysm of nature." Dominating the foreground of the painting—indeed "rising from the scene of desolation and disaster, is 'the calm triumphant image of Aphrodite-Isis'" based on the "Peplos" Kore which is now in the Acropolis Museum. "The tortured landscape with mountains, out-sized statues, and breaking buildings is depicted from a vantage point high above the earthquake which, perhaps, refers to that which ended the Minoan civilization on Crete." When Bakst visited Knossos, Sir Arthur Evans was at work on his reconstruction. Propert wrote that Bakst "would prefer to go down to prosperity as the austere painter of "Terror Antiquus.""[24] Nonetheless, the Peplos Kore also inspired costumes for the nymphs in "The Afternoon of a Faun."

The fact that the Diaghilev company deliberately drew on Russia's legendary past also appealed to Cather. Recall that Bakst entertained Cather during their sittings by telling Russian folk tales. We turn now to *Lucy Gayheart,* which draws on Diaghilev's production of "The Firebird" (Paris, 1910; London, 1911) for which Bakst designed the costume of the Firebird and the Tsarevna. Bakst also designed a second set of costumes for the Firebird and for the Tsarevitch in 1920.[25]

Transmutations of the Firebird, of St. Sebastian, and of Monsters Called Demigods

Lucy Gayheart's characterization is influenced by Bakst's designs for the Firebird in the Stravinsky ballet. The description of Lucy includes frequent references to the color red and to rapid joyous movement, as when she ice skates: "The two ends of a long crimson scarf were floating on the wind behind her, like two slender crimson wings."[26] In her hometown the flying motion of her childhood footprint at thirteen is preserved in concrete—"the print of her toes was deeper than the heel"—and later protected by Harry Gordon (*LG*, 227). When he recalls his happiness as Lucy accompanied him while he hunted ducks—the Tsarevitch in "The Firebird" is a hunter—he felt "it flash by his ear" (*LG*, 223). Indeed Lucy is a firebird at the side of Harry Gordon as hunter and as excellent dancer. When she hastens along the lakefront in Chicago, "the sharp air that blew off the water brought up all the fire of life in her; it was like drinking fire" (*LG*, 47). Moreover, "Her mind had got away from her and was darting about in the sunlight, over the tops of the tall buildings" (*LG*, 40). The singer Clement Sebastian, who loves her, quotes Montaigne about the joy of youth being in the feet. As Lucy mourns the death of Sebastian she finds comfort in a desolate apple orchard in stark contrast to the tree bearing golden apples in Kostchei's enchanted garden within the Diaghilev production.

Lucy Gayheart is the most erotic of Cather's novels, depending as it does on the erotic frustration of unconsummated love. When Clement Sebastian strokes the red feather in Lucy's fur hat or takes her muff, we have transferred episodes of physical lovemaking. While Sebastian and Lucy frequently make melody together as singer and piano accompanist, their congress is not directly physical.

That another ballet influenced the characterization of Clement Sebastian is suggested by Fairy Blair's Freudian slip—"That Mr. Saint Sebastian who was drowned in Italy, wasn't he the singer you played for?" (*LG*, 176)—when she gloatingly confronts Lucy with gossip about her relationship in Chicago. Clement Sebastian's characterization relates to "The Martyrdom of St. Sebastian"—not a Diaghilev production—wherein d'Annunzio's poem was set to music by Debussy to be performed by the mime and art patron, Ida Rubenstein. The ballet continues the Christian legend of the Roman officer transfixed with arrows shot by his soldiers. The sadistic/androgynous aspects of the legend and its interpretations in art[27] relate to Cle-

ment Sebastian's relationship and death with his accompanist James
Mockford.

Visual Artists Cather and Her Russian Contemporaries Admired

Bakst (1866–1924), with Diaghilev, was in a Moscow-based group
that shared the young Cather's attraction to the same innovative
artists in Western Europe. Hence, in their artistic development
Cather and Bakst shared a number of enthusiasms. By 1899 the
variously named Moscow-based Society for Self-Improvement (or
Self-Education), or The Nevsky Pickwickians, was particularly interested in the paintings of Puvis de Chavannes, the Swedish painter
Anders Zorn, and the English Pre-Raphaelites.[28] Cather was in-
sightfully aware of developments in the arts of her time, not only for
aesthetic pleasure but also as sources for structural as well as referen-
tial treatment in her own literary art.

Cather's desire to write in the style of Puvis de Chavannes in *Death
Comes for the Archbishop* needs no repetition here. The windless calm
of his painting doubtless held great attraction for Cather, who as the
child Willie in her Rebel cap had been uprooted to the wind-incised
plains of Nebraska. Furthermore, one sees in Puvis de Chavanne's
paintings dramatic groupings of characters not unlike that of historical paintings or photographs of scenes from ballets. Although ballet
is about movement, the photograph or the costume sketch can in-
duce a stasis from which one may extrapolate what has gone before
and what will come after. Alexandre Benois wrote in the Russian
journal *Retch,* that he "admired Bakst's genius for composing what
might be termed "kinetic" pictures from static and moving elements
in which the extraordinary range of colour, the brilliant draping
and transforming of the human body, established a dichotomous
harmony."[29]

In Cather's fictionalized account written for *The Nebraska State Journal* of her visit to Burne-Jones's studio on her first trip to Europe in
the summer of 1902, we can see that Cather herself came "under the
subtle and melancholy spell" of his art.[30] In Cather's text, Burne-
Jones's valet James, who remains as guardian of the studio, draws her
attention to "a number of studies he made for the mermaid—everybody knows that paintin'. He had great trouble with the pose, and
done them over a good bit, and here's the study for the head of the
dead man she was draggin' under the sea" (*WCE* 74). The structure

of Burne-Jones's painting is implied in Cather's description of Clement Sebastian's descent into the depths: "Mockford must have fastened himself to his companion with a stranglehold and dragged him down" with, perhaps, an expression akin to the mermaid's triumphant smile of satisfaction (*LG*, 138). One might, speculatively, compare descriptions of James Mockford with Bakst's aquarelle of a greenish demigod with a long and curving tail shown in semi-profile from the ballet "Narcisse" (1911). Another such instance is Bakst's brilliantly green although red-tongued "Submarine Monster" designed for an underwater sequence in the 1911 ballet "Sadko."[31] Mockford's eyes "were frankly green . . . with something restless in them." Again: "He looked as if he were made up for the stage, yet there he sat in perfectly conventional clothes, except for a green silk shirt and green necktie" (*LG*, 57, 59). I present the latter instances as matters of synchronicity rather than probable direct influence as in the instance of Burne-Jones's "The Depths of the Sea" (1886).

Cather's picture-making with its arrested dramatic movement has been witnessed to by illustrators of her own time as well as by the tableaux sometimes on display in the old bank building in Red Cloud. Another potent source in Cather's picture-making with its bright colors and arrested dramatic movement can be ascribed in part to Bakst, who also studied and admired the work of the Pre-Raphaelites. But Cather's description of Lucy Gayheart resembles "Portrait of a Girl's Head" by Burne-Jones in red pastel and chalk on paper: "her skin was rather dark, the colour in her lips and cheeks was like the red of dark poppies—deep, velvety" (*LG*, 4–5).[32]

Paintings by Anders Zorn provide precedent for the goddess-like beauty of Thea Kronberg in *The Song of the Lark* as well as the pearlescent glow of Edna, the future Eden Bower, at her Swedish exercises in "Coming, Aphrodite!": "Yonder, in a pool of sunlight, stood his new neighbor, wholly unclad, doing exercises of some sort before a long gilt mirror."[33] Cather's insertion of the sensuous scene with Don Hedger looking through the knothole is skillful. Because Hedger is accustomed to painting from nude models, she is able to depict his voyeurism as an aesthetic experience, the vision of the naked goddess as something "out of the remote pagan past" (*SP&OW*, 366–67). Woodress observes, however, that "The editor who bought the story would have been startled to have a present-day reader point out to him that the explosive and gesture imagery suggests masturbation." An analogy, if not a source of inspiration, can be found in Nijinsky's falling upon the nymph's scarf at the conclusion of the ballet, "The Afternoon of a Faun." Considering the scandal that ensued, there can be no doubt of the intended effect of the balletic movement on the audience in 1912. As Martin Green comments, "Diaghilev found for his Ballets Russes a social space between, or rather above, both the music hall and the Imperial Theatres. It was not socially respectable, but it was aesthetically triumphant."[34]

The Three Erotic Ballets

A major source for the inset story, "The Forty Lovers of the [Aztec] Queen," in "Coming, Aphrodite!" is the Diaghilev productions of "The Three Erotic Ballets": "Cleopatra" (1909), "Scheherazade" (1910), and "Thamar" (1912). As James Laver wrote in 1923: "The frank voluptuousness of 'Scheherazade' was followed by the seductive cruelty of 'Cleopatra.' In all of these Bakst demonstrated the astonishing virtuosity of his handling of colour, and the curious directness and violence of his appeal to the senses. There is little subtlety in his work." "The Forty Lovers of the [Aztec] Queen," sited in "Coming, Aphrodite!" (1920), is replete with "frank voluptuousness" and "seductive cruelty." Indeed the artist Don Hedger uses the story as a strategy to seduce the young singer who has recently exposed herself to exhibitionistic danger by substituting for another woman in a balloon ascent and descent at Coney Island. Woodress correctly cites Cather's claim that she heard the story in Mexico: "she remembered the story of the Aztec Cleopatra. . . . She also thought she remembered reading the tale in Prescott's *Conquest of Mexico*, but Julio's account was much more alive."[35] "The Three Erotic Ballets" are nonetheless a more compelling source.

In "Cleopatra" (1909) the mime Ida Rubenstein was carried onstage in a gold and ebony chest from which she emerged and was set on ivory pattens as a mummy wrapped in twelve veils distinctive not only for their vivid colors but also their designs. Cleopatra offers a handsome slave "a night of love, with death at its end" which he accepts despite his love for the slave, Ta-Hor. It is she who "breaks into frenzied weeping" over his dead body after he has accepted "the poisoned cup" in the morning.[36]

The book of the "Scheherazade" (1910) ballet —*une conte persan*— is ascribed to Leon Bakst (but disputed by Alexandre Benois). The subtitle of this ballet is "*L'Histoire d'une sultane indépendante et d'un petit nègre gris*" which parallels the story of the Aztec queen. Moreover, the independent sultaness has multiple manifestations in various colors during the orgy on stage. "Queen Tamara [Thamar]," according to Spencer, "entices, seduces, and then kills innocent travellers, whose bodies are cast into the River Terek" in the interior of a Georgian castle. Propert writes, "The sheer height of the walls echoed the relentless cruelty of the crowd that filled the room, and the great black coats of the stranger and of the Queen's servants, among the reds and blues of the women, startled one to a sense of impending tragedy." As Gerald Goode recounts the climax: "the green door opens again and the youth staggers backward into the room, dazed. Thamar follows, her voluptuous beauty now a sinister mask. She leans over him, gazes into his face with a smile, and with an arm around his neck drags his unresisting form about the room. Now her hand goes to her girdle, she kisses his eyes, and with a flash she plunges her dagger into his breast. He totters, clutching the air, and falls backward through a swiftly opened panel in the wall, into the torrent below." "Thamar" wrote Propert, "was the third and, so far, the last of the erotic ballets, and dealt again with the love-storms of Eastern queens and their slaughtered lovers. It was the most lurid of the three, and the scenario was of Bakst's own concocting. Our moralists began to assure us that the Russian Ballet was a degenerate affair and Bakst clearly an erotomaniac."[37]

The sexual voraciousness of Cather's Aztec queen combined with her power to drown discarded lovers in an exotic setting, can be paralleled with Bakst's three erotic ballets. Although Cather's subject is punished for her betrayal of her lord, her death by fire brings drought. Hence, the Aztec queen's voraciousness is identified with a force of nature like thunder as well as rain, and the deaths of her lovers recall sacrificial rites of mythic times. The mother of the princess who would become the Aztec queen "dreamed three times that she was delivered of serpents, which betokened that the child she carried would have power with the rain gods. The serpent was the symbol of water" (*SP&OW*, 382–83).

My Mortal Enemy (1926) offers Cather's transposition of Bakst's set for "Le Dieu Bleu" (1912), a ballet set in India about the Hindu god Krishna. Bakst designed the set with immensely long live snakes hung over racks in the viewer's right-hand foreground. In the novel, snake motifs occur in relation to Myra. Other factors are her taste for sumptuous settings as well as her cruelty to her husband, Oswald Henshaw. Myra's taste for sumptuous settings and clothes is, however, also related to the ballet "Scheherazade" (1910). Moreover, Myra can be a seductive teller of tales.

Other Portraits by Bakst

Around 1905 Bakst painted a portrait of Diaghilev. The impresario was in his early thirties when he mounted an extraordinary exhibition of Russian portraiture made possible in large part by the connections he enjoyed as a member of the nobility. It was also the time of the 1905 Revolution. Significantly, Bakst portrays him in his Moscow apartment with his old nurse seated but leaning slightly toward the right in the background. Although Diaghilev stands at three-quarter height in the foreground, his body inclines toward the old woman, so the painting becomes a sensitive double portrait of the nobleman and of his devoted nurse, both separated and united by a grey curtain. "Arnold Haskell thinks there is a conscious symbolism in Diaghilev looking ahead, with his possessions in the background." Bakst also made a drawing of Diaghilev's old nurse which Prince Lieven reproduced in his *The Birth of the Ballet Russe.* When Spencer writes that "Meetings of the Editorial Board [of *The World of Art*] always took place in the dining room at teatime—served by the old nanny . . . ," he suggests that she was a familiar person to the Diaghilev circle.[38]

Around 1905 and 1906 Bakst made portrait pencil sketches of four male colleagues: the painter Alexander Golovin who worked at the Maryinsky Theatre in St. Petersburg and would later work on "The Firebird" in 1910; the composer Balakirev, after whose death his music would be used for the 1912 "Thamar" which Bakst designed; C. A. Somov, a painter and member of *The World of Art* group; and the poet Andrei Bely. Golovin is presented in a large frontal view suggesting affability. While Balakirev and Somov are shown in three-quarter view, only Balakirev, among the four, looks to the side introspectively. In most of the portraits Bakst suggests collars, ties, and jackets with only a few lines except in that of Andrei Bely where the more realized drawing of his jacket, collar, tie, and sweater suggest lines drawn by van Gogh. Bakst also made a charcoal or pencil sketch of the American dancer Isadora Duncan during her second visit to Russia in 1908 when she had dined with Pavlova, Benois, and Bakst. Duncan is not glamorized: a developing double chin and incipient rolls of fat are shown on the neck.[39] Bakst's 1922 portrait of Madame Stravinsky shows a pensive woman with head inclined, shoulders drooping, and heavy arms lying loosely on her lap. There can be no doubt that Bakst was drawn to celebrities. Coco Chanel wrote in her memoirs that Bakst, "that old parrot . . . ran after me to let him do my portrait."[40]

These instances do not exhaust the portraits done by Bakst. There is, for example, a life-sized full-body portrait of *Nijinsky at the Lido* depicting the dancer in scarlet trunks resembling a loin cloth, with another cloth covering his hair. Nijinsky's arm is raised up in a dramatic gesture. It is from a series of three entitled "Lido, Venice—Study of the Bathers."[41]

Nonetheless, two Bakst sketches of peasant women from 1922 for the perhaps unrealized satirical sketch by Potemkine, "Moskwa," induced his biographer, Andre Levinson, to write: "He is completely absorbed by this forgotten world which arises about him as the background of a distant past. He is consumed by an appetite for Russian memories." These drawings bear comparison with Louise Bogan's 1931 description of Cather's predilection for an urbanized version of Russian peasant costume as realized in the late painter's sketches of nearly a decade before: "Her dresses are bright in color; she likes brilliant embroidery, boldly designed materials, and exotic strings of beads." One sketch shows an individualized peasant woman's face of lively humor; the other, a stronger face atop a theatrical peasant costume, recalls Burton Rasco's description of Cather: "her mouth is ample, with full, flexible lips whose movements are as expressive an accompaniment of her speech as the gestures of a Latin; and her nose is a nose, not a tracery."[42] These sketches bring us back to the aptness of Cather's choice of Bakst to paint her portrait. He realized an artistic success because his subject, her tastes, and her accomplishments were akin to his own.

Coda

Cather was not present when her portrait was unveiled in Omaha 30 December 1923, "having been detained in New York," as *The Omaha Bee* reported.[43] Cather's sister was quoted as saying that the picture made Miss Cather "look very much older than she now is." Augustus W. Dunbier, described as "the only Nebraska artist who has exhibited in the Pennsylvania Academy of Fine Arts," declared: "the drawing in Bakst's picture is faulty, and the figure entirely lacking in structural quality. Bakst has made of Miss Cather a Russian peasant. The canvas is not a museum piece, and without Bakst's signature would have no interest whatever. Bakst is a decorative artist, not a portrait painter."[44] Ironically, as Louise Bogan noted, Cather chose to present herself more as a Russian peasant than Bakst portrayed her.

Walter Pach, a visiting lecturer from New York, attacked both the painter and the painting, severely casting doubt on Bakst's abilities and preparation as a portraitist: "Bakst won popularity as a designer of costumes during the craze for Russian dancers. He has been working since then on the strength of that reputation. He has never been a portrait painter; as far as I can see never will be. The painting of Miss Cather is awful. In the French sense of art that painting doesn't exist. . . . Bakst should keep on with his Russian designs that were helped to the front by the dancers and musicians."[45]

Amid newspaper and probably oral reports of dissatisfaction with the Bakst portrait, Cather wrote letters to two prominent Omaha citizens which were quoted in *The Omaha Bee*. To Judge Duncan C. Visonhaler, who had headed the fund raising committee, she wrote: "The Portrait is finished and is satisfactory to me." To Mrs. Guy C. Kiddoo, publicity chairman of the Omaha Society of Fine Arts, Cather expresses reasons for her respect for Bakst as an artist:

> I believe one of the secrets of Bakst's originality, both as a scenic artist and a designer of costumes and stage effects, is that he constantly goes back to the primitive art of half barbarous peoples among whom clothes and ornaments and even architecture were much more matters of personal, individual taste than they are now.
>
> In his portfolios he has many color sketches made in the country districts of Russia, sketches of boys and girls in the homely and home-made costumes they had invented for themselves for a holiday. But, of course, his studies have gone much further back than Russia.
>
> Years ago he spent a long while in the island of Crete, where all that rich and very unconventional art was being unearthed; sculpture and frescoes and pottery that have so influenced our modernists. His splendid production of d'Annunzio's "Phaedra" in Paris last summer was done almost entirely from his studies in Crete. It was by far the richest thing I have ever seen on the stage; enough, one would think to exhaust even a great imagination.[46]

When Bakst entertained Cather with Russian folktales during their sittings, one story may have resembled the firebird Martin Green relates: "the firebird is a village girl with a great gift for the traditional skill of colorful embroidery. When travelling merchants visit her village, they suggest that she come to the city, where rich people will appreciate and reward her skill. But she says she belongs where she was born, where her ancestors live and are buried. Then the sorcerer, Kostchei, begins to practice his deceptions upon her, promising every dazzling prize, but in vain. In fury, he transforms himself into a firebird with brilliant feathers like her own embroidery. Clutching her in his claws, he rises into the air above the village. But she, in despair, plucks out her own brilliant feathers, which fall to earth for men to find." Green adds: "In other words, the folk arts of rural Russia, taken to the metropolis by an impresario like Diaghilev, leave behind brilliant but tragic mementos in the form of these ballets."[47] Yet the folktale of the Firebird is also an allegory of the artist, especially modernist artists like Cather and Bakst, who assuredly draw upon artist-ancestors. While Cather recognized her "home pasture" with *O, Pioneers!*, she, like Bakst, also recognized her role as inheritor. Both Cather and Bakst drew upon art so old it was new.

Notes

I wish to express my thanks to Thomas Heenan, Manager of the History and Social Science Department, and to Linda Trout, Special Projects Manager, at the Omaha Public Library for permission to reproduce the Bakst portrait, which serves as frontispiece for this volume.

1. E. K. Brown, *Willa Cather: A Critical Biography*, completed by Leon Edel (New York: Knopf, 1953), 179.

2. W. D. Edson, "The Editor's Column," *Webster County [Nebraska] Argus* (13 September 1923), reprinted in L. Brent Bohlke, ed., *Willa Cather in Person: Interviews, Speeches, and Letters* (Lincoln: University of Nebraska Press, 1986), 60. When Bohlke is not mentioned in a note, the citation is taken directly from *The Webster County Argus*.

3. Bakst's work was exhibited in 1916 at Scott & Fowles and again in 1922 at the Knoldler Gallery while Cather lived in New York. See Charles Spencer, *Leon Bakst* (New York: Rizzoli, 1973), 241; and Sharon O'Brien, "Chronology," *Willa Cather: Early Novels and Stories* (New York: Library of America, 1987), 1309, 1311.

4. Much of Cather's correspondence to Irene Miner Weisz about Bakst, which is in the collection of the Newberry Library in Chicago, can be found in James Woodress, *Willa Cather: A Literary Life* (Lincoln: University of Nebraska Press, 1987), 339.

5. Willa Cather to Irene Miner Weisz, 11 August 1923.

6. I am indebted to Marvin Friedman, a native Lincolnite, for amplification and corroboration of this idea.

7. Edson, *Argus,* 13 September 1923; Edith Lewis, *Willa Cather Living: A Personal Memoir* (Lincoln: University of Nebraska Press, 1976), 131–32; Lady Duff Gordon, *Discretions and Indiscretions* (London: Jarrolds, 1932), n. p., quoted in Charles Spencer, *Leon Bakst* (New York: Rizzoli, 1973), 190; Spencer, *Leon Bakst,* 239 n. 199; Valerian Svietlov with Louis Reau, Denis Roche and A. Tessier, *Inedited Works of Bakst* (New York: Brentano's, 1927), n. p., quoted in Spencer, *Leon Bakst,* 190.

8. My thanks to Thomas Heenan of the Omaha Public Library for his help in recognizing the ivory or whalebone page cutter in the Bakst portrait; and to him for making available relevant Omaha newspaper accounts from 1923–1924.

9. Woodress, *WC,* 339.

10. Louise Bogan, "Profiles: American Classic," *The New Yorker,* 8 August 1931, reprinted in Bohlke, 113–19. Louise Bogan (1897–1970) was the poetry critic for *The New Yorker* for thirty-eight years (1931–1968). This insightful profile of Cather was the only non-fiction piece she published with the magazine in addition to several

hundred poetry reviews, about a half-dozen short stories, and her own poems. Like Cather, Bogan was elected to the American Academy of Arts and Letters.

11. Brown, *Biography*, 237; Lewis, *Living*, 132; Joan Acocella, "Introduction," *The Diary of Vaslav Nijinsky: Unexpurgated Edition,* trans. Kyril Fitzlyon (New York: Farrar, Straus and Giroux, 1999), xxvi, xliii.

12. Lincoln Kirstein, "Interview" in John Drummond, *Speaking of Diaghilev,* 114, quoted in Acocella, *Nijinsky,* xlii; Ibid., xv, xx; Romola Nijinsky, *The Last Years of Vaslav Nijinsky* (New York: Simon and Schuster, 1952), 361, quoted in Acocella, *Nijinsky,* xx.

13. Willa Cather, *Early Novels and Stories,* ed. Sharon O'Brien (New York: Library of America, 1987), 1246.

14. A chapter of my book in progress on Cather's use of the arts including architecture and dance, is entitled "The Quilt as Structural Metaphor in *One of Ours.*" A preliminary version appears in *The Nebraska Humanist* as "Willa Cather and Women's Art" (Fall 1989), 46–56.

15. R. Nijinsky, 353; quoted in Acocella, *Nijinsky,* 118–19. See two of Nijinsky's drawings reproduced in Acocella, xix and xxviii.

16. Bogan reprinted in Bohlke, *Person,* 118; Alexander Benois, *Reminiscences of the Russian Ballet* (London: Putnam, 1941), quoted in Spencer, *Leon Bakst,* 21. "Prince Lieven adds that in later life Bakst responded to a similar question: "I'm certainly the greatest painter in the world, I am the Russian Veronese." *The Birth of Russian Ballet* (London: Allen and Unwim, 1936), quoted in Spencer, *Leon Bakst,* 218 n. 22; Ibid., 19 and 187; "The Breadth of the Avenue." 2 December 1922; Quoted in Spencer, *Leon Bakst,* 221 n. 37.

17. O'Brien, "Chronology," *EN&S,* 1312; Brown, *Biography,* 180. Compare the verve and insight of the Bakst portrait Brent Bolke chose for the dust jacket of *Willa Cather in Person* with the insipid but jaunty portrait of Cather by Leon Gordon for *Good Housekeeping* (September 1931) which is Bohlke's frontispiece. Notice that the hands in the Bakst portrait are those of a worker, albeit an intellectual one; the hands in the Gordon portrait—tapered, feminine, languid—resemble the ideal of the Virginia lady Bernice Slote thought Cather aspired to be. Bakst had it right. As Louise Bogan observed, "It is impossible to imagine her strong hands in a deprecatory gesture" (Bohlke, *Person,*118). Burton Rasco wrote in *Arts and Decoration* (April 1924): "I believe the first thing I noticed about her was the forceful masculinity of her hands; they are strong hands without the so-called artist taper —which, by the way, I have observed very few artists possess" (Bohlke, *Person,* 65).

18. Conversation with Helen Cather Southwick, n. d.; Acocella, *Nijinsky,* xviii; Alison Settle, *Paris Fashions: The Great Designers and Their Creations,* ed. Ruth Lynam (London: Michael Joseph, 1972); quoted in Spencer, *Leon Bakst,*186.

19. Rasco; reprinted in Bohlke, *Person,* 65; W. A. Propert, *The Russian Ballet in Western Europe, 1909–1920 with a chapter on the Music by Eugene Goossens and Sixty-three Illustrations from Original Drawings* (New York: John Lane; The Bodley Head, 1921), 17; "Miss Cather Writes of the Personality of Bakst," *The Omaha Bee* (13 January 1924) wherein Cather's letter to Mrs. Guy Kiddoo is quoted. Cather may have wanted to diminish possible hostility in the audience that would hear Bakst's lecture on costume and dress under the auspices of the Omaha Society of Fine Arts which was to be held 18 January 1924. Bakst had requested that his portrait of Cather be hung behind the podium.

20. Bakst quoted in Mary Fanton Roberts, "The New Russian Stage: What the Genius of Leon Bakst has done to revivify productions which combine Ballet, Music

and Drama," *Craftsman,* Vol. 29, New York; quoted in Spencer, *Leon Bakst,* 70; Propert, *Russian Ballet* (See Spencer).

21. *Collected Short Fiction 1892–1912,* ed. Virginia Faulkner (Lincoln: University of Nebraska Press, 1970), 530.

22. Bakst was excluded from the St. Petersburg Academy of Arts for submitting in a free competition with the set subject of "The Madonna Weeping over Christ," "an enormous canvas in which all the . . . characters were depicted as peasant Jews. The Virgin was shown as a ragged, dishevelled old woman, her eyes red with weeping." See Spencer, *Leon Bakst,* 17.

23. Willa Cather, *April Twilights,* ed. Bernice Slote (Lincoln: University of Nebraska Press, 1990), ix.

24. The date of 1905 for Bakst's trip to Greece and Crete is tentative. Bakst's brief published account, *Serov and Myself in Greece* (Berlin: Slavo, 1923), gives no date. But Cather is likely to have heard him refer to the trip. Bakst had visited Athens, the Peleponeses, Crete, Aegina, and Corfu; Propert, quoted in Spencer, *Leon Bakst,* 39. Gerald Goode, ed., *The Book of Ballets: Classic and Modern* (New York: Crown, 1939), 63.

25. Propert, *Russian Ballet,* unnumbered plates.

26. Willa Cather, *Lucy Gayheart* (New York: Vintage, 1976), 8.

27. See Richard Kaye, "'A Splendid Readiness for Death': T. S. Eliot, the Homosexual Cult of St. Sebastian, and World War I," *Modernism/Modernity* 6:2 (April 1999): 107–34. On the cover of this issue is a photograph of Eddy Marsh as St. Sebastian.

28. Alan Bird, *A History of Russian Painting* (Oxford: Phaidon, 1987), 176; Spencer, *Leon Bakst,* 19.

29. Spencer, *Leon Bakst,* 72.

30. *Willa Cather in Europe: Her Own Story of Her First Journey,* ed. George N. Kates (Lincoln: University of Nebraska Press, 1988), 73.

31. These images can be seen in *Leon Bakst and the Art of the Ballets Russes: A Book of Postcards* (A649) from Pomegranate Artbooks (San Francisco) made from figures published in Arsene Alexander, *The Decorative Art of Leon Bakst: Notes on the Ballets by Jean Cocteau* (London: The Fine Art Society, 1913) at the San Francisco Performing Arts Library and Museum. The "Submarine Monster" designed for an underwater sequence in the 1911 ballet "Sadko" is also in Spencer, *Leon Bakst,* 148, Plate 21.

32. Edward Burne-Jones' "Portrait of a Girl's Head" in red pastel and chalk on paper is in the Lehman Collection at the Metropolitan Museum in New York.

33. Willa Cather, *Stories, Poems and Other Writings,* ed. Sharon O'Brien (New York: Library of America, 1992), 366.

34. Woodress, *WC,* 313–14; Martin Green and John Swan, *The Triumph of Pierrot: The Commedia dell'Arte and the Modern Imagination,* rev. ed. (University Park: Pennsylvania State University Press, 1993), 72.

35. James Laver, *A Concise History of Costume* (London: Thames and Hudson, 1969), n.p.; quoted in Spencer, *Leon Bakst;* Woodress, *WC,* 7.

36. Goode, *Ballets,* 64–65.

37. Spencer, *Leon Bakst,* 105; Propert, *Russian Ballet,* 19; Goode, *Ballets,* 226; Propert, 19.

38. Spencer, *Leon Bakst,* 30, Plate 12; Arnold L. Haskell, *Balletomania* (London: Gollancz, 1934), n.p., quoted in Spencer, 224, note on Plate 12; p. 29.

39. Spencer, *Leon Bakst,* pp. 36–37, Plates 17, 18, 20, 21; Spencer, unnumbered illustration, 229.

40. Marcel Haedrich, *Coco Chanel: Her Life, Her Secrets* (London: Robert Hale), n.p., quoted in Spencer, *Leon Bakst,* 172.

41. Spencer, *Leon Bakst,* 92, Plate 66 (size 2.03 meters × 1.16 meters).

42. Spencer, *Leon Bakst,* 236, Plates 148 and 149; Andre Levison, *Bakst, the Story of the Artist's Life,* quoted in Spencer, 236; Bogan, quoted in Bohlke, *Person,* 117; Rasco, "Willa Cather," quoted in Bohlke, 65.

43. *The Omaha Bee* (7 December 1923; in *The Webster County Argus,* W. D. Edson commented, "Miss Cather herself is not inclined to enjoy public affairs in her honor, and one is led to suspect that if she should express her inmost desire in the matter, she would inform the Omaha people that she would prefer that they quietly go to the library and suspend the picture in the allotted place rather than to have a big affair with herself as guest of honor" (11 October 1923).

44. Dunbier is quoted in Badollet, "Beaux-Arts," *The Omaha News* (16 January 1924).

45. Walter Pach, quoted in *The Omaha Bee* (11 January 1924).

46. Letters from Willa Cather to Judge Duncan Visonhaler and Mrs. Guy C. Kiddoo, quoted in *The Omaha Bee* (13 January 1924).

47. Green, *Pierrot,* 69.

Bibliography

Acocella, Joan. Introduction to The Diary of Vaslav Nijinsky: Unexpurgated Edition. Trans. Kyril Fitzlyon. New York: Farrar, Straus and Giroux, 1999.

Benois, Alexandre. *Reminiscences of the Russian Ballet.* London: Putnam, 1941.

Bird, Alan. *A History of Russian Painting.* Oxford: Phaidon, 1987.

Bogan, Louise. "Profiles: American Classic." *The New Yorker,* 8 August 1931.

Bohlke, L. Brent. *Willa Cather in Person: Interviews, Speeches, and Letters.* Lincoln: University of Nebraska Press, 1986.

Brown, E. K. *Willa Cather: A Critical Biography,* Completed by Leon Edel. New York: Avon, 1980.

Carter, Huntley. Introductions to Catalogues of Bakst Exhibitions. London: The Fine Arts Society, 1912 and 1913.

Cather, Willa. *April Twilights (1903).* Ed. Bernice Slote. Lincoln: University of Nebraska Press, 1990.

———. *Collected Short Fiction: 1892–1912.* Ed. Virginia Faulkner. Lincoln: University of Nebraska Press, 1970.

———. "Coming, Aphrodite." *Stories, Poems and Other Writings.* Ed. Sharon O'Brien. New York: The Library of America, 1992.

———. *Lucy Gayheart.* New York: Vintage, 1962.

———. *Willa Cather in Europe: Her Own Story of Her First Journey.* Ed. George N. Kates. Lincoln: University of Nebraska Press, 1988.

———. *One of Ours. Early Novels and Stories.* Ed. Sharon O'Brien. New York: The Library of America, 1987.

———. *The Song of the Lark. Early Novels and Stories.* Ed. Sharon O'Brien. New York: The Library of America, 1987.

Drummond, John. *Speaking of Diaghilev.* London: Faber and Faber, 1997.

Edson, W. D. "The Editor's Column." *Webster County [Nebraska] Argus.* 13 September 1923; 11 October 1923.

Goode, Gerald, ed. *The Book of Ballets: Classic and Modern*. New York: Crown Publishers, 1939.

Green, Martin and John Swan. *The Triumph of Pierrot: The Commedia dell'Arte and the Modern Imagination*. University Park: Pennsylvania State University Press, 1993.

Haedrich, Marcel. *Coco Chanel: Her Life, Her Secrets*. London: Robert Hale, 1972.

Haskell, Arnold L. and Walter Nouvel. *Diaghileff, His Artistic and Private Life*. London: Gollancz, 1935.

Kaye, Richard A. "'A Splendid Readiness for Death': T. S. Eliot, the Homosexual Cult of St. Sebastian, and World War I." *Modernism/Modernity* 6: 2 (April 1999): 107–134.

Kirstein, Lincoln. *Dance: A Short History of Classic Theatrical Dancing*. New York: Dance Horizons 1969; reprint of *The Book of the Dance*, 2nd ed., 1942.

Laurin, Carl, Emil Hannover, and Jens Thiis. *Scandinavian Art*. Bronx, NY: Benjamin Blom, 1968.

Laver, James. "The Russian Ballet in Retrospect." *The Studio: An Illustrated Magazine of Fine and Applied Art*. London 93 (1927).

Lewis, Edith. *Willa Cather Living*. Lincoln: University of Nebraska Press, 1976.

Lieven, Prince. *The Birth of the Russian Ballet*. London: Allen and Unwin, 1936.

Nijinsky, Romola. *The Last Years of Vaslav Nijinsky*. New York: Simon and Schuster, 1952.

O'Brien, Sharon. "Chronology." *Willa Cather: Early Novels and Stories*. New York: The Library of America, 1987.

Propert, W. A. *The Russian Ballet in Western Europe, 1909–1920* with a Chapter on the Music by Eugene Goossens and Sixty-three Illustrations from Original Drawings. New York: John Lane; The Bodley Head, 1921.

Rasco, Burton. "Willa Cather." *Arts and Decorations*. April 1924.

Roberts, Mary Fanton. "The New Russian Stage: What the Genius of Leon Bakst has done to revivify productions which combine Ballet, Music and Drama." *Craftsman* 29 (1915).

Settle, Alison. *Paris Fashions: The Great Designers and Their Creations*. London: Michael Joseph, 1972.

Slote, Bernice. "Willa Cather and Her First Book." *April Twilights (1903)*. Lincoln: University of Nebraska Press, 1990.

Spencer, Charles. *Leon Bakst*. New York: Rizzoli, 1973.

Woodress, James. *Willa Cather: A Literary Life*. Lincoln: University of Nebraska Press, 1987.

Part III
City Contacts and Literary Connections

Throw Out the Furniture, Rip Out the Curtains: Cather's Whitman and Whitman's Cather

GLORIA ROJAS

She wouldn't have appropriated *O Pioneers!* for the title of her first prairie novel if she hadn't admired his work. It's obvious that when Willa Cather selected Walt Whitman's words, she was declaring a literary affection, tipping her hat in recognition of America's major poet of the nineteenth century; Walt Whitman had died twenty-one years earlier. The formal dedication of *O Pioneers!*, however, is to Cather's friend, Sarah Orne Jewett. Jewett had died four years before the publication of *O Pioneers!*, and in gratitude for the interest the published writer had taken in the younger writer, Cather honored Jewett's beautiful and delicate work. James Woodress, in his *Willa Cather, A Literary Life,* finds Jewett's letter to a young writer remarkable—it advises Cather to quit the distractions of her job in favor of a quiet center of life.[1]

Carl Van Doren, in his essay "Willa Cather," describes Whitman and Jewett as Cather's "oddly matched progenitors," explaining that Cather has the "delicate tact to paint with clean quiet strokes" like Jewett, and that she has the merit of Whitman's strength.[2] Sharon O'Brien, in *Willa Cather: the Emerging Voice,* sees a parallel in Alexandra Bergson's bonding with both Carl Linstrum and the land, a patrilineal and matrilineal inheritance, and Willa Cather's inheritance from her "literary family headed by Walt Whitman and Sara Orne Jewett."[3] Frankly, I think the baby, while she has a little of her mother, clearly looks more like her daddy.

Had Willa Cather never used the words "O Pioneers," and just named her book *Alexandra's Farm* as she named her previous book *Alexander's Bridge,* it would still resonate with echoes of Whitman. Let's look at the family portraits and see if you don't agree that the child takes after her father. Certainly, she has inherited many of Whitman's important features. Don't you see that she has his adventurous eye, wide open for the possibilities of the open road? Can't you tell that she has his ear for music, particularly opera and the world it encompasses? Notice carefully that she has his nose for news,

193

following him into an early career of criticism, journalism, and editing. His enormous grasp, reaching coast-to-coast and beyond, is also
hers. Most importantly, she shares with Whitman the passion of an
artist, and an obvious sexuality that is handled more subtly by the
female novelist than by the male poet.

Let's look more closely at those eyes, fixed on the road:

> To look up or down no road but it stretches and waits for you,
> however long but it stretches and waits for you,[4]

is part of Whitman's "Song of the Open Road." And from a previous
section of the poem,

> Allons! From all formules!
> From your formules, O bat-eyed and materialistic priests.
>
> (WW, 303)

Cather, too, keeps her eye on the road as she summons her priests. In
Death Comes for the Archbishop, resounding echoes of Whitman practically assault the reader when Jean Latour, encouraging an an-
guished Joseph Vaillant, says lightly, "Allons! L'invitation du voyage!"[5] The challenge issued, the wavering would-be priest climbs
aboard the diligence and onto the road. Later, as an archbishop,
Latour reminisces about the day he uttered the challenge to his
friend Vaillant, and how the invitation to the journey has changed
both their destinies, from small town parish priests to incredible
adventurers in the American West.

Whitman issued his invitations to the journey in French. So does
Cather, twice. "Allons!" says Whitman, and "Allons!" says Latour, a
Frenchman, so that's logical. But in "Old Mrs. Harris," young Vickie
Templeton, living in a barely disguised version of Red Cloud, Ne-
braska, also gets her road test in French. Mr. Rosen, recognizing
Vickie's need to know rather than to be or have, gives her a lesson in
French: "*Le but n'est rien; le chemin, c'est tout.*" The end is nothing; the
road is all. He offers the phrase to Vickie as a meaningful addition to
her college credentials, "an antidote, a corrective to what colleges
might do to her."[6]

The story ends for Old Mrs. Harris with her death, but Vickie, who
is much like the young Willa Cather, "still had to go on, to follow the
long road that leads through things unguessed at and unforeseeable"
(*CS*, 313).

Thea Kronborg is another Cather heroine with many roads to
travel. While her journeys take her to the great cities of the world to

perfect her art, the journey to Panther Canyon leads her to comprehend her art. In *The Song of the Lark,* Thea's dramatic moment of
understanding is one of Cather's most insightful paragraphs. Thea
draws herself up and realizes that art is simply an effort to make a
sheath that imprisons "for a moment, the shining elusive element
which is life itself."[7] In her singing, her throat is a vessel for the
breath, which is the stream of life. In his "Preface" to the first *Leaves of
Grass,* Whitman also appropriated such enclosure: "The American
poets are to enclose old and new for America" (WW, 6). In his poetry,
too, he acknowledges those "words loosed to the eddies of the wind"
(WW, 27).

Panther Canyon is the location of Thea's mythic moment with a
Zeus-like eagle, which swoops down in poetic, aerial seduction. Whitman, too, has a poem about the courtship of eagles, and side by side,
the Whitman poem and the Cather prose offer interesting insights
into the authors' similarities and contrasts. In "The Dalliance of the
Eagles," Whitman's speaker is walking, when his eye is drawn upward
and he hears "a sudden muffled sound, the dalliance of the eagles, /
the rushing amorous contact high in space together." The diction is
vivid in describing the coupling:

> The clinching interlocking claws, a living, fierce gyrating wheel,
> Four beating wings, two beaks, a swirling mass tight grappling,
> In tumbling turning clustering loops, straight downward falling.
>
> (WW, 412)

The poem has the richness of forceful tone, exquisite diction, alliteration, a harsh onomatopoeia in the clinching, interlocking jaws. It
even has a final metaphor, as the eagles break away to pursue "their
separate diverse flight" (412). What the poem lacks is subtlety, and
that is what Cather's eagle most definitely has in *The Song of the Lark.*

In that incredible interlude, Thea is also looking up, but "her
mind, like her body, was full of warmth, lassitude, physical content"
(*SL,* 287). The description is so physical, so full of waiting, that the
appearance of the eagle becomes the appearance of a lover to a
careful Cather reader. Cather's bird of great size sails over the cleft,
wheels as does Whitman's, but her eagle drops into a gulf and then
mounts

> until his plumage was so steeped in light that he looked like a golden bird
> . . . From a cleft in the heart of the world she saluted it. . . . It had come
> all the way. (*SL,* 287–88)

The dalliance of Cather's mythic eagle is the sensuous seduction of the goddess, Thea, and the reader, too. It is an infusion of godliness. Cather does it so smoothly, so elegantly, without the "rumpled sheets" or ruffled feathers of Whitman's eagles. Both excerpts are beautiful, both highly charged and sexual, but one has the brashness of Whitman, and the other the subtle hand of Cather.

> Whatever is felt upon the page without being specifically named there—that, one might say, is created. . . . It is the inexplicable presence of the thing not named, of the overtone divined by the ear but not heard by it, . . . that gives high quality to the novel or the drama, as well as to poetry itself.[8]

In this paragraph from *Not Under Forty,* Cather sets out what distinguishes the two eagle sequences. To Whitman's, I bring the ability to understand words, and react in a pleasurable, visceral way. To the second example, Thea's eagle, I bring my entire history of sensory perception and association, love of myth, and experience. The result is a reading of the exquisite scene unique to me. Cather has truly created more than the literal, because the very process of apprehension creates what is felt on the page.

In "Song of Myself," a section describes twenty-eight young men bathing at the shore. The woman who owns the fine house by the rise of the bank watches them from the window, and desires them. In her imagination, "the lady" joins them, and "seizes fast to them . . . they do not think whom they souse with spray" (WW, 197). The passage is explicitly about repression and fantasy, and it very much reminds me of Marian Forrester and the troop of young boys who come to wade.

In *A Lost Lady,* Marian too sees young men from the window, and watches as they go to the water. But her visit to them is real, and if carefully examined by a reader, also seductive. Marian's tone in talking to the group of boys is "confidential," and she tells them of lifting her skirt and pulling off her stockings to wade, somewhat inappropriate talk for a lady among adolescent boys. Cather studs the prose so we can pick up the signals—bareheaded, unveiled, snakes slithering in symbolism, confidential—and makes the point that the boys are particularly aware that she's different.[9] Afterwards, when Niel has broken his arm in defense of the mutilated female bird, he is rewarded by lying in Marian Forrester's bed, feeling close to her fragrance, being stroked by her soft fingers, seeing her white throat, and finally, being kissed.

Unlike Whitman's metaphor, every action in *A Lost Lady* actually happens. The similarities in the two examples lie in the set-up of the scene, the players themselves; the contrast, however, is in the "thing not named, the emotional aura of the fact," and the doubleness of Cather's prose. While the progenitor Whitman openly and unabashedly tackles the taboos of sex, the offspring prefers a more restrained approach, trusting the reader. Another example of that craft is found in *My Ántonia,* when the sun-silhouetted plough signals the end of Jim Burden's sexually-charged afternoon with the hired girls.[10]

Whitman's "Prairie Sunset" creates strata of "colors till now unknown," as he enumerates the shades of sky-color, "Pure, luminous color fighting the silent shadows to the last" (WW, 632). What the final line effectively produces is a tension between shadow and light. Whitman is a lovely master of suns, moons and sunsets, but Cather takes them farther. Her suns and moons, like Whitman's, are more than just beautiful; in her novels, she gives them personae and power. For example: on the last afternoon of his life, Emil Bergson is wild with joy as the sun flashes on barn windows. Emil, the youngest son in *O Pioneers!* is going to see the woman he loves, Marie Shabata. But the light in the apple orchard foreshadows his doom. "Long fingers of light reached through the apple branches as through a net; the orchard was riddled and shot with gold." Cather's use of "riddled" and "shot" makes the golden light a portent. But it is the moon that Cather provides as an accomplice, lighting Frank Shabata's way to the lovers under the tree, where he murders them.[11]

In *One of Ours,* Cather places the setting sun and the rising moon on opposite sides of the horizon, as though squaring off.

> Except for the place each occupied in the heavens, Claude could not have told which was which. They rested upon opposite rims of the world, two bright shields, and regarded each other,—as if they, too, had met by appointment.[12]

Although her descriptions of both the sun and the moon include color and form, it is this rare positioning that makes the metaphor of threat so effective. The armies are squaring off for the World War. Cather can refract the light of Whitman's glowing suns into beauty, threat or violence.

Still, the prairie and its sunsets were not enough either for Whitman or Cather. He sums it up so well for the both of them in "Give Me the Splendid Silent Sun." The first verse begs for orchards and arbors, serene-moving animals teaching content, solitude, and the primal sanities of nature. Later, surfeited with sunsets, he becomes bereft, bereft of the brashness of Broadway, and he shouts, "Keep your

splendid silent sun / Keep your woods O Nature . . ." (WW, 446).
Instead, "Give me Broadway," and "give me the streets of Manhattan!" (447). To Whitman, the city was people, passions, processions
and pageants, and he bellows his need for "an intense life, full to
repletion and varied!" (WW, 447).

Willa Cather, too, needed The City. Like Thea Kronborg, she may
not always have found urban life easy. Thea discovers that strange
"rooms and strange streets and faces, how sick at heart they made
one!" (SL, 335–36). She asks why she must keep struggling and travel
so far, when all she wanted was a familiar place to hide in. Thea
answers her own question: because otherwise, she would lose her
soul. Willa Cather came to New York for the same reason as Thea—to
perfect her art, to create a perfect sheath for that elusive element,
"life hurrying past us and running away, too strong to stop, too sweet
to lose . . . " (SL, 273).

Nellie Birdseye, in My Mortal Enemy, steps out freely into the air of
the city, like St. Gaudens' Diana. Violet is the color of the sky and the
buildings that surround her, while a vendor sells violets in oiled
paper. Even the trees and shrubbery are sociable, and despite the
falling snow, Nellie says, "Here, I felt, winter brought no desolation; it
was tamed like a polar bear led on a leash by a beautiful lady."[13]

A little alliteration, a lovely alliteration, a rich image tells it all.
Cather accepted the city and the city accepted her. The polar bear
simile is sweetly simple. In the matter of writing, Cather and Whitman share the same standard: "Nothing is better than simplicity"
(WW, 13). Cather, who admires the spare style of Jewett, writes in an
accessible style herself. In Not Under Forty, she wants to simplify what
she sees as the overfurnished novel—she wants to toss the excess
furniture out the window. She bolsters her position with a quote from
Mérimée that "the art of choosing among the innumerable traits that
nature offers, is much more difficult than observing and rendering
all." Selection, she believes, requires a higher level of skill; choosing
what to throw away is craft (NUF, 43–47). Whitman admires that
same virtue, simplicity. In his 1855 preface to Leaves of Grass, he states,
"The art of art, the glory of expression and the sunshine of the light
of letters is simplicity" (WW, 13). While Cather is heaving out the
furniture, Whitman even wants to rip out the curtains which he
claims "hang in the way" (WW, 14). Whitman's interior decorator's
stance is that "I will not have in my writing any elegance or effect or
originality to hang . . . between me and the rest, like curtains." Today's expression "tell it like it is" has a more grammatical antecedent
in Whitman's "what I tell, I tell for precisely what it is" (WW, 14).

Though Whitman is not of the prairie, his reaction to it is much the same as a small boy named Jim Burden. In *Complete Prose Works*, we find an undelivered speech that Whitman wrote and called "The Prairies."

> I have again been most impress'd . . . and shall remain for the rest of my life most impress'd, with that . . . vast Something, stretching out on its own unbounded scale, unconfined." (853)

Cather's own reaction, put into the words of Jim Burden in *My Ántonia*, picks up Whitman's sense of endlessness. Says Jim,

> There seemed to be nothing to see; no fences, no creeks, or trees, no hills, or fields. . . . There was nothing but land: not a country at all, but a material out of which countries are made. (718)

How do you determine exactly what influence Whitman had on Cather, since nothing in writing specifies how extensively she read him? She knew his work, she liked him. Phyllis Robinson writes that when Cather was reporting for *The Journal* in Nebraska, she called Whitman a "joyous elephant" in a piece of criticism.[14] It works. One thing not named is an affectionate image of a trumpeting, loud, boisterous, appealing animal. According to Robinson, Cather found Whitman's primal energy "irresistible." It seems to me that Cather, who was deeply influenced by the work of Whitman, was actually born of the same great soul.

Notes

1. James Woodress, *Willa Cather: A Literary Life* (Lincoln: University of Nebraska Press, 1987), 203.

2. Carl Van Doren, "Willa Cather," *Willa Cather and Her Critics*, ed. James Schroeter (Ithaca: Cornell University Press, 1967), 17.

3. Sharon O'Brien, *Willa Cather: The Emerging Voice* (New York: Oxford University Press, 1987), 439.

4. *Walt Whitman: Complete Poetry and Collected Prose*, Notes and Chronology and Selected Texts by Justin Kaplan (New York: Library of America, 1982), 305.

5. Willa Cather, *Death Comes for the Archbishop* (New York: Vintage, 1971), 285.

6. Willa Cather, *Collected Stories* (New York: Vintage, 1992), 299. Cited as *CS*.

7. Willa Cather, *The Song of the Lark* (Boston: Houghton Mifflin, 1988), 273. Cited as *SL*.

8. Willa Cather, *Not Under Forty* (Lincoln: University of Nebraska Press, 1988), 51. Cited as *NUF*.

9. Willa Cather, *Later Novels*, ed. Sharon O'Brien (New York: Library of America, 1990), 6,7,8,9.

10. Willa Cather, *Early Novels and Stories,* ed. Sharon O'Brien (New York: Library of America, 1987), 864–866.

11. Willa Cather, *O Pioneers!* (New York: Dover, 1993), 102,103.

12. Willa Cather, *One of Ours* (New York: Vintage, 1971), 141.

13. Willa Cather, *My Mortal Enemy* (New York: Vintage, 1990), 22.

14. Phyllis Robinson, *Willa: The Life of Willa Cather* (Garden City: Doubleday, 1983), 75.

Bibliography

Cather, Willa. *Collected Stories.* New York: Vintage, 1992.

———. *Death Comes for the Archbishop.* New York: Vintage, 1990.

———. *Not Under Forty.* Lincoln: University of Nebraska Press, 1988.

———. *O Pioneers!* New York: Dover, 1993.

———. *The Song of the Lark.* Boston: Houghton Mifflin, 1988.

———. *My Ántonia. Early Novels and Stories.* Ed. Sharon O'Brien. New York: Library of America, 1987.

O'Brien, Sharon. *Willa Cather: The Emerging Voice.* New York: Oxford University Press, 1987.

Robinson, Phyllis. *Willa: The Life of Willa Cather.* Garden City: Doubleday, 1983.

Van Doren, Carl. "Willa Cather." *Willa Cather and Her Critics.* Ed. James Schroeter. Ithaca: Cornell University Press, 1967: 13–19.

Whitman, Walt. *Complete Poetry and Collected Prose.* Ed. Justin Kaplan. New York: Library of America, 1982.

Woodress, James. *Willa Cather: A Literary Life.* Lincoln: University of Nebraska Press, 1987.

Willa Cather and Mark Twain: Yours Truly, Jim Burden

ROBERT C. COMEAU

In her preface to a collection of the stories of Sarah Orne Jewett, Willa Cather made a remarkable statement about American writing: "If I were asked to name three American books which have the possibility of a long, long life, I would say at once: *The Scarlet Letter, Huckleberry Finn,* and *The Country of the Pointed Firs.*"[1] While this statement would certainly prove prophetic, it is the more interesting because of the profound influence each of these novels would exert on her own writing, which has certainly enjoyed a long, long life of its own. The mark of Jewett is felt in her early novels, and has been documented and discussed copiously. The themes of Hawthorne, with her fascinating reworkings, are also fairly obvious in these same early works. What has been unnoticed, though, is the enormous influence of Mark Twain and *Adventures of Huckleberry Finn* on Cather's *My Ántonia.*

Mark Twain was the largest figure on America's literary landscape at the beginning of the twentieth century. Early in her literary career, and while she was being courted by S. S. McClure and contemplating the move to join the staff of *McClure's* magazine, Willa Cather was introduced to Twain when a guest at his seventieth birthday party at Delmonico's Restaurant in New York City on December 5, 1905. Of the 170 invited guests, she was one of fifty to meet the author at a special reception prior to the dinner. After her move to New York in May 1906, Cather became an occasional visitor, when her busy schedule at *McClure's* would allow, to Twain's home at 21 Fifth Avenue, in Greenwich Village—not far from Cather's residence on Washington Square. According to James Woodress,

> [Twain] spent a great deal of time in bed in those years and entertained three or four young people at a time, including Cather on occasion, in his bedroom. Cather recalled these sessions when she wrote William Lyons Phelps in 1936 to praise an article he had written on Twain for the *Yale Review.* She was glad he did not accept Van Wyck Brooks's thesis that Twain was a blighted genius. If he had been the imaginary character Brooks created in *The Ordeal of Mark Twain,* she said, he never would have written *Huck Finn;* and if Brooks had ever seen that old lion in bed telling stories, he never could have written his book.[2]

201

E. K. Brown also notes "a brief meeting with Twain, and a morning spent at his bedside listening to him talk."[3]

Apparently, Twain was quite taken with Cather. He praised to his factotum and biographer, Albert Bigelow Paine, Cather's poem "The Palatine," which had appeared in *McClure's* in June 1909. He read the poem to Paine, and Paine included a few stanzas of it in his three volume *Mark Twain: A Biography* when it was published in 1912, quoting Twain as saying, "Here is a fine poem, a great poem, I think."[4] This recognition, unquestionably flattering to the young Cather, was in print six years before *My Ántonia* and was an extraordinary public acknowledgement of the young writer's talent.

Cather had read *Adventures of Huckleberry Finn* as a child, and the memory, as well as the text, remained with her. Woodress notes her re-reading of the novel "for what she thought was the twentieth time," referring to a letter she wrote to Cyril Clemens, Twain's nephew and the first editor of *The Mark Twain Journal,* on November 21, 1934.[5] E. K. Brown tells of childhood adventures on the Republican River near Red Cloud, Nebraska, where Cather and her brothers Roscoe and Douglass played at being pirates, stating that "Stevenson, Mark Twain, and many a humbler source combined with the misshapen roots of trees, the odd configurations of sand and the grotesque contours of the island to make of this retreat a place of high childish romance."[6]

While her years at *McClure's* were important in many respects, they were crucial in consolidating Cather's regard for Twain. Two years before she met Sarah Orne Jewett, she had already begun the process of development into the novelist she would become. It seems that she would occasionally think of Twain and Jewett together, perhaps linking them, along with Hawthorne, as early influences and models of American writing. She mentions Twain quite favorably in her essay entitled "Miss Jewett," which appeared in her 1936 collection, *Not Under Forty:* "It is this very personal quality of perception, a vivid and intensely personal experience of life, which make a 'style.' Mark Twain had it, at his best, and Hawthorne. But among fifty thousand books you will find very few writers who ever achieved a style at all."[7] It is a "style," the quality that Cather perhaps admired most in Twain, that she worked so hard to acquire in the first decade of the Twentieth Century, and which finally rings out at its best in *My Ántonia.*

Cather and Twain share a strong and emotionally-charged attraction to the region in which they came of age, each finding their literary identities in their reminiscences thereof. Both writers had begun their literary careers by examining the tensions between Western life and Eastern life, Twain in such stories as "The Celebrated

Jumping Frog of Calaveras County" and in his first two books, *The Innocents Abroad* and *Roughing It;* and Cather in stories like "A Wagner Matinée" and "Paul's Case" in *The Troll Garden*. They each developed stronger and more assured voices when they wrote about their home towns and the characters therein—Twain in his portions of *The Gilded Age* (co-written with Charles Dudley Warner) and *The Adventures of Tom Sawyer;* and Cather in "The Bohemian Girl" and *O Pioneers!*

When Cather looked back on her girlhood, she remembered the books she had read. In an essay entitled "Old Books and New," written for the Pittsburgh *Home Monthly* (May 1897), she also saluted Twain as part of that reading:

> I got a letter last week from a little boy just half-past seven who had just read *Huckleberry Finn* and *Tom Sawyer.* He said: "If there are any more books like them in the world, send them to me quick." I had to humbly confess to him that if there were any others I had not the good fortune to know of them. What a red letter day it is to a boy, the day he first opens *Tom Sawyer.* I would rather sail on the raft down the Missouri again with Huck Finn and Jim than go down the Nile in December or see Venice from a gondola in May.[8]

Despite some factual inconsistencies, the tone of wistful admiration in the passage is quite clear.

It is a critical commonplace in almost any discussion of *My Ántonia* to note its nostalgic tone and, particularly in Book I, its identification with the pastoral. Cather is unabashedly romantic about the prairie, just as is Twain about the Mississippi River. For each, these natural wonders become dominating images in their literary creations, with Cather often describing the prairie in terms that would suggest water: "The red of the grass made all the prairie the color of wine-stains, or of certain seaweeds when they are first washed up. And there was so much motion in it; the whole country seemed, somehow, to be running."[9] In either sense, the separation from society in general afforded by setting the action on either the prairie or the river will play an important role in each author's ultimate themes of social criticism. Each suggests a setting which is simple, pure or honest, and allows the author space deliberately to evoke a more natural life necessary for the pastoral.

Parallels between the river and the prairie are further established through the perceptions of the two Jims. For example, the characters in both novels depend upon these natural elements for their survival. Huck and Jim can catch fish from the river, and gather up the spoils from wrecks and storms along the way for bartering purposes. Huck can seek freedom from Pap Finn and a restrictive society as well, while Jim can simultaneously attempt to use the river as his pathway to freedom. The Shimerdas and the Burdens depend upon their ability to cultivate the prairie for their survival, and the Shimerdas, newer to prairie life than the Burdens, burrow into the prairie ground for shelter.

The river and the prairie also provide each novel with a measure of conflict. Each set of characters must tame the environment in some way or suffer consequences. The same river which is a highway south is also a graveyard for steamboats and rafts, loaded with snags and tow-heads. The river has violent storms which separate Huck and Jim, just as the prairie is subject to blizzards which lock everyone in homes and away from the community which is so necessary to everyone's survival. The control Nature can exert over people is a theme for each writer. The river plunges inexorably forward, bringing Huck and Jim further south and further away from freedom, though it also supports their idyllic life on the famous raft; and the prairie rolls inexorably onward through seasonal repetitions, though it is brought into some form of controlled usefulness by successful farming symbolized by the famous image of the plow at sunset.

Cather's homage to *Adventures of Huckleberry Finn* begins with her decision to allow a first person narrator to tell the story, the first time she would do so in a novel; she also allows him the name *Jim*, perhaps in further reference to Huck Finn's friend and traveling companion. In earlier editions of *My Ántonia* she stipulates that her narrator's name is James Quayle Burden, or "Jim Burden, as we still call him in the West" (ix); but she would delete the formal name in her subsequent 1926 revision of the Introduction. This deletion has the effect of underscoring any potential allusion to the Twain novel. Jim Burden is also eternally boyish and youthful, never seeming, to the frame narrator, to grow older. Cather accords him high praise by referring to his "naturally romantic and ardent disposition." Jim is constantly looking West, going "off into the wilds or exploring new canyons," and he is "still able to lose himself in Western dreams" (xi), just as Huck closes his narrative by expressing his desire to "light out for the territory ahead of the rest."[10] Considering Cather's criticisms of his marriage, it may be that Jim, too, is trying to run westward to escape the "sivilizing" of the establishment's Genevieve Whitney, his wife.

Significantly, both narrators are introduced early in each novel as a character in their own stories. Huck Finn begins by telling the reader, "You don't know about me without you have read a book by the name of *The Adventures of Tom Sawyer*" (1), making Huck simultaneously more real to the reader while he emphasizes his nature as a fictional character in his own creation. Jim Burden is introduced as a young man of the framing narrator's old acquaintance who is asked to provide his own reminiscences of their childhood friend Ántonia, because he is closer to her. The line between author, storyteller and memoirist gets further blurred by the enormous amount of auto-biographical detail put into each novel by both Cather and Twain. Though Cather seeks to distance herself from Ántonia's story through the device of Jim Burden, he often functions as her spokes-man; and Huck, while obviously more naïve than Jim Burden, also serves as a conduit for many of Twain's observations on his world. Further, despite Cather's title, her novel is as much about the grow-ing up of Jim Burden as it is about Ántonia, and Huck's story is also one of initiation and development. Both narrators tell us their own stories of personal growth through a profound friendship. Cather merely reverses the titling, and adds resonance to her reading of Huck Finn by naming her narrator after Huck's companion.

Twain prefaces his novel with the comic threat that "persons at-tempting to find a plot in it will be shot." Cather, too, disavows traditional plot by allowing Jim, when delivering his memoir to her frame narrator, to say that he "simply wrote down what of herself and myself and other people Ántonia's name recalls to me. I suppose it hasn't any form" (xiii). Both novels pretend their form is incidental. Both dispose of traditional plot by relating incidents in the narrator's life in a highly personal way, though Huck's story becomes a linear river journey punctuated by descriptions of the weather or light, while Jim's repeats the cyclical returns of the prairie seasons and weather, punctuated by journeys.

The characters of Huck Finn and Jim Burden are similar. Huck is, for all intents and purposes, an orphan, with a mother whom we know nothing about and a father who "used to lay drunk with the hogs in the tanyard, but . . . hain't been seen in these parts for a year or more" (10). Pap Finn returns, however, when he hears that Huck has come into money, and wants to claim his rightful share. Huck's response is to fake his own death, recreating himself in a variety of guises until he can safely be himself again. Huck is also, by virtue of his parentage, an outsider, one whose company is forbidden the other boys by their right-thinking parents. This role of outsider al-lows Huck a different perspective from Tom Sawyer, for example, when it comes to observing and commenting upon the culture which shuns him and forbids him real entrance. Mark Twain once stated the theme of *Adventures of Huckleberry Finn* as a "crucial moral emer-gency . . . [in which] a sound heart and a deformed conscience come into collision and conscience suffers defeat."[11] It is this conscience that the dominant culture imposes on all its good citizens which Huck is denied, allowing his sound heart to act in a variety of socially unacceptable ways. He cannot only befriend Jim, but can also, eventually, decide to take positive action in helping him secure his freedom.

Jim Burden is also an outsider. He is a more than symbolic orphan who moves from his birthplace in Virginia to live with his grandparents, first on the prairie in Nebraska and then in the town of Black Hawk, one of Cather's many fictional names for Red Cloud. His displacement is illustrated when he first arrives in Nebraska, far away from home in Virginia and in the middle of the night:

> I had the feeling that the world was left behind, that we had got over the edge of it, and were outside man's jurisdiction . . . I did not believe that my dead father and mother were watching me from up there; they would still be looking for me at the sheep-fold down by the creek. . . . I had left even their spirits behind me. (7–8)

Jim, too, begins his own story by experiencing his own obliteration, his death to an old way of life. He has had the opportunity to leave many of his learned rules and preconceptions behind, making him an innocent with a new identity like Huck, able to deal with the strange new world of the Nebraska prairie with a sound heart.

Jim's grandparents are wise and tolerant, though devout enough to be somewhat reminiscent of the Widow Douglas in *Adventures of Huckleberry Finn*. They are Baptists, a denomination characterized by American democratic feelings; and when the Norwegian cemetery will not allow Mr. Shimerda's body to be buried there because he was a suicide, Mrs. Burden "was indignant. 'If these foreigners are so clannish . . . we'll have to have an American graveyard that will be more liberal-minded'" (108). The Widow Douglas, as Huck reports, "would take me aside and talk about Providence in a way to make a body's mouth water . . . and a poor chap would stand considerable show with the widow's Providence" (14). Unlike the Burdens, however, the widow Douglas lived in a slave-holding society, and her liberalism and tolerance in religion were never stretched, so far as we know, to question human slavery.

Like Huck, Jim Burden finds a friend. In the relative isolation of the prairie, he becomes very close to his near-outcast Bohemian neighbor, Ántonia Shimerda, while his grandparents are also always decent and kind to the Shimerdas. These friendships—Jim and Ántonia, as well as Huck and Jim— must develop in this relative isolation to happen at all. Free from the constraints of the dominant culture's attitudes toward poor immigrants or slaves, these adolescent friendships can form according to the dictates of each character's sound hearts. However, once among "the sivilized," Huck and Jim, and Jim and Ántonia, must revert to socially acceptable roles. Jim must be a slave, Huck a "white gen'l'man," and Jim Burden a school-going and church-respecting townsboy, while Ántonia goes into domestic service, a form of wage-slavery reserved for the daughters of the immigrant farmers. The prairie and the river are further linked as the pastoral environments in which these friendships can be maintained, in direct opposition to shore and town life.

One of the other major themes in *Adventures of Huckleberry Finn* is stated by Huck more than once, most notably when the Duke and the King have been tarred and feathered and are being ridden on a rail. Empathetic Huck observes, "Human beings *can* be awful cruel to one another" (290). Huck's story is loaded with one instance of extreme human cruelty after another, including, but not limited to, murder, thievery, obscenity, double-dealing, lying, slavery, and bounty hunting. The Duke and the King, for all their humorous qualities, are vicious con men capable of duping a family grieving over the death of a husband and father, out of their entire inheritance. It is only through their own overmastering greed and stupidity that they are eventually discovered and forced to flee. At the point that Huck sees the tar-and-feathering, they have used Huck and sold Jim back into slavery, but he can still have pity for them.

Cather, too, uses human cruelty as a theme. Krajiek is more than willing to use his familiarity with compatriots' language to win their trust and cheat them out of their money when selling them his sod-house and inferior goods; and Wick Cutter has no problem lending money to farmers whom he knows can never repay him, thereby allowing foreclosure. Ántonia is brutally jilted by a man whom she loves and who impregnates her. And Pavel and Peter throw a bride to the wolves.

Certainly, social criticism was very firmly in the mind of both Mark Twain and Willa Cather as they wrote these two remarkable books. Twain made his reputation as a writer of satire long before he made a very deliberate turn toward serious artistic literature, of which *Adventures of Huckleberry Finn* is one of the first major examples; and he was well known for his humorous, though often savage, criticisms of politics, journalism, European culture, and effete American culture. Cather, as mentioned earlier, had made her early reputation with stories contrasting Eastern and Western values, often embodied in the passions and lives of a few of the prairie's remarkable citizens with the majority of farmers being "square-headed" and unimaginative.

In *Adventures of Huckleberry Finn*, Mark Twain seriously calls into question the values of the society in which he grew up. It is a society that would not only enslave a gigantic portion of its population, but would also, in the post-reconstruction era, find new and more ingenious ways to prevent its freed slaves from realizing their newly legalized freedom, effectively holding its entire black population in a prison designed by a few powerful people. Tom Sawyer embodies this Southern dominant culture when he keeps Jim prisoner even while he knows that Miss Watson has freed him in her will. Tom commits, as does the South in general, the ultimate act of cruelty in maintaining slavery in all but name, even after its abolition. Huck Finn's sound heart resists, but when he sees that the Tom Sawyers are very much in charge, he lights out for the territory. After their river idyll, Huck can't take this kind of civilization again.

Willa Cather, too, questions the values of the society in which she grew up. Cather, unlike Twain but like Jim Burden, was a transplanted Virginian, making for a distinct similarity between her and her immigrant neighbors. She once said,

> We had very few American neighbors—they were mostly Swedes and Danes, Norwegians and Bohemians. I liked them from the first and they made up for what I missed in the country. I particularly liked the old women, they understood my homesickness and were kind to me.[12]

That the people who were so kind to her could have been so misunderstood by the Americans in town seems to provide the impetus for the diatribe she allows Jim Burden in various parts of Book II, "The Hired Girls," of *My Ántonia*. In this, Jim contrasts the immigrant girls, hired into service and energetic, passionate and full of life, with the town girls, unimpressionable, incapable of enthusiasm and, in short, very lazy. The town's ignorant inability to perceive the fine backgrounds of some of these girls equally galls him.

> I thought the attitude of the town people toward these girls very stupid. If I told my schoolmates that Lena Lingard's grandfather was a clergyman, and much respected in Norway they looked at me blankly. What did it matter? All foreigners were ignorant people who couldn't speak English. There was not a man in Black Hawk who had the intelligence or cultivation, much less the personal distinction, of Ántonia's father. Yet people saw no difference between her and the three Marys; they were all Bohemians, all "hired girls." (194)

What Jim perceives is the snobbery of the East transformed into even greater narrow-mindedness in the West; and how difficult it is to change entrenched ideas in people used to viewing themselves as superior, much like what Twain perceived in the post-reconstruction South. The fools are a majority in any town.

In each writer's mind, the narrative characters become less interesting as they get farther from their respective milieus. Huck's decision, at the end of his book, to "light out for the territory," moving even further in the direction of simplicity and away from civilization, is ultimately flawed, at least in Twain's mind, as is shown in the author's inability to write about Huck convincingly in *Tom Sawyer Abroad, Tom Sawyer, Detective,* and the mercifully unfinished "Huck and Tom Among the Indians." In each instance, Twain attempts to move Huck away from the Mississippi, toward other kinds of adventures. But Twain was unable to sustain a genuine interest in him there. Cather, too, as frame narrator, is uninterested in Jim Burden's life away from the prairie, preferring not to see him in New York because she does not like his new world as personified by his wife. "She is handsome, energetic, executive, but . . . unimpressionable and temperamentally incapable of enthusiasm" (x), in stark contrast to the "naturally romantic and ardent disposition" much preferred by Cather. Jim's marriage to a Whitney is an understandable capitulation to the dominant culture on Jim's part. His way of leaving Black Hawk was through the life of the mind, and even in college he read classics of the Eastern establishment. Despite his romantic liaison with Lena Lingard, he had to look east for the culture he valued. Lena, Tiny Soderball and Ántonia all find success in the west on their own terms; but they occasionally remind Jim, through his intermittent reconnections, of what he left.

In order for Cather to tell Jim's story, she had to access memories of her own childhood in the west, as well as her memories of *Adventures of Huckleberry Finn*—a book which seemed to tell the same sort of story she wanted to tell. She could then appropriate ideas from the novel, note how her themes were similar and different from Twain's, and move forward, creating something new with a distinct awareness of a classic which she admired very much. She is nothing less than a literary descendant of Twain's, grappling with both the technique and the themes of *Huckleberry Finn* in order to realize her own identity as a literary artist.

Notes

1. Willa Cather, "Preface," *The Best Stories of Sarah Orne Jewett, On Writing* (Lincoln: University of Nebraska Press, 1988), 58.

2. James Woodress, *Willa Cather: A Literary Life* (Lincoln: University of Nebraska Press, 1987), 210.

3. E. K. Brown, *Willa Cather: A Critical Biography,* completed by Leon Edel (New York: Knopf, 1949), 152.

4. Albert Bigelow Paine, *Mark Twain: A Biography* (New York: Harper, 1912), 1501.

5. Woodress, *WC,* 51.

6. Brown, *Biography,* 40.

7. Willa Cather, *Stories, Poems and Other Writings,* ed. Sharon O'Brien (New York: Library of America, 1992), 857.

8. Willa Cather, *The World and the Parish,* ed. William M. Curtin (Lincoln: University of Nebraska Press, 1970), 347.

9. Willa Cather, *My Ántonia* (Lincoln: University of Nebraska Press, 1994), 14–15.

10. Mark Twain, *Adventures of Huckleberry Finn,* eds. Walter Blair and Victor Fischer (Berkeley: University of California Press, 1985), 362.

11. quoted in Walter Blair, *Mark Twain and Huck Finn* (Berkeley: University of California Press, 1960), 143.

12. Willa Cather, *The Kingdom of Art,* ed. Bernice Slote (Lincoln: University of Nebraska Press, 1966), 448.

Bibliography

Blair, Walter. *Mark Twain and Huck Finn.* Berkeley: University of California Press, 1960.

Brown, E. K. *Willa Cather: A Critical Biography.* Completed by Leon Edel. New York: Alfred A. Knopf, 1953.

Cather, Willa. "The Best Stories of Sarah Orne Jewett." *Willa Cather on Writing: Critical Studies On Writing As An Art.* Foreword by Stephen Tennant. New York: Knopf, 1949.

———. *The Kingdom of Art: Willa Cather's First Principles and Critical Statements, 1893–1896.* Edited by Bernice Slote. Lincoln: University of Nebraska Press, 1966.

———. *My Ántonia.* Lincoln: University of Nebraska Press, 1994.

———. "Miss Jewett." *Stories, Poems and Other Writings.* Ed.Sharon O'Brien. New York: Library of America, 1992.

———. *The World and the Parish: Willa Cather's Articles and Reviews, 1893–1902.* 2 Vols. Edited by William M. Curtin. Lincoln: University of Nebraska Press, 1970.

Paine, Albert Bigelow. *Mark Twain: A Biography.* 3 Vols. New York: Harper, 1912.

Twain, Mark. *Adventures of Huckleberry Finn.* Ed. Walter Blair and Victor Fischer. Berkeley: University of California Press, 1985.

Woodress, James. *Willa Cather: A Literary Life.* Lincoln: University of Nebraska Press, 1987.

Pernicious Contact: Willa Cather and the Problem of Literary Sisterhood

DEBORAH LINDSAY WILLIAMS

In a 1929 letter to her friend Zona Gale, Willa Cather neatly summed up her ambivalence about being part of a community: one cannot live in a test tube, she wrote, but most contact is pernicious.[1] It is a dilemma with which Cather struggled throughout her career: a tug of war between her need for recognition as an individual artist on the one hand and on the other, her need for support and community. She cannot live in a test tube, but contact is pernicious—and the contact of literary influence perhaps the most pernicious of all. It is in part to escape or avoid pernicious contact that Cather developed a public persona that appeared to exist aloof from and oblivious to contemporary politics, social reforms, and gender issues; it is for this same reason that she attempted to create strong distinctions between herself and other writers, particularly her female contemporaries. Cather's relationship with Gale, a prize-winning playwright and successful novelist, reveals a great deal about Cather's conflicting attitudes towards her literary sisters. When we compare Gale's New York experience with Cather's, we gain a clearer sense of what Cather rejected in order to shape the authorial persona that would become her public image.

New York in the early part of the twentieth century was a city of professional women. Mabel Dodge Luhan, in the third volume of her memoirs, notes that "New York was largely run by women; there was a woman behind every man in every publisher's office, in all the editorial circles, and in the Wall Street offices, and it was the judgement and intuition of these that determined many policies."[2] It was to this city of women that Gale came in 1901 and Cather in 1906, each looking for professional success and freedom—Gale from life in Milwaukee and Cather from magazine work and high-school teaching in Pittsburgh. Upon arrival in New York both women worked as journalists and aspired to be novelists; found mentors in older, more established writers (Gale in Edmund Clarence Stedman, Cather in Sarah Orne Jewett); and achieved their first literary successes while living in the city. Eventually they would share a publisher, Alfred

Knopf; an agent, Paul R. Reynolds; and a literary award: Gale would be the first woman awarded a Pulitzer Prize for drama in 1921, and Cather would be the second woman awarded for literature, in 1923. Further, they shared Midwestern backgrounds, the experience of a university education (Gale at the University of Wisconsin-Madison, Cather at the University of Nebraska), and long literary apprenticeships; even more importantly, each writer published early work that was to be quite different from her later, more successful writing: Gale's rosy short stories are a far cry from the scathing feminist, anticapitalist novels of her later career, and Cather's early poetry and her novel *Alexander's Bridge* do not fully reflect the path her career would later follow. Although each woman saw New York as offering alternatives to traditional expectations and attitudes, they chose to exercise those alternatives in very different ways.

Although Cather lived in Greenwich Village and Gale lived uptown, it was Gale who become involved with the radical political and social movements advocated by Village "bohemians." Gale used the political energy of the Village to build her public identity and to define her ideas about social reform. Cather, on the other hand, professed to be untouched and uninterested in any political or social movements but lived in the very heart of bohemia. By creating a public persona for herself that refused public affiliation with any single group or cause, Cather attempted to remain free of any obligations that might interfere with her writing. As we will see in her letters to Gale, however, preserving this aloofness in private was a more difficult task.

When Gale lived in New York—1901 to 1912, with some extended visits to Portage—she lived uptown at the San Remo, an imposing building on the west side of Central Park, but she spent most of her time downtown, in and around Greenwich Village. Her uptown address served to assuage the worries of her Wisconsin parents, who were alarmed at the list of causes espoused by their daughter, particularly her affiliation with feminism and feminists, which caused her mother to write that she should "leave that mess of women *alone!*" Feminism was only the beginning, however: during her career, Gale wrote and lectured about a variety of radical causes, including equal rights for African Americans, the necessity of pacifism, and the benefits of socialism. Among Gale's closest friends in New York were the women of Heterodoxy, a group of women who met on a bi-monthly basis to discuss politics, feminism, and their own experiences—a prototypical consciousness-raising group. Founded by Marie Jenney Howe, a Unitarian minister (and an early biographer of George

Sand), this group included among its members Mabel Dodge (later Luhan), Crystal Eastman, Charlotte Perkins Gilman, Inez Haynes Irwin (wife of Will Irwin, who worked with Cather and Lewis at *McClure's*), and many others. The women of Heterodoxy were well-known in the Village, as was their support of the lesbian relationships among their members, which were awarded the same respect as heterosexual marriages.[3] For Gale, sisterhood was both political and personal; she anticipated the credo of many mid-twentieth century feminists in her ability to bring her personal experience to bear on political action.

In 1929, sisterhood and the desire to create a female literary community would later prompt Gale, in 1929, to invite Cather to Portage, where Gale lived after she left New York. Gale's invitation is a response to Cather's comment about her wretched existence in New York hotels because her Bank Street apartment had been torn down. Gale suggests that Cather come to Portage and live in her parents' house, which Gale lived in for most of her adult life, leaving it (but not the town of Portage) only after her marriage in 1928, at the age of fifty-four. It is this doubly vacated house that Gale offers to Cather, in an attempt to erase the boundaries between herself and Cather that Cather's letters continually re-establish. Gale does not construct barriers between herself and other women writers; she is not threatened by sororal connections. We could see Gale's gesture as literalizing what had been previously only metaphoric: if Cather were to live in Gale's father's house, it would be as if she really were Gale's sister.

It should not surprise us that Cather refused Gale's offer—although she says it is tempting; Cather spent much of her literary career trying to escape or redefine tradition, an idea strongly symbolized by the image of the father's house. Cather is uncharacteristically effusive about the invitation, gushing that nothing has pleased her as much as the overwhelming proof that Gale would like to have her as a neighbor.[4] She says that she wishes she could take the next train to Portage, and although the word "wish" is underlined, the letter makes no mention of travel plans. Cather ultimately refuses Gale's offer because she is going back and forth to Pasadena to tend to her ailing mother: the role of dutiful daughter takes precedence over literary sister. Although Cather's letter grumbles a bit at the trans-continental train ride, this journey seems part of a clear pattern on Cather's part: she is as often out of New York as she is in residence there. Cather's long sojourns outside the city are well-known—her trips back home, to the Southwest, to Jaffrey, to Grand Manan, to Europe—but she remained always a resident of Manhattan, testament in part to her love for Edith Lewis, whose professional life and livelihood were bound up in the New York worlds of advertising and publishing.

In the letter to Gale refusing her invitation, Cather sounds nevertheless rapturous about Gale's small town. Her doubly underlined "wish" for a long visit to Portage is always deferred, however, always a future possibility. The two women only ever met in New York, a city over which neither had particular dominion. Gale's New York is a socially radical city that allowed her to become increasingly more outspoken and politically active. And while moving to New York was as liberating for Cather as it was for Gale, Cather's New York was very different from Gale's city, despite the fact that Cather's apartment on Bank Street put her at the center of the "new Bohemia" and all that it represented. By 1906, when Cather moved to New York, the Village already symbolized attitudes that challenged conventional bourgeois ideas about everything: politics, sexuality, society.[5]

Despite the controversy, radicalism, and experimentation swirling through the streets of the Village, Edith Lewis says firmly that she and Cather lived in a "sedate Bohemia" where "poor and hardworking" artists lived.[6] Lewis's description implies that she and Cather lived in the Village so that Cather-the-artist could be surrounded by other like-minded artists. Her brief comment gives short shrift to what was actually going on in the Village the entire time that Lewis and Cather lived in its midst.[7] Their first rented rooms, for instance, at 60 Washington Square South, were in Madame Blanchard's rooming house where such writers as Lincoln Steffens, Theodore Dreiser, Stephen Crane, and Frank Norris lived.[8] Around the corner from their Bank Street apartment were the editorial offices of the self-proclaimed "revolutionary magazine," *The Masses,* which would easily be on their daily walking path. Not quite ten blocks from the offices of *McClure's* was 291, Alfred Steiglitz's gallery, which showed some of the most important new art of the twentieth century.[9] Apparently, however, none of these things were worthy of notice. Instead Lewis insists— sounding like Cather herself here—that it was a "youthful, light-hearted, and rather poetic" time when young people were "more ingenuous, less initiated [and] life seemed . . . more boundless."[10] Lewis's silence about their neighborhood seems disingenuous, aimed more at perpetuating Cather's image as a writer uninterested in public life than at accurately characterizing life in the Village in the teens and twenties.[11]

While there is no reason that Lewis *should* describe all that was going on in the Village, the fact that Lewis and Cather lived there as long as they did seems curious, given Cather's professed disdain for political and social activism. In readings and discussions of Cather it is commonly suggested that her New York is the New York of the Opera House, of traditional theater, of the symphony—an idea that Lewis fosters. But the two women lived in a neighborhood full of bohemians at a time when a popular song suggested that "Fairyland's not far from Washington Square" and the presence of "fairies" and "lady lovers" was a well-established fact.[12] Why live in such a neighborhood if fiscal necessity doesn't demand it and one's interests— apparently—are further uptown? Cather and Lewis set up house-keeping together at the same time as "the first visible middle-class gay subculture" in New York began to emerge—in Greenwich Village.[13] If one does not want to be known as a lesbian, then why live in a neighborhood where two women living together stood a far greater chance of being thought of as lesbians? Chauncey points out that while "two women dancing together in a Times Square nightclub elicited no comment . . . in the Village it would be taken as a sign of their lesbianism."[14] It seems most likely that Cather and Lewis were doing what any number of gays and lesbians did: using the "cover story" of village bohemia—the experimental, often radical lives of artists and writers—to mask their own unconventional lives. Lewis's invocation of poor, hardworking artists keeps at bay any suggestion that Cather (or Lewis herself) was anything other than just that— they certainly were *not* members of "Fairyland" or "odd girls," coded descriptions for lesbians.[15]

Having an address in "Bohemia" gave them the benefit of bo-hemia's freedom without having to claim to be, themselves, bohe-mians. Cather's desire to avoid being labeled or categorized— whether as a woman writer, a lesbian, or a bohemian—helps to ex-plain why, in a writer whose work is saturated with a sense of place, the radically experimental and revolutionary "Village" is all but invis-ible in her fiction, except as background in "Coming, Aphrodite!"[16] That story offers further insight to what Cather wanted to create for herself in New York, however, although we might not think of Cather in conjunction with her sexy, somewhat crass heroine, Eden Bower. Cather says of Bower that "she had the easy freedom of obscurity and the consciousness of power. She enjoyed both. She was in no hurry" (*CS* 81). Like Eden, Cather was well-aware of what the public wanted from its artists. Her long apprenticeship as a journalist showed her quite clearly what would and wouldn't sell both in terms of the writ-ing itself and the writers who produced it. And like Eden, Cather wanted success, although on her own terms as an artist (thus also linking Cather with Don Hedger, the story's "real" artist). Unlike Eden, however, Cather was in a hurry, anxious to shed the power of editor in order to gain the power of novelist. Aware of what were to her the pitfalls of becoming too public a figure, Cather managed, through the manipulation of her public persona, to create the "easy freedom of obscurity" for her private self, her private life: the image of the plain-spoken Nebraska writer provided a cover story for the opera-loving lesbian who lived in bohemia.[17]

Gale was more involved with the lesbian community of the Village than Cather, perhaps because Gale felt that she had nothing to hide and thus nothing to lose. It was through the women of Heterodoxy that Gale became a board member of the Women's Peace Party, and served on the committee to help elect Robert La Follette, the Progressive candidate for president. Heterodoxy, according to Luhan, was a group of women who "did things and did them openly . . . whose names were known."[18] It is this sort of public viewing that Cather shied away from, although James Woodress, in his exhaustive biography of Cather, notes that Cather "must have met [Mabel Dodge Luhan] in New York many years before [her trip to Taos and Santa Fe] when she was Mabel Dodge, a rich patron of the arts. She then lived in a mansion on lower Fifth Avenue and kept a salon for the literati of Greenwich Village."[19] If Cather met Dodge in New York, then it is likely that she also met some of the radicals, bohemians, suffragists, and anarchists who attended Dodge's "Evenings."

Gale seems willing to link herself publicly with communal causes and while her writing often portrays the stifling atmosphere of small-town community life, particularly for women, she equally often imagines alternative communities as the solution, communities formed through a shared awareness of life's higher meanings: love and spirituality. The individual as such is almost never a central concern in Gale's fiction or drama; her work more often than not illustrates the damage that can be done when one individual forgets or ignores the community around her.[20] Cather is deeply suspicious about any communal identity that might overwhelm her individuality, however, whether the labels are generated by gender or by politics.[21]

Much has been made of Cather's relationship with Sarah Orne Jewett and Cather's eagerness for the older woman's mentorly advice—a relationship that appears to transcend the boundaries of generation, geography, style. In her relations with her female *contemporaries*, however, Cather seemed significantly less eager for affiliation, advice, or companionship. Some of Cather's friends did make their living as writers, but for the most part, whether coincidentally or not, they stayed away from Cather's literary territory. Cather's intimate female friends—Isabelle McClung, Mariel Gere, Louise Pound, and of course Edith Lewis—were literate and literary, but did not make their living as writers.[22] In her non-fiction prose, Cather habitually emphasized her singularity, her individuality as a writer, whether in her choice of subject, her disdain for popular culture, or her refusal to be linked with other women writers. She rejected literary sisterhood, at least publicly, and often spoke disparagingly about other women writers.

Cather's sense of boundaries is evident in a letter she writes to Gale about Gale's book, *Portage, Wisconsin and Other Essays* (Knopf, 1928). Cather says that Portage haunts her and that it sounds like a lovely place.[23] Gale's essays make her want to move to Portage, she writes, but that would be about the meanest thing one writer could do to another. She goes on to threaten Gale away from her own small Nebraska town, warning her (jokingly, we assume) that she would be furious if Gale came anywhere near her territory. Her letter describes a literary geography in which there can be only one writer for each landscape—a kind of literary quota system. One writer might admire another writer's territory, but only from afar. The letter moves in two directions: Cather reaches out to Gale by praising her writing, invoking its strong pull: Portage haunts her. At the same time, she warns Gale to stay away, insisting on boundaries, divisions, ownership. Nebraska is *her* property, Wisconsin belongs to Gale: there is no possibility of communal possession.

Both Cather and Gale must answer to the public's expectations of women writers, although unlike Cather, Gale does not dislike being categorized as such. In the early part of the twentieth century, women writers were, to some degree, exploring new possibilities for themselves. Should she follow the footsteps of U.S. nineteenth-century women writers, who often claimed to write only to support a family or to promote some social or spiritual message? Should she reject U.S. models altogether and look to Europe, to "the Georges," Jane Austen, or the Brontës? Writers slightly older than Cather and Gale, like Edith Wharton, had begun to make names for themselves, but they were not yet successful enough to be looked to as role models. Gale, whose politics were in some cases quite extreme, shaped a public authorial persona for herself that was more in keeping with her nineteenth-century predecessors. Her fiction often carries a not-very-subtle political message, usually having to do with what she called in a letter to Dorothy Canfield Fisher "the Mother principle": examples of female solidarity and sisterhood. Different from many of her nineteenth-century female predecessors, however, Gale thought of herself as a literary artist, and wrote frequently about the role of art and the literary artist.

Instead of sororal connections, Cather predicates her model of artistic authority on the figure of the solitary artist, aloof from and impervious to political causes, social movements, or literary communities. This model—a traditionally masculine representation of artistic sensibility—revises ideas of female literary authority as it was understood in America in the early part of the twentieth century. And while it may not preclude communal feeling, it certainly precludes communal *participation*. In order to preserve her sense of literary independence, Cather refuses to commit herself publicly to any group, any affiliation—particularly gender-based affiliation. To be seen as a "woman writer" was to be defined by a label that collapsed aesthetic differences under the essentializing rubric of gender: in Cather's eyes, "woman writer" automatically enrolled her in a community that was limiting, public, and belittled, while "artist" was autonomous, private, and celebrated.

Female contemporaries thus form a sisterhood that threatens Cather: the threat of being engulfed by sameness despite her struggle to establish herself as "an artist," separate from and untouched by gender issues. And yet, as we see in Cather's letters to Gale, sisterhood and community are alluring, haunting. Cather's ambivalence about sisterhood and community seems to split along the dividing line between public and private: in private, Cather expresses desire for sisterhood and talks about her wish to come to Portage, or to have Gale visit her (again) in New York. In public, though, Cather is adamantly silent about her friend and her friend's work, as she was about almost all her female peers.[24]

Given Cather's professed aloofness from the world around her, it is all the more startling that she chose to correspond with Gale at all. Gale was an outspoken feminist, pacifist, and activist who often used her literary reputation to increase public attention to her various political causes. Gale's early sentimental short stories are exactly the sort of "women's writing" that Cather abhorred. At the other extreme, Gale's Pulitzer prize-winning play, *Miss Lulu Bett,* has an unequivocally feminist message—something about which Cather was equally unsympathetic. Politics notwithstanding, the two women met together regularly on Gale's visits to New York, month-long trips that she made annually after she had returned permanently in Portage in 1912. Cather speaks fondly about meeting Gale's stepdaughter and her letters to Gale are signed "with love," or "always affectionately yours," a sign of the bond that existed between them.

In her letters Cather speaks highly of Gale's writing, but she never referred to her friends' work in public, a silence that she maintained about the work of almost all her female contemporaries. Gale, on the other hand, praised Cather's work in several different essays, and used *The Professor's House* in a seminar she taught in Colorado. Cather's relationship with Gale reveals her ambivalence towards the larger community of women writers and suggests why she refused to orient herself with the lesbian world of the Village, even as it emerged around her. In all cases, Cather very carefully circumscribed herself and her points of contact with others. Her letters to Gale imagine the possibility of unity, neighborliness, and sisterhood but never quite allow these things to happen. She lives in the Village but does not publicly espouse any of its new ideas: contact, for Cather, seems truly pernicious, particularly contact with communities of women. Although it is possible to argue that Cather helped to expand the possibilities available for women writers in America precisely because she refused to define herself as a "woman writer," the model she offers us instead is a version of the "American Adam," the solitary artist who fears that connection and community will stifle individualism and creativity. Ironically, then, even as Cather goes to great lengths to declare herself free of one tradition, she inscribes herself into another. In Cather's relationship with Gale, and in her attitudes towards her neighbors in the Village, we can see Cather's awareness that there might be other possibilities for redefining the role of woman writer, but that these other avenues represent too great a risk for her to follow. It is possible only for her to admire and observe, but not to participate. As her letter to Gale about the beauty of Portage suggests, Cather's property lines were firmly drawn: boundaries that kept herself in and others out.

Cather's boundary markers seem to have been effective, however: it is Cather who has survived the vicissitudes of changing literary tastes, while Gale has all but vanished from discussions of the period. And the editors, journalists, writers, and reformers who comprised the city of women so proudly described by Mabel Dodge Luhan have also been relegated to the footnotes, for the most part—particularly the women artists and writers. The few artists and writers who remain as "central" are those who were most ambivalent, or even hostile, to being considered with their female peers: Gertrude Stein, Virginia Woolf, Wharton, Cather. Cather, it seems, may have made the correct—if dispiriting—choice: she remains central albeit solitary, while Gale, her epistolary and literary sister, has been all but forgotten. Gale should have perhaps heeded her friend's advice to regard all contact as pernicious.

Notes

1. Unless otherwise noted, all the letters referred to in this essay are in the Zona Gale Collection at the State Historical Society in Madison, Wisconsin. The letters from Cather to Gale are paraphrased rather than quoted directly due to the stipulation in Cather's will that prohibits direct use of material not published in Cather's lifetime. This letter is dated 25 November 1929.

2. Mabel Dodge Luhan, *Intimate Memories* (New York: Harcourt, Brace and Company, 1936), 143.

3. For more about Heterodoxy and its members, see Judith Schwarz, *Radical Feminists of Heterodoxy: Greenwich Village 1912–1940* (Norwich, VT: New Victoria Publishers, 1986).

4. Cather to Gale, 16 October 1929.

5. For more about Greenwich Village and its connections both to the avant-garde and the emergence of gay and lesbian communities, see Steven Watson's book, *Strange Bedfellows: The First American Avant-Garde* (New York: Abbeville, 1991) and George Chauncey's *Gay New York: Gender, Culture, and the Making of the Gay Male World, 1890–1940* (New York: Basic, 1994).

6. Edith Lewis, *Willa Cather Living* (New York: Knopf, 1953), xv.

7. It is interesting, given what was going on in the Village at this time, that Lewis also says her "memories of this time are rather indefinite. I seem to recall it as a period of uncertainty and change, and of somewhat troubled housekeeping" (74). Her indefinite memories seem rather at odds with the other, very detailed descriptions she gives of their living situations and of the nuances of Cather's career. One wonders whether part of what was uncertain and troubling was their decision to keep house together, particularly given that Cather was at this time still seeing a great deal of Isabelle McClung.

8. Watson calls this rooming house the "House of Genius." This further links Cather to the very radicalism that she so fervently denied in letters to friends and family, and in public. (Watson, *Bedfellows*, 126.)

9. Cynthia Griffin Wolff, in this volume, points out that the 1913 Armory show, which caused such a tremendous upheaval—politically, socially, aesthetically—was only a few blocks from the offices of *McClure's* and within walking distance of the Bank Street apartment. In short, the new bohemia was everywhere in the Village, but Cather seems not to have noticed.

10. Lewis, *Living*, xvi.

11. Woodress continues the image of Cather as an artist detached from the experimental world around her when he characterizes the Village, in 1927, as a "backwater." James Woodress, *Willa Cather: A Literary Life* (Lincoln: University of Nebraska Press, 1978), 412.

In fact, by 1927, the Village had become a thriving commercial district due in part to the very subways that drove Cather out of Bank Street.

12. Watson, *Bedfellows*, 144; Chauncey, *Gay New York*, 234.

13. Chauncey, *Gay New York*, 10.

14. Ibid., 234.

15. In her important book, *Odd Girls and Twilight Lovers: A History of Lesbian Life in Twentieth-Century America,* Lillian Faderman suggests that "Cather became very secretive about her private life around the turn of the century because she was cognizant of the fall from grace that love between women was beginning to suffer. . . . She cultivated the image of celibacy and pretended to reject all human ties for the sake of art" (53). While Faderman's description of Cather seems somewhat extreme, her observation about Cather's secret private life is accurate. It raises again the question that I have been asking, however: if Cather wanted to hide her private life, why live in the Village with Lewis?

16. In an astute comment to an earlier version of this paper, Jo Ann Middleton pointed out that in "Coming, Aphrodite!" Cather writes that "nobody had ever taught [Don Hedger] that he ought to be interested in other people; in the Pittsburgh steel strike, in the Fresh Air Fund, in the scandal about the Babies' Hospital." Willa Cather, *Collected Stories* (New York: Vintage, 1992), 69. Subsequent references will be indicated in the text as *CS.* By detailing those things that Hedger is *not* interested in or knowledgeable about, of course, Cather illustrates that she herself is quite aware of the contemporary social and political issues, thus belying to some degree her apolitical public stance.

17. For instance, we might consider Cather's insistence on her artless composition methods, which she makes clear in a late essay (1931) about *O Pioneers!.* She writes that the novel emerged "with no 'arranging' or 'inventing'; everything was spontaneous and took its own place, right or wrong" (*Willa Cather on Writing,* 92). If we are to believe her, the novel sprang fully formed onto paper, an image that seems quite at odds with what we know to be Cather's almost obsessive attention to detail, to craft.

18. Luhan, *Memories,* 143.

19. Woodress, *WC,* 363.

20. The play that won the Pulitzer is one of the few exceptions: Miss Lulu struggles against the confines of her suffocating existence and leaves town alone, on her own adventures (in the version that was first produced) and then with her adventuring husband (in the revised production). Given the privileged position that "the individual" occupies in U.S. literature and thought, it is not surprising that it is this play for which Gale is the best-known today.

21. In her refusal of the label "woman writer," Cather is similar to Gertrude Stein. Stein, however, seems not to have had the same need to distance herself from her sexuality that Cather had.

22. I have discussed these relationships and Cather's attitudes towards her contemporaries in "Threats of Correspondence," in *Studies in American Fiction* (1997) 25: 2.

23. Cather to Gale, 23 October 1928.

24. In a keynote address presented at the Seventh International Willa Cather Seminar (June 1997), Merrill Skaggs discussed the literary rivalry between Ellen Glasgow and Cather. In "Cather, Woolf, and the Two Mrs. Ramsays" (*College English,* September 1998: 29–41). I discuss Cather's attitudes towards Virginia Woolf. Generally, however, Cather's relations with her female literary contemporaries have not been closely scrutinized.

Bibliography

Cather, Willa. *Collected Stories*. New York: Vintage, 1992.

―――――. *On Writing*. Knopf, 1949. Lincoln: University of Nebraska Press, 1988.

Chauncey, George. *Gay New York: Gender, Culture, and the Making of the Gay Male World, 1890–1940*. New York: Basic, 1994.

Faderman, Lillian. *Odd Girls and Twilight Lovers: A History of Lesbian Life*. New York: Oxford University Press, 1991.

Luhan, Mabel Dodge. *Intimate Memories*. New York: Harcourt, Brace, 1936.

Schwarz, Judith. *Radical Feminists of Heterodoxy: Greenwich Village 1912–1940*. Norwich, VT: New Victoria, 1986.

Watson, Steven. *Strange Bedfellows: The First American Avant-Garde*. New York: Abbeville, 1991.

Williams, Deborah. "Threats of Correspondence: The Letters of Edith Wharton, Zona Gale, and Willa Cather." *Studies in American Fiction*. 25 (1997): 2.

―――――. "Cather, Woolf, and the Two Mrs. Ramsays." *College English*. September 1998: 29–41.

Woodress, James. *Willa Cather: A Literary Life*. Lincoln: University of Nebraska Press, 1987.

Meeting in New York:
Willa Cather and Sigrid Undset

MONA PERS

Introducing Sigrid Undset

Early in 1940, "at the height of the Russian invasion of Finland and only a few short weeks before Norway's violation by Germany," Sigrid Undset sent to the editors of *Twentieth Century Authors* an autobiographical sketch in which she declares: "I have always hated publicity about myself. But as things are here . . . I have come to the conclusion that I may just as well tell something about myself whilst I can." All her accounts of herself, however, acknowledged that almost from the beginning, life was tough for her. Her much loved father, a famous archeologist, died when she was still a child. Money grew scarce, and from the age of sixteen, she had to shoulder the role of the family's main breadwinner by working in "the office of an electrical engineers bureau." She minded less because studying would have been a worse alternative: "I hated school so intensely. It interfered with my freedom."[1]

Although she prized freedom highly, Undset's own life did not offer her much of it. At twenty-nine she married a self-centered painter with three children from a former marriage, whom she volunteered to take care of. Before long he and Undset had three children of their own as well. Undset's husband, who was seldom home, did not earn enough to sustain them, and the financial burden again fell on her shoulders. "I wrote books, kept house, and took care of the children," she says.[2] She wrote at night, producing one masterpiece after the other, and in 1928 was awarded the Nobel Prize for Literature. Undset was the second female author to be so honored. To date, the Nobel Prize has been awarded to only six women, two of them Scandinavian.

Undset has been hailed as "the first writer to consecrate her whole life to the study of woman." I myself prefer claims that "her whole life instead has been consecrated to the study of the human soul." That focus is most remarkably displayed in her great novels of thirteenth- and fourteenth-century Norway. In the three-volume *Kristin Lavransdatter* and *The Master of Hestviken* she has, by skilfully applying a

223

modern psychological approach, managed to "reconstruct a dead life in terms of living beings."[3]

Kindred Souls: Sigrid Undset and Willa Cather

In the spring of 1940 the German Nazis occupied Norway. The situation was dangerous for Norwegians like Undset, who had been openly anti-Nazi. Her 26-year-old son had been killed in guerrilla fighting and Sigrid Undset realized that, to save her life, she would have to flee her native country. Moving by way of Sweden, Russia, Japan, and San Francisco, she and her youngest son reached New York on 3 September. One of the few people she knew personally in New York was Alfred A. Knopf, her publisher as well as Willa Cather's. Knopf had already established contact with Undset when his publishing house opened in London in 1919, and had visited her in her native town of Lillehammer in 1922. Through him Undset knew of Willa Cather, with whom she had been corresponding for some time. Knopf recalls that once she reached New York, "Mrs. Undset was very eager to meet Miss Cather, whose work she greatly admired, and I soon brought this about. The two ladies had much in common and became very good friends."[4]

Years before he arranged this meeting, Knopf had written to Cather, "You'll be interested perhaps in knowing that in Sigrid Undset you have a most devoted admirer. She does all she can for you in Norway and even keeps a little picture of you on her desk. She is a most remarkable woman. I'd like to see you together for I think you'd hit it off with each other. You are both such real persons—and her attitude toward her work—the movies, money etc. so much like your own."[5] In the late fall of 1935, in fact, Undset had reported to Knopf that her promotional efforts in Norway on behalf of Cather had met with some measure of success. Knopf, in turn, had forwarded the news to Cather: "Mrs. Undset writes that her sister is to translate *Lucy Gayheart* into Norwegian. She says, 'I am very glad that Nygaards have ventured on a Norwegian edition of one of Miss Cather's books and also that my sister is to do it. She translates well—which some of their latest translators are very far from doing.' "[6] Writing to her childhood friend Carrie Miner Sherwood six days later, Cather recommends reading Undset's latest book in English (probably *The Longest Years*), and hopes that Undset's books are available in the library.[7]

With such high expectations preceding it, the meeting of the two writers could easily have been a letdown for either of them, but it was not. On 16 May 1941, Undset wrote to her Swedish friend, the writer Alice Lyttkens, that "Willa Cather is just as fine and wise a person, and just as full of love of all that is true and human as when she writes, and we like the same things and love the same places in Europe—which are sad to think about now."[8] As promptly, on the following day Cather wrote to Carrie Sherwood to describe the evening that Undset had spent with her the previous night. It had been a peaceful and relaxing evening, as always with Undset, she said, and then continued the account with a long and detailed eulogy of this great Norwegian woman. In addition to being warm, calm, and magnificent, for example, Cather found that Undset was also learned, proficient in no less than four languages, quite a botanist, and a marvelous cook, all qualities and skills that Cather prized highly.[9]

In *Willa Cather: A Memoir*, Elizabeth Shepley Sergeant mentions that Cather often talked with her about her friend Sigrid Undset, "that rock of a Norwegian woman who, during the war, established herself on Brooklyn Heights where she could see the battered ships come in from their dangerous voyages, and keep in touch with the Norwegian underground."[10] Undset certainly put her enforced exile to good patriotic use. A month after her arrival in New York she set out on an extensive, one-year lecture tour of the United States. The main theme for her forty lectures was the effects of World War II on the Scandinavian countries, and especially on their writers. Undset did not enjoy lecturing to crowds, but took on the task for Norway's sake. Women's clubs all over the United States invited her to give lectures in their "Celebrity series." The set-up was one of the oddest things she had come across so far in America, she wrote.[11]

Lecturing was not Undset's only method of propagandizing for her besieged country. During her years in New York she made several radio programs a month and wrote numerous articles about Norway for influential American newspapers and periodicals. Not surprisingly, she also described America and the Americans to her countrymen.

Curious and alert to everything around her, Undset made keen observations about the many people and places she encountered in various parts of America. Her well-known essays "Skjönne America" (Beautiful America), "Amerikansk litteratur" (American Literature), and "Common Ground" were all written during World War II.[12] They disclose that in many respects, both "the country and the people were different from what she expected," claims her first biographer, Professor A. H. Winsnes, referring to lengthy excerpts from her texts. For example, "We come to America," she writes, "with the completely mistaken notion that the whole enormous country is dotted with great towns and huge industrial plants and clusters of chimneys, everything connected by arterial roads with a continuous stream of lorries and cars passing over them, as if they were on conveyor-belts—and we think there is never a glimpse of open country to be seen."[13] This idea, Winsnes suggests, was conveyed to Undset by the type of rather 'hard-boiled' American literature then available in Norway, which "gives an extremely one-sided picture" of the country. But Undset herself clarified her corrective: "It was only just before the outbreak of the war that books by Thomas Wolfe, Willa Cather, Marjorie Kinnan Rawlings and one or two more, had aroused in us the suspicion that America was still a continent which had vast sparsely settled territories and a mighty and varied natural beauty."[14]

Crisscrossing America by train, Undset was often surprised that people only "rarely looked out of the window at the country they were travelling through." But she soon surmised that this did not mean Americans had no feeling for the beauty of their country: "At least, I was lucky enough to meet many American men and women who loved their country and their own districts—the feeling and character of air and sky and contour in the places where they had grown up, the animals and trees, . . . they knew and appreciated all these as happily and deeply as I knew Vestre Aker and Nordmark."[15]

Undset obviously concluded that among the foremost of those Americans loving their country was Willa Cather. Each woman esteemed the other's extensive knowledge of flowers, bushes, and trees. Arne Skouen suggests that the main reason for their friendship, in fact, was their mutual love of flowers.[16] Cather wrote to Carrie Miner Sherwood that Undset knew everything there was to know about both garden flowers and wild flowers; Cather marveled at how Undset's potted plants were thriving.[17] Undset told her sister of a big gardenia that she had given extra love and care, because Cather had given it to her.[18] In her long obituary on Cather, Undset writes that during her stay in America, she herself had grown quite knowledgeable about the magnificent American flora; still, "there was always a blooming tree or a flower plant that Willa Cather said I must see." The last time Cather wrote, she asked whether Undset had seen "the Judas tree in the spring, all covered with cymes of pinkish blue flowers, and the Catalpa tree in the summer, with its screens of big, orchid like flowers."[19]

Among the very first things Undset bought in America was a Flora, a book about native plants. In the spring of 1941 she wrote to a friend in Norway that she wanted to write her own book about America, which was to be mostly about its natural beauty, the American flora.[20] Judging from what she told Eleanor Hinman in 1921, Cather would have liked to do so, too: "There is one book that I would rather have produced than all my novels. That is the Clemens botany dealing with the wild flowers of the west."[21] Undset felt the same way about the writings of Carl Linneaus.

Unfortunately, Undset could never spare the time to write her book about the American flora. As long as the war lasted, she felt it was more urgent to write about Norway in order to support its fight for freedom. Besides all her articles, lectures, and radio programs, she also managed to write three books in America; the first one, *Return to the Future,* deals with her escape from Norway and was published in 1942. Cather disliked the title. On February 16, 1942, Cather wrote Ferris Greenslet at Houghton Mifflin that a much better title for this interesting book would have been "My Escape from Norway."[22] Cather realized, however, that there was no way the "unpersuadable" Undset could be made to change the title. Three days later Cather informed Mary Miner Creighton that Alfred Knopf agreed with her about the title. When she urged him to bring up the subject with Undset, however, he just grinned and suggested that she should be the one to try first, instead. In the end, neither of them dared voice their suggestion about the title to Undset.[23]

Except for its title, Cather liked *Return to the Future.* She told Mary Miner Creighton that the book was both thrilling and very interesting, especially the detailed descriptions of the disgusting living conditions in wartime Russia. The descriptions of Japan and the Japanese seemed by contrast highly affirmative. Cather feared, she said, that this would cause an outcry from the women's clubs in America, which she was sure would have no effect whatsoever on Undset, who would never change a single line in her text for anybody.[24]

A couple of months later, Cather again brought up Undset's descriptions of dirty Russia and clean, elegant Japan. In a letter to Mrs. Whicher, she expressed relief that the book had done well and had been received without prejudice, which Cather thought reflected credit on Americans. She suggested that Mrs. Whicher also read *Gunnar's Daughter,* in her opinion the best book by Undset so far, even though one still practically unknown in America.[25]

Fortaellingen om Viga-Ljot og Vigdis, the original title of *Gunnar's Daughter,* was published in 1909. The English translation did not come until 1936. Elizabeth Shepley Sergeant recalls, "Willa spoke with warmest admiration of *Kristin Lavransdatter* and *Gunnar's Daughter,* books whose inspiration comes from the Sagas and the early

Nordic time. Here, too, was heroic man, pioneer man, exposed to untold danger and peril and resisting and conquering it, creating a new spiritual world. But Mrs. Undset's novels of modern Norway were of no interest to her."[26] Cather no doubt recognized congenial literary themes and characters in Undset's historical novels. The critical acclaim that *Kristin Lavransdatter* offered "a new dimension of historical fiction, with insights into love and marriage realistically portrayed in the context of an essentially moral universe"[27] applies equally well to Cather's *Shadows on the Rock*. Winsnes' assertion that in Undset's work "what is at issue . . . is the question of *loyalty*," could sum up Cather's work, too. As Winsnes contends, Undset's "writing revolves around the central relationships in life in which loyalty is demanded, . . . —between husband and wife, parents and children, the individual and his home, family and country. Most of all it is concerned with man's loyalty towards the Creator, for without loyalty towards Him, no other loyalty is possible."[28] The same is true of most human relations in Cather's fiction. Cather's "gift of sympathy," which Undset was wont to praise, seems in fact all but synonymous with her own sense of "loyalty." Loyalty to their Creator is central to the protagonists of both *Death Comes for the Archbishop* and *Shadows on the Rock*.

Undset, like Cather, has off and on been accused of being both reactionary and escapist. Unset was no more perturbed by those allegations than Cather was. In her article, "War and Literature," Undset makes a clear distinction between vulgar literature of escape, what she calls day-dream literature, and another type, which "turns to history for its subjects, to the duties which have been involved in the struggles of the past" that may also be termed escapist. To this type, Undset argues, "some of the finest literature in the world belongs."[29] She sounds just like Cather.

Cather and Undset also sound alike when praising each other's works and personalities. In her obituary, Undset says of Cather that in her writings, she was unsentimental and never embellished anything.[30] In a letter to Mary Miner Creighton, Cather asserts that, in her writings, Undset never exaggerates anything.[31] In other words, they recognize in each other's works the truthfulness they both strove for in their own. About Cather as a person Undset wrote that "she was as charming and beautiful as she was humorous and wise."[32] Cather informed Carrie Miner Sherwood unequivocally that Undset had all the qualities of a truly great woman.[33]

It did not take the two women long to discover that they were on the same wave length as writers, and that there were many parallels in their lives.[34] Undset, at least, sensed that also on a deeper, more personal level, they had much in common. In both their lives, religion played an important role. So did their childhood memories. They both had experienced the burden and rewards of being the oldest child in their families, painfully aware that their younger sisters were more easy-going and graceful than they were. They had been closely attached to their fathers, and struggled to cope with their spoilt and beautiful mothers. They both developed into high-performing, energetic, impetuous, and unyielding adults. When it came to family and friends they were generous, protective, and supportive. With others, they were fiercely defensive of their personal integrity, and as they grew older, their tendency towards isolation increased. "Sigrid Undset was notoriously hostile to what she saw as unwarranted prying into her private life."[35] She had a high fence erected around her house to ensure her privacy, while Cather entrenched herself in her Park Avenue apartment. They were both reluctant to give interviews, and they wished to prevent further poking into their lives once they were dead. Undset intended to burn "every single piece of paper except one typewritten copy of every book—that was to be the only unprinted 'evidence' she left behind."[36] Cather had similar ideas, but fortunately neither of them had time to carry out in full these autos-da-fé. Thus some of the letters they wrote to each other were saved for posterity.

According to Borghild Krane, the letters Willa Cather wrote to Sigrid Undset are mostly about their "pleasant little meetings and dinners, their mutual hopes for a victorious end to the war, and the very warm feelings they had for each other."[37]

The first letter Undset wrote to Cather after her return to Norway exudes the same warm feelings of friendship: "Very often I think of you and wonder, how are you now? Meeting you was one of the happiest things that happened to me in America, and I cherish the memory of those evenings with you and Miss Lewis so much. When . . . I unpacked your books, it was quite a different thing to handle them . . . , thinking of you as a friend I know now. Your picture which Alfred Knopf sent me from you years ago I also unearthed. . . . It is a little broken and soiled, but all the more dear to me."[38] The rest of the letter is mostly about the postwar situation in Norway. When almost a year later, Cather was going through her letters from Undset, she decided not to destroy this one but to give it to Mary Miner Creighton who, unlike Cather, had once visited Norway.

The last letter Undset wrote to Cather she never sent, because the telegram from Edith Lewis about Cather's sudden death reached her before she had time to do so. Undset wrote her condolences to Lewis on the reverse side of the telegram: "'I am sorry thinking how you must feel the loss of Willa Cather. I also loved her so much."[39]

Notes

1. Stanley J. Kunitz, ed., *Twentieth Century Authors* (New York: Wilson, 1985), 1432–34.

2. Ibid., 1433.

3. Ibid., 1434.

4. Alfred A. Knopf, "Miss Cather," *The Art of Willa Cather,* ed. Bernice Slote and Virginia Faulkner (Lincoln: University of Nebraska Press, 1974), 218.

5. Alfred A. Knopf to Willa Cather, 9 March, n.y., WCPM Archives.

6. Alfred A. Knopf to Willa Cather, 3 December 1935, WCPM Archives.

7. Willa Cather to Carrie Miner Sherwood, 9 December 1935, WCPM Archives.

8. Quoted in Tordis Orjasaeter, *Sigrid Undset—Ett Liv* (Stockholm: Norstedts Förlag, 1993), 321. My translation.

9. Willa Cather to Carrie Miner Sherwood, 17 May 1941, WCPM Archives.

10. Elizabeth Shepley Sergeant, *Willa Cather: A Memoir* (Philadelphia and New York: J. B. Lippincott, 1953), 273.

11. Undset letter to Lyttkens, 13 October 1940, *Ett Liv,* 304.

12. "Sigrid Undset," *Great Women Writers,* ed. Frank N. Magill (London: Robert Hale, 1994), 552.

13. A. H. Winsnes, *Sigrid Undset. A Study in Christian Realism* (New York: Sheed and Ward, 1953), 224–25.

14. Winsnes, *Christian Realism,* 225.

15. Ibid.

16. Arne Skouen, *Sigrid Undset Skriver Hjem* (Oslo: H. Ashehoug & Co, 1982), 80.

17. Willa Cather to Carrie Miner Sherwood, 16 May 1941, WCPM Archives.

18. Letter, 13 October 1940, reported in Skouen, *Undset,* 81.

19. "Willa Cather," *Verdens Gang* (3 May 1947), 11. My translation.

20. Orjasaeter, *Ett Liv,* 318.

21. Eleanor Hinman, "Willa Cather, Famous Nebraska Novelist, Says Pioneer Mother Held Greatest Appreciation of Art—Raps Women Who Devote Themselves to Culture Clubs," *Lincoln Sunday Star,* Arts Section, 6 November 1921: 1, 12.

22. Willa Cather to Ferris Greenslet, 16 February 1942, Houghton Library, Harvard University.

23. Willa Cather to Mary Miner Creighton, 19 February 1942, WCPM Archives.

24. Ibid.

25. Willa Cather to Mrs. Whicher, 22 April 1942, Pierpont Morgan Library, New York.

26. Sergeant, *Memoir,* 273.

27. *Great Women Writers,* 553.

28. Winsnes, *Christian Realism,* 246, 247.

29. Ibid., 249.

30. "Willa Cather," *Verdens Gang* (3 May 1947), 5.

31. Willa Cather to Mary Miner Creighton, 19 February 1942, WCPM Archives.

32. *Verdens Gang,* 11. My translation.

33. Willa Cather to Carrie Miner Sherwood, 17 May 1941, WCPM Archives.
34. Orjasaeter, *Ett Liv,* 320.
35. Gunnel Vallquist, "Sigrid Undset som journalist," *Svenska Dagbladet* (18 April 1982): 10. My translation.
36. Ibid.
37. Borghild Krane, *Sigrid Undset. Liv og Meninger* (Oslo: Gyldendal, 1970) 111. My translation.
38. Sigrid Undset to Willa Cather, 17 March 1946, Newberry Library, Chicago.
39. Quoted in Krane, *Liv og Meninger,* 111.

Bibliography

Unpublished Letters

Cather, Willa. Letters to Carrie Miner Sherwood, 9 December 1935 and 17 May 1941. Willa Cather Pioneer Memorial Archives, Red Cloud.
———. Letters to Mary Miner Creighton, 19 February 1942. Willa Cather Pioneer Memorial Archives, Red Cloud. 26 February 1947. Newberry Library, Chicago.
———. Letter to F. G. Greenslet, 16 February 1942. Houghton Library, Harvard University.
———. Letter to Mrs. Whicher, 22 April 1942. Pierpont Morgan Library, New York.
Knopf, Alfred. Letters to Willa Cather, 9 March, n.y. and 3 December 1935. Willa Cather Pioneer Memorial Archives, Red Cloud.
Undset, Sigrid. Letter to Willa Cather, 17 March 1946. Newberry Library, Chicago.

Books and Articles

Great Women Writers. "Sigrid Undset." Ed. Frank N. Magill. London: Robert Hale, 1994.
Hinman, Eleanor. "Willa Cather, Famous Nebraska Novelist, Says Pioneer Mother Held Greatest Appreciation of Art—Raps Women Who Devote Themselves to Culture Clubs." *Lincoln Sunday Star,* Arts Section, 6 November 1921: 1, 12.
Knopf, Alfred A. "Miss Cather." *The Art of Willa Cather.* Ed. Bernice Slote and Virginia Faulkner. Lincoln: University of Nebraska Press, 1974.
Krane, Borghild. *Sigrid Undset. Liv og Meninger.* Oslo: Gyldendal, 1970.
Kunitz, Stanley J., ed. *Twentieth Century Authors.* New York: Wilson, 1985.
Orjasaeter, Tordis. *Sigrid Undset—Ett Liv.* Stockholm: Norstedts Fšrlag, 1993.
Skouen, Arne. *Sigrid Undset Skriver Hjem.* Oslo: H. Ashehoug & Co., 1982.
Sergeant, Elizabeth Shepley. *Willa Cather: A Memoir.* Philadelphia and New York: Lippincott, 1953.
Undset, Sigrid. "Willa Cather." *Verdens Gang.* 3 May 1947: 5,11.
Vallquist, Gunnel. "Sigrid Undset som journalist." *Svenska Dagbladet.* 18 April 1982: 10.
Winsnes, A. H. *Sigrid Undset: A Study in Christian Realism.* New York: Sheed and Ward, 1953.

Exclusion as Adventure:
Willa Cather and Postmodernism

LAURA WINTERS

Exclusion is a pervasive theme in Willa Cather's fiction. In this essay I will identify and briefly explore this Catherian theme in order to see how Cather's body of work generally (and particularly her theme of exclusion) has been appropriated by contemporary writers in dialogue with Cather's themes, techniques and conclusions. The idea for this essay comes, in part, from my reading four postmodern works, Christopher Coe's 1993 novel, *Such Times;* David Leavitt's *The Page Turner* and Toni Morrison's *Paradise* (both published in 1998); and Alain de Botton's 1997 much less easily classifiable work, *How Proust Can Save Your Life.*

A postmodern reflection on *My Mortal Enemy,* Christopher Coe's *Such Times* begins to explore contemporary novelists' debt to Willa Cather. Coe's narrator Timothy says, "There is an indescribable feeling to holding, reading, and owning forever a first edition of Willa Cather's *My Mortal Enemy.* . . . You need to have the dust jacket to have the full effect, and if the book is signed by the author, that will increase the thrill. But the principal reason that a first edition of a good book imparts an unusual joy is that books were better made around the time that Willa Cather wrote them."[1] Coe's narrator, a gay male Nellie Birdseye, always cruising and always hoping to find identity through others' stories, is not merely a literary dilettante. He is a sometimes loving and sometimes wicked caretaker of his friends who are dying, though he certainly wishes to make beauty out of even that horror, from which he is, in some sense, excluded. In Coe's fiction, the mortal enemy is primarily HIV/AIDS; but the mortal enemy for the community depicted in this novel is also the need to re-envision a fairy-tale world of sexual freedom, as well as the desire to create an aesthetically and emotionally perfect death (or death scene). Coe is signaling his own debt to Cather (whose books were made better than they are today) and the debt of a generation of postmodern novelists who must, from various perspectives and amidst various apocalypses, write about how to survive after the worst has happened; about the radical exclusion that suffering and death can bring.

Before I discuss more fully the postmodern response to Cather's fiction, let me explore briefly that Catherian idea of exclusion which these contemporary writers find so compelling. In Cather's fiction a character is very often outside a window or a door or the slit in the wall of a cave, hoping in some way to get in and wishing for a perceived paradise inside. I acknowledge Cynthia Briggs's interesting work on windows in Cather, as well as Janis Stout's recent book-length study of the role of doors and windows in women writers' narratives of departure. But I'm after something very different here, and it concerns the nature of exclusion.

Sarah Orne Jewett's precept, so essential to Cather, about the importance of "the shapes and scenes that have teased the mind for years"[2] is valuable for me as a critic: that is, the idea of exclusion in Cather's fiction teases my mind because it includes simultaneously the impoverishment of that position of longing, and the enormous freedom of imagination that exclusion often provides for Cather's characters. For them, longing is often the source of the wildest imaginings and the most important plan making. For her characters, the state of exclusion demands that each must try to create a compelling alternate paradise.

I'm interested in Cather's characters' moments of indecision, confusion, or uncertainty. Think of Bartley Alexander, anxious in Bedford Square, waiting for a glimpse of his former lover Hilda, as her hansom cab arrives and she runs up the steps: "In a few moments the lights flared up brightly behind the white curtains and as he walked away he heard a window raised. But he had gone too far to look up without turning around."[3] The centrality of this scene of being on the outside of some warmer, brighter inside begins early in Cather, and continues until the end of her writing life. I think, for example, of Nellie Birdseye outside of Myra's and Oswald's room, overhearing the argument about the safety deposit box key in *My Mortal Enemy;* or of Kathleen suffering outside her father's attic study door, waiting until Godfrey St. Peter's work time is over in *The Professor's House.*

Because I am primarily a teacher, I want to provide a range of models of human behavior for my students (since I believe forthrightly that literary narrative teaches us how to and how not to live our lives). So I began to wonder what wisdom Cather had to teach us about this state of being excluded. Certainly her fiction conveys the enormous freedom and power and control we experience in longing. Being on the outside of tangible places teaches us ways to be existentially on the outside of mystery.

Yet the New York connections for this essay started with a rereading of "Paul's Case" about a year ago. As I read the familiar words concerning Paul's irritability after a wonderful concert—his "feeling of not being able to let down, of its being impossible to give up this delicious excitement which was the only thing that could be called living at all"[4]—I thought of how often that experience occurred in Cather's life and how frequently she tried to describe it in her fiction. And I considered Cather's description of "the [hotel] Schenley," in Pittsburgh, where all "the actors and singers of the better class stayed . . . when they were in the city" (122) and where "Paul . . . often hung about . . . watching the people go in and out, longing to enter and leave schoolmasters and dull care behind him forever" (122). As Paul watches the singer enter this paradise and as he imagines the luxury inside, he "was startled to find that he was still outside in the slush of the gravel driveway; that his boots were letting in the water and his scanty overcoat was clinging wet about him. . . . There it was, what he wanted—tangible before him, like the fairy world of a Christmas pantomime—but mocking spirits stood guard at the doors, and, as the rain beat in his face, Paul wondered whether he were destined always to shiver in the black night outside, looking up at it" (122). This understanding is central to Cather's fiction as well. At moments of greatest longing, at the moments of the need for decision-making, places adhere in the minds of Cather's characters.

For Paul, New York City is the ultimate paradise. New York, particularly the Waldorf and the best shops, represent the other side of the door, and his lack of ability to reside there forever creates the need for death, a drop "back into the immense design of things" (138). The phrasing of this last line of "Paul's Case" is obviously important to Cather since it echoes what would become the inscription on her own tombstone: "that is happiness; to be dissolved into something complete and great."[5]

Another clear Cather literary descendant, David Leavitt's very recent novel *The Page Turner* is a postmodern "Paul's Case." In fact that phrase, "in Paul's case," appears directly in this work about a young, gifted musician who begins an affair with an older virtuoso who is both mentor and teacher. Yet simultaneously as he brings up "Paul's Case," Leavitt rewrites aspects of *The Song of the Lark* and particularly *Lucy Gayheart*, concerning the relationship between a master musician and a pupil. In Leavitt's novel, both master and pupil are men. Paul Porterfield works as a page turner for a great pianist, Richard Kennington, whose need for perfect timing explicitly connects this novel with the key thematic pattern of time in *Lucy Gayheart*. Kennington is tied emotionally to his agent and lover of twenty years,

Joseph Mansourian; they form a pair whose relationship mirrors that of Clement Sebastian and James Mockford in *Lucy Gayheart*. Mansourian in *The Page Turner* is like Mockford (or Edith Lewis, for that matter), and is described by Leavitt as "one of the few friends who have lasted through time and change."[6]

The Page Turner (a novel written by a man who recently experienced a terrible public humiliation when Stephen Spender, I think cruelly, charged Leavitt with plagiarism for stealing and sensationalizing part of Spender's life story for the novel *While England Sleeps*) is explicitly in dialogue with both *Lucy Gayheart* and "Paul's Case." Because of this conflict, David Leavitt is in a unique position to write about the conflicted relationships between older artists and their younger followers.

Leavitt's Paul in *The Page Turner* gets everything Cather's Paul longed for: great hotels, great food, great sex. Paul's mother in *The Page Turner,* convinced that Kennington is in love with her, is literally outside the homosexual bedroom door. Leavitt's Paul gets to the other side of the door sexually, yet finds that the barriers to genuine intimacy and connection remain.

One critical question, certainly for contemporary gay and lesbian studies, involves Cather's alternate narratives, or what Eve Sedgwick calls, in an essay on "Paul's Case," Cather's "refracted plots."[7] In such plots the power of homosexual desire is conveyed through a heterosexual love story. The question is whether refraction of this kind can do less or more that an explicit story of contemporary gay sex and betrayal. For Sedgwick, these "refracted plots" allow Cather both her own enabling privacy (a postmodern phrase if there ever was one) and the "advantage there was to be taken in these plots as aptest carriers, brewed in the acid nuance of centuries, for exposition precisely of exploitation and betrayal."[8] For me as a reader, the very tried and true quality of the heterosexual plot can assume reliable evocations in readers. Cather knew the advantages of literary restraint; she allowed her readers to do the work, and make the metaphorical leaps, on their own.

In Cather's story, Paul's sights are limited—he wants fancy hotels, Negro doormen, wonderful food. But as Cather matures, what her characters find themselves on the outside of becomes much more elemental. For instance, in *The Professor's House*, Godfrey St. Peter lectures on impoverishing science and technology. I would consider this familiar passage one of the most essential in Cather's fiction. Toward the end, St. Peter says, "With the theologians came the cathedral-builders; the sculptors and glass-workers and painters.

They might, without sacrilege, have changed the prayer a little and said, "*Thy will be done in art, as it is in heaven.* How can it be done anywhere else *as* it is in heaven?"[9] Cather considers this one of the most powerful dilemmas of the human condition—to be outside paradise, trying to recreate the best of it.

On some level, my attempt to understand Cather's ideas on exclusion represents an extension of my own long-standing meditations on the idea of exile in Cather's fiction. But I also see that Cather presents those states of being (exclusion and exile) as full of hope and possibility. (At least I can see that in the daylight in a room full of friendly people.)

What hope, then, does Cather provide, what lessons for the excluded—for the poor, for those who are left out, for those not counted in, for those on the outside? Cather explicitly relates the experience of exclusion to her understanding of parting, of leave-taking, of quest, and of journey in her novels—so full of train rides, boat rides, rough and exquisite crossings. Her characters constantly leave and are left. And they must forge new lives and identities to manage those experiences.

One of the most poignant and memorable moments of this kind, from *One of Ours,* involves Claude Wheeler, on a train, on his wedding night, outside the bridal chamber. Cather conveys the desperate disappointment of a person who finds he has longed for the wrong object, when he's made the wrong choice, been longing on the outside of the wrong door. As Claude stands, knocking outside the door of his own train compartment, his wife Enid asks, "would you mind getting a berth somewhere out in the car tonight? . . . I'm not feeling very well. I think the dressing on the chicken salad must have been too rich." The passage continues, "She closed the door, and he heard the lock slip. He stood looking at the highly polished wood of the panel for a moment, then turned irresolutely and went back along the slightly swaying aisle of green curtains."[10] Initially, "on that long, dirty, uncomfortable [train] ride" (168), Claude primarily feels homesickness; but as day breaks, the "dawn-wind brought through the windows the acrid smell of sagebrush: an odor that is peculiarly stimulating in the early morning, when it always seems to promise freedom . . . large spaces, new beginnings, better days."[11] In the course of one painful evening, the "storm of anger, disappointment, and humiliation" becomes, for Claude, the opportunity for new beginnings. Is this possible, Cather's fiction asks? Is this the wisdom of exclusion as opportunity? Does this, in part, cause Claude to go to

France, the most important adventure of his life? In some sense, of course it does.

Cather also realized that sometimes people want in, and sometimes they want out, desperately. Since doubles, pairs, oppositions, and paradoxes abound in Cather's fiction, it is not surprising that on the matter of exclusion, we find opposites everywhere. St. Peter, so connected to the structures he inhabits and so often on the other side of the door—from Tom Outland, from the mesa, from his own family, from his own youthful self—still understands the most important places in terms of a door: "the great fact in life, the always possible escape from dullness, was the lake. The sun rose out of it, the day began there; it was like an open door that nobody could shut. The land and all its dreariness could never close in on you. You had only to look at the lake, and you knew you would soon be free" (30).

Cather also explored the flip side of the outside-the-door, state-of-exclusion dilemma. Near the end of *Shadows on the Rock,* Count Frontenac has a disturbing dream of himself as a child in France. In the dream he is in mortal fear of "[t]hat terrible man on the other side of the door; one could hear him moving about."[12] *Shadows,* like other Cather novels, is really a compendium of doors and windows. In the same novel that holds outside the door the menacing monster, whose exclusion Frontenac is not particularly concerned about, another scene shows the warm, welcoming, sexualized doors of the Cathedral on Christmas eve, doors which open to a "ruddy vault in blue darkness,"[13] toward which the pilgrims journey.

Contemporary novelists have particularly responded to Cather's complex and paradoxical examination of the nature of exclusion. Perhaps the most interesting postmodern response comes in Toni Morrison's novel *Paradise,* which answers *Sapphira and the Slave Girl* regarding the human attempt to create an ideal community from which some are excluded. Both Cather and Morrison interrogate the idea of exclusion.

Morrison has for years taken pains to underestimate, if not dismiss, her debt to the modernists. In a videotaped interview with the novelist A. S. Byatt, when asked directly if she had anybody from whom she'd learned her craft, whose work she admired, or who had influenced her style, Morrison responded that it is from painting she steals (presumably a less threatening theft).[14] In a Spring, 1998, interview at New York's 92nd Street Y, Anna Deavere Smith asked Morrison where her inspiration comes from and whether there have been any outstanding influences for Morrison, in light of Morrison's influence on so many artists from different fields. (Deavere Smith had mentioned that a young choreographer friend of hers had taken inspiration from the novel *Sula*.) Morrison replied, "No. And that's genius, my dear. They call it genius."[15] Obviously, Morrison chooses not to express her debt to other writers directly.

In the most perceptive review of Morrison's *Paradise*, Louis Menand in *The New Yorker* suggests that Morrison's "achievement is to have adapted [the] modernist literary tradition to her own subject matter, which is the experience of African-American women, and thereby to have made it new."[16] Menand defines that tradition in terms of Woolf and Faulkner, the subjects of Morrison's master's thesis at Cornell, and also Joyce and Hemingway; but he could well have included Cather in that list, because Morrison's debt to Cather's literary modernism is profound.

Morrison, in fact, has signaled the depth of her debt to Cather, particularly to the enduring fascination of *Sapphira*, in her critical work, *Playing in the Dark: Whiteness and the Literary Imagination*. Morrison suggests that race has been absent as a category in literary criticism about American literature, resulting in what Morrison calls "a kind of willful critical blindness";[17] and Morrison judges the critical response to *Sapphira* particularly harshly for its cowardice on this matter. Yet Morrison herself deliberately absents race in the novel *Paradise:* the reader must figure out who "the white girl" is who gets shot first, in the opening line of the novel. And there has, of course, been much critical speculation on which character might be this white girl.

In a model class on *Paradise*, held at Princeton and televised by none other than Oprah, Morrison says, "When you know a character's race, what do you know? You don't know anything." In that same class, Morrison essentially appropriates Cather's "the thing not named" (without naming it) when she discusses explicitly her own withholding of information so the reader must do the work. Her words clearly come from "The Novel Démeublé."[18]

Significantly, Morrison's *Playing in the Dark* contains one of the most trenchant and self-revealing critical statements about Cather's last work: Morrison suggests that *Sapphira* is about "the compelling attraction of exploring the possibilities of one woman's absolute power over the body of another woman."[19] *Sapphira* concerns a hellish environment and one woman's power to exclude a person from paradise. Nancy is forced by Sapphira to sleep on a pallet outside of Sapphira's bedroom door, in a place of vulnerability, because Sapphira's sexually irresponsible relative, Martin Colbert, can easily accost her there. The slave Nancy, excluded, menaced and outside of Sapphira's door, could be an image of gay women, outside the protective door of another woman, radically vulnerable there to male violence and privilege. Morrison also explored this area in *Beloved,* which equally concerns the theme of one woman's power over the body of another woman—Beloved's control over Sethe's body particularly, but also Denver's over Beloved's.

Of *Sapphira,* Morrison says, "In her last novel [Cather] works out toward the meaning of female betrayal as it faces the voice of racism."[20] This could easily describe the complexities of Morrison's *Paradise.* The many forms of female betrayal—a mother who leaves her children to suffocate in a locked car, a woman who deserts her daughter, a woman who has complete control over the care and feeding of an elderly mentor figure—these moments are at the heart of *Paradise.* And they represent, in part, Morrison's debt to Cather's themes.

Sapphira and *Paradise* can be paired thematically in the classroom on the issues of race, women's power, and exclusion, to great effect. So can *Lucy Gayheart* and *The Page Turner* on the issues of gender and sexuality, as well as Coe's *Such Times* and *My Mortal Enemy* on the issues of caretaking and death.

On the matter of exclusion as avenue to adventure, Alain de Botton's work *How Proust Can Save Your Life,* both a parody of self-help literature and an instructive, witty manual for life, suggests that Proust's fiction teaches us that "we should learn a lesson from what we naturally do when we lack something and apply it to conditions where we don't."[21] This insight is essential to understanding the moments in Cather's fiction that interest me here. What we do when we lack something is long for it, value it, examine it, scrutinize it, and try to understand it. As de Botton writes, "Deprivation quickly drives us into a process of appreciation."[22] If we could bring this level of appreciation to what lies before us, as Cather did, exclusion truly would become adventure.

Notes

1. Christopher Coe, *Such Times* (New York: Harcourt Brace, 1993), 25.
2. Willa Cather, *On Writing* (New York: Knopf, 1973), 48.
3. Willa Cather, *Alexander's Bridge* (Lincoln: University of Nebraska Press, 1977), 34–35.
4. Willa Cather, *The Troll Garden* (New York: New American Library, 1984), 121.
5. Willa Cather, *My Ántonia* (Boston: Houghton Mifflin, 1954), 18.
6. David Leavitt, *The Page Turner* (Boston: Houghton Mifflin, 1998), 52.

7. Eve Kosofsky Sedgwick, *Tendencies* (Durham: Duke University Press, 1993), 175.

8. Ibid.

9. Willa Cather, *The Professor's House* (New York: Vintage, 1973), 69.

10. Willa Cather, *One of Ours* (New York: Vintage, 1950), 167.

11. Ibid., 169.

12. Willa Cather, *Shadows on the Rock* (New York: Vintage, 1971), 244.

13. Ibid, 113.

14. "Toni Morrison with A. S. Byatt," ICA Video, 42 min., Peas Marsh, 1987, Rye England.

15. New York: YMHA at 92 St., 8:00 p. m., 26 February 1998.

16. Louis Menand, "The War Between Men and Women," *The New Yorker* (January 12, 1998): 78–82.

17. Toni Morrison, *Playing in the Dark: Whiteness and the Literary Imagination* (Cambridge: Harvard University Press, 1992), 18.

18. Aired Wednesday, 11 March 1998, WABC, New York: Channel 7, 4:00 p.m.

19. Morrison, *Playing in the Dark*, 23.

20. Ibid., 28.

21. Alain deBotton, *How Proust Can Change Your Life: Not a Novel* (New York: Random House, 1997), 164.

22. Ibid., 164.

Bibliography

Briggs, Cynthia K. "Insulated Isolation: Willa Cather's Room with a View." In *Cather Studies,* Vol. 1, Ed. by Susan J. Rosowski. Lincoln: University of Nebraska Press, 1990.

Cather, Willa. *Alexander's Bridge.* Lincoln: University of Nebraska Press, 1977.

———. *Lucy Gayheart.* New York: Vintage, 1973.

———. *My Ántonia.* Boston: Houghton Mifflin, 1954.

———. *One of Ours.* New York: Vintage, 1950.

———. *On Writing.* New York: Knopf, 1953.

———. *The Professor's House.* New York: Vintage, 1973.

———. *Shadows on the Rock.* New York: Vintage, 1971.

———. *The Troll Garden.* New York: New American Library, 1984.

Coe, Christopher. *Such Times.* New York: Harcourt Brace, 1993.

de Botton, Alain. *How Proust Can Change Your Life: Not a Novel.* New York: Random, 1997.

Leavitt, David. *The Page Turner.* Boston: Houghton Mifflin, 1998.

Menand, Louis. "The War Between Men and Women." *The New Yorker* (12 January 1998): 78–82.

Morrison, Toni. *Paradise.* New York: Knopf, 1998.

———. *Playing in the Dark: Whiteness and the Literary Imagination.* Cambridge: Harvard University Press, 1992.

Sedgwick, Eve Kosofsky. *Tendencies.* Durham: Duke University Press, 1993.

Stout, Janis P. *Through the Window, Out the Door: Women's Narratives of Departure, from Austin and Cather to Tyler, Morrison, and Didion.* Tuscaloosa: The University of Alabama Press, 1998.

IV
Urban Perspectives

Sapphira and the City

ANN ROMINES

In recent years scholars have begun to recognize Willa Cather's importance as a city novelist, with a particular interest in women's lives in cities. Most of us have agreed with Susan J. Rosowski that Cather's career as an urban novelist ended in 1935 with *Lucy Gayheart,* "her final and darkest novel of the modern city."[1] In this essay, however, I want to suggest something different: that Willa Cather's engagement with the urban novel did not entirely end in 1935. Two years later Cather began writing a novel drawn from family and local histories in the country of her earliest childhood, Virginia's Shenandoah Valley. Surely the process of life review, so often a major task of elderly persons, was a part of writing of this last novel, in which she returned to the rural setting of her first memories.[2]

But Cather herself was an *urban* woman almost all her adult life. In *City Codes,* Hana Wirth-Nesher describes some of the features of life in twentieth-century cities:

> Cities promise plenitude, but deliver inaccessibility. . . . [T]he urbanite . . . is faced with an never-ending series of partial visibilities, of gaps— figures framed in the windows of highrises . . . partly drawn blinds, taxis transporting strangers, noises from the other side of a wall. . . . Because no urbanite is exempt from this partial exclusion and imaginative reconstruction, every urbanite is to some extent an outsider.
>
> Modern urban life, then, is a landscape of partial visibilities and manifold possibilities that excludes in the very act of inviting.[3]

For readers familiar with Cather's fiction and life, this passage will strike familiar chords. Gaps, partial visibilities? A life as a partial, perpetual outsider? A fiction that both welcomes and excludes? Think about it—and bear with me.

For the issue of *Book-of-the-Month Club News* that heralded the publication of *Sapphira and the Slave Girl* in 1940, Elizabeth Sergeant wrote a description of her friend Willa Cather that seems intended to deny that Cather was truly an urban person:

> Metropolitan life has never satisfied her, blunted her impatience with its more cheap and intrusive aspects. One might expect to meet her, any

time in winter, on the windiest corner of Fifth Avenue, rebellion in her
grey eyes, every hair of her fur coat standing on end. But once indoors,
down town or up, her windows look inward. . . . She has always preferred
old books to new, had George Sand (by Courbet) over her mantel, an
orange tree hard by. Always enjoyed fine food and wine and great music,
and taken such pleasures, as a European might, with the spaciousness
they deserve. . . . Maybe homesickness for Eastern culture brought her
here, but surely natal longing for Nebraska and Virginia created her
books.[4]

In fact, this portrait evokes a Willa Cather very like the quintessential
urbanite that Wirth-Nesher describes: permanently displaced, impatient with the limitations of a life in rooms, and filling that life and
those rooms with selections from the plenitude proffered (and withheld) by metropolitan life. But Cather's books, Sergeant asserts,
come from a non-urban *elsewhere*—and *Sapphira,* in particular, was
created from "natal longing" for rural Virginia.

To help persuade you of my premise, let me call in a Virginia
chorus from *Sapphira:*

First, the wise countrywoman Mandy Ringer, who says to Rachel
Blake: "Is that so, Miz Blake! Now nobody but you would a-knowed.
Lordy me, I wisht I could a-had your chance, Mam. It's city life that
learns you, an' I'd a-loved it."[5]

Then, the intrepid African Jezebel, getting her first sight of Baltimore from the deck of a slave ship: she "regarded the water line of
the city with lively curiosity, quite different from the hopeless indifference on the faces of her fellow captives" (94–95).

Next, Sapphira's daughter, Rachel Blake: "To see Mrs. Blake working about her house and garden, a stranger would scarcely guess that
she had lived the happiest years of her life in Washington" (131). If
questioned by a neighbor about city life, "she replied simply: 'I hardly
remember. All that is gone. I'd take it kindly of you not to bring it
back to me'" (145).

For these women, the city is a memory too precious or painful to
recall, a missed chance, a past that they could not hold. For the
young slave Nancy, it is an unimaginable future destination, reached
by an urban Underground Railroad route: Winchester, Philadelphia,
New York, Montreal. Nancy despairs at the prospect of city life: "I
can't go off amongst strangers. It's too hard. . . . I want to go home to
the mill an' my own folks" (237). But Nancy's mother Till, learning
her child is en route to Montreal, concludes gratefully that "up
there," at least, Nancy will "have some chance" (249). For these
women, city life is "a chance"—whether good or ill—to claim the

fuller possibilities of their own lives. It is the same chance Cather herself grasped for in her moves to Lincoln, Pittsburgh, and New York—although she was racked by homesickness as wretched as Nancy's.[7] Like Nancy, she never returned "home" to live.

In fact Willa Cather had grown up in a house with older women who had city histories of their own. Her maternal grandmother, Rachel Seibert Boak, who had married at fourteen, spent a significant part of her adult life in Washington, where her husband, after three terms in the Virginia legislature, worked at the Department of the Interior. When William Boak died in 1854 he left—according to his obituary—"a devoted wife and a large number of children," but no recorded financial resources. According to Seibert family history, Rachel Boak then ran a boarding house in Washington or Richmond.[8] When she returned with her children to the Back Creek community where she had been born, she was apparently without the financial resources to set up a household independently; her father gave her a house. She was still living there, with her daughter Mary Virginia and the daughter's husband, Charles Cather, when the Cathers' first child, Wilella, was born in 1873. The young Cathers soon moved to Willow Shade and "Grandma Boak" assumed the management of their household, a role she maintained almost until her death in Red Cloud in 1893.[9]

Willa Cather grew up attending to her Grandma Boak's stories, and, as Sharon O'Brien has noted, she recognized her maternal grandmother with "the fullest, most affectionate portrait of a family member in her fiction."[10] Having lived in Washington (and perhaps Richmond) as wife, mother, housekeeper, and businesswoman, Rachel Boak must have had a repertoire of city stories to tell, stories that would have been part of Willa's childhood. Or if—like Rachel Blake, the fictional character modelled on her—Grandma Boak withheld the details of her urban life (and family uncertainty about such a basic fact as which city she kept a boardinghouse in suggests this may have been the case), then the withholding itself would have given the untold city stories a powerful attraction for a child as voracious as young Willa.

In addition, Willa's mother Mary Virginia, the middle Boak child, was born in Washington in 1850; certainly she spent her early childhood in the city. The picture Cather sketches in *Sapphira* of the Blake children in Washington shows that their affectionate father lavished them with gifts. It seems likely that Mary Virginia Boak's earliest years were spent in such an indulgent atmosphere, which nurtured her lifelong pleasure in fashion and luxury—although the picture of widowed Rachel Blake's later Back Creek household in *Sapphira* is anything but luxurious. As a teenager, Mary Virginia Boak had another enjoyable urban interlude at a Baltimore boarding school. However, there is no record of Mary Virginia Cather's visiting any of Willa Cather's urban homes. (In *Sapphira*, Rachel Blake gravely slights her mother by failing to invite her to Washington for a visit. "That your own daughter lived there, and you did not visit her, required explanation to your relatives and friends" [144].) In addition, one of Willa Cather's favorite aunts, Franc Cather, had an urban history, evoked in "A Wagner Matinée." So, when Willa Cather returned to Virginia and the cast of characters of her earliest childhood in the writing of *Sapphira*, she also encountered a charged, compelling little trove of fragmentary family stories about girls, women, and cities.

Sapphira and the Slave Girl is set in 1856, a few years before the sea change in American urban life that coincided with the end of the Civil War. As Janis P. Stout and others have well documented, this was a period of "strongly ambivalent, distrustful" American attitudes to cities. Some of the earlier notions of the city as a locus of sexual peril and ruin for women persisted, and by midcentury many bestselling American novels, often by women, represented the city as a hotbed of more amorphous "moral perils," especially for women. At the same time, eastern "seaboard cities served as repositories and nurseries of cultural advance. The rural lack of such cultural accoutrements as theatres and libraries sharpened the division between city and country, and contemporary observers linked urbanism with cultural advantages like those of Europe."[11]

Sapphira displays this range of ambivalent attitudes. When Henry Colbert hears of his daughter Rachel's plan to assist in Nancy's escape, he protests: "Montreal? Now what would a young girl like her do in a big strange city? . . . [S]he'd come to harm, for certain. A pretty girl like her, she'd be enticed into one of them houses, like as not" (226). Henry describes the stereotypical seducer's city of late eighteenth and early nineteenth century fiction, a warmed-over stew of gendered urban stereotypes. The miller apparently never goes to the city himself by choice, not even to the nearby town of Winchester. But, as a man, he can conduct urban business competently, as he proves when he goes to Washington to settle Rachel's tangled financial affairs after her husband's death—since clearly his distraught widowed daughter cannot do so. In the Baptist church he attends faithfully, Henry joins in a favorite hymn that conceives of paradise as a "land of pure delight," a rural "landscape" of "sweet fields" and rivers (78–79),[12] implicitly expressing the antiurban bias of the Back Creek community. But on another level, Henry devotes much of his most vigorously engaged thought to cities. Bunyan's *The Holy War,* a favorite, much-pondered text of Henry's, figures the Christian's contested consciousness as the *town* of "Mansoul." According to Bunyan's editors, this struggle is "emphatically a political transaction," and—in addition to Christian concerns—the allegory also closely addresses an "epoch of municipal revolution" in English towns, including Bunyan's own Bedford.[13] Drawing on Bunyan's military experience, the book discusses moral issues close to Henry Colbert's conscience in the terms of male, homosocial matters of municipal government. The language of *The Holy War* speaks to Henry's condition, "of things about which he could not unbosom himself to anyone" (211)—matters of marriage, property, sexual desire, law, free will and, above all, slavery. Bunyan's text insists that municipal matters are interwoven in that discourse. In fact, when Henry tries to invent a life of freedom for his most able slave, Sampson, he proposes a city life: he will buy Sampson, manumit him, and secure him a job in Philadelphia. In the 1850s, such concerns about slavery were matters of public debate and legislation and were also a great subject of city newspapers. It is while reading such a newspaper, a week-old *Baltimore Sun,* that Henry learns an intimate piece of news: the death of his son-in-law, Rachel's Congressman husband.

City newspapers are the most apparent means by which the "cultural advances" of 1850s eastcoast cities penetrate the rural Back Creek community. The anti-slavery postmistress, Mrs. Bywaters, who by virtue of her position suggests the institutionalized possibilities of exchanges between the largest and smallest U.S. communities, takes advantage of those possibilities by subscribing by mail to a city paper, the New York *Tribune,* edited by Horace Greeley, "one of the most passionate voices in the [1850s] Abolitionist movement."[14] Mrs. Bywaters is based on a favorite Back Creek great-aunt of Willa Cather's, Sidney Cather Gore, who regularly read "the metropolitan dailies" as well as the *Congressional Record* and corresponded with members of Congress, assuming a close and continuous connection between her village life and the nation's cities.[15] In the novel, Mrs. Bywaters strains her limited financial resources and puts her local position in jeopardy by subscribing to the *Tribune,* which she keeps under lock and key. Sometimes she gives interesting issues to her friend Rachel Blake; "they were handy to start a fire with, she said" (145). From the city comes intellectual and political tinder that can start a flame that might ignite even the sleepy rural neighborhood of Back Creek.

I hope I have begun to convince you that subtle but crucial connections between Back Creek women and urban life are integral to the narrative fabric of *Sapphira*. However, the most extended city life attempted by any of these women—Rachel Blake's residency in Washington—was in some ways a disaster. Rachel's youthful marriage was an emotional and sexual awakening; before it, "her heart was cold and frozen," and she was unhappy in her mother's slaveholding household. In Washington, in a narrow rented house, she became entirely her sensual husband's devotee. Since he was "fond of the pleasures of the table," Rachel took "the whole day to prepare his favourite dishes." She did not even venture out to the market;

> Every morning, on his way to the Capitol, Michael stopped at the big market and sent home the choicest food of the season. In those days the Washington markets were second to none in the world for fish and game: wild ducks, partridges, pheasants, wild turkeys . . . Potomac shad, Baltimore oysters, shrimps, scallops, lobsters, and terrapin. In the spring the Dutch truck gardeners brought in the first salads and asparagus and strawberries. (138–39)

This catalog is the most opulent description of Rachel's Washington life; it confirms the rich plenitude of nourishment and sensual pleasures that the city offered to those who frequented its markets. But Michael, not Rachel, is the buyer. She remains in the basement kitchen, devising epicurean dinners for her household patriarch and his circle of Southern male friends. There is no place at the Congressman's dining table for her or any other white woman, until—after dinner, when her work is done—she is brought upstairs for petting and praise, basking in the men's pleasure. Three children are born and are much loved, but Rachel's attempts to curb her husband's expenditures do not hinder his generosities and indulgences; as a wife, she finds herself as financially hamstrung as her mother Sapphira is when she desires to sell Nancy. Michael's last indulgence is a trip to a Southern city, where he and their son die of yellow fever. Rachel's response to this disaster is to intensify the insularity of her Washington life in an episode of anhedonia and denial: she retreats to "her bed, the daylight shut out, her door locked" (143).

The only woman mentioned in Rachel's Washington life is Sarah, a freed mulatto who makes her living "by cooking for dinner parties" (138). It is Sarah who teaches Rachel to cook, serves at her dinners, and—at Michael's death—cares for the two surviving daughters while Rachel is closeted. Without Sarah's assistance, it is hard to see how Rachel could have sustained her Washington life. Despite the obvious limitations of her legal and social status as an African American woman in midcentury Washington, Sarah has freedoms that Rachel lacks: she moves about the city, negotiates the markets, earns her own livelihood, and comes to the aid of a friend in extremity. Indeed Sarah—who is sketched in only a few sentences—might well be a model for the independent life that Rachel Blake constructs for herself as a widow, back in Back Creek. Although Rachel protests that she wishes only to forget her Washington life, it is hard to believe that she has forgotten the example of Sarah.

The presence of women like Sarah in midcentury Washington, both in fact and fiction, is confirmed by the 1868 autobiography of Elizabeth Keckley, a free black woman who had an extremely successful career as a dressmaker during the Lincoln administrations, moving about the city freely and finding customers among the white wives and daughters of members of Congress, the Cabinet, and in the White House: her most famous client was Mary Todd Lincoln, who considered Keckley an intimate friend. Keckley's account of her close relationships with such white Southern women as Lincoln and Mrs. Jefferson Davis is a complex mix of personal history and interracial homosocial romance;[16] traces of these same qualities survive in *Sapphira*.

Rachel's memories of Sarah, I would suggest, are one of the reasons she could bring herself to propose escape to her mother's slave girl. The girl, Nancy, cannot imagine city life; she is a plantation child of the rural "home place," and one of the factors that seem to keep Sapphira's slaves at home (and enslaved) is their fear of city life. Sampson spurns Henry's offer of legal freedom in Philadelphia; Tansy Dave is easily defeated by a change of trains in his attempt to run away to Baltimore and returns home. Inexperienced Nancy can only conceive of distant Montreal as a place where she will still do her mistress's mending and send it home by stage. But what Nancy *can* imagine is something that might seem even more unlikely: a liberating alliance with a white woman who does not own her. Perhaps the family history of Till's alliance with Mrs. Matchem, the white English housekeeper who was her mentor after her mother's death, helped Nancy to approach Rachel with an account of her suicidal despair. When Rachel hears Nancy's story, she determines to help her escape from slavery. To do so, she draws on the various lessons of her city experience: the news from her incendiary New York paper, the example of Sarah's life as a free mulatto, as well as the Underground Railroad network of Northern cities that she accesses through her Baptist and Quaker friends. Another lesson of Rachel's city life was that she was crippled by financial dependence on a man. This time, she approaches her father directly with a request for money for Nancy's needs, and her arguments prevail, as they never did with Michael. On the night of her escape, Nancy appears almost insensible with homesickness and dread. Rachel accompanies her to the edge of the river—then, on the banks of the Potomac, the river so emphatically associated with the city of Washington, the two women part. But Nancy is not too overcome to remember; twenty-five years later, on their reunion, she says to Rachel: "I never forget who it was took me across the river that night, Mrs. Blake" (283).

That night, at the Potomac's edge, Nancy disappears into the North American cities of the second half of the nineteenth century—into the years when Willa Cather herself would come to adulthood. During that time, the possibilities of urban experience for American women drastically changed and expanded, addressing many of Rachel's city problems of access and self-determination. As consumption habits altered, the markets became the milieu of middle-class women, instead of the forbidden territory they were to Rachel. As Christine Stansell argues, by 1860 "America's first great city," New York, supported "a city of women with its own economic relations and cultural forms."[17] By the turn of the century, according to Kathy Peiss, working women "constructed and gave meaning to their lives" not only through their employment but through a highly elaborated visible culture of "cheap amusements"—street life, amusement parks, dance halls, and so forth. Peiss argues that "in many ways, rather than being bystanders in the process of cultural change, working women pioneered new manners and mores."[18] For women, the nineteenth-century American city—and especially working-class New York—was an environment with enormous possibilities, producing, at century's end, figures as different as Sister Carrie and Emma Goldman. As Stansell concludes, "it was a place where the dialectic of female virtue was volatile; where, in the ebb and flow of large oppressions and small freedoms, poor women traced out unforeseen possibilities for their sex."[19]

One of many reminders of these historical conditions in Cather's work is "Coming, Aphrodite!," set around 1900 in Cather's first New York neighborhood, near Washington Square.[20] Consider the story's variety of working women: a professional nurse who collects antique furniture and invests in real estate for her old age, a boardinghouse janitor who also owns real estate in Flatbush, an alcoholic cleaning woman, a series of artists' models, one of whom moonlights by performing at Coney Island, and "the silk-skirt factory girls" who "eat their lunch in Washington Square." Very different from Rachel Blake's Washington, a city in which the female population is almost entirely unindicated! Into this neighborhood comes the spectacular young Eden Bower, an aspiring opera singer, who lights in New York between Chicago and Paris, for a summer of music lessons. Eden is a quintessentially urban woman—although born and reared in a small Illinois town, she "never [really] lived there," instead imagining a glorious internationally urban future for herself. Her room in Washington Square provides "her first taste of freedom," and there—with artist Don Hedger as her accomplice, antagonist, and lover—she confidently confronts key urban issues: access, independence, shared space, permeable boundaries. Alone, she engages her own apartment; she enjoys the outdoor freedoms of the Square; she appropriates the common space of the hallway for her trunk; she confronts Hedger to protest sharing a bathtub with his dog; she breaks open the long-bolted door that separates her apartment from Hedger's and, when their affair ends, she plugs up the knothole that gave him his first views of her unclothed body. She also takes cues from other New York working women—at Coney Island, she conspires with Don's model to take her place (and wear her costume) in a stunningly theatrical balloon descent. Even twenty years later, when Eden Bower returns from her home in Paris for a triumphant New York appearance, she demonstrates masterful access to the city's plenitude. Travelling in her private car to her broker's office, she stops briefly in her old neighborhood, and then impulsively drives to an art gallery for news of her old lover. The city is Eden Bower's oyster—she seems entirely untouched by the fears and uncertainties that trouble Rachel Blake and the terrified young Nancy. And yet, in 1920, Willa Cather presents her not only as a fantastic diva, but also as a credible urban woman.[21]

Such urban women populated Willa Cather's adult life; a very partial list might include Elsie Sergeant, Ida Tarbell, Annie Fields, Cather's cook, Josephine Bourda; her companion Edith Lewis, a highly successful advertising woman; her young niece Mary Virginia Auld, who came to New York on her own, found an apartment and a saleswoman's job at Lord and Taylor, and waited a month before she even let her aunt know she was in the city.[22] Such female independence and self-possession in the city commanded Willa Cather's respect and admiration.

In the autobiographical epilogue to her last novel, Cather inscribes her five-year-old self as she first began to think about such women, women who had left the "ordered and settled" culture of their Frederick County birthplace for an urban route. Nancy was perhaps the first to pose this paradigm for her, and to propose that such a woman could survive to return to her birthplace—although not to stay there.

In the novel, details of Nancy's post-Virginia history are scanty: little Willa knows only that she is housekeeper for a rich Canadian family and is (interracially) married, with three children. For twenty-five years she has not returned to Back Creek, although she occasionally writes to her mother and sends her an annual gift of fifty dollars. Notice the similarities to Cather's own adult life, including the protracted absences and the financial aid to family and friends "back home" in Nebraska. The epilogue's returning Nancy gives little Willa her first intimations of urban, Northern high style, with her long fur-lined coat, elegant turban, and long gold watch chain looped over her black silk dress. "She had, I vaguely felt, presence" (284), and the little girl views her with "astonishment" and approval.[23] But the paradigm of Nancy is troubling as well as gratifying to the child. She is no longer Back Creek's "lissome" "yaller gal," the figure of Willa's father's story and her mother's popular song; she is not "our Nancy," the hereditary property of Willa's family. This woman has her own mysterious presence, and her history is not an open book to the white child. Every precisely articulated word Nancy speaks discredits the local Virginia language, Willa thinks, and that too "repelled me." Willa approves, however, of Nancy's fluency in the local language of caste, class, and race: "I liked . . . the shade of deference in her voice when she addressed my mother," who is the only surviving grandchild of Nancy's former owner (281, 284).

Willa's grandmother, mother, and "Aunt Till"—the major female figures of her young life—conspire so that the child can witness the mother and child reunion of Nancy and Till. That the bonds between mother and daughter can endure the most protracted and extreme separation is a lesson that everyone wants the little girl to learn. But the child picks up other telling lessons as well. This sophisticated woman still longs for some of the flavors of her rural childhood, such as the fresh-roasted coffee. And another shared taste binds the five-year-old to the older woman: Nancy is hungry for the Back Creek stories. She "wanted to know what had happened during the war, and what had become of everybody,—and so did I" (288). That appetite for intimate narrative marked Willa Cather's writing life and, of course, the rural communities where she grew up—Back Creek and Red Cloud—became a sustaining resource of her fiction. In 1923, on a visit to Red Cloud, Cather wrote to Zoë Akins that she was experiencing excitement that she couldn't find in the cities of Paris or New York, as she watched the dramas of lives she had known for decades unfold—unexpectedly, yet predictably, if one knew these lives well.[24] The story of Nancy at the center of *Sapphira and the Slave Girl* is such a continuing drama. In this case, however, Willa Cather did not and could not know all the elements in the case; she could not articulate a nineteenth-century African American woman's story as the "slave girl" grew into a complex and self-possessed Northern, urban, free woman. From the constant oral storytelling of Rachel Blake and Till that was a central feature of her rural Virginia childhood, Willa Cather says that she acquired over time a "complete picture" of her great-grandparents. But Nancy's picture is notoriously incomplete, as many of the critics of this novel have regretted. Instead, Cather's portrayal of Nancy returns us to the *urban* aesthetic that we might derive from Hana Wirth-Nesher's description of city codes: "inaccessibility . . . partial visibilities . . . gaps . . . noises from the other side of a wall . . . partial exclusion and imaginative reconstruction."

My final argument for the importance of cities to Cather's last novel is the total *absence* of city codes in the life of the first title character. Despite her energy, her strong will, and the assured "worldly" bearing that cuts a fine figure on her visits in the town of Winchester, Sapphira Dodderidge Colbert rejects all the features of city life that I have been discussing in relation to the nineteenth-century women in this book. Virtually estranged from Rachel, Sapphira is never invited to visit her in Washington. She reads very little, and is never seen perusing the city newspapers that could give her a fuller sense of the crises of politics and human rights that are closing in on her slave-supported plantation in the Valley of Virginia that will soon become a key battleground of the Civil War. She does not partake of the cultural life of cities—instead of attending plays, for example, she spars with Henry about the disposition of their slaves: "It was almost as good as a play, she was thinking; the way whenever she and her husband were thinking of Nancy, they invariably talked about Bluebell" (199). Although, in an urban setting, her daughter Rachel collaborates and possibly attempts friendship with an African American woman who is not her slave, and later plots Nancy's urban escape, Sapphira remains owner and mistress in all her relations with African Americans. And as mistress, she aspires to absolute access and surveillance of every private space on the plantation: she burns to know what her husband is reading at the mill, what Lizzie is cooking in the kitchen, and who is sleeping where and when and with whom.

Modern urban life, with its gaps and partial visibilities, is an anathema to Sapphira Colbert. Immobilized by her dropsy, she dies in a tiny, static world of her own making.

> When Till came in with the lights, [Sapphira] would let her leave only four candles, and they must be set on the tea-table so placed that the candle-flames inside were repeated by flames out in the snow-covered lilac arbour. . . . When Till peeped in at the door, she would find the Mistress looking out at this little scene; often she was smiling. . . . The Mistress died there, upright in her chair . . . she had preferred to be alone. (294)

It is possible to read Sapphira's very death as resistance to the volatility, contingency, and rapid changes in class, gender, and race relations that were beginning to characterize urban life and that jeopardized the hierarchy of her slaveholding plantation—a fact that Sapphira herself is too astute to ignore.

Sapphira too is partially modelled on a female ancestor of Willa Cather's, Ruhamah Lemmon Seibert, a slaveowner and the mother of "Grandma" Rachel Boak. In the narrative of *Sapphira*, there seems to be nowhere for this character to go but death and historical oblivion. The survivors are the characters with urban connections— Nancy, Rachel, young Willa and her parents. The family prototypes for these characters will move from Virginia to Nebraska in a few years, and it is from Nebraska that Willa Cather will launch her own urban life. I hope I have been able to establish that *Sapphira and the Slave Girl*, with its carefully worked rendering of rural antebellum Virginia, is also a novel in which Willa Cather negotiated obliquely but importantly with cities, both present and imagined, in American history, family history, and her own life.

Perhaps I should let Mrs. Ringer have the last word. As you'll remember, she said: "It's city life that learns you, an' I'd a-loved it." So it was with Willa Cather.

Notes

1. Susan J. Rosowski, "Willa Cather as a City Novelist," in *Writing the City: Eden, Babylon and the New Jerusalem*, ed. Peter Preston and Paul Simpson-Housley (London: Routledge, 1994), 163.

2. "Life review," as identified and defined by psychoanalyst Robert N. Butler in the 1960s, has become an important and widely used concept in recent studies of the

experiences of aging. "The Life Review: An Interpretation of Reminiscence in the Aged," in *Middle Age and Aging: A Reader in Social Psychology,* ed. Bernice I. Neugarten (Chicago: University of Chicago Press, 1968), 486–96.

3. Hana Wirth-Nesher, *City Codes: Reading the Modern Urban Novel* (Cambridge, England: Cambridge University Press, 1996), 8–9.

4. Elizabeth Shepley Sergeant, "Willa Cather," in *Willa Cather* (New York: Knopf, n.d.), 6.

5. Willa Cather, *Sapphira and the Slave Girl* (New York: Knopf, 1940), 126. Further references to this volume will appear parenthetically in the text.

6. John March, *A Reader's Companion to the Fiction of Willa Cather,* ed. Marilyn Arnold (Westport, CT: Greenwood, 1993), 783.

7. In 1897, after her first year in Pittsburgh, Cather wrote to a Lincoln friend that she refused to spend another year away from Nebraska, for it was impossible for her to be happy so far from her home. Willa Cather to Mariel Gere, 19 September 1897. Nebraska State Historical Society.

8. Mildred R. Bennett, *The World of Willa Cather* (New York: Dodd, Mead, 1951), 6.

9. For matters of Willa Cather's family history, I have relied throughout this essay primarily on Bennett, Sharon O'Brien, and James Woodress. Sharon O'Brien, *Willa Cather: The Emerging Voice* (New York: Oxford University Press, 1987). James Woodress, *Willa Cather: A Literary Life* (Lincoln: University of Nebraska Press, 1987). About the Virginia history of Cather's family, I also consulted William Martin Bell, *The Seibert Family* (Washington, PA: 1959).

10. O'Brien, *Voice*, 24.

11. Janis P. Stout, *Sodoms in Eden: The City in American Fiction Before 1860* (Westport, CT: Greenwood, 1976), 15, 26, 6.

12. Also see March, *Companion,* 757.

13. Roger Sharrock and James F. Forrest. "Introduction," John Bunyan, *The Holy War,* ed. Roger Sharrock and James F. Forrest (Oxford: Clarendon, 1980), xxi, xxv.

14. Tomas Pollard, "Political Silence in *Sapphira and the Slave Girl*" (paper presented at Seventh International Willa Cather Seminar, Winchester, Virginia, June 1997), 5–6.

15. James Howard Gore, *My Mother's Story: Despise Not the Day of Small Things* (Philadelphia: Judson, 1923), 49.

16. The elements of romance in Keckley's text are mentioned by James Olney, "Introduction," Elizabeth Keckley, *Behind the Scenes. Or, Thirty Years a Slave, and Four Years in the White House,* 1868 (New York: Oxford University Press, 1988), xxxiii.

17. Christine Stansell, *City of Women: Sex and Class in New York, 1780–1860* (New York: Knopf, 1986), xi.

18. Kathy Peiss, *Cheap Amusements: Working Women and Leisure in Turn-of-the-Century New York* (Philadelphia: Temple University Press, 1986), 3, 8.

19. Stansell, *City of Women,* 221.

20. Woodress, *WC,* 313.

21. Willa Cather, "Coming, Aphrodite!" in *Youth and the Bright Medusa* (New York: Knopf, 1920), 31, 40–41.

22. Woodress, *WC,* 494.

23. In fact, this picture of Nancy reminds me of the famous photograph of an assured Willa Cather at about the same age, as managing editor of *McClure's* Magazine, wearing large hat, dark dress, long looped necklace, and exuding palpable "presence." The photograph appears as frontispiece in O'Brien.

24. Willa Cather to Zoë Akins, 6 December 1923. Henry E. Huntington Library and Museum, San Marino, California.

Bibliography

Bell, William Martin. *The Seibert Family*. Washington, PA: 1959.

Bennett, Mildred R. *The World of Willa Cather*. New York: Dodd, Mead, 1951.

Butler. Robert N. "The Life Review: An Interpretation of Reminiscence in the Aged." *Middle Age and Aging: A Reader in Social Psychology*. Ed. Bernice I. Neugarten. Chicago: University of Chicago Press, 1968. 486–96.

Cather, Willa. "Coming, Aphrodite!" *Youth and the Bright Medusa*. New York: Knopf, 1920. 11–78.

———. Letter to Mariel Gere, 19 September 1897, Nebraska State Historical Society.

———. Letter to Zoë Akins, 6 December 1923, Henry E. Huntington Library and Museum, San Marino, California.

———. *Sapphira and the Slave Girl*. New York: Knopf, 1975.

Gore, James Howard. *My Mother's Story: Despise Not the Day of Small Things*. Philadelphia: Judson, 1923.

Keckley, Elizabeth. *Behind the Scenes. Or, Thirty Years a Slave, and Four Years in the White House*. 1868. New York: Oxford University Press, 1988.

March, John. *A Reader's Companion to the Fiction of Willa Cather*. Ed. Marilyn Arnold. Westport, CT: Greenwood, 1993.

O'Brien, Sharon. *Willa Cather: The Emerging Voice*. New York: Oxford University Press, 1987.

Peiss, Kathy. *Cheap Amusements: Working Women and Leisure in Turn-of-the-Century New York*. Philadelphia: Temple University Press, 1986.

Pollard, Tomas. "Political Silence in *Sapphira and the Slave Girl*." Paper presented at Seventh International Willa Cather Seminar, Winchester, Virginia. June 1997.

Rosowski, Susan J. "Willa Cather as a City Novelist." *Writing the City: Eden, Babylon and the New Jerusalem*, Eds. Peter Preston and Paul Simpson-Housley. London: Routledge, 1994.

Sergeant, Elizabeth Shepley. "Willa Cather." *Willa Cather*. New York: Knopf, n.d.

Sharrock, Roger, and James F. Forrest. "Introduction." John Bunyan, *The Holy War*. Eds. Roger Sharrock and James F. Forrest. Oxford: Clarendon, 1980.

Stansell, Christine. *City of Women: Sex and Class in New York, 1780–1860*. New York: Knopf, 1986.

Stout, Janis P. *Sodoms in Eden: The City in American Fiction Before 1860*. Westport, CT: Greenwood, 1976.

Wirth-Nesher, Hana. *City Codes: Reading the Modern Urban Novel*. Cambridge, England: Cambridge University Press, 1996.

Woodress, James. *Willa Cather: A Literary Life*. Lincoln: University of Nebraska Press, 1987.

City Consciousness: A Comparison of Cather's *The Song of the Lark* and Dreiser's *Sister Carrie*

HEATHER STEWART ARMSTRONG

Attending a dialogue between texts by different authors is always a challenge, particularly when the authors are as disparate in stylistic idiom as Willa Cather and Theodore Dreiser. This critical task gains interest, however, when the novels in question are *The Song of the Lark* and *Sister Carrie*. The similarities between these two novels are very striking. While beneath every similarity lie significant differences, this essay attempts to provide a common language for a dialogue between these two works. In particular, it explores in each novel the portrayal of urban life and its interconnection with the main female character.

As background, it is important to know the pasts out of which Cather and Dreiser wrote. Both belonged to large families and grew up in the midwest, Dreiser in Indiana. Willa Cather was daughter of a poor Virginia family who emigrated to Nebraska, while Theodore Dreiser was son of a poor German immigrant. Dreiser ran away to try his fortune in Chicago when eighteen, while Cather escaped to college in Lincoln. Unlike Cather, Dreiser enjoyed very little formal education; but both writers chose to launch their careers in the same field—journalism. Their careers took them from city to city: Lincoln, Pittsburgh, and New York for Cather; Chicago, St. Louis, Pittsburgh, and New York for Dreiser. Each served as drama critic for a time; each eventually became an acknowledged author. *Sister Carrie* was Dreiser's first novel; *The Song of the Lark,* Cather's third. Dreiser's novel was published originally in 1900, but was little publicized and virtually unnoticed by the public until republished in 1907. Cather's novel reached the public in 1915.

The basic similarities between the novels are readily apparent. The bulk of both plots occurs at the same historic time, in the late 1880s and the early 1890s. Both works focus on a young girl striking out on her own and eventually "making good." Like Thea Kronborg, Dreiser's heroine Carrie Meeber comes from a small midwestern town. Each girl leaves her home and heads for Chicago, Thea at seventeen and Carrie at eighteen, to escape the pressures of a large family and the sordid littleness of a town that is all-in-all to itself. The firmness with which each turns her back on family and home is striking. The narrator says of Carrie:

> Whatever touch of regret at parting characterized her thoughts it was certainly not for advantages given up. A gush of tears at her mother's farewell kiss, a touch in the throat when the cars clacked by the flour mill where her father worked by the day, a pathetic sigh as the familiar green environs of the village passed in review, and the threads which bound her so lightly to girlhood and home were irretrievably broken. (3) [1]

Similarly, when Thea leaves Moonstone the first time, the narrator remarks: "It seemed, on the contrary, as she looked out at the yellow desert speeding by, that she had left very little."[2] This characteristic is even more noticeable in Thea when she leaves for the second and final time. She sobs all night on the train, but recovers by the morning light. "She was going away to fight, and she was going away forever" (508).

Thea and Carrie, filled with longing, seek new lives. Thea's longing, her yearning after art, is documented repeatedly throughout the novel. It is emphasized, for example, in her birthday conversation with Wunsch when he insists, "There is only one big thing—desire" (360); in her passionate discovery and resolution after the concert in Chicago; in her determination before leaving for Germany when she feels "a passion of longing" (616). Similarly, Carrie is consistently pictured as walking about or staring out the window of her apartment, also restless with longing. Her longing is less clearly defined than Thea's, and usually takes the form of desire for material possessions, or for a change in her life that would enable her to acquire more. Towards the end, however, she begins to long for something more—to improve her mind, to be a fine dramatic actress, to find beauty. According to Kenneth Lynn, desire is "the one emotion that exists for Dreiser, once the mind has been exposed to the opium of the city."[3] Carrie epitomizes, as Thea embodies, desire. Late in the novel, Ames tells Carrie that her face continually expresses the world's longing (1957, 437).

Finally, setting Cather's epilogue aside, each woman stands alone at the end. Yet both Thea and Carrie are helped along their way by key men: Drouet and Hurstwood for Carrie; Ray and Fred foremost for Thea, but also Dr. Archie, Wunsch, and Spanish Johnny. Both are deceived and taken advantage of; neither allows herself to become permanently attached. By the end, each performs successfully in the New York theater—Carrie as a famous comedic actress, Thea as a famous opera singer. One could say that Carrie embodies, as Kronborg epitomizes, success. Their professions give them independence. By the final pages, both live in opulent apartments, Carrie at the Waldorf and Thea on Riverside Drive. Both remain unsatisfied. In the uncut version of the novel, the narrator characterizes Carrie's lack of fulfillment at the end thus: "All her nature was stirred to unrest now. She was already the old, mournful Carrie—the desireful Carrie,—unsatisfied" (487). In Dreiser's revised version, the narrator says of Carrie: "Know, then, that for you is neither surfeit nor content. In your rocking chair, by your window dreaming, shall you long, alone" (1957, 454). Thea's dissatisfaction is characterized in the entire last section of the novel—in her confidential chat with Dr. Archie, in her constant desire and feverish preparation for better roles, in her appearance at dinner in the restaurant, when Fred muses that "Even in her most genial moods there was a shadow of restlessness, as if she were waiting for something and were exercising the virtue of patience" (666).

Even though so many emotions and reactions are shared by these heroines, we can find several more points of potential dialogue between the two novels. One of the most interesting is urban life itself, first in Chicago and then in New York. The contrast between Cather's Chicago and Dreiser's is evident in their heroines' first impressions of this city. Before Carrie even reaches Chicago, Dreiser prepares the reader for her reaction, and indeed for one of the novel's main themes, in the following lines:

> The city has its cunning wiles no less than the infinitely smaller and more human tempter. There are large forces which allure, with all the soulfulness of expression possible in the most cultured human. The gleam of a thousand lights is often as effective, to all moral intents and purposes, as the persuasive light in a wooing and fascinating eye. Half the undoing of the unsophisticated and natural mind is accomplished by forces wholly superhuman. A blare of sound, a roar of life, a vast array of human hives appeal to the astonished senses in equivocal terms. Without a counselor at hand to whisper cautious interpretations, what falsehoods may not these things breathe into the unguarded ear! Unrecognized for what they are, their beauty, like music, too often relaxes, then weakens, then perverts the simplest human perceptions. (4)

When Carrie actually begins to see the city, Dreiser captures her wonder, and makes the general statement: "To the child, the genius with imagination, or the wholly untravelled, the approach to a great city for the first time is a wonderful thing. Particularly if it be evening"

(10). In these passages Dreiser highlights the aspects of the city which he is to emphasize repeatedly throughout Carrie's story: the dazzling lure of the city, with its lights and movement, and the irresistibility and emptiness of that attraction. Dreiser makes the city almost a character in this novel. From the first, Carrie wants to make this character's better acquaintance. She wishes to go to the theater almost immediately; when denied this opportunity, she employs her time in walking about the city on her own, getting to know it better.

Cather, on the other hand, denies us access to Thea's first views of the city, noting only that she "arrived in the rain on that first disillusioning morning" (434). The earliest thing we learn about her impression is, "it seemed impossible to keep one's face and hands clean in Chicago" (434). Clearly, Thea has little tolerance for the city, and less enjoyment. Thea has none of Carrie's ranging curiosity. In fact, the narrator notes,

> By the first of February Thea had been in Chicago almost four months, and she did not know much more about the city than if she had never quitted Moonstone. . . . During this first winter Thea got no city consciousness. Chicago was simply a wilderness through which one had to find one's way. She felt no interest in the general briskness and zest of the crowds. The crash and scramble of that big, rich, appetent Western city she did not take in at all, except to notice that the noise of the drays and street-cars tired her. (463)

Carrie, conversely, gets her city consciousness quickly, though this consciousness is by no means entirely pleasant. She is overwhelmed by the size, affluence and self-confidence of the business district, and feels dehumanized when she tries to seek work. Further, like Thea, she is badgered and depressed by the wind and winter weather. Dreiser, in fact, makes a big point of the dispiriting character of cities in the winter (90).

Thea's reactions, of course, do not remain merely blank or negative. She eventually learns more of the city and, partially under Fred's guidance, benefits from urban opportunities. The beginning of her transformation is marked by visits to the Art Institute and the concert at which she hears Dvořák's *New World Symphony*. These events awaken her to the cultural possibilities of the city.

Carrie, in contrast, is never magnetized by the cultural offerings of the city, unless one counts her enthusiasm for the theater. Even with the theater, as elsewhere, a large part of her enjoyment lies in the audience's finery and showiness, and in the sense of advantage to be gained by attending. One of Carrie's chief allures in Chicago is the shop windows and interiors, precisely what does not attract Thea. The narrator says of Thea: "The brilliant window displays, the splendid furs and stuffs, the gorgeous flower-shops, the gay candy-shops, she scarcely noticed" (463). In fact, the only shops which really interest Thea are the jewelry stores, because of her lifelong fondness for the brilliance and beauty of gems. Thea literally avoids the stores, so she will not spend money. Carrie, on the other hand, loves the stores. It is her weakness for them and their wares that draws her into relation with Drouet. Once enmeshed, it is the shops' contents that keep her there. "'My dear,' said the lace collar she secured from Partridge's, 'I fit you beautifully; don't give me up. 'Ah, such little feet,' said the leather of the soft new shoes, 'how effectively I cover them; what a pity they should ever want my aid'" (98).

Clearly Cather and Dreiser use the cities to reveal their heroine's characters. Carrie is impressed and invigorated by bustling crowds, while Thea is tired or annoyed; Carrie is attracted to the shops as Thea avoids them. But the cities also gauge the characters' development. Thus Thea's new interest in cultural opportunities improves her, while Carrie's augmented sense of finery measures the city's infection. In this way, similar details create different effects, because of the disparate nature of the heroines. In addition, Cather and Dreiser sometimes mention similar things (like expensive New York restaurants) with a bias that makes the authors' preferences even more clear than those of their heroines. Each also often chooses urban details quite foreign to the other's novel—Dreiser's factory and Cather's museum, for example.

The greatest difference between Dreiser's portrayal of Chicago and New York and Cather's, however, seems philosophical or ideological. Dreiser, influenced like other American authors by Herbert Spencer's *First Principles*,[4] believed in a cosmic evolution. In fact, Dreiser was so affected by his reading of Spencer that he claimed it "quite blew me, intellectually, to bits."[5] One aspect of current scientific thought, Spencer's and others', was an emphasis on the importance of environment to the organism.[6] For Dreiser, this interconnection of part and whole, of creature and medium, meant that the environment, the city, literally constructed the individual exposed to it. Alfred Kazin, in his introduction to *Sister Carrie,* accordingly describes Carrie as a social construction.[7]

Once within the city's power, Carrie certainly becomes defined by it. Because she internalizes its standards of success and its artificiality, she is condemned to ceaseless longing and emptiness. Richard Lehan puts it this way: "If the city instills desire, Carrie will be subject to desire as long as she is part of her environment. . . . [S]uch desire will never be satisfied; the whole logic of the city is to excite and stimulate."[8]

What has been called Spencer's mechanistic determinism, his emphasis on the "Persistence of Force," minimized individual will in a cosmic scheme where the greatest force acting in a given situation always, naturally, determines the outcome. As one of Dreiser's biographers has noted, reading Spencer destroyed Dreiser's sense of autonomy, of success attained through genius.[9] This can easily be over-emphasized, since Dreiser clung somewhat to the idea that an individual's internal workings and the way in which he/she met impinging forces helped determine that individual's fate. Still, Dreiser continually emphasizes the forces, larger than individual people and often inscrutable, that act upon and influence Carrie's life. As Lehan notes: "The main force at work in the novel is that of the city."[10] The city is not a wholly negative force for Carrie; she is in some ways an improved character at the end. However, Carrie's development, positive and negative, *is* due to the city.

One effect of the city on Carrie is that it nearly obliterates her past, at least as a conscious force. Perhaps this is because Dreiser felt city life, with all its artificiality and false ambitions, "infinitely preferable to the grossness of country life."[11] Despite Thomas Riggio's argument that Carrie's deprived past and familial relations shape her inner life,[12] such conditions are consistently obscured. Carrie never writes and almost never reflects on her family once she leaves them. When she feels uneasy over her conduct with Drouet, the narrator comments: "It was only an average little conscience, a thing which represented the world, her past environment, habit, convention, in a confused, reflected way" (89). This remnant of her past is overcome by the lure of material things made valuable, enviable, and possible by the city. The more Carrie sees of successful city people, the more she wants to be like them. This is especially noticeable when she accompanies Mrs. Vance to the theater in New York for the first time and sees the parade of the well-to-do on Broadway.

Thea, in contrast, increasingly seeks to differentiate herself from both the successful Chicago musicians and the more typical urban dwellers. In fact, she feels antagonistic towards them, as we see when she leaves that awakening concert in Chicago:

> For almost the first time Thea was conscious of the city itself, of the congestion of life all about her, of the brutality and power of those streams that flowed in the streets, threatening to drive one under. . . .

Thea glared round her at the crowds, the ugly, sprawling streets, the long lines of lights. . . . All these things and people were no longer remote and negligible; they had to be met, they were lined up against her, they were there to take something from her. (469–70)

Cather further sets Thea apart from the bulk of the city by designating her as discontent and full of creative power, while "The rich, noisy, city, fat with food and drink, is a spent thing; its chief concern is its digestion and its little game of hide-and-seek with the undertaker. Money and office and success are the consolations of impotence" (522).

Unlike Carrie's, Thea's character is not determined by the cities of which she becomes a part. They contribute to her growth, certainly, but in tandem with her past. Significantly, Thea's greatest moment of creative awakening and personal development takes place in Panther Canyon, not in a city. And as she confesses to Fred and Dr. Archie, she never outgrows some of the standards of Moonstone or the people there who taught her so much. Carrie Lowry La Seur claims that Cather was a creature of both West and East, wilderness and urbanity.[13] This double allegiance and double awareness is evident in the balance of Thea's development. Further, Cather's depiction of Thea shows little of the social construction of character that Dreiser emphasizes.

In addition, Dreiser's cities often exemplify the laws of "Social Darwinism" (actually a Spencerian idea). Carrie rises; Hurstwood falls; and while there is pity for characters like Hurstwood, there are no suggestions for change. Dreiser "looked upon life 'as a fierce grim struggle in which no quarter was either given or taken,' but he had no notion of changing it, because to him fighting and suffering were fundamental to existence—to eliminate them was impossible."[14] While Cather was no social reformer, and while she certainly depicts the artistic world as one of bitter struggle, she does seem to question the "survival of the fittest." In her harsh condemnations of inferior artists and the undiscerning audiences who favor them, Cather acknowledges that the artistic "fittest" are not always, or often, recognized as the best.

Overall, Dreiser gives the city a larger presence in his novel than Cather does in hers. In fact, Dreiser is known for the realism of his urban portraits. When Carrie starts her career in Chicago with a job in a factory, for example, Dreiser depicts even the smells of the workplace and notes: "the whole atmosphere was one of hard contract" (39). Likewise, Dreiser's treatment of the streetcar strikes and his examination of Hurstwood's decline into a homeless man are memorable for their grim detail. Lynn argues that when *Sister Carrie* first came out, "no other American novelist who had dealt with the urban masses had ever presented them with such ruthless honesty; no previous author had been able to free his imagination of all moral preconceptions and confront the culture of the modern American city for what it was."[15]

In light of Dreiser's realism, one might charge that Cather delivered an unrealistic portrait of urban life, as she was also accused of rendering an unrealistic portrait of war in *One of Ours*. However, because Cather did not describe cities in Dreiser's terms does not mean that she was less realistic; similarly, her portrayal of war was not less realistic because it failed to conform to Hemingway's perceptions. On the contrary, Cather touches more sparingly, but just as surely, on the harsh realities of urban existence. The details of Mrs. Lorch's house and the many boarding houses where Thea stays are far from sugar-coated. Further, Cather's vision of the realities of the music world, with its fierce competition, its "stupid faces," and its terrible toll on the artist, is far more convincing and ultimately disturbing than is Dreiser's picture of the theater world.

When all is said and done, one is left with an acute sense of the difference between these two novels. Thea and Carrie, of course, are very different characters, and their reactions to and interactions with Chicago and New York tell us something about them. Even more importantly, however, the cities in the two novels are different in nature, and we see the urban differences through the perspectival and philosophic differences of the authors. Cather's cities are neither so glitteringly attractive, nor so pervasively intrusive upon the soul as are Dreiser's. Even a strong and determined, though unsophisticated, Thea in Dreiser's hands would be corrupted and tainted by the cities. And even a passive Carrie in Cather's hands would be less susceptible to Dreiser's lurid dangers. Like Lucy Gayheart, she would have a wholly different set of dangers with which to contend. Placing the urban portrayals of these two texts in dialogue helps to highlight Cather's unique sense of the urban in *The Song of the Lark*, its hazards, its benefits, and its place in the development of Thea's character.

Notes

1. Because there is considerable scholarly debate about which version of Dreiser's text is the "truer" version, I have availed myself of both. Most of the quotes

come from the Penguin unexpurgated edition (1981). Quotes from the revised edition (Holt, Rinehart, and Winston) are indicated with a "1957" for the publication date.

2. Willa Cather, *The Song of the Lark, Early Novels and Stories,* ed. Sharon O'Brien (New York: Library of America, 1987), 433.

3. Theodore Dreiser, *Sister Carrie,* Introduction by Kenneth Lynn (New York: Holt, Rinehart &Winston, 1957), xiv.

4. James G. Kennedy, *Herbert Spencer* (Boston: G. K. Hall, 1978), 120.

5. Theodore Dreiser, *A Book About Myself* (New York: Boni and Liveright, 1922), 457.

6. Sally Shuttleworth, *George Eliot and Nineteenth Century Science* (New York: Cambridge University Press, 1984), 18–21.

7. Theodore Dreiser, *Sister Carrie,* Introduction by Alfred Kazin (New York: Viking Penguin, 1981), x.

8. Richard Lehan, *"Sister Carrie:* The City, the Self, and the Modes of Narrative Discourse," *New Essays on Sister Carrie,* ed. Donald Pizer (New York: Cambridge University Press, 1991), 72.

9. W. A. Swanberg, *Dreiser* (New York: Scribner's, 1965), 61.

10. Lehan, "Narrative Discourse," 67.

11. Lynn, "Introduction," xi.

12. Thomas P. Riggio, "Carrie's Blues," *New Essays on Sister Carrie,* 27.

13. Carrie Lowry La Seur, "The Allusive World of *The Song of the Lark, Willa Cather Pioneer Memorial Newsletter* XL (1997), 58.

14. Lynn, "Introduction," xi.

15. Ibid., x.

Bibliography

Cather, Willa. *The Song of the Lark. Early Novels and Stories.* Ed. Sharon O'Brien. New York: Library of America, 1987.

Dreiser, Theodore. *A Book About Myself.* New York: Boni and Liveright, 1922.

———. *Sister Carrie.* New York: Holt, Rinehart and Winston, 1957.

———. *Sister Carrie.* New York: Viking Penguin, 1981.

Kazin, Alfred. "Introduction to *Sister Carrie.*" New York: Viking Penguin, 1981.

Kennedy, James G. *Herbert Spencer.* Boston: G. K. Hall, 1978.

La Seur, Carrie Lowry. "The Allusive World of *The Song of the Lark.*" *Willa Cather Pioneer Memorial Newsletter.* XL, No. 3 (Winter 1997): 57–61.

Lehan, Richard. *"Sister Carrie:* The City, the Self, and the Modes of Narrative Discourse." *New Essays on 'Sister Carrie'.* Ed. Donald Pizer. New York: Cambridge University Press, 1991. 65–85.

Lynn, Kenneth. "Introduction." *Sister Carrie.* New York: Holt, Rinehart and Winston, 1957.

Riggio, Thomas P. "Carrie's Blues." *New Essays on 'Sister Carrie'.* Ed. Donald Pizer. New York: Cambridge University Press, 1991. 23–41.

Shuttleworth, Sally. *George Eliot and Nineteenth Century Science.* New York: Cambridge University Press, 1984.

Swanberg, W. A. *Dreiser.* New York: Scribner's, 1965.

Like a Rose Among Thorns: Ethnicity, Demography, and Otherness in Willa Cather's "Old Mrs. Harris"

JESSICA G. RABIN

It all comes down to childhood, or so the depth psychologists would have us believe. And yet so many authors corroborate this idea by incorporating parts of their younger selves into their texts. While the influences that shaped Willa Cather are innumerable and inextricable—history, place, family, mentors, and a good measure of natural genius—it is clear that direct and indirect encounters with the culture of cities impacted formatively on her writing consciousness. Cather chose to spend much of her adult life in New York, a decision that arguably had its roots in early models and dreams. Cather recalls one such influence in "Old Mrs. Harris," a highly-autobiographical story which, according to James Woodress, "might have been subtitled 'Portrait of the Artist as a Teen-ager.'"[1] In the turbulent times which served as the prototype, teenaged Willie was significantly influenced by a European Jewish couple, Mr. and Mrs. Charles Wiener, who appear in this story as Mr. and Mrs. David Rosen. As Woodress explains, the multilingual Wieners "had a large library and gave . . . [Cather] the run of it. . . . They realized . . . [young Willa's] extraordinary talent and encouraged her, as the Rosens do Vickie Templeton, to go to college."[2] Loretta Wasserman's identification of the Wieners as "German Jews educated in the European fashion"[3] illuminates several important dimensions of the cultivated and rich background of Cather's real-life models: the Rosens are well-traveled, highly cultured, and (to their Colorado neighbors, at least) of an almost unimaginably wide-ranging experience.

The Rosens stand in a paradoxical relation to mainstream Skyline. These genteel immigrants have managed to make a good life for themselves in a small Western town, but while they function comfortably within its society, they remain noticeably above it— economically, educationally, and therefore, socially. Still, they do not antagonize their less privileged neighbors; as Marilyn Arnold notes, "Mrs. Rosen holds a superior position among the local women, but she never pushes her advantage."[4] Further, the Rosens do not seem to encounter anti-Semitism, perhaps in part because they do not push their Jewishness either. Some of Cather's representations of Jews draw on common stereotypes, such as her ambivalent depiction of big-nosed, big-moneyed Louie Marsellus in *The Professor's House,* or neuralgic and grasping Miletus Poppas in "The Diamond Mine."[5] The Rosens, however, constitute an almost wholly positive type of otherness. Mrs. Rosen's "slight accent—it affected only her *th's* and, occasionally, the letter *v,*"[6] constitutes the only flaw her neighbors can discern: "people in Skyline thought this unfortunate, in a woman whose superiority they recognized" (262). Her husband, "the only unsuccessful member of a large, rich Jewish family" (274), is nevertheless one of the more well-to-do businessmen in the town. In fact, the Rosens' relatively high standard of living might serve to counterbalance the potentially negative ramifications of their minority status as Jews. In discussing what she terms the "politics of ethnicity," Gillian Bottomley explains that financial achievements can bring societal acceptance for marginalized groups: "ethnics are devalued minorities, not a central part of the nation. Those who are accorded centrality . . . are the economically successful."[7] The Rosens have enough money and class to place them in the upper echelons of Skyline society, but without the showiness of a Louie Marsellus or the physical and social unattractiveness of a Miletus Poppas.

Thus Cather presents the Rosens as reasonable and admirable people. They retain traditional Jewish values, such as respect for the elderly and love of children, but they dismiss the letter of the law and fit comfortably into their adoptive society. Using their outsider status as a way to transcend provincial divisions (and their money to ensure not just acceptance but appreciation), the Rosens "belon[g] to no church, [and] contribut[e] to the support of all, . . . [attending] the church suppers in winter and the socials in summer" (282). These are upper-class, educated German Jews, not embarrassing kerchief- and sidelock-wearing Russian shetl-dwellers.[8] Germany, traditionally considered a cultural and educational center, served as the birthplace of the Jewish enlightenment and the Reform movement (a shift towards cultural assimilation and secular education which began in the late nineteenth century). As exemplars of these trends, the Rosens are learned and culturally refined. They are everyone's rose garden, the thorn in no one's side.

In spite of their assimilationist tendencies, the Rosens remain noticeably Jewish (and even Biblical) in their basic affinities. Many Biblical foremothers (e.g. Sarah, Rebecca, Rachel, and Chana) experience an extended period of childlessness, and Mrs. Rosen similarly grieves over her barrenness: "it was a bitter sorrow to Mrs. Rosen that she had no children. There was nothing else in the world she wanted so much" (273). Mr. Rosen patiently listens to his wife's running commentary about the comings and goings of the Templetons because he realizes that this house full of children serves—at least on some level—as a surrogate family for his wife, who compares them favorably to the Rosens' own thankless and self-centered nieces and nephews. At the same time, Mrs. Rosen's interest in the seemingly-overlooked Grandma Harris reflects the respect for older people which marks Biblical stories from Noah to Moses.[9] Without preaching or even articulating her beliefs outright, Mrs. Rosen communicates a reverence for the elderly which is a hallmark of Jewish culture. Although Mrs. Harris accepts her old woman's position as one of relative powerlessness, she deduces that "Jewish people had an altogether different attitude toward their old folks" (272). The Rosens are assimilated Jews, but Jewishness remains an integral part of their identity.

Otherness can easily be cause for condemnation in a small town, but not for the Rosens, whose distinctly Jewish name is also a tag for a central image in the medieval symbol system of courtly love.[10] Medieval romance places the rose image beyond the confines of time and natural decay, creating a world in which "roses do not die, [and] dreams become reality."[11] As perhaps the only Jews in Skyline, the Rosens represent an ancient nation still alive today; as the friends and neighbors of the Templetons, the Rosens introduce new and limitless possibilities, a world in which "if you want [something] without any purpose at all, you will not be disappointed" (299). Furthermore, Douglas Kelly explains that the rose derives figurative significance from the contrast "between its appearance and the configuration in which it is placed."[12] The Rosens, whose house provides "the nearest thing to an art gallery and a museum that the Templetons had ever seen" (274), join the symbolism of medieval Europe to that of Jewish mysticism: "like a rose among thorns, so is my beloved among the daughters" (Song of Songs 2:1).[13] Jewish tradition interprets this verse in Solomon's Song of Songs as an allegory in which the rose symbolizes the Jewish people, while the thorns represent the other nations of the world. Mr. and Mrs. David Rosen, whose name also invokes that of King David, shine out from their surroundings. Their name is regal, and their neighbors seem to appreciate their worth.

If the Rosens use the otherness of their ethnicity towards positive ends, they also benefit from a cosmopolitan and international background, which once again differentiates them from their fellow residents. Accepting Bruce Robbins's contention that the cosmopolitan or international position tends to be considered as core in our culture,[14] we then see that the Rosens occupy yet another privileged position. Even though they have presumably resided in Skyline for some time, the Rosens retain a metropolitan ethos, corroborating sociologist and urban theorist Robert Park's claim that the city is "a state of mind, a body of customs and traditions, and of the organized attitudes and sentiments that inhere in these customs and are transmitted with this tradition."[15] The Rosens can be taken out of the city, but the city cannot be taken out of the Rosens. Park also points out that this ethos is often found in Jews, who "are, before all else, a city folk."[16] The Rosens' insider/outsider status in Skyline also suggests the prototype of the Wandering Jew, a figure whose detachment from people and places promotes transcendence of petty preoccupations. Mr. Rosen is a paragon of this type: "all countries were beautiful to Mr. Rosen. He carried a country of his own in his mind, and was able to unfold it like a tent in any wilderness" (282–83). As Park would say, he has clearly "acquire[d the] abstract terms with which to describe the various scenes he visits."[17] For her part, Mrs. Rosen has all the sensibilities and tendencies required of metropolitan life, as delineated by Park's mentor, Georg Simmel: "punctuality, calculability, [and] exactness."[18] From her "symmetrically plaited coffee-cake, beautifully browned, delicately peppered over with poppy seeds, with sugary margins about the twists" (262) to "her kitchen [left] in a state of such perfection as the Templetons were unable to sense or admire" (275), Mrs. Rosen is clearly a person who values "order and comeliness" (264). The Rosens' ability to transplant themselves and to thrive in a very different cultural climate from that of European capitals and fine opera suggests that they possess "cosmopolitan mobility."[19]

Although we are never actually told where the Rosens lived before Skyline, we can infer that they have connections to New York. First of all, we have the popular myth that all American Jews are former New Yorkers (and Brooklyners, to be specific). Beyond this folk wisdom, Cather's text provides more tangible evidence through Mrs. Rosen's associations. The moon in Skyline prompts Mrs. Rosen to think about "the Adirondacks, for which she was always secretly homesick in summer" (282), allowing us to reasonably conclude that she and her husband had spent the winters in New York City and the summers upstate. In any case, it is a combination of the Rosens' different identities—Jewish, European, and cosmopolitan—that makes them so important to the Templetons and to the text. These cultured immigrants serve as a counterpoint to the equally displaced and in many ways equally foreign Templetons. In this position, they can serve as validators, bridge-builders, and enablers.

Mrs. Rosen's traditional Jewish enjoyment of children, respect for the elderly, and belief in education forge a bond between herself and all three generations of Templeton women. Yet not one of these relationships is uncomplicated, a truth embodied by the cross-stitch, Mrs. Rosen's avocation and her method of relating to those she values. In Cather's always-significant opening line,[20] "Mrs. David Rosen, cross-stitch in hand, [sits] looking out of the window across her own green lawn to the sunburned yard of her neighbours on the right" (262), crossly waiting for an opportune time to run "across the alley-way" (270) to see Mrs. Harris. This scene provides an early intimation of the cross-purposes which will characterize neighborly relations, as Mrs. Rosen continually crosses or criticizes Grandma Harris, Victoria, and Vickie.

Watching baby Hughie nurse on her first visit to her neighbor's house, Mrs. Rosen "could not help admiring him and his mother" (280). This Madonna-like depiction constitutes perhaps the most powerfully positive image of Victoria in the story, and Cather accomplishes several aims by including this imagery. First of all, the fact that Mrs. Rosen, a Jew, can appreciate the figure of the mother and child suggests the potential for bridging the gaps created by ethnicity and religion. Secondly, Mrs. Rosen's aesthetic appreciation for an image which has so frequently been the subject of art testifies to her cosmopolitan cultivation. Finally, Mrs. Rosen is a person who "gave credit where credit was due" (295); her own disappointing childlessness does not keep her from admiring a mother of many beautiful children. Thus Mrs. Rosen's first impression of Victoria serves to somewhat counterbalance her clear disapproval of her neighbor's mothering techniques: "'dat woman takes no more responsibility for her children than a cat takes for her kittens'" (273). As she gets to know the family better, Mrs. Rosen finds herself wanting desperately to "for once . . . get past the others to the real grandmother" (265) and pays court to Mrs. Harris with coffee cakes, cookies, and sweaters. Always "on her guard" (265), Mrs. Harris exasperates Mrs. Rosen with her continual deference to her daughter and grandchildren and her willingness to carry their burdens. Mrs. Harris claims not to mind working for the younger generations, but Mrs. Rosen resists "the chain of responsibility . . . the irritating sense of being somehow responsible for Vickie" (277). Nevertheless, although she "hated the girl's bringing-up so much that she sometimes almost hated the girl" (274), Mrs. Rosen's appreciation for scholarship makes her a patient listener to Vickie's Latin translations and a fervent advocate for Vickie's ambitions to attend college.

The Rosens encounter a culture clash, however, when they encourage Vickie to try for a college scholarship. When Mrs. Rosen reminds Mr. Templeton that his daughter "'has finished de school here, and she should be getting training of some sort'" (277), he merely laughs. Later, the dogged Mrs. Rosen brings up Vickie's studying over tea with Victoria and Mrs. Harris and is politely informed that "none of our people, or Mr. Templeton's either, ever went to college" (295)—the implication here being, "you are foreign and other, and we do things our way." Education may be second nature to these multilingual Europeans Jews, but their country neighbors do not share their enthusiasm or ambition.

Thus the Rosens bring a different set of ethnically based values to their relationship with the Templetons, creating both bonds and tensions. Another element that the Rosens bring into this cultural cross-stitch is demography. The Rosens have internalized the standards of their more urban and northern background, while the Templetons reflect their rural southern roots.[21] Like most women of her age and class, Mrs. Harris "believe[s] that somebody ought to be in the parlour, and somebody in the kitchen" (288). Conversely, Mrs. Rosen feels that Mrs. Harris should be accorded more respect in her household. It becomes crucial for Mrs. Harris to show Mrs. Rosen that she is not "'put upon' . . . [, for] to be pitied was the deepest hurt anybody could know" (272). A stalwart Yankee, Mrs. Rosen feels no affection for typically "willowy or languishing" (279) Southern ladies and refuses on principle to acknowledge "a silly, Southern name" (278) like Adelbert. The Templetons are equally mystified by the way Mrs. Rosen "wasted so much pains and good meat" (298) on her clear soups. Nevertheless, it is interesting that despite Mrs. Rosen's northern affiliations, Mrs. Harris does not classify her with Skyline's "meddlesome 'Northerners' [who] said things that made Victoria suspicious and unlike herself" (288). Furthermore, although Mrs. Rosen worries that old Mrs. Harris is inadequately honored in the Templeton household, she takes pains to work within the system, limiting her response to muttered expressions of indignation and affronted complaints to Mr. Rosen. Mrs. Harris knows that Mrs. Rosen "understood how it was" (271) and appreciates her efforts to avoid alienating Victoria.

This knowledge of how things are and the attendant willingness to play along allows the Rosens to validate the Templetons in important ways. Having the benefit of a wider experience, the Rosens can affirm some of the Templeton norms which seem so foreign to the Main Street denizens of a "snappy little Western Democracy" (288). The transplanted Templetons try without success to recreate a courtly code right out of the Arthurian legend. For example, Victoria, "who had been a belle in . . . Tennessee" (286) where she was "admired and envied" (288), acts the part of the Lady of a courtly romance. Her "tall figure and good carriage" (295), along with her "training . . . to the end that you must give a guest everything you have" (285) suggests noblesse oblige. Her lover and husband—"people usually called him 'young Mr. Templeton'" (278–9)—"came of a superior family" (287), if not wholesale aristocracy. He has a "boyish, eager-to-please manner . . . [, a] fair complexion and blue eyes" (279) and chivalrous, "lovely manners" (300), much like Fair Welcome in Guillaume De Lorris's "The Romance of the Rose."[22]

Also like a traditional knight-errant, Hillary Templeton spends a significant amount of time away from home, allowing the Rosens to step in and effectively pay obeisance to the ladies of his house. As if living out the symbolic roots of their name, the Rosens validate the rules of the "feudal society" (288) to which the Templetons still adhere, injecting elements of courtly love into their interactions with the family. Mr. Rosen, perhaps the only non-family member in all of Skyline who truly appreciates Victoria, is essential to her self esteem. Observing and enjoying that Victoria is still a "handsome woman" (262), Mr. Rosen displays his regard by closing "his store half an hour earlier than usual for the pleasure of walking home with her" (267). At the Methodist ice cream social, Victoria's children are proud and happy to notice "how nicely he placed a chair for her and insisted upon putting a scarf about her shoulders" (284). Although he is not a man of many words, he "in his quiet way ma[kes] Mrs. Templeton feel his real friendliness and admiration" (284). When this elicits a negative response from the malicious Mrs. Jackson, Mr. Rosen, albeit unsuccessfully, tries to distract Victoria and protect her from hurt.

Mrs. Rosen is the similarly self-appointed champion of Mrs. Harris. Although Mrs. Harris' "friendship with this kind of neighbour was almost as disturbing as it was pleasant" (272), Marilyn Arnold goes so far as to suggest that "it is partly Mrs. Rosen's appreciative point of view that accords Grandma dignity and personal worth."[23] Mrs. Rosen considers Mrs. Harris "impressive" (264), and seeks to enjoy her company alone whenever possible. Like the Lover in "The Romance of the Rose," Mrs. Rosen finds her "advances . . . alternatively welcomed . . . and discouraged,"[24] as when Mrs. Harris first accepts the gift of the nephew's forgotten sweater and then guardedly parries Mrs. Rosen's questions while barely nibbling her coffee cake. In the end of both De Lorris's poem and Cather's story, however, "love is stronger than reason . . . in spite of the obstacles that separate."[25] This kind of love and validation leads Marilyn Arnold to conceptualize the Rosens' role as the "healer."[26]

Thus while other townspeople laugh at Mr. Templeton, scorn Victoria, and pity Mrs. Harris, the Rosens behave in a manner the Templetons can for the most part understand. At times, however, the habits and capabilities of the Rosens exceed even Mrs. Harris's capacity for psychological assimilation, and in these instances she accommodates their idiosyncracies through the rubric of "foreignness." For example, Mrs. Harris concludes "that Mrs. Rosen managed to be mistress of any situation, either in kitchen or parlour . . . because she was 'foreign.' Grandmother . . . knew well enough that their own ways of cooking and cleaning were primitive beside Mrs. Rosen's" (289). In this way, Mrs. Harris both explains Mrs. Rosen's capabilities and excuses herself from trying to emulate them. Mrs. Harris' conception of herself as "primitive" further invokes the insurmountable gaps in sensibility between a pioneer community in Colorado and the civilized background of thousands of years in Europe. On another occasion, Mrs. Rosen's effusiveness leaves Mrs. Harris "looking down at her hand [and thinking] how easy it was for these foreigners to say what they felt!" (304). Just as the Rosens' awareness of their own otherness provides them a certain measure of distance from the people around them, so Mrs. Harris uses this otherness as a means of achieving detachment from a personal relationship that might become threatening.

The irony, of course, is that the southern-born Templetons are at least as foreign as the European-born Rosens. Both are outsiders, though they seem to be on opposite ends of the spectrum: the Rosens are above Skyline and the Templetons are below it. Indeed, in the context of Cather's story, it would seem possible to argue for "southern" as an ethnicity.[27] Sollors paves the way for this sort of reading when he points out that White Anglo-Saxon Protestant is also an ethnicity, although "it is a widespread practice to define ethnicity as otherness." Using Sollors's characterization of "ethnic" as denoting "nonstandard, or, in America, as not fully American,"[28] we can insist that the southern Templetons experience the difficulties of their status as a marginalized minority in Skyline. Through their cosmopolitan advantages, the Rosens win a position of acceptance in their Colorado community (and one not usually available to Jews). Instead of reinforcing their own position by pushing the Templetons down further, the Rosens use their liminality to heal, so that the otherness they share cements a bond between them. The complexity of this bond is once again embodied in the cross-stitch.

Although the task of forming innumerable small, meticulous *x*-shapes can seem arduous or meaningless, the resulting gestalt is often beautiful. Mrs. Rosen's impatience with and criticism of the Templetons also eventually gives way to what Marilyn Arnold identifies as the "rather marvelous friendship" that evolves between Mrs. Rosen and Mrs. Harris (150). Mrs. Rosen transcends and exceeds blood ties when the torn sweater she gives to Mrs. Harris "become[s] the dearest of Grandmother's few possessions. It was kinder to her . . . than any of her own children had been" (271). Further, Mrs. Harris demonstrates a real trust in Mrs. Rosen by turning to her for help when Vickie reveals that her father will not fund her college education. In a rare expression of emotion, "Mrs. Harris's red-brown eyes slowly [fill] with tears . . . [and she says] 'Thank you, ma'am. I wouldn't have turned to nobody else'" (304). Mrs. Harris treats Mrs. Rosen like family. Mrs. Rosen's response, "that means I am an old friend already, doesn't it Grandma?" (304), does not receive direct affirmation from Mrs. Harris, though she does later think to herself "with modest pride that with people like the Rosens she had always 'got along nicely'" (306). On her deathbed, Mrs. Harris reflects that "she didn't have to see Mrs. Rosen again to know that Mrs. Rosen thought highly of her and admired her—yes admired her. Those funny little pats and arch pleasantries had meant a great deal" (313).

Although Mrs. Rosen claims to help Vickie solely out of a desire to please Mrs. Harris, Cather indicates that Mrs. Rosen the cross-stitcher might also be stitched into the web of life by others; if Mr. Rosen has adopted Victoria and Mrs. Rosen has adopted Mrs. Harris, it would seem that Vickie has adopted the Rosens. In their relationship with her, they become enablers, and these childless members of an ancient nation forge a link with the future. Vickie, who "never paid compliments, absolutely never" (277), verbally expresses her desire to emulate the Rosens, admitting, "I want to pick up any of these books and just read them, like you and Mr. Rosen do" (277). Similarly, a frustrated Vickie reacts to her family's apparent indifference to her needs with the pouting observation that "nobody but Mr. Rosen seemed to take the least interest" (312). Although "sometimes Vickie Templeton seemed so dense, so utterly unperceptive, that Mrs. Rosen was ready to wash her hands of her" (277), the relationship triumphs, and the Rosens encourage, inspire, and enable Vickie to take the road out of Skyline that "led toward the moon" (282).

When Vickie receives her acceptance letter, she goes first to the Rosens with the good news. Mrs. Rosen, "delighted[,] . . . squeeze[s] the girl's round, good-natured cheeks, as if she could mould them into something definite then and there" (298). For his part, Mr. Rosen looks at Vickie "through his kind, remote smile" (299); then trying "to distract her and help her to keep back the tears" (299), he gives Vickie her first French lesson: " *'Le but n'est rien; le chemin, c'est tout.'* That means: The end is nothing, the road is all' " (299). In this scene, it becomes clear that the biologically barren Rosens have figuratively created a child in their own image. The Rosens then take the step of putting this new-born creation on its feet, so to speak, by granting Vickie an unsecured loan that will enable her to actually attend the university. Now Vickie "won't just sit on de front porch" (298), but will make something of her life, and through her, the Rosens will help create the future.

It is worth noting that Vickie's future success will also be brought about through migration, and specifically through migration to a city. In facilitating Vickie's move to Ann Arbor, the Rosens point her in the direction of the cosmopolitan and also towards another degree of otherness. As Judith Fetterley and Marjorie Pryse point out, "Vickie . . . move[s] outside the home, beyond female community, and into the larger male-dominated world of the university."[29] Furthermore, this entrance will bring both freedom and conformity, as Mrs. Rosen makes clear. Since Mrs. Rosen comes "from a much wider experience" (296) than the Templetons, she takes it upon herself to teach Vickie the proper etiquette, informing her: "if you are going off into the world, it is quite time you learn to like things that are everywhere accepted" (300). Ironically, Mrs. Rosen prepares Vickie for moving into the world by making her more conformist, but perhaps Mrs. Rosen aims to save Vickie from the future embarrassment of being viewed as a country-bumpkin. In finding her niche in Skyline, Mrs. Rosen has clearly discovered that gaining respect requires a measure of conformity.

The Rosens—Jewish, cosmopolitan, and foreign—compose a crucial element of this story by virtue of the tension they create, the bonds they form, and the roles they play. Instead of submerging or smoothing over their multiple identities, the Rosens nurture and utilize their otherness as a "ditch to build bridges over" (282). Although they are drawn from Cather's real-life neighbors in Red Cloud, Cather infuses them with the permanent vitality of art. Today, so many years after "Old Mrs. Harris" was first published, Mr. and Mrs. David Rosen continue to show how, in a world marred by divisiveness and hatred, and in spite of human quirks and shortcomings, individuals can cross cultural barriers to stitch permanent ties.

Notes

1. James Woodress, *Willa Cather: Her Life and Art* (Lincoln: University of Nebraska Press, 1970), 39.

2. Woodress, *Life and Art*, 39–40.

3. Loretta Wasserman, *Willa Cather: A Study of the Short Fiction* (Boston: Twayne, 1991), 56.

4. Marilyn Arnold, *Willa Cather's Short Fiction* (Athens: Ohio University Press, 1984), 142.

5. About Louie Marsellus, Cather writes, "there was nothing Semitic about his countenance except his nose—that took the lead" (Willa Cather, *The Professor's House* [New York: Vintage, 1973], 43). Louie's nouveau-riche extravagances strike his brother-in-law, Scott McGregor, as "outlandish" (43), and he, in turn, blackballs Louie from the Arts and Letters club. In Cather's "The Diamond Mine," the Jewish Miletus Poppas is described as having "an indescribably foreign quality in his voice" (Willa Cather, "The Diamond Mine," *Collected Stories* [New York: Random, 1992],103). Further, he has a "lupine" face, along with a "cold, supercilious manner . . . [and] alarming, deep-set eyes,—very close together . . . and always gleaming with something like defeated fury" (103–4). It is interesting that Mrs. Rosen's accent is treated much more sympathetically than Poppas's, while no mention is made of either of the Rosens' noses.

6. *Collected Stories*, 262. Hereafter cited in the text.

7. Gillian Bottomley, *From Another Place: Migration and the Politics of Culture* (Cambridge, England: Cambridge University Press, 1992), 63.

8. As a group, German Jews came to America first, assimilated and succeeded. When their less-educated Russian counterparts arrived and isolated themselves in ghettos, many German Jews tried to distance or distinguish themselves from what they perceived as an embarrassing connection.

9. Ham and his descendants are subjected to a curse because of the lack of respect Ham shows his father, Noah, by gazing on him drunk and naked (Genesis 9: 21–26); Moses demurs from being chosen as the leader of the Jewish people because he believes that it would be an affront to his older brother, Aaron (Rashi, Exodus 4:10).

10. Cather's use of the courtly love tradition in other works is noted in Merrill Maguire Skaggs, *After the World Broke in Two: the Later Novels of Willa Cather* (Charlottesville: University Press of Virginia, 1990), 195 n. 2.

11. Douglas Kelly, *Medieval Imagination: Rhetoric and the Poetry of Courtly Love* (Madison: University of Wisconsin Press, 1978), 178.

12. Kelly, *Medieval*, 93.

13. Cather lived for several Nebraskan months with her paternal grandfather, a Baptist minister, so it is reasonable to suppose that she would have been familiar with this Scriptural reference.

14. Bruce Robbins, "The Weird Heights: On Cosmopolitanism, Feeling, and Power," *differences* no. 1 (Spring 1995): 172.

15. Robert Park, "The City: Suggestions for the Investigation of Human Behavior in the Urban Environment," in *Classic Essays on the Culture of Cities*, ed. Richard Sennett (New York: Appleton Century Crofts, 1969), 91.

16. Park, "The City," 106.

17. Ibid.

18. Georg Simmel, "The Metropolis and Mental Life," in *Classic Essays on the Culture of Cities*, 51.

19. Robbins, "Weird Heights," 172.

20. Arnold, *Cather's Short*, 141.

21. Ibid., 152.

22. In Guillaume De Lorris, *The Romance of the Rose*, ed. Frances Horgan (New York: Oxford University Press, 1994), the narrator describes Fair Welcome as "a handsome and pleasant and quite irreproachable young man" (ll. 2763–64) and informs us that he is "the son of generous Courtesy" (ll. 2765–66).

23. Arnold, *Cather's Short*, 143.

24. Horgan introduction, *The Romance of the Rose*, xii–xiii.

25. Ibid., xiii.

26. Arnold, *Cather's Short*, 152.

27. Taking Gillian Bottomley's definition of ethnicity as "'a consciousness of kind' . . . constructed and reconstituted in relation to specific political and economic circumstances" (Bottomley, *Migration*, 57) along with Lawrence Fuchs's insistence that ethnicity implies ancestral traditions (Lawrence Fuchs, *The American Kaleidoscope: Race, Ethnicity, and the Civic Culture* [Hanover: University Press of New England, 1990],177), we can argue that the Templetons are southern in all of these ethnic ways.

28. Both references to Sollors come from Werner Sollors, *Beyond Ethnicity: Consent and Descent in American Culture* (New York: Oxford University Press, 1986), 25.

29. Judith Fetterley and Marjorie Pryse, introduction to Willa Cather, *American Women Regionalists, 1850–1910* (New York: Norton, 1992), 596.

Bibliography

Arnold, Marilyn. *Willa Cather's Short Fiction*. Athens: Ohio University Press, 1984.

Ben Isaiah, Rabbi Abraham and Rabbi Benjamin Sharfman. *The Pentateuch and Rashi's Commentary: A Linear Translation into English*. New York: S. S. and R. Publishing, 1950.

Bottomley, Gillian. *From Another Place: Migration and the Politics of Culture*. Cambridge, England: Cambridge University Press, 1992.

Cather, Willa. "Old Mrs. Harris." 1932. In *Collected Stories*, 262–314. New York: Random, 1992.

———. "The Diamond Mine." 1920. In *Collected Stories*, 102–36. New York: Random, 1992.

———. *The Professor's House*. 1925. New York: Vintage, 1973.

De Lorris, Guillaume. *The Romance of the Rose*. Ed. Frances Horgan. New York: Oxford University Press, 1994.

Fetterley, Judith and Marjorie Pryse. Introduction to Willa Cather. In *American Women Regionalists, 1850–1910*, Ed. Judith Fetterley and Marjorie Pryse, 593–96. New York: Norton, 1992.

Fuchs, Lawrence H. *The American Kaleidoscope: Race, Ethnicity, and the Civic Culture*. Hanover: University Press of New England, 1990.

Horgan, Frances. Introduction. *The Romance of the Rose*. By Guillaume De Lorris. New York: Oxford University Press, 1994.

Kelly, Douglas. *Medieval Imagination: Rhetoric and the Poetry of Courtly Love*. Madison: University of Wisconsin Press, 1978.

Park, Robert. "The City: Suggestions for the Investigation of Human Behavior in the Urban Environment." In *Class Essays on the Culture of Cities*. Ed. Richard Sennett, 91–130. New York: Appleton-Century-Crofts, 1969.

Robbins, Bruce. "The Weird Heights: On Cosmopolitanism, Feeling, and Power." *differences* 7, no. 1 (Spring 1995): 165–87.

Simmel, Georg. "The Metropolis and Mental Life." In *Classic Essays on the Culture of Cities*. Ed. Richard Sennett, 47–60. New York: Appleton-Century-Crofts, 1969.

Sollors, Werner. *Beyond Ethnicity: Consent and Descent in American Culture*. New York: Oxford University Press, 1986.

Song of Songs. As found in Harold Fisch, ed. *The Jerusalem Bible*. Jerusalem: Koren Publishers, 1992.

Wasserman, Loretta. *Willa Cather: A Study of the Short Fiction*. Boston: Twayne Publishers, 1991.

Woodress, James. *Willa Cather: Her Life and Art*. Lincoln: University of Nebraska Press, 1970.

Success and Willa Cather: The Uncelebrated Victories in *Obscure Destinies*

JOANNE STONE MORRISSEY

> Success is counted sweetest
> By those who ne'er succeed.
> To comprehend a nectar
> Requires sorest need.
>
> —Emily Dickinson

Definitions of "success" are as varied as the attempts to achieve it.[1] Success is neither an absolute ideal nor a fact unfailingly recognized by common sense. It is therefore impossible to use the word in a way that seems valid for long. Yet this essay will suggest an interpretation of success as Willa Cather characterized it in personal conversations and depicted it in her work. It will then examine the three short stories in *Obscure Destinies*, focusing on the perspectives of the primary characters. Perhaps ironically, the forms of success Willa Cather explores in this collection were realized in the most affluent setting in which she ever lived, her Park Avenue apartment; perhaps the poignancy of the contrast between her opulent New York setting and life on the plains vitalized Cather's book about obscure, prairie successes. Finally, this essay will connect the seeming disparities of Cather's fictions into her cohesive definition of success.

Whatever Willa Cather thought of success, it seems today that she had her share of it. According to James Woodress, Cather "had achieved most of the things she wanted from life and knew that her professional career had been a success."[2] Edith Lewis wrote shortly after the death of Cather's father that "his gentle, modest pride in [Willa's] achievements, and the high esteem they had won, were one of the chief satisfactions she got from what is known as success."[3] Cather was especially pleased when Justice Oliver Wendell Holmes gave his highest praise to her writing.[4]

Elizabeth Shepley Sergeant (Elsie), a long time literary companion and friend of Willa's, writes about her reluctance to visit the successful Cather at her ritzy new Park Avenue address:

> Willa had said so much across the years to the effect that smug success and easy money were not real aims in human life; about the hostility of

comfortable, self-satisfied people to any serious effort of the artist, that I wondered how she would tolerate the masked faces she would meet going in and out.

If Neighbour Rosicky ventured into this lobby with its repressed attendants in uniform, whose chief job seemed to be to tend an excluding telephone board, would he reach his goal? Grandma Harris, even Mr. Trueman and Mr. Dillon, in this setting would remain indistinguishable.[5]

After going into the apartment, Shepley found that Willa was still her old self, values intact. Cather was never smug about her own worldly success, nor was she self-important about attaining it, however self-protective she may have become about freeing herself to do her work.

But for what success did Willa Cather aim? She wished to produce fine art, of course.[6] She associated artistic success with inner strength, devotion, and struggle.[7] On the other hand, she knew that fame and success are often corrupting or disillusioning. Cather discovered that while the drive toward success could be internalized, and joy could come from experiencing something done exceptionally well by oneself or another, fame and its accompanying notoriety could be a nuisance.[8] She also found that success in one's art was incomplete until one accepted the responsibility of that success; and completeness was important to Cather.

On September 11, 1906, William James included in a letter to H. G. Wells the following disconcerting comments about success and American society: "[The problem is] moral flabbiness born of the exclusive worship of the bitch-goddess SUCCESS. That—with the squalid cash interpretation put on the word success—is our national disease."[9] I believe that Cather would enthusiastically concur with James because, as Sergeant points out, "Willa believed in the early American virtues, courage, sturdiness, tough endeavor."[10] She believed in the success that comes from hard work and commitment, defining an artist's success as the ability to deliver himself completely to his art.[11] It is this complete delivery of one's self to one's art, including the arts of living and of loving, that Cather celebrates in *Obscure Destinies*. She applauds the artistry in successful living.

Genuine artistry is rare, difficult to imagine and arduous to attain or to repeat. The same is true of successful living. In Cather's case, her daily life became painful as she reached her fifties, when parents and friends began to die. She wrote Dorothy Canfield Fisher that they were now the older generation.[12] Without parents or children, Cather's links to her past and future became more tenuous. As James Kirschke writes, "the successes and insights that coincide happily in a work of literary art serve as no necessary proof of an artist's ability to master the daily problems of life."[13] Cather, however, used the daily problems of her complicated life and her debilitating physical and emotional traumas to write a cathartic and insightful tribute to her parents, her grandmother Boak, and to Red Cloud, to which she would never return. *Obscure Destinies,* comprised of three splendid and gracious narratives, is considered by many to be her finest book of short stories[14] and a great success.[15]

Success in "Two Friends" is tangible, as easily tallied as money. It is a more traditional kind than that of the volume's other two stories, and is identified immediately:

> Long ago, before the invention of the motor car . . . in a little wooden town in a shallow Kansas river valley, there lived two friends. They were "business men," the two most prosperous and influential men in our community, the two men whose affairs took them out into the world to big cities, who had "connections" in St. Joseph and Chicago. In my childhood they represented to me success and power.[16]

Eventually this kind of success disintegrates, though the unexpected triggering event is a personal quarrel. While all three stories in *Obscure Destinies* are considered autobiographical, this one gives a perspective on Cather's discrepant childhood and adult understandings of success. Cather said, in fact, that the story was not about two men, "but about a picture they conveyed to a child."[17] While the picture includes this snapshot of success, the photographic negative reveals an opposite side. The friends are secure and established, solid as the brick wall against which they lean. They enjoy the privileges of success: travel to faraway places, fine dress, even fur coats, silk shirts, and jeweled rings. They are respected, intelligent, listened to. They like and esteem each other. Then their communion founders on a political disagreement and the drive for political rightness. They allow competing ideas to destroy friendship.

Cather appears to be the curious child playing jacks on the sidewalk, infatuated with and awed by the two friends. Because they symbolize success and power to her, Sergeant postulates that they give the youth a sense of spiritual anchorage and connection with a wider world.

> The little girl had a lively curiosity about the personalities and the talk of these local potentates, and would walk through the general store of a winter evening, watching the two able men playing checkers behind the wire screening. . . . [T]he girl would sit on the sidewalk [and listen] to

Mr. Dillon talking, and Mr. Trueman making an occasional teasing, sting-
ing answer.[18]

The two men literally "voice" their experiences and their successes.
They talk for hours about places, plays, and other topics rich in
exotic interest for a small town girl. They even sound successful,
albeit in different ways. Trueman's voice is thick and low: "There was
a curious attitude in men of his class and time, that of being rather
above speech." Dillon's voice is crisp and clear: "Every sentence he
uttered was alive, never languid, perfunctory, slovenly, unaccented.
When he made a remark, it not only meant something, but sounded
like something,—sounded like the thing he meant" (678). They are
successful communicators. The narrator hears them discuss a play
and thinks:

> It was curious a third person, who had never seen these actors or read
> the plays, could get so much of the essence of both from the comments of
> two businessmen who used none of the language in which such things are
> usually discussed. . . . In some way the lives of those two men came across
> to me as they talked, the strong, bracing reality of successful, large-
> minded men who had made their way in the world when business was still
> a personal adventure. (678)

These two friends become the child's window, as well as her "audio" on the world. She loves to listen to them good-naturedly arguing
about important issues. One day, however, the banter ceases and the
years-long friendship ends over an argument about William Jennings
Bryan and the free silver issue.[19]

This story is unusual for Cather. Not only does it employ a political
sub-plot while it highlights a politician; it also deals with monetary
issues and economics, subjects Cather eschews in her public letter on
"Escapism."[20] In the story, the child openly admires a conservative
and financial view of success. What she observes, however, is pros-
perous men who somehow forget their mutual regard and lose the
most successful camaraderie of their lives. Sadly, neither is ever again
as whole as he once was. This awful destruction of something wonderful and complete leaves "the feeling of something broken that could
so easily have been mended; of something delightful that was sense-
lessly wasted, of a truth that was accidentally distorted—one of the
truths we want to keep" (690). Although the two men were financially
successful and had created a successful relationship, they failed when
required to put ego aside.

James Woodress calls "Old Mrs. Harris," the middle story in *Obscure
Destinies,* "a major accomplishment, perhaps the best story Cather

ever wrote"; Blanche Knopf thought it might be one of the greatest stories of all time; and even Willa Cather thought "the right things had come together in the right combination."[21] Success in "Old Mrs. Harris" is not as tangible as in "Two Friends," however, because it is defined privately. Its ingredients are grace, good manners, usefulness, and respect. It can be muted, and is not simple for others to acknowledge.[22] Cather focuses on seemingly trivial events to highlight the dignity of each Templeton family member, but especially to stress the achievements of Grandma Harris.[23]

Grandma exemplifies a noble and self-sacrificing success attained without fanfare or accolade. She takes satisfaction in what her quiet victories achieve for her family. When the Templetons move from Tennessee where household help and friendships are abundant, to a much smaller house in Nebraska, money and help are scarce and times are difficult. The ensuing culture clash causes each Templeton emotional pain, for Nebraska townsfolk don't understand their ways. Wagenknecht sees the underlying theme of the story as a drama of the generations:

> At the beginning we see Mrs. Harris from Mrs. Rosen's point of view, as the family drudge who wears herself out looking after the Templeton children while her daughter, Victoria Templeton, plays the fine lady. . . . [T]hough it is quite true that Mrs. Harris is being much imposed upon with looking after the little Templetons, whom she dearly loves, . . . her situation is quite what elderly women in her class accepted in her time and place.[24]

Yet this is more than a generational saga. It is also a tale of protecting and providing for the family, while also maintaining the name and reputation of the clan. Mrs. Harris is doing what she has been raised to do, as are Victoria, Vickie, and even the boys. Mrs. Rosen once asked Grandma why she didn't get Vickie to help in the kitchen, to which Mrs. Harris replied, "We are only young once, and trouble comes soon enough." Cather explains,

> Young girls, in the South, were supposed to be carefree and foolish; the fault Grandmother found in Vickie was that she wasn't foolish enough. When the foolish girl married and began to have children, everything else must give way to that. She must be humoured and given the best of everything, because having children was hard on a woman, and it was the most important thing in the world. In Tennessee every young married woman in good circumstances had an older woman in the house . . . who managed the household economies and directed the help. (646)

When a southern woman of those times and circumstances was widowed she was expected to grow old quietly and without complaint. It
was anticipated that she would become the housekeeper for her
daughter or daughter-in-law.

Respectability is more important to Mrs. Harris than her own physical comfort. For the household to be respectable, Victoria must have
proper clothing and a parlor in which to receive guests. Mrs. Harris
never questions this arrangement, nor challenges her own place in
the kitchen. She cooks, cleans, and cares for the children, allowing
Victoria to perform her social duties and Vickie to do "foolish
things." Grandma is, by her own standards, successful. Mrs. Rosen
enjoys visiting because, "There was something easy, cordial, and
carefree in the parlour that never smelled of being shut up, and the
ugly furniture looked hospitable. One felt a pleasantness in the human relationships. . . . The Templetons were not selfish or schem-
ing. . . . Victoria might eat all the cookies her neighbor sent in, but
she would give away anything she had" (635–36).

Success characterizes this family, for each member contributes to
the clan. Gentlemanly Mr. Templeton models good manners for his
wife and children. Vickie reads to the boys and wins a university
scholarship for herself. When Grandma is weary, Mandy rubs her
feet, and the boys do yardwork around town and contribute money
to their mother. Baby Hughie contributes golden beauty and happy
smiles. Seeing his mother nurse him, Mrs. Rosen thinks, "They are so
comfortable and complete" (637). This simple statement defines the
household.

As she lies dying, Mrs. Harris reflects. She is glad Mrs. Rosen is in
Chicago, for she hates pity. She knows that Mrs. Rosen, at her
deathbed, would discover her embarrassing little secrets, like the
hard bed and the patched nightgown. Then Mrs. Rosen would be
angry with Victoria and Victoria would be cross. Grandma protects
both herself and her daughter, her family, as long as she is conscious.
Besides, "She didn't have to see Mrs. Rosen again to know that Mrs.
Rosen thought highly of her and admired her—yes, admired her.
Those funny little pats and arch pleasantries had meant a great deal
to Mrs. Harris" (671). Grandma dies satisfied, a success.

"Neighbour Rosicky" is one of Cather's most beautiful and successful stories. As Brown says, "There is nothing simpler in Willa Cather's
fiction than 'Neighbour Rosicky'; the tone is quietness itself, and
perfectly sustained; the emotion has a flawless purity."[25] It is a tale
about people with clear values and virtues and worries. It is a very
human success story in which the engaging characters triumph. The

protagonist Rosicky is successful in his friendships, his marriage, and in raising his family. Subsequently, his family members successfully face economic difficulty, disillusionment, potential disaster, and death. As her father-in-law lies ill, Polly thinks to herself: "It was as if Rosicky had a special gift for loving people, something that was like an ear for music or an eye for colour. It was quiet, unobtrusive; it was merely there" (616). Rosicky makes a successful art of living.

Anton Rosicky assumes mythic proportions in this story. He is good, he is giving, he is happy. He is also dying. Dr. Burleigh may even envy him a bit as he tries to reason with Rosicky to slow down: "[Y]ou are one of the few men I know who has a family he can get some comfort out of; happy dispositions, never quarrel among themselves, and they treat you right. I want to see you live a few years and enjoy them" (588). After Rosicky leaves, the successful doctor muses on their lot. Jamie Ambrose summarizes,

> The entire Rosicky family—and Anton in particular—have prospered less than their more materialistic neighbors; but to Anton, the well being of his family has always been more important than making money. As the doctor who examines him reflects: "People as generous and warm-hearted and affectionate as the Rosickys never got ahead much; maybe you couldn't enjoy your life and put it in the bank, too."[26]

Anton and Mary Rosicky have a successful marriage; they complete each other. After she hears of his heart trouble, Mary scrutinizes Anton's face to locate any changes, but finds none: "It is hard to see anyone who has become like your own body to you," she thinks. "They agreed, without discussion, as to what was most important and what was secondary. . . . They had been at one accord not to hurry through life, not to be always skimping and saving. They saw their neighbors buy more land and feed more stock than they did, without discontent" (596). A landowner, Rosicky defines success for his sons as he tells them, "You boys don't owe nobody, you got plenty to eat an' keep warm, an' plenty water to keep clean. When you got them, you can't have it very hard" (606).

At the end of this richly textured story, Anton sits by his window to do some patchwork. He asks Mary to thread a needle for him before she goes to feed the chickens. He is smiling as she leaves, thinking about how sweet Polly is and that he doesn't have to worry about his son's marriage anymore. Then he dies, alone with his memories, without any fuss.[27] A few weeks later, Dr. Ed Burleigh stops at the graveyard:

Nothing could be more undeathlike than this place; nothing could be more right for a man who had helped to do the work of great cities and had always longed for the open country and had got to it at last. Rosicky's life seemed to him complete and beautiful. (618)

A mythic Rosicky successfully achieves here the ultimate completion.

Notes

1. Social anthropologist Margaret Mead defined success as fulfilling the expectations of one's parents. Mead satisfied both. (Margaret Mead, *Blackberry Winter: My Earlier Years* [New York: William Morrow, 1972], 3–22). Children in two stories within *Obscure Destinies* also successfully fulfill the expectations of their parents. Rudolph, in "Neighbour Rosicky," is inherently kind and dependable while making a good marriage with Polly, both conditions being desires of his father. Victoria Templeton fulfills the expectations of her mother Mrs. Harris, in "Old Mrs. Harris," by behaving as a Tennessee belle who is different from ordinary Western women.

Unlike Mead, John O'Neil defines success as the simple attainment of a goal, or as doing a good job at any endeavor. He characterizes "mythic success" as "a potent elixir compounded of wealth, power, privilege and freedom from care," and explains that "in every age success has been either celebrated or painted in the darkest of colors." Cather describes both kinds of success in *Obscure Destinies*. In O'Neil's terms, Rosicky exemplifies a simple success which she celebrates; Mr. Dillon and Mr. Trueman exemplify a "mythic" success she deplores. (John R. O'Neil, *The Paradox of Success* [New York: G. P. Putnam's Sons, 1994], 25–26). Perhaps, as we shall see, she also redefines such terms.

2. James Woodress, *Willa Cather: A Literary Life* (Lincoln: University of Nebraska Press, 1987), xvii. Two sentences later Woodress adds, "Her literary reputation was secure and that was what really mattered."

3. E. K. Brown, *Willa Cather: A Critical Biography,* completed by Leon Edel (Lincoln: University of Nebraska Press, 1953), 274–75.

4. Holmes wrote to Ferris Greenslet, in a letter dated 25 July 1930, thanking him for his gift of *My Ántonia:* "It lifts me to all my superlatives. I have not had such a sensation for a long time. . . . I think it a prime mark of a real gift to realize that any piece of the universe may be made poetical if seen by a poet. But to be more concrete, the result seems to me a wonderful success." On 24 March 1931, Holmes wrote to Cather regarding *Death Comes for the Archbishop,* "What to another would be prose, under your hand becomes poetry without ceasing to be truth." (Elizabeth Shepley Sergeant, *Willa Cather: A Memoir* [Athens: Ohio University Press, 1953], 254–55.)

5. Sergeant, *Memoir,* 261.

6. Perfect art might be defined as an ideal, or even as the flawless human imitation of an ideal. Cather, however, was attentive to imperfection. She called the Chicago Art Institute's French painting after which she named her third novel, *The Song of the Lark,* "rather second rate." (Willa Cather, *Early Novels & Stories,* ed. Sharon O'Brien [New York: Library of America, 1987], 1328). Cather also recorded the difference between highest achievement in singing and the public successes of so imperfect a singer as Jessie Darcy in *The Song of the Lark.* Cather looked beyond acclaim to an idea of highest art for which one could sing or perform.

7. In Cather's preface to the revised text of *The Song of the Lark,* published for the 1937 Autograph Edition, she says, "Success is never so interesting as struggle—not even to the successful, not even to the most mercenary forms of ambition." (*EN&S,* 1328)

8. Cather recoiled from the intrusive attention brought on by her literary success. After being awarded the Prix Femina Americain for *Shadows on the Rock* in 1933, she was pressured into attending a ceremony in her honor. She consented to the appearance so long as photographers would be kept at bay. "This was agreed; but all at once, the vandals were pointing their lenses at her and flashing lights. And there was Willa Cather, who expected others to keep faith, shrinking into a frozen statue" (Sergeant, *Memoir,* 256–57). Woodress adds, "Cather resented the fact that she could not sit on a bench in Central Park without being recognized and accosted by strangers" (Woodress, *WC,* xiv).

9. The appropriateness of a cash interpretation of success is an issue in Cather's fiction. The free coinage of silver versus a gold-only American monetary standard was the issue on which William Jennings Bryan ran for president in 1896, 1900, and 1908. This is the issue which split Cather's "Two Friends."

10. Sergeant, *Memoir,* 271.

11. Cather believed that the successful artist depicted in *The Song of the Lark* reversed Oscar Wilde's *The Portrait of Dorian Gray.* "As Thea is more and more released into the dramatic and musical possibilities of her profession, as her artistic life grows fuller and richer, it becomes more interesting to her than her own life. . . . Thea Kronborg . . . becomes somewhat dry and preoccupied. Her human life is made up of exacting engagements and dull business detail, of shifts to evade an idle, gaping world which is determined that no artist shall ever do his best. Her artistic life is the only one in which she is happy, or free, or even very real" (*EN&S,* 1328–29).

12. Phyllis C. Robinson, *Willa: The Life of Willa Cather* (New York: Holt, Rinehart and Winston, 1983), 260.

13. James J. Kirschke, *Willa Cather and Six Writers from the Great War* (Lanham: University Press of America, 1991), 88.

14. *Obscure Destinies* "is her finest book of short stories and in its minute realism and sharpness of outline invites comparison with Flaubert's *Trois Contes.* The three tales are of a piece; they were the synthesis, after many years, of old experiences; and they are filled with a humanity and gentleness and feeling which demonstrated that . . . she could still confront her own past and draw great art from it" (Brown, *Biography,* 294).

15. Even the President of Czechoslovakia, Tomas Masaryk, admired her work. He liked "Neighbour Rosicky" and could quote the last page of "Old Mrs. Harris." *Obscure Destinies* had great success in London. When Myra Hess came to New York, she told Willa that all her musical friends were talking about it. (Robinson, 161–62)

16. Willa Cather, *Stories, Poems and Other Writings,* ed. Sharon O'Brien (New York: Library of America, 1992), 673.

17. Edward Wagenknecht, *Willa Cather* (New York: Continuum, 1994), 121.

18. Sergeant, *Memoir,* 259.

19. Woodress points out that this could not have happened in the way Cather depicts it, for these events occured after she left Nebraska (Woodress, *WC,* 52–53). He explains, however, that Cather's Bryan symbolized "the entire Middle West; all its newness and vigor, its magnitude and monotony, its richness and lack of variety, its egotism and its nobility" (Woodress, *WC,*101–2).

20. *Willa Cather on Writing* (Lincoln: University of Nebraska Press, 1988), 18–29.

21. Woodress, *WC*, 441.

22. Cather said of Katherine Mansfield, "It was usually [her] way to approach the major forces of life through comparatively trivial incidents. She chose a small reflector to throw a luminous streak out into the shadowy realm of personal relationships" (*OW*, 108). Cather uses this technique to emphasize the actions of Grandma Harris and often utilizes Mrs. Rosen as the "reflector."

23. "Willa Cather's use of detail and small dramatic incident was never more felicitous, whether in giving us the portrait of Mrs. Harris through the kindly eyes of Mrs. Rosen . . . or describing the strivings of the daughter. . . . Such small matters as picnics and serving tea, the routine of the kitchen, or the death of the cat take on a distinct importance because they are important to Mrs. Harris, who goes about her appointed tasks, emerging from her shadowy existence only to arrange quietly with her neighbor for Vickie to have a loan to supplement the scholarship she has won that will take her to college" (Brown, *Biography,* 293).

24. Wagenknecht, *Cather,* 120.

25. Brown, *Biography,* 276.

26. Jamie Ambrose, *Willa Cather: Writing at the Frontier* (New York: Berg, 1988), 133.

27. Neighbour Rosicky's death is eerily similar to Cather's. As Ambrose says, "Death took her gently, almost unawares" (Ambrose, *Frontier,* 147).

Bibliography

Ambrose, Jamie. *Willa Cather: Writing at the Frontier.* New York: St. Martin's, 1988.

Blanchard, Paula. *Sarah Orne Jewett: Her World and Her Work.* Reading: Addison-Wesley, 1994.

Brown, E. K. *Willa Cather: A Critical Biography.* Completed by Leon Edel. Lincoln: University of Nebraska Press, 1953.

Cather, Willa. *Early Novels & Stories.* Ed. Sharon O'Brien. New York: Library of America, 1987.

————. *Later Novels.* Ed. Sharon O'Brien. New York: Library of America, 1990.

————. *Not Under Forty.* Lincoln: University of Nebraska Press, 1988.

————. *Stories, Poems, and Other Writings.* Ed. Sharon O'Brien. New York: Library of America, 1992.

Fetterley, Judith & Marjorie Pryse, eds. *American Women Regionalists: 1850–1910.* New York: Norton, 1992.

Johnson, Thomas H. *The Complete Poems of Emily Dickinson.* Boston: Little, Brown, 1960.

Kirschke, James J. *Willa Cather and Six Writers from the Great War.* New York: University Press of America, 1991.

Mead, Margaret. *Blackberry Winter: My Earlier Years.* New York: Morrow, 1972.

Middleton, Jo Ann. *Willa Cather's Modernism: A Study of Style and Technique.* Rutherford: Fairleigh Dickinson University Press, 1990.

O'Neil, John R. *The Paradox of Success.* New York: Putnam, 1994.

Robinson, Phyllis C. *Willa: The Life of Willa Cather.* New York: Owl, 1983.

Sergeant, Elizabeth Shepley. *Willa Cather: A Memoir.* Athens: Ohio University Press, 1953.

Wagenknecht, Edward. *Willa Cather.* New York: Continuum, 1994.

Woodress, James. *Willa Cather: A Literary Life.* Lincoln: University of Nebraska Press, 1987.

Thea Kronborg, a Distinguished Provincial in New York: or, Willa Cather's Cultural Geography of Humor

SUSAN J. ROSOWSKI

On the face of it *New York, Cather,* and *humor* seem incongruous terms. The cosmopolitan Cather who belongs in New York is not a comic Cather, even if such a being exists (another unlikely proposition, one infers from Cather criticism). Yet I propose that Cather's greatness sprang from a finely tuned comic sensibility, and that New York City was essential to her in claiming the comic spirit for her art. In this Cather literary biography the preface to New York is long, for the comic Cather forms in her childhood reading, develops further in her university years, and makes her debut in *O Pioneers!* and *The Song of the Lark.* By the time she began writing her novels, Cather was measuring a nation's literature by its comedy; she both believed that American literature suffered from the immaturity of its humor, and also set out to remedy that situation. In *The Song of the Lark,* the focus of this paper, Cather described how she did so. She claimed comedy for America by creating Thea Kronborg from the materials of her own life, then by taking Thea from the province to the city, from Red Cloud (renamed Moonstone) to New York. In the process, Cather created a cultural geography of humor.

As background to this journey, we might remember that Cather's childhood reading included George Meredith's *The Egoist: A Comedy in Narrative,* with its prelude conjuring the "comic spirit"—that notion of a living spirit that Meredith expanded upon in "An Essay on Comedy" (1877) and that Henri Bergson developed also in "Le Rire" (1900), translated as *Laughter* in 1911.[1] We might also remember that while she was a student at the University of Nebraska from 1890–95, Cather wrote comic sketches and satiric profiles, fables, jokes, and tall tales, as well as commented in reviews upon the cultural and social functions of humor. She was keenly aware of humor's role in relationships of power: "It is a terrible curse to lack a sense of humor, for it reacts on one and makes one gratify the humor of every other living creature," she wrote during this time. It was during this period that she began linking the development of humor to a national self-consciousness. "American writers seeking to escape a European influence have yet to learn that there is nothing excruciatingly funny in a dozen people falling down stairs without any particular cause," Cather wrote; "but give us time, we will learn to appreciate a more delicate and insinuating class of comedy." As for what America needs, Cather was clear about that as well, calling for "a class of comedy" that aligns itself with art as "a deeper comedy, . . . a humor that takes in all the great jests of this world and the next, the whole gigantic joke of the creation." She responded to her own call by adopting in *O Pioneers!* the "comic spirit" familiar from George Meredith and Henri Bergson, and then exploring the "social game" of comedy in *The Song of the Lark.*

We might begin—as Cather did—with Henri Bergson, whose notions of comedy proceed from his contrast between life and machine. He describes Life—whether in nature or society—by an élan, a "vital spirit" characterized by unexpectedness and change. "What life and society require of each of us" in response, Bergson writes, "is a constantly alert attention that discerns the outlines of the present situation, together with a certain elasticity of mind and body to enable us to adapt ourselves in consequence."[6] In contrast, "[t]he comic is that side of a person which reveals his likeness to a thing, that aspect of human events which, through its peculiar inelasticity, conveys the impression of pure mechanism, of automatism, of movement without life."[7] Working (as I have argued elsewhere) from Bergsonian principles of comedy in *O Pioneers!,* Cather named her characters *Bergson* and developed them by their contrasting responses to life. On the one hand there is Alexandra, in whom her father, John Bergson, recognizes "resourcefulness and good judgment," who "learned by the mistakes of her neighbors," and who could intuitively "guess the weight of a hog before it went on the scales." On the other hand, "Lou and Oscar were industrious, but he could never teach them to use their heads about their work."[8]

While a quality is comic when it is habitually (that is, mechanically) present, Bergson explains that "still more laughable will be [a quality] we have seen springing up and growing before our very eyes, with whose origin we are acquainted and whose life-history we can reconstruct."[9] It is precisely the principle by which Cather develops Lou and Oscar who, as Alexandra reflects in "Neighboring Fields," "had been growing more and more like themselves" (93) over the years. Their rigidity takes the physical form of Lou's "stiff, yellow hair that would not lie down on his face, and [his] bristly little yellow mustache," and Oscar's face that was "as bare as an egg." Rigidity appears also in their habits. Oscar, for example, was "the sort of man you could attach to a corn-sheller as you would an engine. . . . he worked like an insect, always doing the same thing over in the same way, regardless of whether it was best or no" (55–56). Contrasted to Lou's and Oscar's rigidity, Cather develops élan or a vital spirit in Alexandra, who is as sensitive to nuance in conversation as she is to the land she is farming. Alexandra orchestrates a dinner party in one of the novel's comic set pieces reminiscent of Twain's humor in its misapprehensions and double entendres.

In comedy marriage creates the union by which a new society emerges, and in this sense plot as well as character development follow comic principles in *O Pioneers!* When Carl returns to the Divide from Alaska, he offers an attentiveness and flexibility complementary to that of Alexandra. In classic comic fashion, the couple must first confront and defeat representatives of the old order—here the Bergson brothers of low comedy whose wives, in growing older, are beginning to resemble them. Alexandra breaks with her brothers and a new society gathers around her.

Though Cather knew that she had hit the home pasture by aligning herself with the Comic Spirit in *O Pioneers!,* she hadn't yet drawn directly from her own life for her humor. To do so, she needed to acknowledge her attitude toward her materials and to reconcile herself with them by confronting the disparity between her ideals and the reality of her background. She felt herself destined for uncommon things in the world, yet she also felt herself painfully and awkwardly ill equipped by having come from the province.

Cather faced a dilemma. Impersonality was the premise of comedy, where the spectator must be disinterested and the comic person unconscious;[10] yet Cather was personally invested in her comic materials. More troublesome, she was aspiring to serious art, yet her Nebraska materials were the stuff of comedy and the consensus was that comedy and art are incompatible. Cather structured *The Song of the Lark* as both an exploration and a rejoinder. In it she would write of comedy from the inside by grounding her story in Nebraska; moreover, she would include among her Nebraska characters someone who, very much like herself, wants, "more than anything else in the world . . . to be an artist" (190). She would then follow her young artist's growth, detail her movement from the province to the world, and by doing so, reconcile comedy and art.

To read *The Song of the Lark* for its laughter, we might begin with the clown that appears briefly on its pages. He enters the text as "a

particularly disgusting sort of tramp" (122) who is walking on the
street alongside the Kronborgs' house, in one hand carrying a bundle and in the other carrying a box. When she sees him slow to sniff
the aromas of suppers cooking, Thea hopes he will "not stop at their
gate, for . . . this was the dirtiest and most utterly wretched-looking
tramp she had ever seen." Then, suddenly aware of the "terrible
odour about him," she "put her handkerchief to her nose. A moment
later she was sorry, for she knew that he had noticed it. He looked
away and shuffled a little faster" (123).

That exchange of glances makes it impossible for Thea to dismiss
this tramp when she hears of him in following weeks. He has "traveled with a circus," she learns, and he has brought to Moonstone the
tools of his trade: "a filthy clown's suit" in his bundle, and "half a
dozen rattlesnakes" in his box (123). As if following him, Cather
describes his uneasy negotiation with the community. He moves into
an empty shack on the edge of town, where he tries "to give a miser-
able sort of show" (123). Unsuccessful there, he brings his show into
town, where Thea again sees him. On her way to the butcher one
Saturday night she "heard the whine of an accordion and saw a crowd
before one of the saloons. There she found the tramp, his bony body
grotesquely attired in the clown's suit, his face shaved and painted
white—the sweat trickling through the paint and washing it away—
and his eyes wild and feverish" (123). He offers a deal to the specta-
tors: pay him, and he will entertain them by eating a live rattlesnake.
The community responds by arresting, then banishing, him; he re-
taliates by chalking an expletive upon the standpipe reservoir and
then drowning himself in the town's water-supply. By the time his
body is discovered, "the fever had already broken out, and several
adults and half a dozen children died of it" (124).

As the tramp affected Thea, rereading *The Song of the Lark* for what
it reveals about laughter created in me discomfort so acute that I
wanted to avert my face. In this novel in which she drew most directly
upon Red Cloud experiences, Cather explores victimization, then
confronts its human consequences in the ugliest of actions and
meanest of emotions. The tramp scene's exchange of glances initi-
ates questions radiating through the text. Haunted by the tramp,
Thea asks how people could "fall so far out of fortune?" and tries "to
make herself realize what pitch of hatred or despair could drive a
man to do such a hideous thing" (125). What kind of society encour-
ages entertainment in which a man takes venom into himself? See it
clearly, she challenges us, against a backdrop of butcher shop and
saloon; trace its course to a decomposing body that poisons a com-

munity. As the butt of laughter in society, her clown introduces comedy that is not really funny—but instead is sad, even frightening. As William Lynch reminds us in *Christ and Apollo: The Dimensions of the Literary Imagination,* the clown figure "remembers the human condition, but is it not clear to all at times that he feels he is *trapped* in that situation, and really feels he is crucified?"[11]

"To understand laughter, we must put it back into its natural environment, which is society," Bergson wrote;[12] by moving inside the comic situation and presenting it from within, Cather complicates his formula. It is one thing to describe the comic action from a theater box, as a disinterested spectator; it is quite another to recognize that according to comic conventions, you belong among the rustics on the stage. In response to Bergson, Cather drew upon her experience of Nebraska, a state providing a code for comic conventions, and upon the people and places she knew from her childhood who filled out those conventions; then she explored the consequences those conventions had on members of the comic cast.

Cather presents the Kronborgs as familiar comic types of small town life: the ineffectual preacher/father and his pragmatic wife, the priggish elder daughter, the dull brother, and the addle-pated spinster aunt. The family develops according to Bergson's principles, with the mechanical encrusted upon life, the habitual replacing flexibility, the rigid where life demands spontaneity. The family unit resembles a regiment: Anna considers herself her mother's "lieutenant"; the assembled family is a "troop," and seeing them marching to Sunday School "was like watching a military drill" (17). Aware of their position in Moonstone as the Methodist pastor's family, the Kronborgs respond by assuming variations of mechanical encrustation. As if preparing the carapace that will encase her living husband in the role of pastor, Mrs. Kronborg irons her husband's "stiff shirt and white neckties" so that they will appear "correct and spotless in the pulpit" (11); as if looking to rules of decorum to protect the unit from the personalities of its members, the eldest daughter Anna considers herself the family's "obstinate contender for proprieties" (17). To fit himself into the role of pastor, Mr. Kronborg calls on "his habitual pulpit manner" (5), which Cather explains in Bergsonian terms as the "somewhat pompous English vocabulary he had learned out of books at college," quite devoid of any "natural, spontaneous human speech" (14). Even the "blissfully lazy" baby fulfills his public function of being perpetually on view by sitting contentedly in his wagon while he is pulled about Moonstone by his sister. As assiduously as the other Kronborgs work to honor the proprieties, Tillie Kronborg can be counted upon to unsettle them, for she is irrepressibly given to making an exhibition of herself.

Outside the Kronborg household, Cather populates Moonstone with a plethora of comic types. At one extreme, there are the mechanical figures of Mrs. Archie, whose "clicking laugh sounded like a typewriting machine in action" (31), and Lily Fisher, whose "pink-and-white face, her set smile of innocence, were surely born of a colour-press" (56–57). Then there are the romantics who foolishly perform roles they have unwittingly assumed: Doctor Archie "often dodged behind a professional manner. There was sometimes a contraction of embarrassment and self-consciousness all over his big body, which made him awkward—likely to stumble, to kick up rugs, or to knock over chairs" (13). Ray Kennedy talks about mastering metals in "bookish phrases," for "the stiffness of his language" is as inflexible as his subject (105). The musicians Professor Wunsch and Spanish Johnny exhibit idealism that breaks into madness (*folle*); and as Mistress of the Revels, Tillie Kronborg is perpetually organizing them all into performances of the Moonstone Drama Club.

Here, in short, is God's plenty of comic potential. The complication is that Cather has grounded Thea so personally in the comic material of her own plot: the flighty preacher is *Thea's* father; the sanctimonious girl and dull boy, *her* sister Anna and brother Thor; the eccentric spinster *her* aunt Tillie; the music teacher and doctor *her* mentors, Professor Wunsch and Doctor Archie. And behind Thea, there is Cather herself with *her* family and *her* Red Cloud friends serving as her models.

Having established the type, Cather frees her materials from it by "dissolving . . . the outer crust," thereby bringing "us back to the inner core."[13] Like the clown returning the spectator's gaze, she sets in motion questions concerning the social utility of laughter. It is an interrogation that Cather announces in her opening scenes. When Doctor Archie is fetched by Thea's father to attend to Thea's mother, characters are true to type: the small-town doctor, young as doctors usually are in western towns, is called by a husband, nervous as men usually are upon such occasions, to attend his wife in labor. Then, Doctor Archie sees Mr. Kronborg *and himself* caught in a performance and—as the tramp exchanged glances with Thea—reveals his awareness of being trapped within the type: "It did seem that people were stupider than they need be; as if on a night like this there ought to be something better to do than to sleep nine hours, or to assist Mrs. Kronborg in functions which she could have performed so admirably unaided" (5).

To experience society's laughter as victim is to know pain and humiliation, shame and anger. To follow its consequences is to understand that humiliating laughter contaminates a community, even as the humiliated clown's body poisoned its water supply. Belle Archie illustrates the principle. In a classically Bergsonian manner, Cather gives Belle Archie a history by writing that she was once Belle White, who "used to play heavy practical jokes which the young men thought were very clever" (31). Demonstrating the repetition that, Bergson argued, provides the basis for humor, Belle's practical joke against Howard Archie repeats itself when the Archies' marriage becomes an ongoing and very heavy joke in Moonstone. Again, however, Cather moves inside the comic situation to describe it from the victim's point of view. Dr. Archie "knew that everyone was curious about his wife, that she played a sort of character part in Moonstone, and that people made fun of her, not very delicately"—for they recognized her stinginess and amused themselves in getting her to perform to type: "Her own friends . . . liked to ask her to contribute to church charities, just to see how mean she could be. The little, lopsided cake at the church supper, the cheapest pincushion, the skimpiest apron at the bazaar were always Mrs. Archie's contribution" (77). "Respectability was so necessary to Archie that he was willing to pay a high price for it" (78), Cather comments, implicitly challenging her reader to consider the price extorted by a society where friends, under the guise of a church charity, plot mean-spiritedly.

No one is immune from the laughter or its costs, as the provincialism of Thea's preoccupations demonstrates. Thea also plays to placate a Moonstone audience, for she is "very sensitive about being thought a foreigner," and is "proud of the fact that, in town, her father always preached in English; very bookish English, at that, one might add" (14). She suffers from being bested by Lily Fisher and the Baptists, is proud of her brother Thor in the "imitation tiger-skin coat and cap" she purchased for him (94), and thinks she "could never bear the disgrace" of Mrs. Livery Johnson's withdrawing her daughter as Thea's piano pupil (96). Her unconsciousness of her provincialism may be endearing, but within the claustrophobic world of Moonstone it is also dangerous.

"The story set out to tell of an artist's awakening and struggle; her floundering escape from a smug, domestic, self-satisfied provincial world of utter ignorance," Cather reflected in her 1932 preface to *The Song of the Lark*. She then added fiercely, "What I cared about, and still care about, was the girl's escape."[14] That Thea's escape takes the form of accidents is very much in the comic mode: an inheritance from an accident enables Thea to study music in Chicago, where a sympathetic teacher recognizes her talent and a wealthy patron befriends her. Most important, Destiny has granted Thea a voice, and "Destiny in the guise of Fortune is the fabric of comedy," writes the American philosopher Susanne Langer: "it is developed by comic action, which is the upset and recovery of the protagonist's equilibrium, his contest with the world and his triumph by wit, luck, [and] personal power."[15]

Thea's resistance is easy against her "natural enemies." When, for example, Mrs. Livery Johnson "so enjoyed an opportunity to rebuke Thea, that, tightly corseted as she was, she could scarcely control her breathing," Thea simply "turned away and walked slowly homeward" (54). More difficult by far is resisting her family and friends. Tillie, for example, enlists Thea's help when she performs in the Moonstone Drama Club:

> Tillie always coaxed Thea to go "behind the scenes" with her when the club presented a play, and help her with her make-up. Thea hated it, but she always went. She felt as if she had to do it. There was something in Tillie's adoration of her that compelled her. There was no family impropriety that Thea was so much ashamed of as Tillie's "acting," and yet she was always being dragged in to assist her. Tillie simply had her, there. She didn't know why, but it was so. There was a string in her somewhere that Tillie could pull; a sense of obligation to Tillie's misguided aspirations. (61)

We are comic to the extent that we resemble a puppet, Henri Bergson maintains, then explains that "the passions we have brooded over, the actions we have weighed, decided upon and carried through, in short, all that comes from us and is our very own, these are the things that give life its ofttimes dramatic and generally grave aspect." (In other words, that makes life suitable for art.) "What, then, is requisite to transform all this into a comedy?," he asks, then suggests it is "[m]erely to fancy that our seeming freedom conceals the strings of a dancing-jack."[16] More than any other character, Tillie Kronborg serves as a means by which Cather explores Bergson's idea that someone is laughable in proportion as she reminds us of something mechanical such as a puppet or a machine. As if drawing directly upon Bergson, Cather explains that Tillie's "mind was a curious machine; when she was awake it went round like a wheel when the belt has slipped off" (60). Her eccentricities and extravagances are those of Moonstone society magnified. Happy in the "social advantages" of membership in the Kronborg household, "She thought her brother the most important man in Moonstone" (18); she revels in performances in which (as Thea's mother remarked) she makes an exhibition of herself: "Much to the embarrassment of the children, she always 'spoke a piece' at the Sunday-School concerts." "The Moonstone Drama Club," Cather writes (62), "was the pride of Tillie's heart, and her enthusiasm was the principal factor in keeping it together. Sick or well, Tillie always attended rehearsals, and was always urging the young people, who took rehearsals lightly, to 'stop fooling and begin now'" (61).

Cather's genius enabled her to reconcile her comic materials to her serious ambition. She probed beneath the comic surface of an addle-pated spinster and retrieved Folly from its classical and folk traditions. "In older countries, where dress and opinions and manners are not so thoroughly standardized as in our own West, there is a belief that people who are foolish about the more obvious things of life are apt to have peculiar insight into what lies beyond the obvious" (60), Cather writes, then specifies that Tillie "had intuitions," and her romantic imagination found possibilities where others didn't. In the manner of Erasmus, Cather praises Folly, setting in motion language of *the fool, foolishness, fooling around,* and *folly* as variations of life spirit erupting in the manner of carnival. Spanish Johnny "is always fooled," his wife explains of his "wildness"; "He is good at heart, but he has no head. He fools himself," so that when he hears the sound of the sea in a conch-shell, "To him, it is the sea itself. A little thing is big to him" (41). Hearing the same siren song, Professor Wunsch, who "came from God knew where—follow[s] Spanish Johnny into town when that wanderer came back from one of his tramps" (21).

Paradoxically, Moonstone's misfits are Cather's heroes, for to join Folly's retinue is to be saved. The point is so important that Cather expounds upon it in Ray Kennedy's reflections as he lies dying: "The gold mine, the oil well, the copper ledge—all pipe-dreams, he mused, and this was a dream, too. He might have known it before. It had always been like that; the things he admired had always been away out of his reach: a college education, a gentleman's manner, an Englishman's accent—things over his head. And Thea was farther out of his reach than all the rest put together. He had been a fool to imagine it, but *he was glad he had been a fool.* She had given him one grand dream" (134, emphasis mine).

Thea's escape from a "smug, domestic, self-satisfied provincial world of utter ignorance," at first takes the form of inchoate longings. She likes "There was a sound of revelry" among Byron's poems (14), and feels that "something" separates city people from country people. When Doctor Archie describes *A Distinguished Provincial in Paris* as "a history of a live city . . . all the kinds he knew," Thea asks,

> "City people or country people?"
> "Both. People are pretty much the same everywhere."
> "Oh, no, they're not. The people who go through in the dining-car aren't like us."
> "What makes you think they aren't, my girl? Their clothes?"
> Thea shook her head. "No, it's something else. I don't know." (37)

To understand this "something else," Thea must learn that leaving the province does not ensure freedom. Thea goes to Chicago to study music, and she realizes there that roles projected upon her in the city are from scripts she had learned in Moonstone. The daughter of her landlady "tries to make a heroine of her, just as Tillie Kronborg had always done, and Thea is conscious of something of the sort" (157). Through this period Thea's contest with the world increasingly resembles a carnival's fun house with distorting concave mirrors reflecting faces adjusted to meet other faces, all to the effect of making things small, mocking, and mean. Fear of being the object of ridicule becomes "humor as inverse sublimity," writes Jean Paul,[17] and understanding that the "Sickly, uncertain flicker smile" of Mrs. Andersen in Chicago is the kind of a smile "that so often comes from a secret humiliation" (156) means knowing that secret humiliation exists in Moonstone faces too—behind Doctor Archie's "contemptuous smile" (4) and "mirthless little laugh" (78), and Wunsch's "coarse, scornful mouth" (24) and "loose, sarcastic smile" (66), for example.

"Destructive humor"—the "reduced form of laughter, a cold humor deprived of positive regenerating power" has the effect of turning "the entire world . . . into something alien, something terrifying and unjustified," writes Jean Paul, whose *Welverlachung* is remarkably close to the alienating humor Cather describes.[18] Thea extends her lessons in the contaminating effect of the sneer under Madison Bowers in Chicago. Without the leavening of compassion the glance between performer and audience is mean-spirited and ugly. Bowers' audiences are "always aware of the contempt he felt for them" (226), and he describes himself as selling "tricks for stupid people," provided they were able to pay. "They fed his pockets, and they fed his ever-hungry contempt, his scorn of himself and his accomplices" (227). Cather probes the darkest potential of humor when Bowers engages Thea in a "rough game of banter" (228). He "liked to watch the germination and growth of antipathies" (230), and "[f]or the first time Thea had a friend who, in his own cool and guarded way, liked her for whatever was least admirable in her" (227).

In its annihilating energy, "[s]kepticism is also similar to humor. . . . It is a kind of psychic vertigo which suddenly transforms *our* own rapid motion into an *external* one affecting the whole steady world."[19] Jean Paul could be describing changes in Thea: "With that increased independence of body there had come a change in her face; an indifference, something hard and sceptical" (231). Thea's clothes change also, "like the attire of a shopgirl who tries to follow the fashions: a purple suit, a piece of cheap fur, a three-cornered purple hat with a pompon sticking up in front" (231). Having described a costume marking Thea as a comic type, Cather goes beneath the type to describe the experience from within: "I keep wanting to tell them how stupid they are" (233), Thea says of popular singers of the day. She "was moody and contemptuous toward her fellow boarders," Cather writes; and they eventually felt that "under her jocularity, [she] was cold, self-centred, and unimpressionable" (235). Desperately unhappy, Thea "was more influenced by Bowers than she knew." Cather explains: "Unconsciously she began to take on something of his dry contempt" (239).

In exploring the skeptic's corrosive influence, Cather probes the Romantics' fear of being discovered for their ideals, then ridiculed and mocked as pretentious, and finally pitied for failing to meet them. From fear of humiliation, Mrs. Andersen has allowed her husband's brothers to defraud her; Doctor Archie lives at the mercy of the jokers who deride his marriage; and the newly married Fred Ottenburg "became absolutely reckless" from humiliation over "the ignorance and the fatuous conceit which lay behind [his wife's] grimacing mask of slang and ridicule" (302).

Appropriately to an exploration of comedy, Cather uses the body as a site to play out the tension between artificial versus natural, between life-denying versus regenerative impulses. Clothing is to the individual body what ceremonies are to the social body, both reflecting the original idea of comedy, that of a mechanism superimposed upon life.[20] Describing Anna's priggishness, for example, Cather writes, "Scarcely anything was attractive to her in its natural state—indeed, scarcely anything was decent until it was clothed by the opinion of some authority" (120). And Cather records Thea's sensitivity to costumes imposed upon the body in remarkable detail: we know her response to the tramp's dirty clown suit, her resistance to Tillie's love for costumes ("'Tillie,' Thea used to cry impatiently, 'can't you see that if Miss Spencer tried to make one of those things, she'd make

me look like a circus girl' " [139]); and her realization that the costume that the German dressmaker in Chicago "achieved" for her is "a
horror"—in that it includes every known fabric. In the background
of these scenes is the long tradition of folly: that is, the Fool's "servants at one time wore motley, emblem of breakdown."[21]

Against the artifice of clothing, the body exerts itself as a fundamental law of comedy. Certainly, that is the case in *The Song of the
Lark,* where Thea's emerging physicality affirms the life-affirming
and regenerative impulses of the narrative. Thea's mother enters her
bedroom and, feeling her breasts beneath her nightgown, advises
her to leave off her buttons so that her chest might develop. Remarkable for its forthrightness, the scene anticipates others in which
Cather releases the body. Singing for the Nathanmeyers, for example, Thea "laughed and drew herself up out of her corsets, threw her
shoulders high and let them drop again. She had never sung in a low
dress before, and she found it comfortable" (251–52). Similarly,
Cather confirms Thea's desire to "have" Fred as her lover, acknowledges her hearty appetite, and describes her pleasure at feeling the
warm water penetrate her body in the bath.

Whereas the comic spirit springs from bodily regeneration and
renewal, its release is signaled by laughter. In Cather's narrative this
release comes with Thea's "deep laugh" that springs from the deep
sources of life and of art. Hearing her sing for the first time, Harsanyi
wonders why he hadn't guessed it before: "Everything about her
indicated it—the big mouth, the wide jaw and chin, . . . *the deep laugh.*
The machine was so simple and strong, seemed to be so easily operated. She sang from the bottom of herself. Her breath came from
down where her laugh came from, the deep laugh which Mrs. Harsanyi had once called 'the laugh of the people'" (171, emphasis
mine). In not performing, Thea is freed of others' expectations, and
she embodies the truth that "Laughter is essentially not an external
but an interior form of truth. . . . Laughter liberates not only from
external censorship but first of all from the great interior censor; it
liberates from the fear that developed in man during thousands of
years: fear of the sacred, of prohibitions, of the past, of power. It
unveils the material bodily principle in its true meaning."[22]

Comedy has to do with radical and structural matters rather than
surface features such as relative levity or pathos, according to Susanne Langer. Whereas tragedy concerns "the personal sense of life,
or self-realization" with "a beginning, efflorescence, and end," "[t]he
pure sense of life is the underlying feeling of comedy . . . to maintain
the pattern of vitality in a non-living universe is the most elementary

instinctual purpose."[23] By such a principle, laughter "seems to arise from a surge of vital feeling" (340). Cather's Panther Canyon section provides a radical and structural break in the narrative that releases the pure sense of life with which comedy is most significantly concerned, and that confirms Thea's vocation in art. Bathing in the stream that is "the only living thing left of the drama that had been played out in the canyon centuries ago," Thea experiences "a continuity of life that reached back into the old time" (273). There, standing upright and naked in the pool, Thea understands: "what was any art but an effort to make a sheath, a mold in which to imprison for a moment the shining, elusive element which is life itself" (273). The moment signals Cather's union of art and comedy. In it Cather gives to Thea the conception of art as springing from the comic spirit informing folk rituals and classical texts that celebrate the regenerative cycles of life. Fred Ottenburg arrives in Panther Canyon to demonstrate the difference. On a hike and telling Thea to go on ahead if she liked, he says,

> ". . . but I'm here to enjoy myself. If you meet a rattler on the way, have it out with him." She hesitated, fanning herself with her felt hat. "I never have met one."
> "There's reasoning for you," Fred murmured languidly. (286)

Fred's reference to the rattler recalls Thea's Moonstone experience of the clown who ate rattlers as entertainment; but whereas in Moonstone the tramp (AKA clown) illustrates the contaminating venom of laughter based on victimization, in Panther Canyon Fred's humor is liberating. The point is not that Thea becomes witty, which she doesn't; the point is that in Panther Canyon Fred's languid enjoyment of the absurdity of her logic exists at the other end of the comic spectrum from the ridicule, practical jokes, and the sarcasm of Moonstone and Chicago. Again, Cather uses Fred to interpret:

> He discovered . . . that she had a merry side, a robust humour that was deep and hearty, like her laugh, but it slept most of the time under her own doubts and the dullness of her life. She had not what is called a 'sense of humour.' That is, she had no intellectual humour; no power to enjoy the absurdities of people, no relish of their pretentiousness and inconsistencies—which only depressed her. But her joviality, Fred felt, was an asset, and ought to be developed. . . . She was still Methodist enough to believe that if a thing were hard and irksome, it must be good for her. And yet, whatever she did well was spontaneous. (304)

Distancing liberates in comedy, providing the necessary impersonality. It is a point Cather acknowledges in New York City. In her last

section Doctor Archie asks of Fred, "these people all look happier to
me than our Western people do. Is it simply good manners on their
part, or do they get more out of life?" (327–28). "New York people
live a good deal in the fourth dimension," Fred responds; "I mean
that life is not quite so personal here as it is in your part of the world.
People are more taken up by hobbies, interests that are less subject to
reverses than their personal affairs."

> The doctor looked at him narrowly. "You think that's about the princi-
> pal difference between country people and city people, don't you?"
> Fred was a little disconcerted at being followed up so resolutely, and he
> attempted to dismiss it with a pleasantry. "I've never thought much about
> it, doctor. But I should say, on the spur of the moment, that is one of the
> principal differences between people anywhere. It's the consolation of
> fellows like me who don't accomplish much. The fourth dimension is not
> good for business, but we think we have a better time." (328- 29)

"What you want more than anything else in the world is to be an
artist; is that true?" Harsanyi once asked Thea, who in responding
"Yes, I suppose so" reveals the secret she has so carefully protected
(190). Becoming an Artist was serious business for Willa Cather, who
in 1915 knew that behind her lay the frantic pace of *McClure's,* and
behind that, the grind of teaching, the mind-numbing domestic pap
of *Home Monthly,* then the struggle to escape from Red Cloud, where
in 1895 she had retreated following her graduation from the University of Nebraska. She gave her dilemma to her character. To reveal
her dream is to risk humiliation; yet to become an artist, Thea must
respond to and release the Comic Spirit within herself—that is, the
regenerative, vital life force. Thea's growth as an artist involves her
coming to understand "the absurdity of trying too hard. Up to a
certain point, say eighty degrees, artistic endeavour could be fat and
comfortable, methodical and prudent. But if you went further than
that, if you drew yourself up toward ninety degrees, you parted with
your defences and left yourself exposed to mischance. The legend
was that in those upper reaches, you might be divine, but you were
much likelier to be ridiculous" (368).

In her epilogue Cather returns to Moonstone and to the novel's
comic material. The scene is familiar—an ice cream sociable attended by "a fair-haired dimpled matron who was once Lily Fisher"
and "a spry little old spinster," Tillie Kronborg (413). For the first
time, Cather's narration moves inside Tillie, and Cather gives us
Moonstone not as seen by a Bergsonian disinterested spectator viewing the comic players on a stage, but seen instead by Folly, who is the

romantic figure within that comic cast, and who vindicates the conceits of Folly. "Tillie is trying not to hurt their feelings by showing too plainly how much she realizes the superiority of her position," Cather writes; "[s]he tries to be modest when she complains to the postmaster that her New York paper is more than three days late" (414). Tillie reads of Madame Kronborg's "having sung for the King at Buckingham Palace and having been presented with a jewel by His Majesty," and "[o]nce more she has to remind herself that it is all true, and is not something she has 'made up.' Like other romancers, she is a little terrified at seeing one of her wildest conceits admitted by the hard-headed world" (416–17).

Your talent for comedy is measured by your "being able to detect the ridicule of them you love, without loving them less: and move, by being able to see yourself somewhat ridiculous in dear eyes, and accepting the correction their image of you proposes,"[24] George Meredith wrote in the book that Cather included in her personal library when she was a girl growing up in Red Cloud. By writing of the comedy of herself as a youth in ways recognizable to those who knew her then, Cather proved her talent for *comedy*. Her genius for *art* lay in converting her Nebraska materials from the stuff of comic conventions into the high art of an American epic, and it has to do with the way Willa Cather forged her journey between the province and the city, from Red Cloud to New York.

Notes

1. George Meredith, *The Egoist: A Comedy in Narrative* and "An Essay on Comedy," *Comedy,* Introduction and Appendix by Wylie Sypher (Garden City: Doubleday, 1956), 3–57.

2. *Courier,* November 23, 1895, in Bernice Slote, ed., *The Kingdom of Art: Willa Cather's First Principles and Critical Statements* (Lincoln: University of Nebraska Press, 1967), 408.

3. Willa Cather, *Nebraska State Journal,* 10 October 1895, in Slote, *Kingdom,* 242–43.

4. *Courier,* 14 September 1895, in Slote, *Kingdom,* 281.

5. In referring to the influence of Henri Bergson, I refer also to the influence of Loretta Wasserman and Tom Quirk in Cather studies, the scholars who have established the importance to Cather of Bergsonian philosophy. Wasserman, for example, interprets Bergson's ideas of unconscious memory and of contrasting time—chronological time and lived time—as they influenced *My Ántonia* and *The Professor's House;* and Quirk demonstrates Cather's interest in the scientific character of Bergson's *Creative Evolution,* particularly as it emerged in the vitalistic scheme of her fiction beginning with *O Pioneers!* I suggest that Henri Bergson's ideas of comedy were equally important to Cather as he presented them in *Le Rire* (1900), translated

as *Laughter* in 1910—at precisely the time that Cather was preparing to leave *Mc-Clure's* and to write *O Pioneers!*.

6. Henri Bergson, *Laughter: An Essay on the Meaning of the Comic,* Authorized translation by Cloudesley Brereton and Fred Rothwell (New York: Macmillan, 1911), 72.

7. Mary Ann Gillies, *Henri Bergson and British Modernism* (Montreal, Canada: McGill-Queen's University Press, 1996), 171.

8. Willa Cather, *The Song of the Lark* (Boston: Houghton, Mifflin, 1988), 28.

9. Bergson, *Laughter,* 68.

10. Ibid., 16.

11. William F. Lynch S.J., *Christ and Apollo: The Dimensions of the Literary Imagination* (New York: Sheed and Ward, 1960), 99.

12. Bergson, *Laughter,* 8.

13. Ibid., 160.

14. Cather, Preface, *The Song of the Lark* (London: Jonathan Cape, 1932).

15. Suzanne K. Langer, *Feeling and Form: A Theory of Art* (New York: Scribner's, 1955), 331.

16. Bergson, *Laughter,* 79.

17. Jean Paul, *Horn of Oberon: Jean Paul Richter's School for Aesthetics,* Introduction and Trans. by Margaret R. Hale (Detroit: Wayne State University Press, 1973), 91.

18. Ibid., 93–94.

19. Ibid.

20. Bergson, *Laughter,* 44–45.

21. Marcel Gutwirth, *Laughing Matter: An Essay on the Comic* (Ithaca: Cornell University Press, 1993), 43.

22. Mikhail Bakhtin, *Rabelais and His World,* Trans. Helene Iswolski (Cambridge: MIT Press, 1968), 94.

23. Langer, *Feeling and Form,* 327–28.

24. Meredith, *Comedy,* 42.

Bibliography

Bakhtin, Mikhail. *Rabelais and His World.* Trans. Helene Iswolsky. Cambridge: MIT Press, 1968.

Bell, Robert H. *Jocoserious Joyce: The Fate of Folly in "Ulysses."* Ithaca: Cornell University Press, 1991.

Bergson, Henri. *Laughter: An Essay on the Meaning of the Comic.* Authorized translation by Cloudesley Brereton and Fred Rothwell. New York: Macmillan, 1911.

Cather, Willa. *My Ántonia.* Ed. Charles Mignon, with Kari Ronning; Historical essay by James Woodress; Explanatory notes by James Woodress, with Kari Ronning, Kathleen Danker, and Emily Levine. Lincoln: University of Nebraska Press, 1994.

———. *O Pioneers!* Ed. Susan J. Rosowski and Charles Mignon, with Kathleen Danker. Historical essay and explanatory notes by David Stouck. Lincoln: University of Nebraska Press, 1992.

———. *The Song of the Lark.* 1915. Boston: Houghton Mifflin, 1987.

Galligan, Edward L. *The Comic Vision in Literature.* Athens: University of Georgia Press, 1984.

Gillies, Mary Ann. *Henri Bergson and British Modernism.* Montreal, Canada: McGill-Queen's University Press, 1996.

Gutwirth, Marcel. *Laughing Matter: An Essay on the Comic.* Ithaca: Cornell University Press, 1993.

Huizinga, Johann. "The Comedy of Life." In *Twentieth Century Interpretations of "The Praise of Folly."* Ed. Kathleen Williams. Englewood Cliffs, NJ: Prentice-Hall, 1969. 61–67.

Kaiser, Walter. *Praisers of Folly: Erasmus, Rabelais, Shakespeare.* Cambridge, Mass.: Harvard University Press, 1963.

Langer, Susanne K. *Feeling and Form: A Theory of Art.* New York: Scribner's, 1953.

Lewis, Paul. *Comic Effects: Interdisciplinary Approaches to Humor in Literature.* Albany: State University of New York Press, 1989.

Lynch, William F. S. J. *Christ and Apollo: The Dimensions of the Literary Imagination.* New York: Sheed and Ward, 1960.

Meredith, George. "An Essay on Comedy." In *Comedy.* Introduction and Appendix by Wylie Sypher. Garden City, NY: Doubleday, 1956.

Paul, Jean (pseudonym of Jean Paul Friedrich Richter, 1763–1825). *Horn of Oberon: Jean Paul Richter's School for Aesthetics.* Introduction and Translation by Margaret R. Hale. Detroit: Wayne State University Press, 1973.

Slote, Bernice, ed. *The Kingdom of Art: Willa Cather's First Principles and Critical Statements 1893–1896.* Lincoln: University of Nebraska Press, 1966.

Swabey, Marie Collins. *Comic Laughter.* New Haven: Yale University Press, 1961.

Welsford, Enid. "*The Praise of Folly* and the Tradition of the Fool." in *Twentieth Century Interpretations of 'The Praise of Folly'.* Ed. Kathleen Williams. Englewood Cliffs, NJ: Prentice-Hall, 1969. 101–105.

Contributors

Heather Stewart Armstrong received her Ph.D. in English from Drew University's Caspersen School of Graduate Studies in 1997. She lives with her husband and toddler son in Etna, Maine, and maintains her research interests in George Eliot and her contemporaries, as well as in Willa Cather.

Robert C. Comeau teachers English and American Literature at Union County College in Cranford, New Jersey. Presently he is completing his doctoral program at the Caspersen School of Graduate Studies at Drew University and is writing his dissertation on Willa Cather and Mark Twain.

Kathryn H. Faber is completing her Doctor of Letters degree at Drew's Caspersen School of Graduate Studies. Former Director of the Upper School at the Kent Place School in Summit, N.J., she is mother of two sons, grandmother of three, and a resident of Madison, N.J.

Evelyn Haller is Professor and Chair of English at Doane College in Crete, Nebraska, near Lincoln. She has published articles on Cather, Virginia Woolf, and Ezra Pound, and is completing a book on Cather's use of the arts including architecture and dance.

Sherrill Harbison is an Associate of the Five Colleges, Amherst, Massachusetts, and a Visiting Lecturer at Trinity College, Hartford. Her work has been supported by the Fulbright Commission, the National Endowment for the Humanities, and the Norwegian Marshall Fund, and she is a three-time winner of the Aurora Borealis Prize from the five Nordic governments. She has edited Penguin Classics editions of Cather's *The Song of the Lark* and of Sigrid Undset's *Gunnar's Daughter.*

Jo Ann Middleton is author of *Willa Cather's Modernism: A Study of Style and Technique* and contributed the bibliographical essay on "Fiction: 1900–the 1920s" to *American Literary Scholarship* from 1990 to 1996. She presently directs the Medical Humanities Program at Drew's Caspersen School of Graduate Studies and the Raritan Bay Medical Center.

ROBERT K. MILLER, Professor of English at the University of St. Thomas in St. Paul Minnesota, has published essays on Cather in *Cather Studies, WCPM Newsletter, Willa Cather: Family, Community and History,* and *Willa Cather's Southern Connections.* He has edited *Great Short Works of Willa Cather* for HarperCollins and is presently researching a book focused on Cather's conception of virtue.

JOANNE STONE MORRISSEY had been a successful entrepreneur and Wall Street financial analyst for over twenty years when she decided to seek a new career in literature and education. She is now completing her doctorate at Drew's Caspersen School of Graduate Studies where she is concentrating in American Studies. Her dissertation will trace Walt Whitman's influence on Flannery O'Connor's work.

JOHN J. MURPHY, Professor of English at Brigham Young University, is the author of *My Ántonia: The Road Home* (1989) and over sixty essays on Cather and other American writers, as well as the annual "Fiction: 1900 to 1930s" bibliographical essay in *American Literary Scholarship* (1981–87). He is volume editor of the Scholarly Edition of *Death Comes for the Archbishop* (1999) and of Penguin's *My Ántonia* (1994). His collections of Cather criticism include *Critical Essays on Willa Cather* (1984) and *Willa Cather: Family, Community and History* (1990). Currently he edits *Literature and Belief,* a journal devoted to religious values in literature.

MONA PERS is Professor of English at Mälardalen University in Sweden. She obtained her Ph.D. degree from Uppsala University in 1975, and has since written many articles and two books on Willa Cather, *Willa Cather's Children* (1975) and *Willa Cather's Swedes* (1995). She edited "Scandinavian Contributions" in *American Literary Scholarship* from 1981–1985.

JESSICA G. RABIN (B.A., Drew University 1994) completed her Ph.D. degree at Emory University in Atlanta, in autumn 1999. Her field of concentration is American modernism and ethnic literature, and her dissertation examines how Cather employs multiple subject positions to trace and represent her own shifting sense of alliances.

GLORIA ROJAS spent most of her professional life as a broadcast journalist at ABC, CBS, and NBC. A veteran reporter of natural disasters, crimes, political chicanery, as well as the arts, she became a student of literature at Drew University when she retired from television. She now enjoys investigating and reporting on the work of Willa Cather.

ANN ROMINES is Director of Graduate Studies and Professor of English at the George Washington University. She is the author of numerous essays on U.S. women's writing and culture. She has also published two books, *The Home Plot: Women, Writing and Domestic Ritual* (1992) and *Constructing the Little House: Gender, Culture, and Laura Ingalls Wilder* (1997). She is editor of *Willa Cather's Southern Connections: New Essays on Cather and the South* (2000) and of the Scholarly Edition of *Sapphira and the Slave Girl*.

SUSAN J. ROSOWSKI, University Professor and Adele Hall Distinguished Professor at University of Nebraska, is general editor of the Willa Cather Scholarly Edition and editor-in-chief of Cather Studies. She has written many essays on Cather and other plains writers, as well as *The Voyage Perilous: Willa Cather's Romanticism* (1986) and *Birthing a Nation: Gender, Creativity, and the West in American Literature* (1999). She has also served as president of the Western Literature Association and as academic director for several international Cather seminars.

MERRILL MAGUIRE SKAGGS, contributor to and editor of this volume, is Professor of English at Drew University and a frequent plenary speaker at Cather colloquia. Among the three dozen essays and several books on American literature she has published is *After the World Broke in Two: The Later Novels of Willa Cather* (1990). It is one of six books on Cather to emerge, under her pen or direction, from Drew's Caspersen School of Graduate Studies.

JOSEPH R. URGO, Professor and Chair of the Department of English at the University of Mississippi in Oxford, is the author of *Novel Frames: Literature as Guide to Race, Sex, and History in American Culture* (1991), *Willa Cather and the Myth of American Migration* (1995), and most recently, *In the Age of Distraction* (2000).

GRETEL D. WEISS, a sociologist, has taught at Douglass College, Drew University, and Monmouth University. Since her retirement she has enjoyed renewing her study of American literature and especially of Willa Cather.

DEBORAH LINDSAY WILLIAMS is Assistant Professor of English at Iona College, where she teaches twentieth-century American literature, women's studies, and literary criticism. She has published essays about a number of American women writers, including Edith Wharton and Zona Gale; she is currently completing a book entitled *Not in Sisterhood: Edith Wharton, Willa Cather, Zona Gale, and the Politics of Female Authorship, 1900–1940.*

LAURA WINTERS is Chairperson of the English/Communication Department and Professor of English at the College of Saint Elizabeth in Morristown, N.J. She teaches twentieth-century literature, creative writing, and film at both the College of Saint Elizabeth and the Caspersen School of Graduate Studies at Drew University. She is also author of *Willa Cather: Landscape and Exile* (1993).

CYNTHIA GRIFFIN WOLFF teaches at MIT where she holds the "Class of 1922 Professorship of Humanities." She has edited more than a dozen books and published several dozen essays—all on the subject of women writers and women characters. Her authored books include *A Feast of Words: The Triumph of Edith Wharton* and *Emily Dickinson,* both currently in print in the Radcliffe Biography Series of the Addison-Wesley Press. She is currently writing a book-length study of Willa Cather.

Index